THE NEW

LEXINGTON PRESS

COOPERATIVE STRATEGIES

North American Perspectives

COOPERATIVE STRATEGIES

North American Perspectives

Paul W. Beamish

J. Peter Killing

Editors

o

The New Lexington Press
San Francisco

Substantial discounts on bulk quantities of The New Lexington Press books are available to corporations, professional associations, and other organizations. For details and discount information, contact the special sales department at (415) 433–1740; Fax (800) 605–2665.

For sales outside the United States, see the last page of the book for contact information.

The New Lexington Press Web address: http://www.newlex.com

△ Manufactured in the United States of America on Lyons Falls
TCF Turin Book. This paper is acid-free and 100 percent totally chlorine-free.

Library of Congress Cataloging-in-Publication Data

Cooperative strategies / Paul W. Beamish, J. Peter Killing, editors.
    p. cm. — (The New Lexington Press management series)
  Includes bibliographical references and indexes.
  Contents: v. 1. North American perspectives—v. 2. European perspectives—v. 3. Asian Pacific perspectives,
   ISBN 0-7879-0812-6 (v. 1 : alk: paper).—ISBN 0-7879-0813-4 (pbk. : v. 1 : alk. paper)
   1. Strategic alliances (Business) 2. Joint ventures. 3. Foreign licensing agreements. 4. International business enterprises.
I. Beamish, Paul W., 1953– II. Killing, J. Peter. III. Series.
HD69.S8C665   1997
658'.044—dc21   96-50092

FIRST EDITION

HB Printing 10 9 8 7 6 5 4 3 2 1

PB Printing 10 9 8 7 6 5 4 3 2 1

THE NEW LEXINGTON PRESS MANAGEMENT SERIES

The Cooperative Strategies Series

Cooperative Strategies: North American Perspectives
Cooperative Strategies: European Perspectives
Cooperative Strategies: Asian Pacific Perspectives

To the memory of my godfather,
Austin O'Boyle:
soldier, scholar, wizard, inspiration—
the spark who ignited my "international" life.
P.W.B.

CONTENTS

PART THREE
Dynamics of Partner Relationships

PART FOUR
The Role of Information and Knowledge in Cooperative Alliances

PART FIVE
Strategy and Performance of Cooperative Alliances

PREFACE

THIS THREE-VOLUME SERIES focuses on the most current theory and research on new cooperative international business arrangements and the most up-to-date assessments of them. Since the early eighties there has been growing recognition of cooperative efforts in international business and of negotiated alliances between two or more firms. This has led to an impressive amount of research on the extent and nature of such strategies and the conduct, operations, and mandate of the companies that pursue them. These arrangements include joint ventures, strategic alliances, R&D partnerships, and consortia and involve technology transfers, licensing agreements, management service and franchising agreements, cross-manufacturing agreements, and other strategically innovative business transactions. The changing balance of world economic power and resources, rapid technological change, and new participants in world markets and R&D are all developments that have increased management researchers' interest in the different ways international firms adapt to a rapidly changing environment. These new cooperative strategies are the outgrowth of the push toward globalization during the last decade.

The editors and contributors to these three volumes include top experts in international strategy and management. They provide extensive conceptual insight and present empirical evidence for analyzing the environments in which these new international strategies and linkages among firms operate. The geographically focused volumes highlight the commonalties and differences among different nations, cultures, and trade zones. The chapters in each volume highlight the body of theory and research on global cooperative strategies. The volumes are designed as resources for researchers, students, practitioners, and managers who have a need to know more about the latest collaborative arrangement on the international business scene and who are interested in international business and management strategy.

How the Series Is Organized

For any undertaking of this magnitude, an obvious question is how to organize the material. With forty-five contributions to be spread across three books, the possibilities were endless. Various approaches were considered.

We could have organized the contributions according to the functional topic they address (that is, grouping discussions of marketing together, discussions of strategy together, and so on). However, this ran counter to our desire for a cross-functional approach. We could also have organized the series according to empirical versus theoretical contributions; however, we felt it was more interesting to mix these together.

Our solution was to provide sufficient detail to readers so that they can decide which chapters are of greatest relevance to their interests. We do this in three ways. First, summary tables are included that list the chapters in the three books (in alphabetical order, according to first author), with an analysis detailing whether the chapter is empirical or not, and if it is, the regional base of the data. Second, at the start of each chapter, the abstract of the paper on which the chapter is based is reprinted. Third, the preface to each volume explains how we have grouped its chapters according to their major themes. We hope that together these devices will allow the reader to quickly understand the breadth of the contributions.

Overview of Volume One

The chapters in this volume are broadly grouped into five often overlapping categories:

- Advances in theories of cooperation
- The formation of alliances
- The dynamics of partner relationships
- The role of information and knowledge in alliances
- The performance of cooperative strategies

One of the overarching emphases of this volume is on the role of trust. No fewer than five chapters consider it in part.

Advances in Theories of Cooperative Strategies

Numerous theoretical lenses can be employed to increase our understanding of cooperative strategies. Each theory has both advantages and limitations, and each represents a unique way of helping us link observed practice to a conceptual underpinning. The chapters in this volume are anchored in a very wide set of theoretical approaches, conceptual frameworks, and models. These include social exchange, prospect theory, agency theory, property rights, transaction costs, procedural justice, and dominant versus peripheral games. This wide range of approaches illustrates just how rich the area of cooperative strategies is for academic study.

The Formation of Alliances

A key consideration in any cooperative strategy is its formation. A number of fundamental questions must be considered: Why cooperate and form an alliance at all (versus going it alone)? What are the primary characteristics to seek in any partner? How should the alliance be configured in terms of responsibilities? The chapters in this volume address why increasing numbers of industries are employing cooperative strategies, when it makes sense to undertake technology development within a cooperative format, and the implications for R&D consortia performance of differences in nationality and research location.

The Dynamics of Partner Relationships

Central to every cooperative strategy is a relationship between two or more partners. The form and frequency of partner interaction is constantly changing, influenced by issues such as the development and maintenance of trust and commitment, as well the inevitable occasional conflicts. The chapters in this volume consider the antecedents of trust in cross-border marketing partnerships, the impact of joint venture managers' perceptions of procedural justice on organizational commitment, the importance of partners' cultural sensitivity in building trust, successful interfirm exchanges, various process patterns in cooperative interorganizational relationships, and trust and its role in the process of international joint venture management. Collectively, these behavioral considerations can teach us much about partnership dynamics.

The Role of Information and Knowledge in Alliances

A characteristic concern of nearly every organization contemplating forming an alliance is whether its potential partner will gain access to its core assets and resources. In increasing numbers of organizations, these core assets are knowledge-based. Not surprisingly, a stream of research has emerged that looks at the acquisition and management of knowledge in joint ventures. Two chapters in this volume explore this phenomenon. One identifies organizational processes used by firms to access and exploit knowledge within an alliance; the other provides a framework that maps the transfer of knowledge in alliances, the transformation or creation of new knowledge in such ventures, and the harvesting or active and conscious integration of knowledge into parent company routines.

The Performance of Cooperative Strategies

Without superior performance—however it is defined—most organizations will neither establish nor maintain cooperation. Thus two of the chapters in this volume place a particularly strong emphasis on alliance performance. These chapters examine the relationships linking the strategic motivations, structure, and performance of joint ventures and whether joint venture formation announcements affect the capital market value of participating firms.

Development of the Series

In late 1986, we were each invited to present a paper of our choice at a conference dealing with the then-emerging field of cooperative strategies in international business. The resultant compilation, edited by Farok Contractor and Peter Lorange, was the best book of its day on this subject. Practitioner and academician interest in cooperative strategies has exploded in the past decade, in all disciplines. In fact, some have called this the "age of alliance capitalism." From what had been an original focus on equity joint ventures, the field has grown to include consideration of nonequity forms of cooperation, shorter-term alliances, and so forth. A significant portion of the research published in the major academic journals focuses on cooperative strategies. With that context, we set as our objective to consolidate the current and future thinking on this important subject.

To do so, we decided to host three conferences on cooperative strategies, focusing in turn on North American, European, and Asian Pacific perspectives. Each conference included papers by authors from the specific region under consideration or about cooperative strategies involving that region. Authors from outside these three regions were encouraged to submit to the conference on the region of their choice.

We decided to host three, rather than one, conferences in order to attract the maximum number of high-quality submissions. To minimize travel, time requirements, and expense for the authors, the editors decided that they would go to the authors. This approach was quite effective, as we received submissions from authors in twenty-two countries. The conferences were held in all three regions: the conference on North America was held in London, Ontario; the conference in Europe in Lausanne, Switzerland; and the conference on Asia in Hong Kong.

All papers submitted underwent an initial double-blind review by three reviewers. Approximately fifteen papers per region were selected, and their authors were invited to participate in the conferences. After the conferences, the authors were given several months to revise their papers before publication in these three volumes. A small number of papers were also selected by the editors for inclusion in a special issue of the *Journal of International Business Studies (JIBS)*, approved for publication in late 1996 by the Academy of International Business (AIB).

Expenses for each conference (for food, accommodations, and materials) were provided free to the participants, who also received copies of the three books and the special issue of *JIBS*. All AIB members received the special issue of *JIBS* at no additional cost. This was made possible through the financial support of the Royal Bank of Canada. As we think you will agree, the final products are excellent.

The Call for Papers

In early 1995, we issued a call for papers. Our intent was to cast a broad, multifunctional net. To that end, we took two steps. First, we compiled a list of 218 scholars who had recently published in the international alliances area and encouraged them to prepare and submit a paper. At the same time, we asked if they would be willing to also (or instead) serve as a reviewer. Second, we advertised in *JIBS,* the newsletter of the Academy of International Business, the American Management Association Global Marketing Interest Group's newsletter, the *Academy of Management Journal,* and the *Journal of Marketing.* We explained that the deadline for submissions was September 1, 1995, that papers must be original, and that they should not exceed thirty double-spaced pages in length, including exhibits. Preparation following the *JIBS* style guide was requested.

We encouraged submission of the following types of materials:

- Papers dealing with any of the traditional nonequity cooperative strategies—such as licensing, the adoption of common technical standards, long-term OEM arrangements, joint research, joint distribution, and so on—and with equity arrangements such as minority equity positions and joint ventures.

- Papers having implications for managers.

- Papers dealing with some aspect of parent company performance or with the performance of free-standing alliance entities, if established. We were particularly interested in papers that examined performance over time.

- Papers dealing with international cooperative strategies, in which the partners and their alliance entity were not all in the same country. Papers prepared for each regional conference were to have particular relevance to managers in that region. For example, for the Asia conference we encouraged papers identifying factors that affect the performance of various cooperative strategies within Asia or, equally, papers considering the experience of Asian companies cooperating with partners in other parts of the world. Studies without a regional focus were also welcome, however.

- Papers dealing with firms that were entering or exiting cooperative alliances.
- Papers dealing with cooperative strategies designed to foster innovation.
- Papers dealing with situations in which the nature of an alliance was being changed.
- Papers comparing cooperative arrangements based on harmony with those that were more contentious.

We equally encouraged three other types of submissions:

- Papers discussing the experiences of two or more partners.
- Papers examining cooperative strategies between competitors, between suppliers and customers, or involving government agencies.
- "Think pieces," based on either large- or small-sample research. Papers in which information was collected from both partners and the alliance entity, if there was one, were particularly welcome.

The Review Process

All articles in the three books and the special issue of *JIBS* underwent a double-blind review process. As much as possible, a *JIBS*-style review process was followed.

Nearly eighty articles were submitted. While some were rejected at the point of submission as not appropriate, most went out to three reviewers. These reviewers had been selected on the basis of their previous contributions to the literature. The reviewers were a mix of those who had submitted papers plus subject matter experts who agreed to serve as part of an editorial panel.

On the basis of the first round of reviews, the authors of forty-five papers were invited to participate in one of the three conferences. Most of the forty-five papers went out for a second review in early 1996, and where reviewer comments were received, these were forwarded to the authors.

By March 1996 it was not possible to always maintain both sides of the double-blind review process. While the authors never knew who their reviewers were, by this time some of the reviewers (those attending the conferences) knew who the authors were. This was because all presenters received binders containing the (revised) papers presented at the conferences.

The authors of each paper (one to four authors per paper) attended each conference, as did the series editors. Up to sixteen papers were presented at each conference. During each of the three conferences, there were no concurrent sessions. Each paper was presented over a thirty- to forty-five-minute period. There were numerous stimulating questions, and all authors were encouraged to consider where linkages existed to other papers being presented in the three meetings. Based on the input received, all papers were revised—sometimes substantially—and resubmitted. They were then copyedited for consistency. Papers were selected for inclusion in the special issue of *JIBS* on the basis of the standard *JIBS* criteria of being exceptional in one or more of the areas of theory, evidence, methodology, or innovation. Additional criteria used for inclusion in the *JIBS* special issues were these:

- A desire for some regional representation (this occurred naturally).
- A desire for different functional perspectives (for example, economics, marketing, strategy, organizational behavior).
- A desire to see new theoretical lenses applied.
- Input from the other presenters regarding which papers should be included in the special issue.
- Length (some excellent work could not be condensed to journal article length).

There were many more excellent papers than journal space available. Some of the authors whose papers were not among the nine selected for the special issue were understandably frustrated, given the academic tendency to accord journal articles much greater importance than book chapters. As the above process description suggests, however, these chapters are different. We feel that they are much stronger than those contained in most collections. Many are tier-one journal quality, as readers will discover.

Acknowledgments

From idea to inception, this project has taken large portions of the past two years. We received a lot of assistance from a lot of individuals and institutions. For this, we are most grateful. The Royal Bank of Canada provided the lion's share of the substantial financial cost. They allowed a large portion of the funds they provide to Paul Beamish, Royal Bank Professor in International Business, to be used for this initiative. We believe this has been an effective use of their support and in fact can serve as a model for corporate-academic interaction. Three universities provided both financial and administrative support. At IMD, Professor Peter Killing received able assistance from President Peter Lorange (we considered the fact that Peter is now managing IMD to be a very happy coincidence, given his early work in this field) and, at an operational level, from Cindy Panettieri, who managed all of the details for the Lausanne conference. IMD provided significant financial assistance for the European conference.

In Hong Kong, Professor David Tse facilitated local arrangements. We are most appreciative of the efforts put forth by Professor Tse, his students, and City University of Hong Kong. In Canada, we received substantial assistance on many levels at the Richard Ivey School of Business (formerly called the Western Business School). Dean Larry Tapp provided the welcome to the participants. Associate Dean of Research Ken Hardy was fully supportive from the very beginning. Numerous faculty, doctoral candidates, and staff provided assistance at various stages. David Sharp, Doug Reid, and Barbara Nelson copyedited papers on a tight deadline.

A particular thanks must go to Jean Fish and, especially, Mary Roberts. Nearly all the paper flow for the three conferences, three books, and special issue of *JIBS* was coordinated at Ivey through Mary's very competent hands.

We had a large pool of article reviewers who gave us their input, and a group of authors who shared our vision about the importance of the subject. The dynamic at the conferences was terrific: challenging, supportive, invigorating, and fun. This would have been impossible without the full participation of so many scholars.

At each conference we benefited immensely from the input we received from the invited senior executives. In Canada, Christopher Garmston (retired from Kentucky Fried Chicken International) not only shared his experiences with various joint ventures, he sat through all of the presentations in London, providing very helpful input. In Switzerland, Dr. Oyvind Fyllong Jensen, executive vice president of Dynal A.S., provided a most informed presentation about the challenges of a bioscience joint venture. In Hong Kong, Peter Lau, CEO of Giordano International Ltd., reviewed his company's very interesting alliance experiences in Asia.

The board of the Academy of International Business graciously accepted our proposal for the first special issue of *JIBS* in twelve years. As a consequence of this experience, a protocol was approved for considering further special issues.

Finally, Bill Hicks of The New Lexington Press shared our excitement for this project. Four publishers offered to publish the three books. We selected The New Lexington Press because it most closely matched our selection criteria of publishing the books quickly after the conferences, having a good international distribution network, and showing a willingness to price the books such that they would be accessible to as many people as possible.

Reviewer Acknowledgments

Sanjeev Agarwal
Azimah Ainuddin
Jay Anand
Africa Ariño
Preet S. Aulakh
Don Barclay
Marilyn W. Barrett
C. Christopher Baughn
Paul W. Beamish
Francis Bidault
Julian Birkinshaw
Linda L. Blodgett
Judith Blumenthal
Larry Browning
Peter J. Buckley
Jonathan L. Calof
Mark Casson
S. Tamer Cavusgil
Peggy E. Chaudhry
John Child
John B. Cullen
Refik Culpan
Tina Dacin
Andrew Delios
Christiane Demers
Johannes G. Denekamp
Gregory G. Dess
M. Krishna Erramilli
Carl Fey

Eileen Fischer
William H. Friedman
John Garland
J. Michael Geringer
Keith W. Glaister
Knut Haanes
Louis Hébert
Gunnar Hedlund
Duane A. Helleloid
Graham Hooley
Veronica Horton
John Hulland
C. L. Hung
Andrew C. Inkpen
Marko Jaklic
Johny K. Johansson
Jean L. Johnson
Julius H. Johnson Jr.
David H. Kent
J. Peter Killing
W. Chan Kim
Yui Kimura
Stephen J. Kobrin
Masaaki Kotabe
Harry Lane
Donald Lecraw
Chol Lee
Kwok Leung
Jiatao Li

Bente Lowendahl
Yuan Lu
Marjorie A. Lyles
Anoop Madhok
Shige Makino
Zaida Martinez
Alfredo Mauri
Martha Maznevski
Stuart McFadyen
Rod McNaughton
Richard W. Moxon
Kent E. Neupert
William Newburry
Jarmo Nieminen
Detlev Nitsch
Paul Olk
Richard N. Osborn
Yongsun Paik
Yigang Pan
Dorothy Paun
Jone L. Pearce
Laura Poppo
B. J. Punnett
U. Srinivasa Rangan
Doug Reid
Peter Smith Ring

Johan Roos
Kendall Roth
Alan M. Rugman
Jane E. Salk
Mitrabarun Sarkar
David M. Schweiger
Sanjay Sharma
Bernard L. Simonin
Fredric William Swierczek
Stephen Tallman
Hildy Teegan
Iris Tiemessen
Honorio Todino
Brian Toyne
David K. Tse
Christopher L. Tucci
Alain Verbeke
Ilan Vertinsky
Mary Ann Von Glinow
Alan William Wallace
Patrick Woodcock
Richard Wright
Aimin Yan
Henry Wai-Chung Yeung
Udo Zander
Liming Zhao

London, Ontario
Lausanne, Switzerland
December 1996

PAUL W. BEAMISH
J. PETER KILLING

	Global	North America	Asia	Europe	Specify	Not Empirical
Aulakh, Kotabe, and Sahay* Trust and Performance in Cross-Border Marketing Partnerships: A Behavioral Approach	x				US and Global	
Demers, Hafsi, Jørgensen, and Molz Industry Dynamics of Cooperative Strategy: Dominant and Peripheral Games	x				Canada	
Florin Organizing for Efficiency and Innovation: The Case for Nonequity Interfirm Cooperative Arrangements						x
Hébert and Beamish Characteristics of Canada-Based International Joint Ventures		x		x	Canada	
Horton and Richey On Developing a Contingency Model of Technology Alliance Formation						

Cooperative Strategies: North American Perspectives Data Focus
*Included in Special Issue of JIBS.

	Global	North America	Asia	Europe	Specify	Not Empirical
Inkpen An Examination of Knowledge Management in International Joint Ventures		x	x		NA and Japan	
Inkpen and Currall International Joint Venture Trust: An Empirical Examination		x	x		NA and Japan	
Johnson Procedural Justice Perceptions Among International Joint Venture Managers: Their Impact on Organizational Commitment	x					
Johnson, Cullen, Sakano, and Takenouchi* Setting the Stage for Trust and Strategic Integration in Japanese-U.S. Cooperative Alliances		x	x		US Japan	
Madhok Economizing and Strategizing in Foreign Market Entry						x
Merchant International Joint Venture Performance of Firms in the Nonmanufacturing Sector		x			US+	

		US+
Olk	The Effect of Partner Differences on the Performance of R&D Consortia	x	
Ramanathan, Seth, and Thomas	Explaining Joint Ventures: Alternative Theoretical Perspectives		x
Ring	Patterns of Process in Cooperative Interorganizational Relationships	x	
Sarkar, Cavusgil, and Evirgen	A Commitment-Trust Mediated Framework of International Collaborative Venture Peformance	x	
Tiemessen, Lane, Crossan, and Inkpen	Knowledge Management in International Joint Ventures		x

Cooperative Strategies: North American Perspectives Data Focus (*continued*)

*Included in Special Issue of JIBS.

THE AUTHORS

Preet S. Aulakh is assistant professor of marketing and international business at Michigan State University. His research interests include control issues in international business, strategic alliances, and entry strategies in foreign markets. His previous articles have appeared in the *Journal of Marketing,* the *Journal of International Business Studies,* and the *Journal of International Marketing.* He earned his doctorate at the University of Texas, Austin.

Paul Beamish is Royal Bank Professor in International Business at the Richard Ivey School of Business, University of Western Ontario. He serves on various editorial boards and is editor in chief of the *Journal of International Business Studies* for the 1993–1997 period.

S. Tamer Cavusgil holds the John William Byington Endowed Chair in Global Marketing at the Eli Broad Graduate School of Management, Michigan State University. Cavusgil also serves as executive director of the Michigan State University Center for International Business Education and Research and is editor in chief of the *Journal of International Marketing.*

Mary M. Crossan is the F.W.P. Jones Faculty Fellow at the Richard Ivey School of Business, University of Western Ontario, where she teaches strategic management. Her research on organizational learning and strategic renewal has been published in the *Journal of Management Studies, Organizational Dynamics,* the *International Executive,* the *International Journal of Organizational Analysis,* and the *Journal of Organizational Change Management.*

John B. Cullen is professor of management and systems at Washington State University. His current research focuses on the management structure of international strategic alliances and cross-cultural studies of ethical climates. His work has appeared in three monographs and numerous journals, including the *Journal of International Business Studies, Administrative Science Quarterly,* and the *Academy of Management Journal.*

Steven C. Currall is assistant professor of administrative science and psychology at the Jones Graduate School of Administration at Rice University. His current research interests include organizational boundary role persons, boards of directors, and psychometrics. He earned his doctorate in organizational behavior from Cornell University and holds a master's degree in social psychology from the London School of Economics.

Christiane Demers is professor of organizational strategy at École des Hautes Études Commerciales in Montreal, where she earned her doctorate. Her research interests include globalization in service industries and strategic change.

Cuneyt Evirgen is general manager of Bilesim Market Research Center, Ltd., in Istanbul, Turkey. He received his doctorate in marketing and international business from Michigan State University. He holds an undergraduate degree in engineering and an MBA from Bosphorus University in Turkey.

Juan M. Florin is a doctoral candidate at the University of Connecticut with research interests in international management strategy, cooperative ventures, and cross-cultural issues in management. His work experience includes fifteen years in international business with management positions in Latin America and the United States.

Taïeb Hafsi is professor of organizational strategy at École des Hautes Études Commerciales in Montreal. His research interests include strategic management of complex organizations, national strategies, and strategic change. He earned his doctorate in business administration at Harvard.

Louis Hébert is associate professor of strategy and international business at the Faculty of Commerce and Administration at Concordia University. He received his doctorate in business administration from the Richard Ivey School of Business, University of Western Ontario. His research interests include the management of joint ventures, strategic alliances, and mergers and acquisitions, and he currently heads a major project on strategic alliances in high-tech industries, particularly software and environment technology. He also has interests in the economic integration of the Americas and the restructuring of South American economies. He has published and presented several award-winning papers on the management of joint ventures around the world.

Veronica Horton is assistant professor of management at Middle Tennessee State University. Her research focuses on issues related to collaborative alliances and on assessing the impact of country-of-origin on the international marketing of hybrid products. She earned her doctorate at Ohio State University.

Andrew C. Inkpen is assistant professor of management at Thunderbird, the American Graduate School of International Management. He earned his doctorate in business policy at the Richard Ivey School of Business, University of Western Ontario. His research interests include the transfer of knowledge across borders by multinational firms, organizational learning, and knowledge management in international strategic alliances.

Jean L. Johnson is associate professor of marketing at Washington State University. Her research interests include the development, management, and strategic role of interfirm relationships and strategic alliances in the firm. In addition to the *Journal of International Business Studies,* her work has appeared in the *Journal of Marketing, Journal of the Academy of Marketing Science,* and *International Marketing Review.*

James P. Johnson is assistant professor of management and international business at Old Dominion University, Norfolk, Virginia. He received his doctorate in international business from the University of South Carolina.

Jan Jørgensen is professor of organizational policy at McGill University Faculty of Management in Montreal, where he received his doctorate. His current research interests include organizational responses to globalization, public sector divestment and restructuring, and management in developing countries.

J. Peter Killing is a professor at the International Institute for Management Development (IMD) in Lausanne, Switzerland. He has worked as a teacher, consultant, and researcher in the area of international management since 1975. He is coauthor of several international business strategy texts, and has written widely on the design and management of alliances.

Masaaki Kotabe is associate professor of international business and Ambassador Edward Clark Centennial Fellow in Business at the University of Texas, Austin. His research interests include global sourcing strategies, product and process innovation management, international alliances, and trade practices. His research has appeared in such journals as the *Journal of International Business Studies, Strategic Management Journal,* the *Journal of Marketing,* and the *Columbia Journal of World Business,* among others. He is the author of *Anticompetitive Practices in Japan* (Westport, Conn.: Praeger, 1996).

Henry W. Lane is the Donald F. Hunter Professor of International Business at the Richard Ivey School of Business, University of Western Ontario, where he is the program manager of the Doing Business in North America Program as well as associate editor of the *Journal of International Business Studies (JIBS).* His research interests are intercultural management, organizational learning, and strategic renewal. His articles have appeared in *JIBS* and in *Management International Review, Organizational Dynamics,* the *Journal of Business Ethics,* and the *International Journal of Organizational Analysis.*

Anoop Madhok is currently assistant professor at the David Eccles School of Business, University of Utah. He obtained his doctorate from McGill University, Montreal. His interests include global strategic management, foreign market entry, interfirm collaborations, and the theory of the firm. His articles on these topics have been published in the *Strategic Management Journal, Organization Science,* the *Journal of International Business Studies,* and the *Scandinavian Journal of Management.*

Hemant Merchant is the Dean's Endowed Research Fellow and assistant professor of international business at Simon Fraser University. He received his doctorate from Purdue University. His research focuses on issues related to the economic performance of international joint ventures involving firms in both manufacturing and nonmanufacturing sectors.

Richard Molz is professor of strategic management at Concordia University in Montreal. He received his doctorate from the University of Massachusetts. His research interests include organizational responses to globalization, industry structures, and strategic management in Eastern European countries.

Paul Olk is assistant professor at the Graduate School of Management of the University of California, Irvine. His research interests include the formation, management, and performance of strategic alliances. He received his doctorate from the Wharton School of the University of Pennsylvania.

Kannan Ramanathan is a doctoral candidate in strategy and international business at the University of Illinois, Urbana-Champaign. His research interests include organizational economics, with particular emphasis on property rights, interfirm collaboration, and strategy issues related to technology. His dissertation explores the economic value created by pharmaceutical firms at different stages in the new drug development process and identifies the factors that influence the extent of value creation at each stage.

Brenda Richey is assistant professor of international business at Florida Atlantic University. She received her doctorate at Ohio State University. In addition to strategic alliances, her research interests focus on questions of industrial policy and corporate governance.

Peter Smith Ring is professor of strategic management in the College of Business Administration at Loyola Marymount University in Los Angeles. He received his doctorate at the University of California, Irvine. His research explores the structures and processes of cooperative interorganizational relationships, as well as interorganizational trust and public-private interactions. He is currently investigating these issues in the context of networks among professional services firms.

Arvind Sahay is assistant professor of marketing at London Business School. He received his doctorate at the University of Texas, Austin. His research interests include technology licensing, product and competitive strategies, and new product development, and his research has appeared in the *Journal of Marketing*.

Tomoaki Sakano is professor of management at Waseda University, Tokyo. His research focuses on organization restructurings and interfirm buyer-seller relationships in the Japanese manufacturing and distribution sectors as well as strategic alliances. His research has appeared in the *Journal of Marketing*, the *Journal of Applied Psychology*, and the *Journal of International Business Studies*.

Mitrabarun Sarkar is a doctoral candidate in marketing and international business at Michigan State University. He holds an undergraduate degree in economics from St. Stephen's College, New Delhi, and a master's degree in business management from the Indian Institute of Management, Ahmedabad, India.

Anju Seth is associate professor of strategic management at the University of Illinois, Urbana-Champaign. She serves on the editorial board of the *Strategic Management Journal* and has received numerous research awards. She brings a multidisciplinary perspective to her research, drawing from organizational economics and financial economics. She has published several articles on value creation in corporate strategy via acquisitions, restructuring, corporate governance, joint ventures, and globalization, and on philosophy of science issues within the research tradition of strategic management.

Hideyuki Takenouchi is a doctoral student at the Graduate School of Commerce, Waseda University, Tokyo. His primary research interests include strategic alliances and other international management issues.

Howard Thomas is dean of the College of Commerce and Business Administration at the University of Illinois, Urbana-Champaign, as well as James F. Towey Professor of Strategic Management, professor of business administration, and director of the Office of International Strategic Management. Currently he serves on the editorial boards of the *Strategic Management Journal,* the *Journal of Strategic Change, Planning Review,* the *British Journal of Management,* the *Quarterly Review of Economics and Business,* and the *European Management Journal* and is associate editor of the *British Journal of Management*. He has published a wide range of articles on many topics, including competitive strategy, risk analysis, managing change, and decision theory.

Iris Tiemessen, having completed a doctoral thesis at the Richard Ivey School of Business, University of Western Ontario, is assistant professor of management at Bentley College in Waltham, Massachusetts. Her research interests are in the areas of knowledge management, international alliances, and employee competencies.

COOPERATIVE STRATEGIES

North American Perspectives

PART ONE

ADVANCES IN THEORIES OF COOPERATIVE STRATEGIES

1

ORGANIZING FOR EFFICIENCY AND INNOVATION

The Case for Nonequity Interfirm Cooperative Arrangements

Juan M. Florin

THIS CHAPTER DEVELOPS *a conceptual framework to explain interfirm cooperative arrangements in terms of efficiency and innovation. Efficiency of the exchange, measured as a reduction of transaction costs and operating costs, and innovation are proposed as performance outcomes, mediated by a relational exchange based on trust, specialization, and efficient experimentation.*

ONE OF THE MAIN hypotheses of transaction cost economics (TCE) is that as investments in assets specific to a transaction increase, contracting and monitoring costs also increase to safeguard against opportunistic behavior (Williamson 1989). This relationship results in a tradeoff between the efficiency of operations and the efficiency of the exchange. In other words,

I am grateful to Michael Lubatkin, Peter Lane, Patricia Gorman Clifford, the participants in the brown-bag seminar at the University of Connecticut, and the editors and three anonymous reviewers for their helpful comments and suggestions on earlier versions of this chapter.

investment in specific assets to meet a customer's needs may increase productivity (Parkhe 1993), but will also increase the transaction costs involved, sometimes offsetting the benefits from specialization.[1] The theory rests on the assumption that people and organizations act opportunistically and will take advantage of vulnerabilities displayed by the other party to a transaction.

Alternative forms of exchange based on interfirm cooperation challenge both the assertions of opportunism (Hill 1990) and the tradeoff between asset specificity and transaction costs expected by TCE (Dyer 1995; Parkhe 1993). In particular, cooperative arrangements possess certain structural characteristics, such as effective communication and information sharing systems between the parties, that make these transactions less exposed to opportunistic behavior. Furthermore, cooperative arrangements based on long-term relationships between partners function as hierarchies, in that they reduce the complexities of monitoring and control mechanisms (Jarillo 1988).

Given that TCE's relationships may not hold in cooperative arrangements (Dyer 1995), a new model of interfirm cooperation is warranted. Toward that end, this chapter develops an efficiency model of exchange to explain the potential performance benefits from interfirm cooperation. Building on Zajac and Olsen's definition (1993) of transaction value as joint value maximization, this model is based on the concept of cooperative efficiency at the exchange level. (Throughout this chapter, efficiency is understood as economy in the use of assets, time, and management effort to achieve a certain objective.) Transaction value is maximized in this model through the simultaneous reduction of transaction costs and operating costs, and an increase in innovation.

Innovations by either of the partners in a cooperative arrangement contribute to the competitive advantage of the dyad (Abrahamson 1991). An increase in innovations can result from shifts in the investment strategies of the individual firms as a result of the partnership. For example, resources previously locked into monitoring and control activities can be redirected into the development of core capabilities (Quinn 1992; Yoshino and Rangan 1995) and experimentation. This redeployment of resources to experimentation, with a focus on specialization, provides an efficient approach to innovation. Hence this chapter contributes to the understanding of performance in cooperative arrangements from the point of view of efficiency and innovation.

The purpose here is not to reject or disprove economic theories of exchange. Rather, it is to propose a model of efficient exchange that integrates economic theories (TCE and game theory) and management theories (resource based), focusing on the exchange relationship as the unit of analysis. The theories are extended by the model's consideration of both parties in the exchange, the nature of the relationship developed between them, and the analysis of the value added at the dyad level in addition to the individual firm level.

The rest of this chapter is organized in three sections. I begin with a brief review of the literatures, their limitations, and their contributions to this model. The second section introduces the model and the concept of transaction value, analyzing the dimensions and performance implications of the relational exchange process in cooperative arrangements. This is followed by a conclusion with suggestions for research and implications for managers.

Literature Review

The following discussions briefly review the literatures as they contribute to the understanding of cooperative arrangements and propose extensions to support the efficient model of exchange developed here. Cooperative arrangements are defined here as *essentially* nonequity relationships, either because there is no equity investment in the partner's business or because such investment is small and irrelevant to the issues of control and decision making in the partnership. Cooperation is understood in structural terms, that is, as the pooling of *complementary* firm-specific capabilities with the objective of improving the competitive advantage of the dyad.

Transaction Cost Economics

A basic assumption in TCE literature is that organizations and managers will act opportunistically to maximize utility, even at the expense of the other party. At the industry level, research has focused on the definition of organizational boundaries (that is, make or buy decisions). The basic argument is that markets are the ideal form of exchange, but when markets fail, organizations are more efficient (Williamson 1985). The literature accepts the dichotomy of markets and hierarchies as the primary alternatives for exchange, and opportunism as the assumption explaining the behavior of the parties to the exchange. Some authors have argued that hybrid types (Borys and Jemison 1989) and contracts (Hennart 1989) are alternatives available between markets and hierarchies. However, as the basic assumptions of opportunism regarding the nature of the exchange remain unchanged, hybrids and contracts are a middle ground in a continuum between markets and hierarchies.

TCE examines the exchange attributes that differentiate markets from hierarchies, identifying which forms of exchange are more efficient depending upon the characteristics of the transaction (Williamson 1991). One of the main determinants of the make-buy choice identified by TCE is the cost of the transaction. Transaction costs include the costs of searching for new suppliers or customers, negotiating, writing contracts, monitoring the other party's performance, and enforcing the contracts. When these costs become so high as to offset fully the benefits of the transaction, markets are said to fail. Hierarchies are said to be more efficient and thus are preferred. An example of imperfect markets leading to internalization is that of international competition where economic, institutional, and cultural barriers increase the cost of the exchange. The transaction cost theory of the multinational enterprise suggests that foreign direct investment, as an extension of a hierarchy across borders, reduces the cost of international coordination, facilitates knowledge transfer, and increases the efficiency of the exchange (Hennart 1989; Kogut 1986; Kogut and Zander 1993). More recently, however, globalization trends have set the stage for new nonequity-based agreements grounded instead on cooperation (Yoshino and Rangan 1995). Traditional theories of the firm are unable to explain this new trend. The new cooperative forms, developed around trust as opposed to opportunism, do not fit well on the continuum between markets and hierarchies.

An important contribution of TCE is the insight that investments in specific assets result in more efficient operations by lowering production costs (Parkhe 1993). However, the incentive to make investments to boost productivity is tempered by the opportunistic presumption that as assets become more specific to a particular customer's needs, they expose the owner to greater risk of opportunism (Klein, Crawford, and Alchian 1978). Thus the main relationship between transaction costs and asset specificity is that as investments in specific assets increase, transaction costs also increase, sometimes offsetting the efficiency benefits derived from specialization. Simply put, according to TCE, investing in specific assets enhances efficiency in operations (such as production or distribution), but there is a tradeoff between the efficiency of operations and the efficiency of the exchange due to the potential for opportunistic behavior.

The efficiency model of cooperation presented here rests strongly on the concept of specialization-based efficiency supported by TCE. However, recent empirical evidence on the relationships between auto makers and their suppliers (Dyer 1995; Helper and Sako 1995) has shown that the tradeoff predicted by TCE may not hold for transactions based on cooperative arrangements. Specifically, Dyer (1995) found evidence that transaction costs do not necessarily increase with an increase in asset specificity. Taking these conclusions a step further, it appears that firms engaging in cooperative arrangements can expect to realize simultaneous efficiency gains in the form of reduced transaction costs and reduced operating costs.

Dyer (1995) does not attempt a theoretical explanation of how or why this phenomenon may occur. Developing such a theory requires assuming a different perspective on transactions. Game theory looks more generally at exchange relationships at the individual level and helps us understand which characteristics of an exchange make cooperation possible.

Game Theory

Game theory looks at rational behavior in situations involving interdependence of outcomes (Camerer 1991). It considers the possible outcomes from interdependent exchanges under different payoff structures, different time horizons, and various frequencies of repetition and communication between players (Fudenberg and Maskin 1990). Significant research on game theory explores the Prisoner's Dilemma game, where defection is the dominant outcome when a single interaction is played. However, variations to this game have been developed that result in cooperation as a possible outcome (Oye 1986). One example is the Stag Hunt game that is structured in such a way that cooperation is the most likely outcome. When analyzing the Stag Hunt game, called the Coordination Game in recent writings (Camerer 1995), one finds many features of the cooperative exchange.

The structure of the Coordination Game is one in which the parties value the payoff from cooperation more than the potential gains from unilateral defection. These costs of defection include issues such as reputation effects, the potential gains from an evolving history of cooperation, and the commitment of partner-specific investments (Parkhe 1993). Thus in coordination-type games, the payoff of defection is smaller than that of cooperation. Furthermore, qualitative incentives such as reputation and trust lead to cooperation as a stable outcome in these relational exchanges (Hill 1990; Ring and Van de Ven 1992). These motives to cooperate generate action in the best interest of the relationship, breeding trust and reciprocity, and coordinating action (Blau 1964).

Another aspect of game theory that supports interfirm cooperation is the repetitive nature of the exchange. Empirical evidence suggests that even with noncooperative kinds of games, repeated interaction and communication between the players may result in cooperation (Axelrod 1984). Again, cooperation results when partners compare short-term payoffs from defecting with long-term payoffs from cooperating (Telser

1980). The explanation of such behavior is called the "tit-for-tat" effect, where cooperation in the current exchange will be matched by cooperation in the next one, and most importantly, defection in the current move will result in defection in the next move by the opponent (Axelrod 1984). This relationship between potential common future benefits and present actions has been called "the shadow of the future." Empirical evidence shows that cooperative performance is stronger the longer the shadow of the future (Heide and Miner 1992; Parkhe 1993).

In summary, recent work on game theory supports the notion that cooperation is a stable outcome given a long shadow of the future (long-term benefits), repeated interactions, and good communication between the players. These are the main features of a cooperative arrangement that lead to the development of trust in a relational exchange. Furthermore, these characteristics will contribute to the efficiency of the exchange by minimizing transaction costs.

While the previous theories have addressed the economics of the exchange process, at the firm level the resource-based view supports the notion that cooperation within the firm and the ability to develop trust-based relationships are capabilities that lead to competitive advantage (Barney and Hansen 1994). In the next subsection I present the basic assumptions of that theory, and propose an extension to interfirm cooperation by focusing on the dyad as the unit of analysis.

Resource-Based View of the Firm

Researchers adopting the resource-based view (RBV) of the firm argue that firm-level variances in capabilities better explain "buy versus make" decisions than traditional economic views (Kogut and Zander 1992; Teece and Pisano 1994). As with TCE, RBV also supports the notion that investments in specific assets improve efficiency of operations. However, RBV's focus on the firm explains how internal routines, skills embedded within the organization, and common language result in a set of capabilities unique to the firm that explain its competitive performance. This unique set of capabilities will also influence which activities of the value chain should be internalized and which should be acquired from outside. Ideally, an organization may generate value by integrating activities that leverage its firm-specific capabilities (Poppo and Zenger 1995), and subcontracting the less critical ones to partners specialized in those activities (Quinn 1992; Yoshino and Rangan 1995).

Although the RBV focus is on firm-specific capabilities, its concepts can be extended to the cooperative arrangement dyad. The competitive performance of the dyad can then be improved by the development of shared routines (such as integrated systems or cross-boundary teams), complementary capabilities (as a parallel to embedded skills), and trust as the basis for interfirm cooperation (the common language), all of which would afford competitive advantage. Hence, by extending the RBV to the dyad level, the theory helps us understand the competitive advantage of cooperation based on trust. The model presented in the next section develops the concept of relational exchange based on trust and its role in cooperative arrangements.

A Model of Efficient Interfirm Cooperation

The international business literature has observed the importance of process issues, such as the nature of the relationship, in determining performance in foreign direct investment and international joint ventures (Beamish and Banks 1987; Geringer and Hébert 1991; Madhok 1995; Parkhe 1993). These studies have advanced our knowledge of trust-oriented cooperation in interfirm equity-type arrangements. However, very little has been done to explain performance of nonequity type cooperation (Tallman and Shenkar 1994). Madhok (1995) hints at the potential efficiency implications of trust-based relationships in equity-based cooperation. This chapter also contributes to the international business literature by examining transaction costs, operating costs, and innovation as the performance drivers for the formation of nonequity-based cooperative arrangements, a relationship that has not received much attention to date.

Current trends in the business environment illustrate the need for new forms of exchange, such as cooperative arrangements, to create value and develop a competitive edge (Daft and Lewin 1993). One trend is the globalization of markets (Auster 1987; Levitt 1983), which continues in the 1990s at an even greater pace. Barriers to trade are falling dramatically in developing countries, not only opening these markets to foreign competitors but also forcing organizations in these regions to become international in scope in order to survive. These new players are becoming formidable competitors outside their markets and are avidly searching for partners to expand their operations.

Another accelerating trend is the increased speed of technological change that makes it impossible for any organization to single-handedly take advantage of all the opportunities available to it for creating value. These trends define competition in terms of global scope and speed. They require efficient but flexible forms of cooperation to enable firms to stay abreast of technological change and quickly tap into global markets.

These benefits of scope and speed have previously been established as reasons for interfirm cooperation (Bleeke and Ernst 1992; Hamel, Prahalad, and Doz 1989; Harrigan 1987; Harrigan and Newman 1990; Jones and Shill 1991; Kanter 1994). In this chapter, I develop a model to explain how cooperation can also lead to improvements in the bottom line in terms of efficiency and innovation, defining these performance outcomes of a cooperative exchange as transaction value.

Transaction Value as a Measure of Performance

The measurement of performance in strategic alliances has been elusive because of the difficulty in comparing financial statements before and after the formation of a joint venture or merger. In the case of international joint ventures, difficulties in establishing reliability and comparability of measures are magnified (Geringer and Hébert 1991). This is not a constraint in cooperative arrangements where the boundaries of the partner organizations have not changed. However, to this author the interesting question is not whether one of the firms to a transaction is performing better (the TCE approach), but whether and why cooperative arrangements may perform better than markets or hierarchies for the sum of the transactions between the partners (Helper and Sako 1995).

Zajac and Olsen (1993) point out that TCE ignores this joint value creation by focusing the analysis at the single firm's cost minimization efforts, without considering the interdependent nature of interorganizational strategies. They define transaction value in cooperation as, first, joint value maximization and, second, as the processes by which the exchange partners create and claim value. However, the authors still assume TCE's trade-off between the efficiency of specialization and transaction costs; they state that joint value creation outweighs the transaction inefficiencies that may result from supporting the cooperative effort.

The correct unit of analysis to evaluate performance in cooperative arrangements is the exchange itself. Contrary to TCE's expectations that asset specificity will increase transaction costs, it is proposed here that *transaction value* in cooperative arrangements results from the simultaneous reduction of transaction costs and operating costs, and an increase in innovation through efficient experimentation (experimentation is efficient if the resources allocated to it are directed toward specialization that results in innovation). Figure 1.1 depicts a model where a relational exchange based on trust, specialization, and efficient experimentation mediates the relationship between certain structural characteristics of interfirm cooperation and transaction value. The performance dimensions of transaction

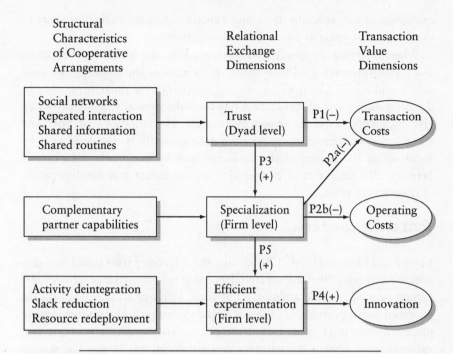

Figure 1.1. A Model of Efficient Interfirm Cooperation.

value in cooperative arrangements are identified as transaction costs, operating costs, and innovation.

The remainder of this section is devoted to the development of propositions linking the characteristics of cooperative arrangements with the dimensions of transaction value. The dynamics of the relational exchange construct are explored as well.

Relational Exchange Dimensions and Performance

It has been said that "competitive advantage increasingly depends not only on a company's internal capabilities, but also on the types of its alliances and the scope of its relationships with other companies" (Parkhe 1991: 579). Larger global companies have been the first to identify these trends and embrace cooperation as an alternative form of exchange (Beamish 1988), relying on trust in relationships as the means of controlling and reducing risk (Madhok 1995). This relational exchange is characterized in the model as the dynamic interaction of trust at the exchange level, specialization on complementary capabilities at the firm level, and efficient experimentation at the firm level. These three dimensions of the relational exchange—trust, specialization, and experimentation—each contribute to the creation of value in cooperative arrangements.

When referring to theory construction, Bacharach (1989: 498) states that "[the] primary goal of a theory is to answer the questions of *how, when,* and *why.*" The question of why cooperative arrangements may be an interesting form of transaction has been theoretically defined from an efficiency perspective as transaction value. The questions of how and when value is created in cooperative arrangements is discussed next by focusing on the nature of the exchange and its role in the relationship between characteristics of cooperative arrangements and the dimensions of transaction value.

Trust at the Dyad Level

Barney and Hansen (1994: 176) identify three levels of trust based on a definition of trust as "the mutual confidence that no party to an exchange will exploit another's vulnerabilities." The three levels of trust depend on the potential for opportunistic behavior in the exchange and the safeguards in place. The first level, weak form trust, occurs when there are no significant vulnerabilities among the partners in a particular exchange. The second level, semistrong form trust, exists under significant exchange vulnerabilities; economic models propose governance mechanisms to prevent opportunistic behavior under these conditions. Under the highest level, strong form trust, trust emerges as a result of the values, principles, and standards of behavior held by the parties. Barney and Hansen (1994) consider the concept of trust as essentially an attribute of a relationship and trustworthiness as an attribute of the individual firms (the exchange partners). Developing a reputation for trustworthiness and having the ability to cooperate based on trust are both viewed as potential sources of competitive advantage. However, the potential for opportunistic behavior by the partner may counter a firm's willingness to become exposed to such behavior.

The economics literature tells us that when markets are inefficient, for example due to information asymmetry or asset specificity, opportunities develop for one party to take advantage of another party's vulnerabilities in a transaction (Williamson 1985). Thus, market inefficiency leads to increased potential for opportunistic behavior. It is under such conditions that the concept of trust in an economic exchange becomes relevant. The following sociological perspective on trust accounts for this opportunistic context and complements Barney and Hansen's definition (1994).

According to Gambetta (1988: 217), trust is "a particular level of the subjective probability with which an agent assesses that another agent or group of agents will perform a particular action, both before he can monitor such action and in a context in which it affects his own action." In other words, trusting a person means *believing* that when offered a chance, he or she is not likely to behave in a way that is damaging to us. Furthermore, the willingness to become vulnerable to the other party's actions is a key factor of trust in the context of an exchange (Mayer, Davis, and Schoorman 1995). Thus, trust is not offered here as a replacement for opportunistic behavior, but rather as a characteristic of the relationship that helps avoid the costs that one may incur using other mechanisms (such as contracts and hierarchies) to control for opportunistic behavior.

In this way, trust operates as a social control mechanism in a relational exchange (Hamel, Prahalad, and Doz 1989), and as such operates as a risk reduction device (Gambetta 1988; Meadows 1995). More precisely, the reduced perception of risk entices managers to run the risks involved in developing a cooperative arrangement, even though traditional control mechanisms may be absent. In economics terms, trust reduces the perceived risk, helping an agent cope with uncertainty and seek cooperation.

It has been suggested that for trust to exist in a relationship it is necessary to establish structural mechanisms that will lower the possibility of opportunistic behavior (Madhok 1995). Four structural characteristics of cooperative arrangements, identified in the literature review, facilitate the development of trust as a mediator between cooperation and transaction costs: social networks, repeated interaction, shared routines, and shared information. Social networks provide information from previous interactions with other partners. These social interactions result in the development of a reputation as a trustworthy partner (Barney and Hansen 1994; Gulati 1995; Zaheer and Venkatraman 1995), and as possessing moral integrity and goodwill (Ring and Van de Ven 1992). The information gained through a network may help in the initial steps that partners take when entering into a cooperative arrangement. Higher levels of trust will develop over time as social bonds strengthen through shared norms and, possibly, similar values (Granovetter 1985). This higher form of trust may lead to sustainable competitive advantage (Barney and Hansen 1994).

According to game theory, repeated interaction can also influence transaction costs. Although the theory does not rely on the concept of trust to explain the bases of cooperation, one can conclude from the previous review that to build trust, partners need to establish a history of successful cooperation (Yoshino and Rangan 1995). Recent empirical evidence supports the notion that repeated ties influence the choice of nonequity-based alliances over those that are equity based—in other words, familiarity breeds trust (Gulati 1995). Hence, long-term relationships in the form of repeated interactions between partners will facilitate the development of cooperative arrangements between them when new opportunities arise.

In addition to the previous two structural antecedents to trust, which are well supported in the literature (Camerer 1991; Gulati 1995; Madhok 1995; Zaheer and Venkatraman 1995), this model provides a richer explanation of how trust is developed in cooperative arrangements by including two variables occurring at the dyad level and derived from the RBV. Shared routines (internal to the exchange) and information sharing (a common language) have the effect of developing trust and cooperation through everyday interactions at all levels of the organizations (Hamel, Prahalad, and Doz 1989; Ohmae 1989). These antecedents foster reliability, cooperativeness, and openness and are the basis for the existence of trusting relationships between partners (Quinn 1992). This social context in a relational exchange is key to the success of interfirm cooperation (Beamish and Banks 1987) and for capability building from a resource base perspective (Barney 1992).

A final consideration deriving from Gambetta's definition (1988) is that trust is a risk-taking behavior from the perspective of the party granting the trust. Hence willingness to take risks is an important component of trust (Johnson-George and Swap 1982). In other words, trust in a relational exchange means that the parties are willing to grant trust, and that this trust entails the belief that the other parties can and will perform their part of the exchange (Meadows 1995). In summary, it is the reliance on trust as a risk reduction mechanism that makes cooperative arrangements efficient. This efficiency derives from the minimization of monitoring and enforcing mechanisms (such as complicated contracts) that otherwise would drive transaction costs up (Hennart 1989). The following proposition formally establishes the mediating role of trust in the relationship between characteristics of cooperative arrangements and transaction value:

PROPOSITION I: The level of trust between partners in a cooperative arrangement mediates the negative relationships between social networks, repeated interactions, shared information, and shared routines, and the transaction costs of the exchange.

Following Barney and Hansen's classification (1994) of levels of trust, it appears that a semistrong form trust is sufficient for a cooperative arrangement to be efficient. According to those authors, this level of trust results from the structural characteristics of cooperation which relate social and economic costs to opportunistic behavior. One such cost, an opportunity cost, derives from the foregoing of efficiencies from specialization. The role of specialization in a relational exchange is central from an efficiency perspective.

Specialization at the Firm Level

Specialization is defined here as possessing two attributes: focus in the core business and quality in terms of product, service, process, or technology (see Note 1). Both TCE and RBV support the notion that investments leading to specialization result in efficient outcomes (Poppo and Zenger 1995). The theories differ, however, in identifying the antecedents of specialization. RBV suggests that specialization results from the need to focus on the development of core capabilities that will provide competitive advantage to the firm. TCE theory looks at the characteristics of the exchange and predicts that firms will internalize those activities that are not available or too costly to obtain in the marketplace. The model presented here considers both concepts and suggests that firms will seek partners with complementary capabilities to perform value chain activities outside their own core capabilities. This strategic choice can lead to the specialization of each partner and, in turn, to the improvement of the competitive advantage of the dyad as measured in terms of efficiency.

The literature reviewed supports the notion that cooperation results in a shadow of the future that prevents opportunistic behavior. One way of creating this effect is through cooperation with partners that have complementary capabilities, as such partnerships will result in interdependent outcomes. Empirical investigation has also shown that specialization improves efficiency by reducing production costs (Parkhe 1993). Consequently, firms that concentrate on performing the activities they perform best will become more efficient (Kotabe 1990). These arguments lead to the proposition that a relational exchange that fosters specialization in complementary capabilities will contribute to the value of the transaction by lowering both transaction costs and operating costs. More formally:

PROPOSITION 2A: Specialization by the partners in a cooperative arrangement mediates the negative relationship between complementary partner capabilities and the transaction costs of the exchange.

PROPOSITION 2B: Specialization by the partners in a cooperative arrangement mediates the negative relationship between complementary partner capabilities and the operating costs of the partners.

The degree of specialization will be accentuated through the evolution of cooperation as the levels of trust increase. In other words, because increased levels of trust reduce the perceived level of risk (Gambetta 1988; Meadows 1995), managers will be encouraged over time to increase their investments in assets specific to the relationship. Hence, the interaction of trust with complementarity of capabilities will also influence the level of specialization of the partners.

PROPOSITION 3: Trust will moderate specialization so that the greater the level of trust between partners in a cooperative arrangement, the greater the degree of specialization by each partner.

Taking the second and third propositions together, one can better understand the role of specialization as a moderated mediation between complementary capabilities of the partners and the efficiency of the exchange (James and Brett 1984). I now turn to the third component of a relational exchange, efficient experimentation, and its mediating role between cooperation and innovation.

Efficient Experimentation at the Firm Level

Efficient experimentation is defined here as the allocation of resources to the development of capabilities to improve the firm's areas of competence. Within a cooperative arrangement, this results in the intentional and directed use of resources toward experimentation related to the exchange. The literature on innovation has related innovation to organizational slack (Sharfman, Wolf, Chase, and Tansik 1988). Recently, Nohria and Gulati (1995: 32) defined slack as "the pool of resources in an organization that is in excess of the minimum necessary to produce a given level of organizational output." Some examples are redundant employees, less than full-capacity utilization, and unnecessary capital expenditures. The authors include, within the definition of slack, unexploited opportunities for increased outputs such as increased sales and access to innovations. This forgoing of opportunities is key to the reasons for cooperation, and to the concept of innovation as a performance outcome for cooperative arrangements.

Slack can facilitate or inhibit experimentation. It facilitates it by providing resources that otherwise would not be available. On the other hand, it may reduce the need to innovate or result in undisciplined experimentation, which rarely yields positive results (that is, innovation). "The literature provides no clear answer," according to Nohria and Gulati (1995: 32), "because theorists stand divided on whether slack facilitates or inhibits innovation." This model builds upon the notion that increased slack may lead to more experimentation but not necessarily to innovation. Thus the concept of slack is relevant to this analysis because if one considers organizational slack as a measure of inefficiency, then innovation is a tradeoff to efficiency of operations.

This view of slack as an antecedent to innovation complements the RBV notion of purposeful allocation of resources to the development of core capabilities (Yoshino and Rangan 1995). As with specialization, firms can uncover such resources by transferring value-chain activities to specialized partners through cooperative arrangements (activity deintegration), and redirect resources to experimentation (Quinn 1992). The relational exchange environment encourages this activity deintegration and the redeployment of slack to experimentation in complementary capabilities.

Nohria and Gulati (1995) found empirical evidence in a sample of multinational corporations to support the proposition that there is an optimal amount of slack that will foster experimentation. They depict the slack-innovation relationship as an inverted U-shaped curve in which both too little and too much slack result in less innovation. Building on this conclusion, I propose that cooperative arrangements allow for the reduction of the optimal slack within each organization in the partnership. Furthermore, slack can be allocated to experimentation focused on complementary capabilities. This experimentation, if well managed and applied to core capabilities, results in value creation through innovation (Haspeslagh and Jemison 1991). More formally:

PROPOSITION 4: Efficient experimentation by the partners in a cooperative arrangement mediates the positive relationships between activity deintegration, slack reduction, and resource redeployment, and the level of innovation.

Contrary to Parkhe's argument (1991) that diversity of objectives hinders cooperation, it is proposed here that diversity of capabilities improves the competitive advantage of the dyad through efficient experimentation. This complementarity becomes a structural component to the cooperation, which in turn promotes further experimentation. As the partners become more specialized through outsourcing of noncore activities, experimentation can become more focused and efficient. Hence, the degree of specialization influences the efficiency of the experimentation processes of each partner.

PROPOSITION 5: Specialization moderates efficient experimentation, so that the greater the degree of specialization by the partners in a cooperative arrangement, the more efficient they will become in their respective experimentation processes.

Taken together, Propositions 4 and 5 describe a moderated mediating role of efficient experimentation in the relationship between cooperation and innovation. Furthermore, the roles of trust and specialization as moderating variables (Propositions 3 and 5) depict the relational exchange as a dynamic concept (Baron and Kenny 1986).

Conclusion

In this chapter I have developed an efficiency model of cooperation as an alternative explanation of performance in cooperative arrangements to the traditional transaction cost economics perspective. Three dimensions of a relational exchange, trust between the partners, specialization, and efficient experimentation, have been suggested to mediate the relationship between distinct characteristics of a cooperative arrangement and the transaction value of the exchange. Building on Zajac and Olsen (1993), I defined transaction value as the reduction of transaction costs and operating costs, and the increase of innovation. In addition to their mediating effects, the dimensions of the relational exchange interact with each other, with trust increasing partner specialization and specialization increasing the efficiency of a firm's experimentation. Taken together, this set of relationships can create value for firms developing cooperative arrangements.

Current theory appears unable to completely explain cooperative arrangements; these limitations have been discussed and extensions proposed to narrow this gap. The trade-off between efficiency of the exchange and efficiency of operations established by TCE theory is no longer applicable under cooperative arrangements. In a relational exchange context, firms can achieve higher levels of efficiency by reducing transaction costs and operating costs simultaneously. Furthermore, the redeployment of resources to efficient experimentation in core capabilities facilitates innovation in each of the organizations in the dyad, adding value to the exchange. Transaction cost economics theory, game theory, and resource-based theory all focus on the individual firm outcomes, ignore the other party in the transaction, and do not consider the mediating effect that the nature of the relationship itself has in the exchange. Contrary to Williamson's assertion (1993) that the study of organizations is not well served by introducing the concept of trust, this chapter has posited that the concept of trust is at the root of efficiency and innovation and is thus absolutely necessary to understand performance in exchange relationships (Jarillo and Bidault 1995).

The process of cooperation is not strictly economic, but also social, psychological, and emotional (Tallman and Shenkar 1994). Economic models do not explain all the interpersonal and organizational factors at play inside organizations. A research agenda for cooperation should focus on how cultural differences affect trust and cooperation, and which organizational practices may foster these types of relationships in interorganizational exchanges. Empirical research on trust has only recently begun to appear in major management journals and at conferences. The most simple approach has been to survey participants in a cooperative arrangement, asking them whether they trust their partner or whether their partner is trustworthy (Dyer 1995). More complex instruments have been developed in the psychology field for interpersonal relationships (Cook and Wall 1980; Johnson-George and Swap 1982; Rempel and Holmes 1986; Rotter 1967), and in sociology for intergroup trust (Lewis and Weigert 1985). These measures were recently adapted by Zaheer and Venkatraman (1995) to compare interpersonal trust with interorganizational trust in buyer-supplier relationships. Other chapters in this volume provide new and interesting approaches to understanding and measuring the trust construct (see Chapters Seven, Nine, Twelve, and Ten).

New ways of competing globally have been developed in recent years that can provide interesting venues for research on cooperation. One example is the convergence of technologies to develop new applications. Cooperative arrangements based on converging technologies are an interesting venue to research the impact of trust, complementary capabilities, and efficient experimentation discussed here. Another example is the outsourcing of industrial design by developing partnerships with specialized suppliers. The service industries present yet another interesting context to research cooperation. In particular, service networks (referral-based alliances) are proliferating in this industry (Bamford 1995). Finally, the functional area most heavily targeted by researchers interested in cooperation is procurement and the buyer-supplier relationship (Dyer 1995; Heide and Miner 1992; Helper and Sako 1995).

The implications for management practice are significant. If managers' mental models follow assumptions of opportunism and mistrust, their strategic choices will be limited to the development of controlling mechanisms that increase transaction costs and dissuade specialization. Only if managers are able to consider trust as an alternative control mechanism to reduce risk and uncertainty can their strategic options expand through the development of cooperative arrangements.

The challenge is then to practice the relational exchange developed in this model across organizations and across borders. Cultural considerations, both organizational and national, will have a significant impact on a manager's ability to develop trusting relationships. Those organizations that learn how to develop these types of exchanges will benefit from efficiency and innovation. Learning to compete globally through cooperation may be the only viable long-term strategy.

NOTE

1. Asset specificity and specialization are related but different concepts. Asset specificity refers to the commitment of resources to a certain customer or relationship that cannot be readily redeployed or applied to alternative use. Economic theory posits that asset specificity makes a company vulnerable to its customers. Specialization refers to a company's focus on a certain process or technology in which it develops a special competence. The expected benefit of specialization is becoming the best at what one does (that is, being the lowest-cost producer or marketer, being at the forefront of technology, and the like).

BIBLIOGRAPHY

Abrahamson, E. 1991. Managerial fads and fashions: The diffusion and rejection of innovations. *Academy of Management Review,* 16(3): 586–612.

Auster, E. 1987. International corporate linkages: Dynamic forms in changing environments. *Columbia Journal of World Business,* Summer 1987: 3–6.

Axelrod, R. 1984. *The Evolution of Cooperation.* New York: Basic Books.

Bacharach, S. B. 1989. Organizational theories: Some criteria for evaluation. *Academy of Management Review,* 14(4): 496–515.

Bamford, J. 1995. Service networks: Hearing the hoofbeat of history. *The Alliance Analyst.*

Barney, J. B. 1992. Integrating organizational behavior and strategy formulation research: A resource based analysis. *Advances in Strategic Management,* 8: 39–61.

Barney, J. B., and M. H. Hansen. 1994. Trustworthiness as a source of competitive advantage. *Strategic Management Journal,* 15: 175–190.

Baron, R. M., and D. A. Kenny. 1986. The moderator-mediator variable distinction in social psychological research: Conceptual, strategic, and statistical considerations. *Journal of Personality and Social Psychology,* 51(6): 1173–1182.

Beamish, P. W. 1988. *Multinational Joint Ventures in Developing Countries.* New York: Routledge.

Beamish, P. W., and J. C. Banks. 1987. Equity joint ventures and the theory of the multinational enterprise. *Journal of International Business Studies,* 18(2): 1–16.

Blau, P. M. 1964. *Exchange and Power in Social Life.* New York: Wiley.

Bleeke, J., and D. Ernst. 1992. The way to win in cross-border alliances. *The McKinsey Quarterly,* 1: 113–133.

Borys, B., and D. B. Jemison. 1989. Hybrid arrangements as strategic alliances: Theoretical issues in organizational combinations. *Academy of Management Review,* 14(2): 234–249.

Camerer, C. F. 1991. Does strategy research need game theory? *Strategic Management Journal,* 12 (Summer): 137–152.

Camerer, C. F. 1995. Mental models and strategic decision making (Workshop). Paper read at Academy of Management Annual Meeting, Vancouver, BC.

Cook, J., and E. Wall. 1980. New work attitude measures of trust, organizational commitment and personal need nonfulfillment. *Journal of Occupational Psychology,* 53: 39–52.

Daft, R. L., and A. Y. Lewin. 1993. Where are the theories for the "new" organizational forms? An editorial essay. *Organization Science,* 4(4).

Dyer, J. H. 1995. Maximizing transaction value: How transactors simultaneously achieve high asset specificity and low transaction costs. Paper read at Academy of Management Annual Meeting, Vancouver, BC.

Fudenberg, D., and E. Maskin. 1990. Evolution and cooperation in noisy repeated games. *American Economic Review,* 80(2): 274–279.

Gambetta, D. 1988. Can we trust trust? In D. Gambetta, editor, *Trust: Making and Breaking Cooperative Relations.* Cambridge, Mass.: Blackwell.

Geringer, J. M., and L. Hébert. 1991. Measuring performance of international joint ventures. *Journal of International Business Studies,* 22(2): 249–263.

Granovetter, M. 1985. Economic action and social structure: The problem of embeddedness. *American Journal of Sociology,* 91: 481–510.

Gulati, R. 1995. Does familiarity breed trust? The implications of repeated ties for contractual choice in alliances. *Academy of Management Journal,* 38(1): 85–112.

Hamel, G., C. K. Prahalad, and Y. Doz. 1989. Collaborate with your competitors—and win. *Harvard Business Review,* January-February: 133–139.

Harrigan, K. R. 1987. Strategic alliances: Their new role in global competition. *Columbia Journal of World Business,* Summer: 67–69.

Harrigan, K. R., and W. H. Newman. 1990. Bases of interorganization co-operation: Propensity, power, persistence. *Journal of Management Studies,* 27(4): 417–434.

Haspeslagh, P. C., and D. B. Jemison. 1991. *Managing Acquisitions.* New York: Free Press.

Heide, J. B., and A. S. Miner. 1992. The shadow of the future: Effects of anticipated interaction and frequency of contact on buyer-seller cooperation. *Academy of Management Journal,* 35: 265–291.

Helper, S. R., and M. Sako. 1995. Supplier relations in Japan and the United States: Are they converging? *Sloan Management Review,* 36 (Spring): 77–84.

Hennart, J. F. 1989. Can the "new forms of investment" substitute for the "old forms?" A transaction costs perspective. *Journal of International Business Studies,* 20(2): 211–234.

Hill, C. 1990. Cooperation, opportunism, and the invisible hand: Implications for transaction cost theory. *Academy of Management Review,* 15(3): 550–513.

James, L. R., and J. M. Brett. 1984. Mediators, moderators, and tests for mediation. *Journal of Applied Psychology,* 69: 307–321.

Jarillo, J. C. 1988. On strategic networks. *Strategic Management Journal,* 9(1): 31–41.

Jarillo, J. C., and F. Bidault. 1995. Opportunism, trust, markets and hierarchies. Paper read at Strategic Management Society Annual Conference, Mexico City.

Johnson-George, C., and W. Swap. 1982. Measurement of specific interpersonal trust: Construction and validation of a scale to assess trust in a specific other. *Journal of Personality and Social Psychology,* 43: 1306–1317.

Jones, K. K., and W. E. Shill. 1991. Allying for advantage. *The McKinsey Quarterly,* 3: 73–101.

Kanter, R. M. 1994. Collaborative advantage. *Harvard Business Review,* March-April: 96–108.

Klein, B., R. G. Crawford, and A. A. Alchian. 1978. Vertical integration, appropriable rents, and the competitive contracting process. *Journal of Law and Economics,* 21: 297–326.

Kogut, B. 1986. On designing contracts to guarantee enforceability: Theory and evidence from East-West trade. *Journal of International Business Studies,* 17(1): 47–61.

Kogut, B., and U. Zander. 1992. Knowledge of the firm, combinative capabilities, and the replication of technology. *Organization Science,* 3(3): 383–397.

Kogut, B., and U. Zander. 1993. Knowledge of the firm and the evolutionary theory of the multinational corporation. *Journal of International Business Studies*, 24(4): 625–645.

Kotabe, M. 1990. Linking product and process innovations and modes of international sourcing in global competition: A case of foreign multinational firms. *Journal of International Business Studies*, 21(3): 383–408.

Levitt, T. 1983. The globalization of markets. *Harvard Business Review*, May-June: 92–102.

Lewis, J. D., and A. J. Weigert. 1985. Social atomism, holism, and trust. *Sociological Quarterly*, 26: 455–471.

Madhok, A. 1995. Revisiting multinational firms' tolerance for joint ventures: A trust-based approach. *Journal of International Business Studies*, 26(1): 117–137.

Mayer, R. C., J. H. Davis, and F. D. Schoorman. 1995. An integrative model of organizational trust. *Academy of Management Review*, 20(3): 709–734.

Meadows, C. J. 1995. Global collaboration: A proposed framework for forging cooperative relationships. Paper read at the Organizational Dimensions of Global Change: No Limits to Cooperation conference at Weatherhead School of Management, Case Western Reserve University, Cleveland, Ohio.

Nohria, N., and R. Gulati. 1995. What is the optimum amount of organizational slack? A study of the relationship between slack and innovation in multinational firms. Paper read at Academy of Management Best Papers Proceedings, Vancouver, BC.

Ohmae, K. 1989. The global logic of strategic alliances. *Harvard Business Review*, March-April: 143–154.

Oye, K. A., editor. 1986. *Cooperation Under Anarchy*. Princeton, N.J.: Princeton University Press.

Parkhe, A. 1991. Interfirm diversity, organizational learning, and longevity in global strategic alliances. *Journal of International Business Studies*, 22(4): 579–601.

Parkhe, A. 1993. Strategic alliance structuring: A game theoretic and transaction cost examination of interfirm cooperation. *Academy of Management Journal*, 36(4): 794–829.

Poppo, L., and T. Zenger. 1995. Opportunism, routines, measurement, and boundary choices: A test of transaction cost and resource-based explanations for make-or-buy decisions in information services. Paper read at Academy of Management Best Papers Proceedings, Vancouver, BC.

Quinn, J. B. 1992. *Intelligent Enterprise*. New York: Free Press.

Rempel, J. K., and J. G. Holmes. 1986. How do I trust thee? *Psychology Today*, February: 28–34.

Ring, P. S., and A. H. Van de Ven. 1992. Structuring cooperative relationships between organizations. *Strategic Management Journal*, 13: 438–498.

Rotter, J. B. 1967. A new scale for the measurement of interpersonal trust. *Journal of Personality*, 35: 651–665.

Sharfman, M. P., G. Wolf, R. B. Chase, and D. A. Tansik. 1988. Antecedents of organizational slack. *Academy of Management Review*, 13(4): 601–614.

Tallman, S. B., and O. Shenkar. 1994. A managerial decision model of international cooperative venture formation. *Journal of International Business Studies*, 25(1): 91–113.

Teece, D., and G. Pisano. 1994. The dynamic capabilities of firms: An introduction. *Industrial and Corporate Change*, 3(3): 537–555.

Telser, L. G. 1980. A theory of self-enforcing agreements. *Journal of Business*, 53: 27–41.

Williamson, O. E. 1985. *The Economic Institutions of Capitalism*. New York: Free Press.

Williamson, O. E. 1989. Transaction cost economics. In R.D.W. Schmalensee, editor, *Handbook of Industrial Organization*. Amsterdam: North-Holland.

Williamson, O. E. 1991. Comparative economic organization: The analysis of discrete structural alternatives. *Administrative Science Quarterly*, 36(2): 269–296.

Williamson, O. E. 1993. The logic of economic organization. In O. E. Williamson and W. G. Winter, editors, *The Nature of the Firm: Origins, Evolution, and Development*. New York: Oxford University Press.

Yoshino, M. Y., and U. S. Rangan. 1995. *Strategic Alliances: An Entrepreneurial Approach to Globalization*. Boston: Harvard Business School Press.

Zaheer, A., and N. Venkatraman. 1995. Relational governance as an interorganizational strategy: An empirical test of the role of trust in economic exchange. *Strategic Management Journal*, 16(5): 373–392.

Zajac, E. J., and C. P. Olsen. 1993. From transaction cost to transactional value analysis: Implications for the study of interorganizational strategies. *Journal of Management Studies*, 30(1): 131–145.

2

ECONOMIZING AND STRATEGIZING IN FOREIGN MARKET ENTRY

Anoop Madhok

THE INTERNALIZATION AND *competitive strategy perspectives, which are based respectively on economizing and strategizing logic, have been dominant in addressing the foreign entry mode decision. Yet, differences in their level of analysis and orientation toward competitiveness have resulted in their approaching the issue only partially and in mutual isolation. This chapter first compares the two perspectives and their approaches toward underlying areas of common concern, such as risk minimization and the earning of rents, and then addresses how macroenvironmental factors, central to competitive strategy, interact with specific transaction characteristics to affect multinational firms' choice of mode of foreign market entry. It is argued that an exploration of the interface between the two perspectives provides the basis for a more comprehensive theoretical understanding.*

GLOBAL COMPETITION AND technological developments have fundamentally and irrevocably altered the way firms conduct business. To meet the multiplicity of pressures they need to manage simultaneously—geographic, product, market, technological, competitive—corporations are extending their presence all over the globe for a multitude of purposes and through a multitude of forms (Contractor and Lorange 1988; Hagedoorn 1993). In this context, the mode of foreign market entry has become an important strategic decision with critical implications for competitive advantage. In line with this, scholarly interest in the topic has increased (Anderson and Gatignon 1986; Gomes-Casseres 1989; Hill, Hwang, and Kim 1990; Contractor 1990; Osborn and Baughn 1990; Anderson and Coughlan 1987; Erramilli and Rao 1990; Kim and Hwang 1992).

The entry mode decision has been addressed predominantly from an economizing logic or a strategizing logic. The logic of economizing has been applied primarily by the internalization perspective, which is closely related to transaction cost (TC) theory (Rugman [1986] refers to internalization theory as the transaction cost theory of the multinational firm; here, the two are used interchangeably). The gist of the argument is that, depending on the characteristics of the transaction, each mode of involvement in a particular market involves a different level of transaction costs. A fit between the transaction characteristics and the mode of ownership (also called entry mode, governance mode, and ownership form in this chapter) results in economically efficient governance and makes the firm more competitive. The logic of strategizing has been applied primarily by the competitive strategy (CS) perspective, which is oriented toward the competitive positioning of the firm in various product markets. From this perspective, each mode of involvement entails a different level of resource commitment and, relatedly, a differing degree of flexibility for entry and exit (Harrigan 1985, 1988; Porter 1980; Contractor and Lorange 1988; Hill, Hwang, and Kim 1990). A fit between various environmental characteristics and the extent of firm involvement results in effective strategic positioning and makes the firm more competitive.

Both the economizing and strategizing logics provide unique and interesting insights into firms' choices regarding the mode of entry. However, with the economic rationale underlying the boundaries of the firm being different for these two perspectives (Hagedoorn 1993), as both are rooted in different theoretical traditions (institutional and industrial organization economics, respectively) and differ in their emphasis (governance cost efficiencies and competitive positioning, respectively), each approaches the issue of entry mode choice only partially. This chapter was motivated by the concern that continuation of the two perspectives along their respective parallel paths is hindering the development of a more sophisticated understanding of the entry mode phenomenon. It seeks to review briefly (as the basics are well known) the literature on the mode of foreign market entry from the TC-internalization and competitive strategy perspectives (other perspectives exist but are not the focus here), primarily with the intention of highlighting the key issues in the choice of entry mode. Further, it compares the two perspectives and their approach toward underlying areas of common concern, such as risk minimization and the earning of rents, and also conceptualizes the entry mode decision in a more comprehensive manner by exploring aspects of the interface between the two.

Basically, differences in level of analysis and competitive orientation have resulted in the two perspectives developing in mutual isolation. In its preoccupation with the economic efficiencies obtained through minimization of transaction costs, the internalization perspective ignores corporate strategic motives driving the choice of governance mode, which may override cost minimization and efficiency considerations. This is one of its major shortcomings (Contractor 1990). For example, rapid market entry to preempt competition may drive a firm to seek a partner, even if this is not the transactionally least-cost mode of governance. CS, on the other hand, is oriented toward firm positioning and the strategic benefits obtained through a particular mode of involvement, such as preemptive access to resources or leveraging of the firm's source of competitive advantage. It tends to neglect the underlying transaction-related issues. For example, from the TC point of view, in a collaboration formed for the purpose of technology development, complexities in pricing and transferring know-how would be major considerations influencing ownership mode preference. These complexities can increase transaction costs and create inefficiencies in transferring the know-how, thus negating many potential benefits and preventing the consummation of the transaction. The issue of market failure, however, is not addressed by the CS perspective.

In brief, economizing and strategizing have tended to be treated as competing logics where internalization emphasizes (transaction) cost minimization and CS emphasizes the benefits associated with strategic product-market positioning (Kogut 1988). Yet, with the essence of firm strategy being ultimately the search for rents (Bowman 1974; Rumelt 1984), these rents can be earned through developing cost efficiencies, greater benefits, or a combination of the two. Therefore, both transactional and strategic considerations need to be factored into the ownership mode decision. The importance of both is affirmed by Porter and Fuller's statement that "the choice of a coalition implies that it is perceived as a less costly *or* a more effective way to configure than the alternatives" (1986: 321; emphasis added). An insightful paper that weaved in elements from strategic and TC arguments, though in the different context of the strategy-structure choice, was that of Jones and Hill (1988). Some authors (Kogut 1988; Kim and Hwang 1992) have addressed both CS and TC perspectives, but they treat them as contending and alternative explanations. The position taken herein, however, is that economizing and strategizing are not competing arguments, but need to be addressed jointly, not additively, in order to attain a more thorough and comprehensive understanding of entry mode decisions. In line with this, this chapter also addresses how macroenvironmental factors, central to CS, interact with specific transaction characteristics to affect such decisions.

Mode of Entry

TC logic (Williamson 1975) views the transaction as the basic unit of analysis. A particular transaction's characteristics determine the choice of the most efficient institutional mode by which to manage it.

The Internalization Perspective

Under the assumptions of bounded rationality and opportunism, the presence of certain characteristics creates contracting problems that increase the cost of transacting through the market. Beyond a certain point, it would be in the firm's interest to reduce the TC by internalizing the transaction. Internalization theory is a variant of TC theory specifically concerned with the multinational firm (Buckley and Casson 1976; Rugman 1980). Essentially, the multinational firm is deemed to possess some rent-yielding firm-specific advantage, primarily some form of know-how. Multinational activities are driven by the objective of exploiting this advantage abroad in the most efficient manner (Hymer 1976), namely internalization (a subsidiary), quasi-internalization (joint ventures), or arm's-length contracting (such as licensing). Imperfections in the market for knowledge can result in market failure, in which case internalization is more efficient. Internalization theory has been criticized by Teece (1986a) for being not only rather general but also too predominantly concerned with the market for knowledge. Though both internalization and TC theory revolve around the concept of market failure, the former pays inadequate attention to the more specific contextual conditions, such as asset specificity, that influence the nature of a transaction and that TC theory emphasizes.[1]

With a few prominent exceptions (Hennart 1988; Gomes-Casseres 1989), the internalization literature on entry mode has tended to concentrate primarily on the choice between equity ownership (subsidiary) and licensing (for example, Davidson and McFetridge 1985; Telesio 1979; Rugman 1986). This is probably because licensing has tended to be the most common form of nonequity or contractual collaboration. Here, licensing is used as representative of all nonequity collaborative agreements.

A major argument, put forward to explain why a firm would prefer an internalized governance structure to licensing, concerns the nature of know-how. First, it is difficult to arrive at a market clearing price for know-how, especially where it is tacit and difficult to articulate. Due to informational asymmetries, the buyer is uncertain of the value of the know-how and has apprehensions about misrepresentation of its value by the seller. On the other hand, greater revelation of the know-how in order to convince the prospective licensee of its intrinsic value actually reduces the income-earning potential of the know-how, as the buyer now possesses it without paying for it. This paradoxical situation is known as the buyer uncertainty problem, and is a driving force toward internalization (Buckley and Casson 1976; Teece 1981). Though this dilemma can potentially be resolved through patent protection, patents are often difficult to enforce and easy for others to circumvent (Hennart 1982). Second, the knowledge is frequently the outcome of joint team input and comes as a composite package that includes both the tangible embodiment of the technology and the associated tacit managerial know-how (Teece 1981). In such situations, denser interaction and involvement is required to transfer the know-how to a partner effectively, which then raises transfer costs. Arm's-length contractual mechanisms are unsuitable for such transfer. Besides the evaluation problem, the difficulty in observation and measurement of tacit know-how makes it difficult to specify adequate contractual stipulations determining the exact mechanisms of its transfer, the exact extent of its transfer, the exact responsibilities of each party in this regard in order to effectuate successful transfer, and even when such transfer has been completed. In addition to these difficulties, there is little incentive to provide more than is set out in the contract (Davies 1977). A subsidiary provides superior incentives and more efficient mechanisms for such transfer.

While tacitness is concerned with difficulties in measurement and ambiguities surrounding transfer, another argument deals with the specificity of the investment to a particular transaction in terms of the ease and extent to which it can be redeployed to alternative uses. Transaction-specific investments render the firm vulnerable to self-interested behavior by a partner who could act opportunistically to the extent of the switching costs between the current and the next best use of the asset (Williamson 1985). Therefore, in the presence of such specific investments, firms prefer entering a market through a subsidiary (Anderson and Coughlan 1987).

The above arguments deal with the preference for equity over licensing. Joint ventures are regarded as an intermediate and quasi-internalized form of governance structure. Being characterized both by equity as well as collaboration with a partner, the arguments and concerns above are equally applicable to JVs after making the necessary modifications arising from their peculiar status (Hill, Hwang, and Kim 1990). For example, although there may be concerns about opportunistic behavior by a partner, an advantage of the JV over licensing is that performance and behavior specifications need not be made in as detailed a manner *ex ante* (Kogut 1988). The reason is that not only does an equity joint venture provide superior avenues for monitoring but, more importantly, shared ownership results in goal congruence through the alignment of incentives (Hennart 1988).

The Competitive Strategy Perspective

The competitive strategy perspective is concerned with the attainment of competitiveness through the strategic positioning of a firm within a product-market (Porter 1980; Harrigan 1983; Contractor and Lorange 1988; Hagedoorn 1993).[2] Entry, exit, and mobility barriers are a critical part of the theory due to their effect on strategic flexibility. Different ownership forms offer varying degrees of strategic flexibility for entry and exit (Harrigan 1985; Hill, Hwang, and Kim 1990) and, either by reducing risk, pooling complementary know-how, or facilitating rapid market presence, are useful alternative vehicles through which a firm can choose to engage in competitive interaction.

The choice of a firm's boundaries becomes an important strategic decision, as boundary choices such as the extent of vertical integration and the nature of contracts are an important source of difference among firms and have a critical impact on firms' mobility (McGee and Thomas 1985). Porter (1980) specified three kinds of vertical integration: full, tapered, and quasi-integration (joint ventures); Harrigan (1983) added a fourth: contracting (nonownership). Both Porter and Harrigan argued that an ability to achieve objectives while maintaining strategic flexibility through lesser levels of integration could be a source of competitive advantage.[3] As the nature of entry and exit barriers and the maintenance of flexibility are two major concerns for multinational firms, entry through a wholly owned subsidiary can be an overcommitment in uncertain environments (Oman 1984; Harrigan 1983). It requires a greater dedication of resources and, by creating higher exit barriers, reduces the firm's strategic flexibility.

Basically, through sharing costs and risks, combining synergistic product-market complementarities, and reducing the time to market, among others, collaborations facilitate both rapid entry and exit from various product-markets and enable a firm to leverage its source of advantage (Hagedoorn and Schakenraad 1994; Contractor and Lorange 1988; Porter and Fuller 1986). They also enable the achievement of a rapid presence in multiple markets when competitive exigencies make such presence important (Oman 1984). Collaborative action can also influence the structure of the industry by creating barriers to entry as a result of various monopolistic first-mover advantages (such as early market share or preemptive access to superior distribution networks).

In brief, a collaboration is a useful means for improving competitive positioning in dynamic environments characterized by intense competitive rivalry, rapid technological change, and uncertain demand. Here, nonequity collaborations are an even less committed form of involvement than JVs and offer greater flexibility, as entry and exit barriers are even lower (Harrigan 1983; Osborn and Baughn 1990). They enable a firm to position itself rapidly through a multitude of arrangements with various partners, with minimal commitments by the firm relative to other forms.

The wholly owned subsidiary, though an overcommitment in an uncertain environment, is preferable in a more benign environment where there is greater scope for profit-making and demand is less uncertain (Harrigan 1983), as it enables a firm to capture more value with greater certainty. Moreover, due to the availability of sufficient slack in benign environments, exit barriers and the lack of flexibility are no longer so important an issue. This increases the attractiveness of subsidiaries, as it lowers risk.

A Comparison of the Two Perspectives

Both the internalization and CS perspectives provide useful insights into firm choices regarding the entry mode decision. However, they differ fundamentally in their level of analysis. Consequently, each has a principal focus on a different aspect of the environment and differs in the primary means by which firms attain competitiveness. CS is primarily concerned with the firm's macrolevel external environment, characterized by the competitive interaction among firms in a context of technological dynamism and changing demand conditions. As each mode of involvement possesses a differing degree of flexibility for entry and exit, the fit between the environmental characteristics and the extent of firm involvement is an important aspect of a firm's ability to position itself strategically and compete successfully in various product-markets. The assumption is that such a fit can be a source of competitive advantage. On the other hand, TC is oriented toward the characteristics of a particular dyadic relationship. It focuses on the microlevel transactional context and is primarily concerned with the minimization of TC. The fit between the transaction characteristics and the mode of ownership is a critical aspect of the firm's ability to conduct economic activity in an efficient manner. The assumption is that this fit is the source of its competitiveness.

As a result of their differing orientations, CS focuses on the management of competition and is concerned with the structural elements of the macro-environment within which it competes. Here, strategic action, whether through sole entry or collaboration, can create or overcome structural market imperfections. Given the environmental conditions, the key question here is the extent of resource commitment that the firm is willing (or able) to undertake in order to attain the desired position. On the other hand, internalization focuses on the management of the transaction and is concerned with informational market imperfections and the costs related to the dyadic relationship with a partner. The considerations in determining the appropriate mode of operating in a product-market are therefore quite different.

In spite of their different levels of analysis and orientations, it is important to realize that the two are not independent of one another. The firm, or business division, is basically a collectivity of transactions, with the transactions possessing common characteristics being included under a single subunit (Ulrich and Barney 1984). TC considerations, therefore, also have an impact on the firm's competitive environment. For example, internalization of a transaction in order to minimize TC also has the effect of raising barriers to entry. This could occur because of the greater capital requirements needed to be competitive in the case of vertical integration, or, in the case of horizontal integration, because information not only acts as a firm-specific advantage but also as a barrier to entry (Casson 1983).

TC and CS clearly address important micro- and macrolevel considerations, both of which apply to various phenomena such as knowledge complementarities, earning rents, and managing risk, in which the two share a common interest. However, due to their fundamentally different orientation, each illuminates a different aspect of these phenomena. At times, they reinforce one another's argument. At other times, as a result of their differing orientations, they diverge in their ownership preferences.

Complementarities in Knowledge

Stopford and Wells (1972) and Franko (1971) investigated the ownership preferences of multinational firms (subsidiaries or JVs) and found a preference for JVs in situations where firms possessed product knowledge but lacked the necessary market knowledge. CS reasoning would suggest a preference for JVs so as to access complementary resources required to fill strategic gaps, whether of a product or market nature. Here, JVs facilitate more effective and rapid entry into a market (Stopford and Wells 1972).

TC would argue for JV formation here because frequently the respective product know-how and the knowledge of the market are both difficult to articulate. In other words, there are tacit knowledge flows in both directions. Tacit knowledge transfer is best handled through an equity relationship, not only due to the superior alignment of incentives but also to the more intimate mechanisms it presents for the transfer of knowledge (Vernon and Wells 1986; Killing 1994).

Though the above-mentioned studies did not address nonequity collaborations, research into collaborations (such as Hagedoorn 1993) has revealed that JVs tend to be prevalent in the case of collaborations driven by both market and technology objectives. This contrasts with the dominance of contractual forms of cooperation used in the case of unidirectional knowledge flows, ostensibly because JVs are a stronger form of cooperation and provide superior governance mechanisms. The nature of the exchange is therefore important. When there is complex interdependence, firms tend to prefer JVs over nonequity collaborations (Hagedoorn 1993; Osborn and Baughn 1990), unlike in situations of unidirectional flows. The key difference between CS and TC is that CS addresses the potential synergistic outcomes arising from the structural complementarities between partners' respective firm-specific advantages, whereas TC directs itself toward the factors underlying the synergistic process. One addresses the potential scope for mutually synergistic rents, the other addresses the governance mechanisms needed to capture these rents. In sum, though differing in their theoretical focus, the two perspectives converge in their preference and complement one another.

Risk Minimization

Both TC and CS are oriented toward minimizing risk. However, consistent with their unit of analysis and orientation, what they mean by risk is completely different. For CS, the source of risk lies in uncertain demand and in the competitive and technological conditions within which the firm operates. These could be the risks inherent in technology development, which derive from the enormous cost of development and the relatively high probability of failure. They could be the risks associated with variable and fluctuating demand. They could be the risks associated with competitors' moves. The presence of such risks makes risk sharing, and hence collaboration, attractive. But though CS concerns address the benefits of collaborating in managing macrolevel risks, they do not address the microlevel risk involved in the very act of collaborating itself. This risk arises from the inclination of actors to engage in self-interested behavior, which is not only an intrinsic part of any transaction but is the central issue with which TC is concerned.

The reduction of risk is important to both perspectives. However, due to the differences in the meaning of risk, at times they converge and at other times they contradict. For example, according to CS, technological convergence in many industries (for example, computers and communications) and a blurring of industry boundaries has resulted in preference for collaborations that minimize the risks inherent in technology development and bring benefit from the knowledge overlap. In TC theory, information asymmetries increase the perceived risk of opportunism and, consequently, affect the choice of governance structure. Information asymmetries are lower in the case of closely linked activities due to greater knowledge overlap. This in turn enables more effective monitoring of important aspects of the relationship and a reduced scope for opportunism, thereby lowering the perceived level of risk and the associated TC (Ring and Van de Ven 1992). Furthermore, the relatedness of the know-how decreases the cost of transfer due to greater commonality between the underlying routines. Both these aspects increase the likelihood that collaborative modes will be chosen. Though both TC and CS focus on different aspects of the phenomenon and differ in their reasoning, they complement one another and manifest a degree of convergence with respect to the decision to collaborate.

At other times, due to their differing macro- and microlevel considerations, the two make different recommendations regarding the preferred extent of internalization. For instance, in the early volatile stages of the product life cycle, CS favors collaborations in order to avoid a premature overcommitment through high sunk investments, thus retaining greater flexibility for exit in case the potential is unrealized. For mode of entry, on the other hand, internalization logic would argue for greater internalization for two reasons. First, at that stage, protection of know-how through a complete contract is difficult. Second, the pricing and transfer of the transaction would be especially difficult because the knowledge has not been codified and its value not yet proven. Consequently, the buyer uncertainty problem is exacerbated (Davidson and McFetridge 1985). This results in a preference for internalization. The contradiction has also been pointed out by Hill, Hwang, and Kim (1990).

Earning of Rents

Broadly speaking, both CS and TC are interested in the earning of economic rents through a company's specific advantage. Rents can be earned through both (transaction) cost efficiencies or the creation of strategic advantages. The key difference between the TC and CS perspectives lies in what they are trying to optimize. Rents come from two sources: the size of the pie and its distribution. The strategizing CS perspective emphasizes the former. The rent pool can be secured, for example, through creation of entry barriers against other competitors, be it through sole entry or, where resources are more constrained, through partners. Therefore, collaborations are valuable, and may even be essential, for the earning of rents. The economizing TC perspective, on the other hand, emphasizes the distribution of rents (that is, share of the total pie). The pie already exists in that the internalization perspective assumes the existence of a rent-yielding firm-specific advantage, the exploitation of which is the driving force behind internationalization. Therefore, rather than creating rents, TC is more concerned with preventing them from dissipating due to hazards and costs of contracting with a partner.

Once again, due to their differing focus, the two perspectives can contradict each other about ownership preference. Therefore, where CS may recommend a collaboration for the creation and realization of rent potential, the TC perspective may recommend the use of subsidiaries. This would happen when imperfections in the market for know-how increase both the cost of contracting and the potential for opportunism, with its implications for rent distribution, beyond the benefits of rent creation believed to result through collaboration. At other times, though, the two converge. For example, in her study on international JVs, Hladik (1985) found a number of R&D-driven JVs where greater information sharing occurred due to rent creation effects (for example, setting of technological standards and consequent first-mover advantages), as the benefits of joint technological development and rapid market penetration were greater than the negative externalities arising from the leakage of know-how. Here, JVs are a useful vehicle to attain strategic ends such as technology development (Hladik 1985; Osborn and Baughn 1990); they create and secure the rent stream through monopolistic first-mover advantages and entry barriers. On the other hand, TC would be highly concerned in such situations with maintenance of greater discretion over the use (and abuse) of such technological assets and would argue, at minimum, for use of an equity relationship (such as a joint venture) in order to align incentives, create mutual hostages, and better oversee how the technology was being used, thus guarding against the dissipation of the rent stream. Of course, there is always the possibility of unintended spillovers of know-how, and firms need to make cost-benefit trade-offs (Harrigan 1988). However, the ultimate goal of the two perspectives, capturing the rent stream, is broadly the same, although the focus is different.

In sum, both the micro- and macrolevels of analysis are important and relevant to firms. They both lend unique and important insight into a number of shared concerns, although they approach them differently. A fuller elaboration of how elements of the two perspectives inform and interact with one another would facilitate a richer and more comprehensive understanding of firms' governance choices.

Economizing, Strategizing, or Both: Toward an Integration

Anderson and Gatignon (1986) attempt to integrate the literature on entry mode decisions using long-term efficiency criteria within a TC framework. However, long-term efficiency of the firm lies in global optimization and not in local suboptimization, as they subsequently acknowledged (Gatignon and Anderson 1988), and is frequently governed by strategic action that outweighs purely transactional considerations. A conspicuous weakness of TC is its basic inability to distinguish between the efficiency of an organizational form and its effectiveness in the light of overall corporate strategy. For example, in its global rivalry with Komatsu, Caterpillar formed a JV with Mitsubishi, the number two player in the Japanese construction equipment industry. The strategic purpose of the venture was to limit Komatsu's earnings (and engage attention) in its primary market, which would then impede its ability to compete in other markets of significance to Caterpillar. Even though the JV did not make much money, it had a high strategic value to Caterpillar; TC minimization was not the driving issue behind its formation. In other words, entry decisions can be governed by more global considerations driven by strategy (Kim and Hwang 1992; Kogut 1988), regardless of the least cost mode.

According to Robins (1987), a major flaw of TC analysis is that it applies an efficiency maximizing argument to an environment of imperfect competition. TC is most applicable under equilibrium conditions. However, where such conditions do not hold, the level of competitive pressures faced by a firm determines the extent to which it is pushed toward attaining TC economies through governance efficiencies. In other words, where efficiency pressures are not so strong, there is no compulsion for a tight correspondence between transaction costs and the governance mode. If a firm's competitive environment has a certain level of slack, it creates room for transactional inefficiencies (Osborn and Baughn 1990; Jones and Hill 1988) and increases the firm's tolerance for partners (Doz 1988).

Williamson acknowledges that firms may engage in strategizing instead of economizing through TC minimization, but posits that strategic behavior is "the exception rather than the rule" (1981: 1564; 1985, 1991) and that such behavior is limited to the small number of firms with market power advantages. This limits the argument about the infeasibility of strategic behavior only to small firms in fragmented markets and not to the larger firms in the economy, especially those belonging to oligopolistic strategic groups with high entry or mobility barriers. The significance of such firms in the economy is much greater than their numbers suggest.

Such firms also tend to be multinational and to dominate international investment. In global oligopolies, firms face greater discretion over important strategic choices as a result of the greater degree of slack in such environments arising from entry barriers (Yoffie 1993). Moreover, as mentioned, transactional inefficiency in organizational form for any one particular operation may not be globally inefficient for the multinational firm, especially when driven by strategic considerations. The concern of large and diversified global firms with overall positioning rather than with the TC associated with any one collaboration (Osborn and Baughn 1990; Porter and Fuller 1986) suggests the prevalence of such strategizing. In this regard, Buckley and Casson (1985) draw a distinction between creating and responding to market imperfections; they emphasize that excessive focus on responding to (knowledge) market imperfections has left a gap in internalization theory through the failure to address the creation of market imperfections. Strategic behavior, then, is far more prevalent than Williamson acknowledges, especially at the level of individual investment or entry decisions.

Knudsen (1995: 204), in interpreting Winter's argument (1988), makes a similar case for viewing the firm as a collectivity of transactions that cannot be isolated from one another. He states, "Since a complex network of interdependent transactions occurs within the firm, the totality of transactions, and not the individual transactions, are subject to a 'market test' of efficiency. We must thus assume that if a firm is characterized by such a bundle of interdependent transactions, some of the transactions will prove to be inefficient." It can safely be surmised that a firm will choose to engage in transactionally inefficient forms mainly for effectiveness reasons arising from deliberate strategizing considerations. In general, a firm may consciously trade off or sacrifice transactional efficiencies, or current savings in TC, depending on the impact of such a decision on future earnings. This essentially is a trade-off between immediate term TC optimization and longer-term competitive positioning.

There is another issue here. With its emphasis on cost minimization, TC essentially ignores the notion of value or rent creation and is therefore unable to fully appreciate the rent-creating role of a particular form of organizing (Madhok 1996a, 1996b). The sole benefit of a governance mode from a TC perspective is the extent of reduction in TC (Hill and Kim 1988; Madhok 1996a, 1996b). Consequently, Williamson casts strategic behavior in a purely negative light where dominant firms primarily (ab)use their market power with the objective of artificially inflating their rents. To him, therefore, strategizing essentially undermines economizing. Such a constrained perspective toward strategizing ignores the essential notion that it may result in a choice to form a collaboration not for nefarious reasons associated with the deliberate exploitation of market power but, rather, with the objective of true (that is, not artificial) value creation through the combination of synergistic and complementary productive resources of firms (Lazonick 1991).

From the standpoint of value creation, firms can be motivated to enter into collaborations to develop their capabilities, which enhances future rent-earning potential. For example, besides the fact that a firm may choose to engage in multiple collaborations in order to "hedge its bets" positionally as the technological and competitive scenario unfolds (Mytelka 1991), equally important is the explanation that each of these collaborations increases the robustness of the firm's own knowledge base and consequently enables it to exploit future developments in an intrinsically superior manner than would have been the case otherwise (Cohen and Levinthal 1990). TC ignores this dynamic aspect of firm activity, thus impeding the recognition of trade-offs—between static and dynamic, short-term and long-term, exploitation and development.

The essential point is that both transactional and strategic considerations need to be simultaneously factored into the ownership mode decision. Harrigan (1986) criticized earlier treatment of vertical integration for promoting a static view and emphasized the need for a contingency perspective on the integration strategy. Similarly, in a TC interpretation of earlier work on multinational strategic management, Rugman and Verbeke (1992) argued that the examination of contingencies was useful for appreciating the compatibility of the respective theories. In the more specific context of this chapter, Hill, Hwang, and Kim (1990) concluded by suggesting that an important and worthwhile research direction pertaining to entry mode lay in synthesizing the concerns of different perspectives through exploring some of the contingencies involved. This is the focus of the following sections, which also address how macroenvironmental factors central to CS interact with specific transaction characteristics to inform firms' ownership mode choices.

Contingency One:
Environmental Dynamism and Asset Specificity

The pace and complexity of technological change in a firm's environment is a key source of uncertainty. For TC, this creates difficulties in contracting and increases the risk of opportunism; for CS, it increases the risk of overcommitment of scarce resources due to greater exit barriers. However, as Zajac and Olsen (1993) point out, the TC counterpart of CS's exit barriers is asset specificity (that is, the extent of the dedicatedness of the investment to a single purpose).

Anderson and Gatignon (1986) addressed the issue of asset specificity and environmental volatility (referring primarily to country risk); their argument is basically that in the presence of highly specific investments a more risky environment would drive a firm to internalize transactions because the level of exposure to opportunism becomes unacceptable. However, the extent of commitment of highly specific assets by the firm is a strategic variable that is within the firm's control and can be managed (Teece 1986b). Typically, in the early and more volatile stages of an industry, know-how, standards, and demand are still evolving and therefore the operating context is uncertain. In such a situation, firms would tend to avoid investing in specialized assets, instead favoring more generalized and fungible assets that are more easily transferable across a variety of uses (Teece 1986b), to the extent that this is technologically feasible. Such investments could then be deployed through arm's-length contractual arrangements.

On close scrutiny, Teece's argument (1986b) addresses both TC and CS concerns. As mentioned, in contrast to the pressures of transactional efficiency, CS is more concerned with the maintenance of strategic flexibility in uncertain environments. TC, on the other hand, is essentially concerned with minimizing losses from opportunism. As Hill and Kim (1988) point out, the expected loss from opportunistic behavior is a function of the probability of opportunism as well as the actual loss should such opportunism occur. On one hand, a fast-changing environment makes contracting more difficult, which would result in a greater probability of opportunism. However, when a firm simultaneously lowers the extent of potential losses due to opportunism by "managing" the level of dedicated investments, there is minimal change in the expected loss. Also, the level of TC is further contained in a situation of limited exposure because it is no longer so urgent to devise a complete contract. Not only does collaboration therefore have a minimal impact on TC, but the firm enjoys the strategic benefits of flexibility and access to the expertise of a partner in a situation of limited exposure. In this manner, the firm manages both microlevel and macrolevel risk while also expanding avenues for it to earn rents.

Contingency Two: The Nature of the Know-How

CS and TC considerations suggest that the firm has a simultaneous dual focus: on other competitors in the external environment, and on the partner in the dyadic relationship (Madhok 1996c). Of course, a competitor could also be a partner, in which case the situation becomes more complex. The nature of the know-how is directly relevant to the concerns of both CS and TC and is a major factor in deciding how to best exploit it.

With the earning and appropriation of rent being of central importance, the scope for opportunism and its impact becomes an issue of considerable significance. The nature of the know-how significantly affects both the ease with which it can be comprehended by a partner, and hence the probability of leakage as well as the impact of such leakage. Take the situation where the firm's know-how is tacit. Tacit knowledge is embedded within the firm, so it is more difficult for others to understand and appropriate it and, consequently, both the risk and the impact of leakage is lower. In essence, tacitness behaves as a protective umbrella (Madhok 1996c). In a situation where the know-how is composed of both tacit and articulable components, even if some of the know-how were exposed to the partner and the more tangible aspects were to leak, the opportunistic firm would find it difficult to generate rents from it in isolation from the rest of the know-how (Cantwell 1991; Madhok 1996a, 1996b). Of course, the opportunistic firm could develop the missing knowledge, but this is an uncertain, costly, and imperfect process. Such a situation, therefore, lowers the returns of opportunism and the incentive to behave opportunistically. Moreover, where the state of the know-how is progressing rapidly, even if the know-how were to leak, it may not have a serious negative impact. The reason for this is that by the time the partner is able to master the know-how and become competitive using it, it would be relatively obsolete and the focal firm would have moved one step ahead. Of course, the sophistication of the partner also matters in this regard.

By a similar logic, the extent to which the know-how is tacit or embedded within the firm is also critical to macrolevel competitive dynamics. As mentioned, being firm-specific and difficult to articulate, tacitness forms a natural barrier to entry by others, thus buffering the firm against competitive pressures and extending the competitive lag. In such circumstances, a firm would tend to prefer internalization in order to both benefit from the experience curve and capture the idiosyncratic rents arising from the know-how. On the other hand, competitive pressures are accentuated when a firm's knowledge is less tacit, facilitating rapid entry by potential competitors (Teece 1986b). In such situations, the transient nature of the rents motivates a firm to enter into multiple collaborations, both equity and nonequity, in order to establish a wider market presence and enjoy preemptive first-mover advantages before these are competed away. Collaborations therefore provide the opportunity for rapid exploitation of ephemeral rents. Also, collaboration is facilitated by the nontacit nature of the know-how. Because such know-how tends to be codified and standardized, the cost of transfer is lower (Davidson and McFetridge 1985), which reinforces the disposition toward collaboration. Of course, such know-how is easier for a partner to appropriate. At the same time, being of a generic nature, it tends to be less valuable. Furthermore, the risk of opportunism can be reduced through tighter contracting.

Contingency Three: The Capability Gap

The capabilities of a firm, measured by possession of the necessary resources (temporal, financial, managerial, technological) required for a particular operation and coupled with the firm's ability to generate rents through the commitment of such resources, are important considerations in decisions about ownership mode. They also help explain a seeming paradox in this regard. As already explained, in the early stages of an industry's life cycle, TC considerations tend to drive a firm toward internalization, due to the exacerbation of the buyer uncertainty problem and the added difficulty in contracting. Typically, in this stage, the future earnings stream tends to be high, though fluctuating (Hill, Hwang, and Kim 1990). To protect this rent stream, a firm prefers to enter through subsidiaries.

This, however, contradicts the empirical evidence, namely the phenomenal increase of collaborative activity both within and across borders. In fact, an overwhelming concentration of this activity is found in sectors characterized by intense global competition and rapidly changing technologies (Hergert and Morris 1988; George 1995; Hagedoorn 1993). The weakness of the argument for internalization in the face of high TC is that it implicitly assumes that a similar stream of rents could be generated by a firm whether it chose to internalize the transaction or to seek out a partner (Conner 1991; Madhok 1996b; Demsetz 1988). This is clearly not the case. Where the firm is unable to do so within an acceptable time frame or cost (that is, in the presence of a capability gap), the desire to realize rents may drive it to form collaborations for strategic reasons, even though this may require some TC-related trade-offs. This argument is supported by

Hagedoorn's finding (1990, 1993) that in the more demanding environments characteristic of high-tech industries, more than 85 percent of collaborations are strategically rather than transactionally motivated. Such considerations of capability constraints were less relevant in more mature industries such as food and beverages. Similarly reflecting capability considerations, George (1995) found a greater prevalence of international as contrasted to domestic (U.S.) collaborations in industries where the U.S. was technologically weak relative to foreign competitors, and the reverse where it was strong.

Contingency Four: Interdependence

Another factor important to the entry mode decision is the role of a particular operation in the firm's overall strategy. This influences the extent of interdependence between that operation and other operations of the firm. International competition often necessitates the pursuit of more global optima by multinational firms. When this is so, a high level of coordination between different operations is required so that different parts of the organization do not operate at cross-purposes or suboptimize. This increases the potential for conflict with partners pursuing more local optima.

Though authors have tended to treat such interdependence as a strategic variable (Kim and Hwang 1992), clearly it is not so. Both transactional and strategic considerations are intertwined here. As Jones and Hill (1988) point out, highly interdependent operations can be afflicted by a high level of transaction costs due to ambiguities in the measurement of performance and consequent difficulties in monitoring and enforcement. Furthermore, for tightly knit strategies where interdependencies are high, negative externalities from opportunistic behavior become magnified, as the effect of self-serving behavior can have a strong adverse impact on other operations of the firm. Here, dyadic conflict has an impact not only on the rent distribution concern of TC, but on the CS concern of rent size, especially where speed of decision making is critical (as in the case of a first-mover advantage). In such situations, a firm may decide that any strategic benefits, such as flexibility or access to a partner's source of advantage, may not be worth the potential sacrifices required. It would therefore prefer a subsidiary to assure the superior control and authority relationship needed for flexibility and speed in decision making.

The above discussion makes it quite clear that it is not particularly meaningful to evaluate an entry decision only on the basis of one perspective or the other. The respective nature of the investment, of the environment, and of the know-how are all highly relevant because they influence the underlying transactional properties and the competitive characteristics surrounding the decision. The external environmental and internal exchange conditions need to be coupled in considering the governance mode decision.

Conclusion

In summing up, a discussion of the literature indicates that the TC-internalization and competitive strategy perspectives, with their respective economizing and strategizing logics, provide rich insights into understanding entry mode decisions. However, differences in their level of analysis, the primary environment of concern, and their orientation toward competitiveness make the two conceptually distinct. One rather unfortunate consequence is that the perspectives have developed independently. In addition, neither explicitly recognizes its own limitations nor the complementarities of the other. Therefore, TC researchers have tended to neglect CS considerations that can influence the choice of organizational form without being transactionally optimal. A mode of organization that has inferior transaction cost properties may be superior, both in a strategic and a long-term efficiency sense, than one that merely economizes on TC. On the other hand, CS researchers have been prone to overlook TC-related issues pertinent to the management of dyadic collaborative relationships that have implications for CS-related concerns.

Pure economizing or pure strategizing thus becomes somewhat limiting. This does not deny the importance of either pure form but, rather, suggests that placing sole emphasis on economizing through the choice of the transactionally optimal governance form, at the cost of strategizing, may render a firm vulnerable to competitors who are more strategically adept. Similarly, placing sole emphasis on strategizing may be inadequate if transactional inefficiencies are continually ignored. In short, it is important to incorporate both transactional and strategic considerations into an analysis of entry mode, because competitive advantage is a function of both economizing and strategizing. Approaching the two jointly, rather than additively, and exploring how both perspectives inform and interact with one another provides the basis for a more comprehensive framework for understanding the foreign market entry phenomenon. Without doing so, transaction-related issues such as tacitness may not get the deserved level of attention by CS theorists. Conversely, issues such as the impact of competition may continue to be neglected as important predictors of foreign market entry by TC-internalization theorists.

This does not mean that strategizing and economizing are equally important in every transaction. When does a firm strategize? When does a firm economize? When and under what conditions does the balance tilt toward one or the other? In his discussion of JVs, Kogut (1988) suggested that strategic considerations would dominate in the decision to form a JV, even if this were not the least cost mode, following which TC considerations could be applied to the dyadic context to determine more specific governance mechanisms. Whether an entry mode is dominated by one or the other in a two-step decision process, or whether firms make simultaneous trade-offs in determining entry mode, is an issue that needs to be researched further. As Mytelka (1991: 7) puts it, the calculus involves "not only trade-offs between internalization, which increases the inertia of firms, and the higher TC of arm's-length relationships but also between short-term financial gain and long-term positional advantages." These trade-offs, such as the dynamic between the long-term and the short-term, efficiency and effectiveness, flexibility and inertia, size and distribution of rents or, in general, economizing and strategizing, have a direct and decided impact on organizational form and the mode of entry. On what basis are these trade-offs made? How are they managed? These are important issues for research.

In spite of elegant conceptual explanations of the internalization framework, empirical studies of mode of foreign market entry have tended to yield mixed results. For example, some studies (such as Gatignon and Anderson 1988; Davidson and McFetridge 1985), using proxy measures for tacitness like the R&D-to-sales ratio, found support for the argument that the level of tacitness of the firm's know-how results in a preference for subsidiaries, although others have found that this had the reverse or no influence (Swedenborg 1979; Lall and Siddharthan 1982). Perhaps additional insights can be gained by more systematically incorporating external environmental factors into the analysis. There is potential for greater enrichment of our theoretical understanding of firms' governance mode choices by simultaneously addressing both micro- and macrolevel issues and the interface between the two. This chapter is a step in that direction.

NOTES

1. Teece (1986a) argued that both of the theories need to be interwoven in order to extend the understanding of the range of choices available to the multinational firm, a gap that has since being addressed in the literature (for example, Gatignon and Anderson 1988; Hennart 1988).

2. In the realm of international investment, Knickerbocker's follow-the-leader study (1973) and Graham's exchange-of-threats study (1974) were two of the early works that examined strategic behavior by multinational firms.

However, these studies have more to do with entering a particular market than with the mode of entry per se. Furthermore, these studies were conducted more than two decades ago, before globalization of business and competition resulted in the mode of entry decision becoming such a critical issue. In our use of competitive strategy in this chapter, we are concerned with those aspects most relevant to entry mode.

3. Porter and Harrigan's arguments were made largely in the context of integration. Though these were not specifically addressed toward the international domain, they are general enough to be equally applicable to the international arena. Hill, Hwang, and Kim (1990) make the same point. In a similar vein, many of the arguments in this chapter can be more generally applied not just to foreign market entry but to mode of ownership in general.

BIBLIOGRAPHY

Anderson, E., and A. Coughlan. 1987. International market entry strategies and expansion via independent or integrated channels of business. *Journal of Marketing*, 51: 71–82.

Anderson, E., and H. Gatignon. 1986. Modes of foreign entry: A transaction cost analysis and propositions. *Journal of International Business Studies*, 17: 1–26.

Bowman, E. H. 1974. Epistemology, corporate strategy, and academe. *Sloan Management Review*, 15: 35–50.

Buckley, P. J., and M. Casson. 1976. *The Future of the Multinational Enterprise.* New York: Holmes and Meier.

Buckley, P. J., and M. Casson. 1985. *The Economic Theory of the Multinational Enterprise.* Old Tappan, N.J.: Macmillan.

Cantwell, J. C. 1991. The theory of technological competence and its application to international production. In D. McFetridge, editor, *Foreign Investment, Technology and Economic Growth,* 33–67. University of Calgary Press.

Casson, M. 1983. *The Growth of International Business.* London: George Allen and Unwin.

Cohen, W. M., and D. A. Levinthal. 1990. Absorptive capacity: A new perspective on learning and innovation. *Administrative Science Quarterly,* 35: 128–152.

Conner, K. R. 1991. An historical comparison of resource-based theory and five schools of thought within industrial organization economics: Do we have a new theory of the firm? *Journal of Management,* 17: 121–154.

Contractor, F. J. 1990. Contractual and cooperative forms of international business: Towards a unified theory of modal choice. *Management International Review,* 30: 31–54.

Contractor, F. J., and P. Lorange. 1988. Why should firms cooperate? The strategy and economics basis for cooperative ventures. In F. J. Contractor and P. Lorange, editors, *Cooperative Strategies in International Business,* 3–30. San Francisco: New Lexington Press.

Davidson, W. H., and D. G. McFetridge. 1985. Key characteristics in the choice of international technology transfer mode. *Journal of International Business Studies,* 16: 5–21.

Davies, H. 1977. Technology transfer through commercial transactions. *Journal of Industrial Economics,* 26(2): 161–175.

Demsetz, H. 1988. The theory of the firm revisited. *Journal of Law, Economics and Organization,* 4: 141–161.

Doz, Y. L. 1988. Technology partnerships between larger and smaller firms: Some critical issues. In F. J. Contractor and P. Lorange, editors, *Cooperative Strategies in International Business,* 317–338. San Francisco: New Lexington Press.

Erramilli, M. K., and C. P. Rao. 1990. Choice of foreign market entry modes by service firms: Role of market knowledge. *Management International Review,* 30: 135–150.

Franko, L. G. 1971. *Joint Venture Survival in Multinational Corporations.* New York: Praeger.

Gatignon, H., and E. Anderson. 1988. The multinational corporation's degree of control over foreign subsidiaries: An empirical explanation of a transaction cost explanation. *Journal of Law, Economics and Organization,* 4(2): 305–336.

George, V. P. 1995. Globalization through interfirm cooperation. *International Journal of Technology Management,* 10: 131–145.

Gomes-Casseres, B. 1989. Ownership structures of foreign subsidiaries: Theory and evidence. *Journal of Economic Behavior and Organization,* 11: 1–25.

Graham, E. M. 1974. Oligopolistic imitation and European direct investment in the United States. Unpublished Ph.D. dissertation, Harvard University, Cambridge, Mass.

Hagedoorn, J. 1990. Organizational modes of interfirm co-operation and technology transfer. *Technovation,* 10: 17–30.

Hagedoorn, J. 1993. Understanding the rationale of strategic technology partnering: Interorganizational modes of cooperation and sectoral differences. *Strategic Management Journal,* 14: 371–386.

Hagedoorn, J., and J. Schakenraad. 1994. The effect of strategic technological alliances on company performance. *Strategic Management Journal,* 15: 291–310.

Harrigan, K. R. 1983. *Strategies for Vertical Integration.* Lexington, Mass.: Heath.

Harrigan, K. R. 1985. *Strategic Flexibility.* Lexington, Mass.: Heath.

Harrigan, K. R. 1986. Matching vertical integration strategies to competitive conditions. *Strategic Management Journal,* 7: 535–555.

Harrigan, K. R. 1988. Joint ventures and competitive strategy. *Strategic Management Journal,* 9: 141–158.

Hennart, J.-F. 1982. *A Theory of Multinational Enterprise.* Ann Arbor: University of Michigan Press.

Hennart, J.-F. 1988. A transaction costs theory of equity joint ventures. *Strategic Management Journal,* 9: 361–374.

Hergert, M., and D. Morris. 1988. Trends in international collaborative agreements. In F. J. Contractor and P. Lorange, editors, *Cooperative Strategies in International Business,* 99–111. San Francisco: New Lexington Press.

Hill, C. W., P. Hwang, and W. C. Kim. 1990. An eclectic theory of the choice of international entry mode. *Strategic Management Journal,* 11: 117–128.

Hill, C. W., and W. C. Kim. 1988. Searching for a dynamic model of the multinational enterprise: A transaction cost model. *Strategic Management Journal,* 9: 93–104.

Hladik, K. 1985. *International Joint Ventures: An Economic Analysis of US-Foreign Business Partnerships.* Lexington, Mass.: Heath.

Hymer, S. H. 1976. *The International Operations of National Firms: A Study of Direct Foreign Investment.* Cambridge, Mass.: MIT Press.

Jones, G. R., and C.W.L. Hill. 1988. Transaction cost analysis of strategy-structure choice. *Strategic Management Journal,* 9: 159–172.

Killing, J. P. 1994. The design and management of international joint ventures. In P. W. Beamish, J. P. Killing, D. J. Lecraw, and A. J. Morrison, editors, *International Management.* Boston: Irwin.

Kim, W. C., and P. Hwang. 1992. Global strategy and multinationals' entry mode choice. *Journal of International Business Studies,* 23: 29–54.

Knickerbocker, F. T. 1973. *Oligopolistic Reaction and Multinational Enterprise.* Cambridge, Mass.: Harvard Business School Division of Research.

Knudsen, C. 1995. Theories of the firm, strategic management, and leadership. In C. A. Montgomery, editor, *Resource-Based and Evolutionary Theories of the Firm: Towards a Synthesis.* Boston: Kluwer.

Kogut, B. M. 1988. Joint ventures: Theoretical and empirical perspectives. *Strategic Management Journal,* 9: 319–332.

Lall, S., and N. S. Siddharthan. 1982. The monopolistic advantages of multinationals: Lessons from foreign investment in the U.S. *The Economic Journal,* 92: 668–683.

Lazonick, W. 1991. *Business Organization and the Myth of the Market Economy.* New York: Cambridge University Press.

Madhok, A. 1996a. The organization of economic activity: Transaction costs, firm capabilities and the nature of governance. *Organization Science,* 7(5): 577–590.

Madhok, A. 1996b. Cost, value and foreign market entry: The transaction and the firm. *Strategic Management Journal,* 16(9), forthcoming.

Madhok, A. 1996c. Know-how-, experience- and competition-related considerations in foreign market entry: An exploratory investigation. *International Business Review,* 5(4): 339–366.

McGee, J., and H. Thomas. 1985. Strategic groups: Theory, research and taxonomy. *Strategic Management Journal,* 9: 319–332.

Mytelka, L. K. 1991. Crisis, technological change and the strategic alliance. In L. K. Mytelka, editor, *Strategic Partnerships: States, Firms and International Competition.* London: Pinter.

Oman, C. P. 1984. *New Forms of International Investment in Developing Countries.* Paris: OECD.

Osborn, R. N., and C. C. Baughn. 1990. Forms of interorganizational governance for multinational alliances. *Academy of Management Journal,* 33: 503–519.

Porter, M. E. 1980. *Competitive Strategy: Techniques for Analyzing Industries and Competitors.* New York: Free Press.

Porter, M. E., and M. B. Fuller. 1986. Coalitions and global strategy. In M. E. Porter, editor, *Competition in Global Industries,* 315–342. Boston: Harvard Business School Press.

Ring, P. S., and A. H. Van de Ven. 1992. Structuring cooperative relationships between organizations. *Strategic Management Journal,* 13: 483–498.

Robins, J. A. 1987. Organizational economics: Notes on the use of transaction-cost theory in the study of organizations. *Administrative Science Quarterly,* 32: 68–86.

Rugman, A. M. 1980. Internalization as a general theory of foreign direct investment: A re-appraisal of the literature. *Weltwirtscaftliches Archiv,* 116: 365–379.

Rugman, A. M. 1986. New theories of the multinational enterprise: An assessment of internalization theory. *Bulletin of Economic Research,* 38: 101–118.

Rugman, A. M., and A. Verbeke. 1992. A note on the transnational solution and the transaction cost theory of multinational strategic management. *Journal of International Business Studies,* 23: 761–772.

Rumelt, R. P. 1984. Toward a strategic theory of the firm. In R. B. Lamb, editor, *Competitive Strategic Management,* 566–570. Englewood Cliffs, N.J.: Prentice Hall.

Stopford, J. M., and L. T. Wells Jr. 1972. *Managing the Multinational Enterprise.* New York: Basic Books.

Swedenborg, B. 1979. *The Multinational Operations of Swedish Firms.* Stockholm: Almqvist and Wicksell.

Teece, D. J. 1981. The multinational enterprise: Market failure and market power considerations. *Sloan Management Review,* 22: 3–17.

Teece, D. J. 1986a. Transaction cost economics and the multinational enterprise: An assessment. *Journal of Economic Behavior and Organization,* 7: 21–45.

Teece, D. J. 1986b. Profiting from technological innovation: Implications for integration, collaboration, licensing and public policy. *Research Policy,* 15: 286–305.

Telesio, P. 1979. *Technology Licensing and Multinational Enterprises.* New York: Praeger.

Ulrich, D., and J. B. Barney. 1984. Perspectives in organizations: Resource dependence, efficiency, and population. *Academy of Management Review,* 9(3): 471–481.

Vernon, R., and L. T. Wells. 1986. *The Economic Environment of International Business.* Englewood Cliffs, N.J.: Prentice Hall.

Williamson, O. E. 1975. *Markets and Hierarchies: Analysis and Antitrust Implications.* New York: Free Press.

Williamson, O. E. 1981. The modern corporation: Origins, evolution, attributes. *Journal of Economic Literature,* 19: 1537–1568.

Williamson, O. E. 1985. *The Economic Institutions of Capitalism: Firms, Markets, Relational Contracting.* New York: Free Press.

Williamson, O. E. 1991. Strategizing, economizing, and economic organization. *Strategic Management Journal,* 12 (Special Issue): 75–94.

Winter, S. G. 1988. On Coase, competence and the corporation. *Journal of Law, Economics and Organization,* 4: 163–180.

Yoffie, D. B. 1993. *Beyond Free Trade: Firms, Governments and Global Competition.* Boston: Harvard Business School Press.

Zajac, E. J., and C. P. Olsen. 1993. From transaction cost to transaction value analysis: Implications for the study of interorganizational strategies. *Journal of Management Studies,* 30: 131–145.

3

EXPLAINING JOINT VENTURES

Alternative Theoretical Perspectives

Kannan Ramanathan, Anju Seth, and Howard Thomas

IN THIS CHAPTER *we critically analyze the contributions of the transactions cost approach to the strategic management literature on joint ventures. We suggest that alternative perspectives from property rights, agency theory, and prospect theory address some of the limitations of the transactions cost perspective on joint ventures. We identify research propositions from these theories that represent useful avenues of research inquiry for joint ventures in general and international joint ventures in particular.*

THE PRESENT AGE OF "alliance capitalism" (Dunning 1995) is distinguished by a radical change in the organization of productive activity by multinational enterprises (MNEs) toward collaborative arrangements between firms. The steep rate of alliance formation during the last two decades clearly demonstrates that an either-or choice between market and hierarchy for the organization of productive activity is descriptively oversimplistic. Recent research in international business has provided numerous

We would like to thank Paul Beamish, John Easterwood, Jean-Francois Hennart, Peter Killing, Huseyin Leblebici, Joe Mahoney, Tom Roehl, Sarabjeet Seth, participants at the 1996 Global Perspectives on Cooperative Strategies seminar in London, Ontario, and three anonymous referees for their helpful comments.

insights in explaining the advantages of interfirm collaborative arrangements over the more traditional market-hierarchy dichotomy. These explanations for the most part have been framed within the internalization model of MNEs, with collaborative arrangements being described as a point on a so-called continuum between arm's-length trading and an administrative hierarchy (such as Beamish and Banks 1987; Buckley and Casson 1988; Jarillo 1988). At one extreme of the continuum, firms interact with each other using spot markets: market prices act as the only coordination mechanism. At the other extreme, the interaction is characterized by internalizing the transaction, where internalization involves the "absorption of other organizations or their tasks" (Thorelli 1986). The location of productive activity at some point on this continuum is considered to be determined by efficiency considerations, and that point will be selected to minimize the sum of transactions costs and production costs. For example, at an intermediate point in the continuum, firms may engage in joint ventures (JVs), which are collaborative arrangements involving a hybridization of market and hierarchy forms of governance. More formally, an international joint venture (IJV) is "a separate legal organizational entity representing the partial holdings of two or more parent firms, in which the headquarters of at least one parent firm is located outside the country of operation of the joint venture. This entity is subject to the joint control of its parent firms, each of which is economically and legally independent of each other" (Shenkar and Zeira 1987: 547).

Two related criticisms have recently have been leveled at the transactions cost explanation of IJVs: first, it fails to address important organizational factors that affect JV formation, and second, it focuses too strongly on control through hierarchical fiat that becomes possible as a result of internalization. One approach taken by critics to bring descriptive and predictive realism to research on JVs is to incorporate organizational and behavioral factors such as social dynamics (for example, Madhok 1995), corporate culture and structure (such as Tallman and Shenkar 1994), and societal culture (Parkhe 1991, for example).

Although we, in general, concur with the criticisms, we adopt a somewhat different approach toward adding explanatory and predictive richness to the extant explanations of JVs. The scope of our discussion is represented by two questions: Why are JVs formed? and What factors influence the nature of the JV partnership? In exploring these questions, we, like previous researchers, adopt a cost-benefit mode of analysis. However, our analysis highlights the potential of JVs and IJVs to effectively manage different kinds of risk and uncertainty, an issue that the aforementioned critics of the transactions cost perspective appear to have considered only tangentially. We examine the explanatory contributions of two theories of the firm in the economics tradition, specifically, the property rights approach and the agency theory approach, which explicitly address issues of risk and uncertainty but in a manner different to the transactions cost perspective. Further, we examine how a branch of decision theory that is also intimately concerned with risk-related issues (that is, prospect theory) can contribute to our understanding of JVs. We demonstrate that these perspectives provide significant insights into JVs while taking into account important organizational and behavioral issues associated with effective management of risk and uncertainty. Each of the theories we discuss provides insights on JVs in general as well as the specific case of IJVs. We highlight the contributions of the theories to both the general and the specific case.

Before proceeding further, a clarification is in order. The theories we discuss here as relevant to developing a deeper understanding of JVs are essentially metaphorical. A metaphor implies a way of thinking and seeing that abstracts and highlights certain characteristics of the phenomenon while downplaying others (Morgan 1986). For the understanding of complex organizational phenomena, any theoretical lens by itself, by virtue of its metaphorical nature, is necessarily incomplete. We believe that by virtue of applying multiple theoretical lenses, which highlight and explain different aspects of complex organizational phenomena, our understanding of these phenomena advances (as demonstrated by Kogut [1988] in his discussion of alternative theoretical explanations of JVs). Theoretical pluralism is necessary to avoid the risks of premature closure of promising areas of inquiry (Seth and Thomas 1994).

Thus, one important objective of this chapter is to explain, from the viewpoints of the different theoretical perspectives we consider, what the roles of risk and uncertainty are with regard to the questions raised above. In some cases, the different theories make opposing or inconsistent predictions about the relationships of interest, and in others, similar predictions. Although some theories might make similar predictions about the *what* of a postulated relationship, as we shall see, each theory employs a different rationale for *why* the relationship might exist. The *why* is "probably the most fruitful but also the most difficult avenue of theory development. It commonly involves borrowing a perspective from other fields, which encourages altering our metaphors and gestalts in ways that challenge the underlying rationales supporting accepted theories. This profound challenge ... generally affects a broad reconceptualization of affected theories" (Whetten 1989: 493).

A second important objective here is to address this challenge. Because our intention is to stimulate interesting debate, and thus facilitate new areas of inquiry into JVs, we trace and compare the assumptions and logical arguments from each theory that comprise its answer to the *why* issue.

In the next section, we briefly describe the transactions cost perspective, outline its predictions with regard to JVs, and highlight some important issues regarding JV formation that traditional transactions cost theory does not directly address (note that throughout we make the simplifying assumption that an IJV is a partnership between two parents, but the arguments also apply to multiparent IJVs). In the following section, we describe alternative theoretical approaches, with a view toward developing a research agenda for the future. We identify and state research propositions derived from each of the theories we discuss, and highlight their similarities and differences. Finally, we summarize our conclusions.

The Transactions Cost Approach to the Choice of Governance

In his seminal work *The Nature of the Firm,* Coase (1937) offered a new explanation for the existence of firms. Simply stated, he suggested that the essence of economic activity is the transaction; hierarchies manage productive activity because transactions costs make spot market transactions relatively more costly, and therefore less efficient under certain circumstances.

Key Points

The considerable power of the transactions cost (TC) approach to explain whether a transaction will occur across a market interface or be internalized within a hierarchy rests upon its explicit recognition of the thinking, planning, contracting, monitoring, and enforcing costs that accompany any transaction. Specifically, the TC approach makes four important assumptions or propositions regarding the features of transactions and alternative governance modes, as follows:

- Each transaction can be separated from, and is independent of, other transactions conducted by a transacting partner (as inferred from the contention of transactions cost economics, following Commons [1934], that the appropriate unit of analysis is the transaction; see Williamson [1991]).

- Administrative fiat is the key feature that distinguishes hierarchical from market modes of governance.

- There exists a nontrivial degree of behavioral uncertainty (that is, uncertainty attributable to the opportunism of motivationally complex transacting partners) that characterizes transactions.

- The central problem is to align the features of the transaction with an appropriate governance mode such that the sum of transactions costs and production costs is minimized.

Embedded within these propositions are three important behavioral assumptions:

- One or more transacting partners may behave opportunistically (that is, engage in self-interested behavior with guile).
- While transacting partners are intendedly rational, limits on human rationality constrain the writing of contracts contingent on all possible states of the world.
- Decision makers are risk-neutral.

Given these assumptions, the TC approach predicts that a transaction will be carried out within a firm rather than across a market interface if the former governance mode reduces the sum of production and transaction costs (Williamson 1975, 1985). (Note that though production costs are relevant, the analytical focus here is on transaction cost.) As described in Williamson (1985), two critical dimensions on which transactions differ, and which are deemed to drive transactions costs, are asset specificity and frequency. A central conclusion of the TC approach is that two joint conditions are necessary and sufficient to cause transaction costs to be sizable if the transaction occurs across a market interface, but subject to reduction if the transaction is internalized within a hierarchy: first, assets needed to complete the transaction are transaction-specific, and second, the transaction is of a recurrent nature.

The reasons for this are twofold. First, the bounded rationality of the economic agents limits their ability to write *a priori* contracts that cover all possible contingencies; hierarchies eliminate the need to anticipate all contingencies by resorting to administrative fiat. Second, the opportunism that economic agents are prone to is mitigated by resorting to administrative fiat. A special significance is attributed to the first condition (asset specificity), which refers to the degree to which an asset cannot be redeployed to alternative uses without loss of productive value. When only one of the above conditions is met, other forms of governance that are less costly than internalization will suffice (Williamson 1991).

The Transactions Cost View of IJVs

Just as the transactions cost approach is extremely influential in describing the genesis of the multinational enterprise (Caves 1982), the transactions cost framework has also been used fruitfully to explain the existence of JVs in general and IJVs in particular. In the general case, it has been argued that "all JVs can be explained as a device to bypass inefficient markets for intermediate inputs" (Hennart 1988: 364); the presence of inefficiencies in transferring factors of production across a market interface gives rise to significant transactions costs, and is a necessary condition for JVs to emerge. Specifically, given a high degree of behavioral uncertainty, when a transaction is recurrent and the assets involved are highly idiosyncratic to the transaction, the hazard of negative externalities is present with the potential to diffuse the value of the assets of the transacting parties. A JV with shared equity ownership holds the parties to mutual hostage positions, thus attenuating these transactional hazards (Kogut 1988). For example, where the transaction involves the transfer of tacit knowledge—which is difficulty to codify and specify in a contract—the transaction will be more efficiently handled through common ownership. As another example, when distribution networks are subject to economies of scale or scope, they may be characterized by a small-numbers bargaining situation. An equity participation in the distributor allows the manufacturer to avoid a possible hold-up problem and the bargaining stalemates that could result.[1]

However, not only must the JV governance mode have superior cost-reducing properties relative to markets, it must be more efficient than complete internalization. In the situations described above, complete internalization of the transaction by one party is a feasible alternative means to economize on transactions costs. In fact, the traditional TC calculus predicts that complete internalization is a more efficient mode than shared ownership: administrative fiat by virtue of full ownership resolves the hazards of opportunism more efficiently than shared ownership. If internalization is the best solution to market failure, the question arises as to why partners in a JV choose (or are forced to choose) to share ownership rather than full acquisition of the other partner. To resolve this conundrum, some assumptions contained in the traditional version of the TC model must be relaxed or new assumptions introduced.

For example, Buckley and Casson (1988) consider the case of a new facility that is jointly owned by two partners with equal equity. They suggest that there must be an element of economic indivisibility in a new facility arising from economies of scale, economies of scope, or technological inseparability. However, this explanation is not very satisfying: even in the presence of such indivisibilities, given a high potential for value-reducing externalities to exist, the transactions cost perspective would still predict that the assets of one of the parent firms be acquired by the other (such that a facility with unitary ownership is set up in lieu of one with joint ownership) or that both parent firms merge.

So why does an acquisition of assets or a merger not occur? New assumptions may be introduced to resolve this issue; as Buckley and Casson state: "The answer must be that there is some net disadvantage to such a merger. It may be managerial diseconomies arising from the scale and diversity of the resultant enterprise, legal obstacles stemming from antitrust policy or restrictions on foreign acquisitions, difficulties of financing because of stock market skepticism, and so on" (1988: 41).

In sum, the transactions cost model of JVs appears to predict that JVs are formed when transactional hazards suggest that internalization is efficient (the transactions cost approach specifies these conditions well), but constraints of various kinds prohibit full internalization (the transactions cost approach does not systematically address these conditions). Also, even if such constraints did not exist, there may be more efficient ways to resolve the problem of transactional hazards than internalization, solutions that the transactions cost perspective does not consider as first-best because of the assumptions and predictions of the theory. Transactions cost theorists have devoted much attention to distinguishing between different kinds of asset specificity, given the special significance and explanatory power attributed to this dimension of transactions (assuming the potential for opportunism) for determining transactions costs and therefore the optimal governance mode.[2] At the same time, other technological, strategic, motivational, and political factors that affect production costs or revenues and are likely also to affect the choice of governance mode have received less than systematic attention.

The empirical evidence similarly suggests that the TC approach is well suited to explain the reasons underlying the existence of fully owned subsidiaries, but less informative about the reasons for joint venture formation. For example, as Gatignon and Anderson (1988) described it, full ownership of overseas subsidiaries is more likely in the presence of high transactions costs (proxied by R&D/sales and advertising expenditures/sales). However, other explanations appear to be responsible for the existence of IJVs. Similarly, Gomes-Casseres (1989) concluded from his empirical study that transactions cost arguments were useful but not sufficient to explain the rationale for IJVs.

It therefore becomes imperative to systematically examine the conditions under which IJVs emerge, beyond the insights contributed by the transactions cost perspective. This chapter provides such a systematic examination with particular reference to the property rights perspective, agency theory, and prospect theory. In the following section, we highlight the contrasts between the TC view and other theoretical perspectives by comparing the key assumptions of the TC perspective with those of other approaches.

Overview of Contrasting Theoretical Perspectives

Whereas the TC view of the rationale for JVs focuses on the mitigation of the hazards of opportunism, other theoretical perspectives such as property rights and agency theory suggest that a JV is formed to capitalize on the latent value-creating potential of the strategic assets owned by different parties, in the presence of environmental risk and uncertainty. Uncertainty in a transaction may stem from two sources, the transaction partner's actions and the environment. With its emphasis on the dangers of opportunistic behavior by the transaction partner, the literature on transactions cost economics has emphasized the former source of uncertainty over the latter. Although environmental uncertainty has not been ignored, it has generally been characterized by reference to the limits that bounded rationality places on writing complete contracts. We suggest that the possible impact of an uncertain environment on the decision to form a JV warrants greater attention than it has received in the TC perspective.

Separability of Transactions
Versus Separability of Property Rights

The traditional TC approach predicts that transactions will be aligned with governance structures (that is, markets versus hierarchies) in a transaction-cost economizing way. Fundamental to the TC view is that the relevant unit of analysis is the transaction, and governance choices are made to economize primarily on the characteristics of that transaction (Williamson 1991). The implicit assumption is that transactions costs are dependent (only) on the governance structure and production costs are dependent (only) on technology. However, production and transaction costs generally vary both with the organization as well as the technology, and it may be inappropriate to treat the two as independent (Williamson 1985, Milgrom and Roberts 1992).

Moreover, even if we could separate production and transaction costs, in reality it may not always be possible to separate one transaction from others carried out by a potential JV partner. While transactions costs pertain to a single transaction, the hierarchy form of governance structure pertains to groups of transactions. It may be infeasible for a governance choice to be made relative to a single transaction conducted by two transacting entities, independent of other transactions conducted by them. In the face of this reality, if the traditional TC approach predicts that a certain transaction is conducted most efficiently through internalization, the entire nexus of linked transactions would have to be internalized. As previously discussed, the TC explanation of JVs recognizes that constraints exist that prevent complete internalization, leading to the formation of JVs (Buckley and Casson 1988; Hennart 1989). However, in doing so, it departs from the assumption of traditional TC theory that each transaction can be separated from, and is independent of, other transactions conducted by a transacting partner.

An alternative viewpoint, the property rights perspective, suggests that the choice of governance mode is more complex than merely one between market and hierarchy, and it sheds light on this complex choice. The property rights literature views assets as bundles of rights. If the focal firm acquires the right to the specific use of an asset, even though the asset continues to be owned by another, internalization then may not be necessary (rather than necessary but impossible due to constraints, as the TC view suggests). Indeed, it is this sharing of rights—an asset being used by two or more firms but owned by only one—that forms an important conceptual basis for the formation of JVs, and indeed many other hybrid forms of governance. In addition, the property rights perspective highlights that uncertainty may cause optimal asset uses to be unknown *ex ante,* facilitating the formation of JVs. Below we develop a property rights perspective on the question "Why are JVs formed?"

Administrative Fiat Versus
Sharing Residual Claims and Residual Risk

The TC view essentially suggests that if assets of strategic importance to a firm's activities are owned by another firm, then the focal firm may be subject to a hold-up problem. The TC solution to this threat is to internalize the transaction. The rationale in this lies in the TC perspective of the firm as fundamentally comprising authority relationships, which are considered to be more efficient in resolving the potential hold-up problem than market transactions. The advantage of organizations over markets lies in "overcoming human pathologies through hierarchy" (Ghoshal and Moran 1996: 42). The substitution of an administrative interface for a market interface is proposed to have beneficial effects regarding goal pursuit, monitoring, staffing, and resource allocation, which serve to attenuate the hold-up problem.

Whereas the TC approach proposes that internalization reduces opportunistic behavior, Grossman and Hart (1986: 692) pointed out that there is no reason to assume that the scope for such behavior changes when "one of the self-interested owners becomes an equally self-interested employee of the other owner." Internalization simply replaces what was, perhaps, a supply contract by an employment contract. If administrative fiat does not have the property of efficiently resolving conflicts of interest, how then might the hold-up problem be resolved? Agency theory provides useful insights into the answer. The perspective of agency theory is that the firm is essentially a "nexus of contracts" (Alchian and Demsetz 1972; Jensen and Meckling 1976; Fama 1980). As stated by Alchian and Demsetz, the firm has "no power of fiat, no authority, no disciplinary action any different from ordinary market contracting" (1972: 777). The central problem of agency theory, then, is how the interests of parties to a contract may be aligned under conditions of environmental uncertainty. We develop an agency perspective on JVs that addresses both the questions of interest in this chapter (Why are joint ventures formed? What factors explain the nature of the JV partnership?) This perspective describes how, under conditions of environmental uncertainty, the sharing of residual claims and residual risk (achieved by shared equity ownership) have important incentive-alignment features and thus may underlie the formation of JVs and influence the nature of the JV partnership.

The differences in the predictions of the TC perspective and the agency theory perspective in part rely upon their different assumptions about human motivation. TC assumes the strongest form of self-interest seeking, that individuals may act opportunistically (that is, in a self-interested manner that includes "lying, stealing, cheating . . . [and] subtle forms of deceit" [Williamson 1985: 47]). In contrast, agency theory subscribes to a semi-strong form of simple self-interested behavior. Given that the TC perspective assumes opportunism, the sheer force of administrative fiat is necessary to quell this opportunism. Given that agency theory assumes simple self-interest seeking, contractual mechanisms are sufficient to align interests.

Risk Neutrality Versus Framing of Risk

The TC approach considers that two dimensions of the transaction (asset specificity and frequency) are of paramount importance in predicting the choice of governance mode (it also assumes behavioral uncertainty to a nontrivial but nonparamount degree). As such, each transaction is treated independently of the decision maker's cognitive frame of reference. The identity of the decision maker is assumed not to matter, as any rational person would behave in the same manner. In contrast, the implication of another approach, prospect theory, is that transactions need to be understood as being contingent on the cognitive framing of the environment, and that the choice may vary as a function of how the environment is perceived (Tversky and Kahneman 1981). Again, the predictions of the two theories regarding whether a firm should internalize are associated with the behavioral assumptions underlying the decision-making process. While in the TC perspective decision makers are subject to risk neutrality and bounded rationality, prospect theory finds that a decision maker may exhibit either risk-averse or risk-seeking behavior depending on how the risky choice is framed. Prospect theory shows that decision making under risk is frequently characterized by a violation of the axioms of expected utility theory: the decisions made are, from the perspective of expected utility theory, irrational.

In emphasizing the characteristics of the transaction, the TC approach not only downplays the characteristics of the transactors but also ignores the possible influence of competitors in the market. The formation of JVs by one or more competitors may serve as a reference point for the actions of a firm. DiMaggio and Powell (1983) point out that the social legitimacy and security derived from imitative behavior may serve to override economic rationales in making a decision, and may account for systematic biases in the decision maker's "frames."

Implications of the Different Theoretical Perspectives

The above brief review suggests that there are a number of alternative perspectives that address gaps in the transactions cost explanation of JVs. In this section we discuss these perspectives in greater detail and provide an inventory of propositions based on them. We show that different perspectives make, in some cases, opposing or inconsistent predictions, and in other cases, make similar or consistent predictions but with different rationales. The assumptions and key features of the theories we discuss are summarized in Table 3.1.

Property Rights and Optimal Asset Usage
Under Uncertainty

Whereas the TC approach compares different governance modes for efficient handling of a transaction, the focus of property rights is on optimal ownership arrangements for the efficient usage of productive assets: "Property rights affect economic behavior through incentives. They delineate decision-making authority over economic resources, determine time horizons, specify permitted asset uses, define transferability, and direct the assignment of net benefits. Because they define the costs and rewards of decision making, property rights establish the parameters under which decisions are made regarding resource use" (Libecap 1986: 229).

Theory	Central research problem	Conceptualization of JV	Goals of JV	Key explanatory concepts	Nature of environment	ASSUMPTIONS REGARDING MANAGERS		
						Motives	Behavior	Attitude to risk
Transaction cost economics	Optimal governance mode	Authority relationship	Minimize sum of production and transaction costs	Asset specificity, frequency of transaction, separability and independence of transactions	Behavioral uncertainty	Opportunistic	Bounded rationality, information asymmetry between transacting partners	Risk-neutral
Property rights	Optimal ownership arrangements	Bundle of property rights	Maximize firm value	Asset complementarity, asset non-separability, divisibility of property rights	Uncertainty of optimal asset usage	Maximize firm value	Rational	Risk-neutral

Agency theory	Optimal contracting relationships	Nexus of contracts	Maximize firm value	Reduction of agency (monitoring, bonding and residual) costs	Uncertainty of value of residual claims	Self-interest seeking	Rational, information asymmetries between agent, effort-averse	Risk-neutral or risk-averse
Prospect theory	Managerial decision-making processes	—	Formation of JV (although risky) preferred to sure loss of not forming JV	Frames, choice heuristics and cognitive biases	Uncertainty of loss or gain	Seek gains or avoid losses	Subjective decision making	Risk-seeking (with sure losses), or risk-avoiding (with sure gains)

Table 3.1. Joint Ventures: Assumptions and Key Features of Alternative Theoretical Perspectives.

The scope and content of property rights over resources affect the way people behave in a world of scarcity. The notion of property as a bundle of rights suggests that the focus of ownership is not the property itself, but the bundle of rights to exercise control over various attributes of the property. A property may have several attributes—for instance, being unique or ubiquitous, or transferable to other owners or users—that under appropriate circumstances generate an income stream. Control over these attributes— the right to use the resource, to appropriate returns from it, to change its form or substance—are called property rights (Furubotn and Pejovich 1974). If the bundle of rights associated with a resource is divisible and assignable, each right may have a different owner, and the structure of ownership can have important consequences for the generation of rents.

In the context of the rent-generating potential of a property, appropriability refers to a firm's ability to capture rents from it. However, mere ownership of a property does not guarantee rent-generating use; the property has to be put to appropriate use. Although a firm may own a particular property, it may not have the capability to use the property in a fashion such that its rent-generating potential is fully exploited. But other firms may, and clear ownership of a property facilitates its transfer to another owner, such that complementary properties are owned together. If the asset is essential to the original owner's operations, then rather than transfer the entire asset it may be possible to transfer specific rights over it to another firm. The notion that a resource can be partitioned among several people, and that more than one party can claim some ownership interest in the same resource, stems from the fact that it is not the resource itself that is owned, but rather a bundle of rights to use it.

Property Rights and Joint Ventures

The property rights perspective provides rich insights into the first of the two questions that represent the scope of this chapter (Why are joint ventures formed?) The owner of any firm controls the property rights over the firm's assets. In a JV some rights over certain assets are shared and others are retained by the firm owning them. For instance, the right to use the asset and the right to appropriate returns from the asset may be shared, but the right to change the form or substance of the asset may be retained by the owner firm. Thus, the property rights perspective is more specific than the TC view in describing how exactly JVs lie between markets and hierarchies. See, for example, Child, Yan, and Yu (1997) for an interesting discussion of different kinds of ownership rights over assets, specifically in Sino-foreign JVs. Two key concepts underlying this perspective of JVs are nonseparability of assets and uncertainty regarding the optimal production-investment decisions to maximize the value of assets.

First, as previously mentioned, the property rights perspective recognizes that, although some assets may not be separable, the rights to them may indeed be divisible and assignable. In the course of various activities that constitute the rent-seeking process, a firm may gain exclusive property rights to resources that have rent-generating potential. These resources may be physical, such as an exclusive or cheap supply of a particular input, or knowledge-based, such as patents or competence in a particular strategic or functional area. However, realizing the full rent potential of them may require the use of complementary resources owned by another firm. (Indeed, it has been argued [Hennart and Reddy, 1994] that one of the benefits of JVs is that they allow firms to share in assets without owning them.) If these assets were not idiosyncratic to the asset-owning firm they could possibly be sold in a market transaction. But the strategic nature of some assets implies that the firm cannot afford to lose control over them. Hence the owner firm needs to retain control while combining the use of the assets with those of another firm. By doing so, the owner firm shares the right to use and the right to appropriate rents from the assets, but retains residual control rights. Stopford and Wells (1972) propose a similar argument: they suggest that JV formation reflects an underlying trade-off between the drive for unambiguous control and the quest for additional resources.

Given that some combination of the resources owned by parent firms may be potentially valuable, contributors to the JV share rights in the JV. If the contributions made by either partner are in the form of assets that cannot be separated from the operations of the owner firm, then the owner firm retains residual control rights to the asset, and only specific rights are shared with the JV partner. On the other hand, if assets are separable from the parent firm without threatening its productivity, the control will be shared with the JV partner. In fact, if all assets necessary for the operation of the JV were freely separable and assignable, they would be owned by only one of the potential JV partners—the one to whom they are more valuable. Retaining control rights in a JV protects those assets strategic to either firm's operations; sharing specific rights provides an incentive for both parents to invest in the JV. Hence:

PROPOSITION R1: All else being equal, an investment opportunity is more likely to be pursued as a shared investment (as in a JV) than as a wholly owned investment when the critical inputs required to pursue the opportunity are owned by different parties and when these inputs are inseparable from the other assets of the owner firms.[3]

Uncertainty about the optimal usage of complementary assets owned by different parties also underlies the formation of JVs. A specific type of uncertainty is important from the property rights perspective: uncertainty about the strategic and operational decisions that will lead to optimal usage of complementary assets owned by two firms (in terms of creating value). This kind of uncertainty makes it difficult to assign an accurate value to the complementary assets. To understand why this uncertainty is a key concept underlying a property rights approach to JVs, let us consider an extreme case where there is no uncertainty associated with a project calling for inputs from two firms. When an accurate value can be assigned to each firm's input (which depends on knowing with certainty the decisions required for optimal usage of the assets), the party that benefits the most can simply pay the other firm for its inputs (though the payout need not correspond exactly to their value if the firm has enough bargaining power).

In contrast, consider the situation when the value of the inputs cannot be accurately assessed. This is particularly likely in the case of intangible assets such as intellectual property, brand name, reputation, and the like, which also are often not separable from the owner firm's other activities. Uncertainty regarding the value of each partner's assets leads to questions about which organizational form will best govern productive activity. It may not be feasible for either firm to internalize the other if the utility of the other's contribution remains to be determined. In this circumstance, it may be useful for the firms to share residual control rights over an asset. Residual control rights govern "all usages of the asset in any way not inconsistent with a prior contract, or custom" (Hart 1995: 30). Sharing the rights allows decisions on usage of these assets to be deferred at the time of formation of the JV until optimal usage can be determined. This also preempts other potential claimants from staking their rights to the assets.

In general, property rights tend to be made more precise as resource values are recognized—that is, when resource values can be accurately assessed (Libecap 1986). However, the recognition of the value of a resource attracts additional claimants to the resource, thereby leading to two problems: possible losses resulting from a common pool situation, and an increase in the costs of defining property rights. The common pool situation arises when an increase in resource value attracts a large number of claimants who, in competing for the use of these resources, may drive down their value. At the same time, the cost of defining and enforcing property rights is likely to be increased by the larger number of claimants to the resource. It may therefore be efficient for a firm to establish its claim to a potentially valuable resource *ex ante* of its value being realized by other possible claimants. However, when the costs of establishing these rights are nontrivial, the firm may share these costs with another firm. Thus, an investment opportunity is more likely to be pursued as a shared investment (as in a JV) than as a wholly owned investment when the critical inputs required to pursue the opportunity are owned by different parties, and when the optimal usage of these inputs for the investment opportunity cannot be discerned *ex ante*. This suggests:

PROPOSITION R2: All else being equal, relative to wholly owned investments JVs are more likely to be formed in industry sectors that present considerable technological uncertainty (such as the high-tech sector) or demand uncertainty (such as airlines) than in industry sectors with stable cash flows.

PROPOSITION R3: All else being equal, relative to wholly owned investments JVs are more likely to be formed in periods of economic and competitive volatility than in periods of stability.

Once the uncertainty over optimal usage is resolved, property rights tend to be fully defined, allocated, and enforced. As Coase (1960) points out, in the absence of transactions costs, these rights will be reallocated to their highest-valued use regardless of their initial assignment. This suggests that JVs have limited lives, lasting only until the relative value of property rights to their joint owners has been determined.

We note that the property rights perspective on JVs is an interesting and useful way to conceptualize the underlying basis of change processes and flux in multinational enterprise IJVs. In discussing the high rate of gross turnover in IJVs, Caves (1994) refers to the evidence from Franko (1971) that governance costs and problems of opportunism cause JVs to be dissolved. As Caves also points out, this suggests that the transactions cost explanation for the formation of IJVs is somewhat unsatisfying, as it implies that the venture partners sign up in ignorance of the hazards ahead. We add that it is equally problematic that in spite of repeated so-called failures, firms continue to participate in JVs; this carries the troubling implication that firms are incapable of learning much from their mistakes. Caves (1994: 20) suggests that "it would be attractive to test an explanation resting on news (good or bad) that is revealed to the JV partners after they have committed resources to the venture." We propose that the property rights perspective provides a theoretical rationale for this explanation.

Agency Theory and the Incentive Properties
of Sharing Residual Claims and Residual Risk

The agency theory perspective firmly rejects the TC view that the firm is a fundamentally different type of governance mechanism from the market or that in the firm, contractual relations are replaced by administrative fiat. Instead, in agency theory the firm is viewed as merely a nexus of contracts (Jensen and Meckling 1976) between owners of the factors of production and customers. A firm is characterized not by the presence of authority relationships but by team use of inputs (Alchian and Demsetz 1972). Whereas in the TC perspective hierarchies are employed to minimize the sum of production and transactions costs, according to agency theory firms come into existence to exploit the advantages of teamwork while controlling agency costs (given informational and other functional inseparabilities). The key features of team production are that several types of resources (not all of which are owned by one party) are used, and the product is greater than the sum of the separable outputs of each resource. However, this team effort gives rise to agency problems that arise because contracts between agents are not costlessly written and enforced. Agency costs include "the costs of structuring, monitoring, and bonding a set of contracts among agents with conflicting self-interests, plus the residual loss because the cost of full enforcement of contracts exceeds the benefits" (Fama and Jensen 1983b: 327; see also Jensen and Meckling 1976).[4]

In the agency framework, agents are assumed to pursue self-serving goals. The problem posed by agents having different goals is compounded by information asymmetry and environmental uncertainty. Information asymmetry means that agents have different information about each others' efforts. If the environment in which contracts between agents are written were deterministic, all outcomes could be predicted with certainty. In such an environment, any deviation in a task performed by an agent that would detract from the optimal outcome could readily be attributed to the agent. Similarly, in an environment that produces stochastic outcomes, if one agent had complete information about another's effort, then the former could easily determine if the outcome of the latter's actions are attributable to the agent or to environmental uncertainty.

However, when the agent's effort is not fully transparent and the environment is uncertain, it is frequently impossible to determine with certainty whether an agent is consuming on-the-job perquisites, with negative consequences for efficient team production: this is the agency problem. Agents must incur costs to reduce the magnitude of this problem. Monitoring costs include not only supervision but the setting up of systems to align the incentives of agents. Knowing that other agents are aware of their divergent interests, each agent attempts to demonstrate good faith and thereby incurs bonding costs. Despite monitoring and bonding activities undertaken by agents, there might still be some disparity between the actual outcome and the best possible outcome if the agent had acted in good faith. This disparity contributes to residual loss.

Agency theory explains how specific types of organizational forms arise and survive with reference to the efficiency of the organizational form in coordinating the activities of self-interested parties (Alchian and Demsetz 1972; Fama and Jensen 1983a, 1983b). As Alchian and Demsetz (1972) describe for the example of the classical capitalist firm, problems with team production arise because it is difficult to observe each individual's output or input, thus making reward allocation imprecise. As a result, shirking on the part of team members is likely. Lacking adequate individual incentives, teams therefore require central monitors to control actual or potential shirkers. But if the central monitor consists of a person who is also a team member, the benefit of his performance is a public good. Thus, it is desirable to adopt institutional forms where the full benefits of monitoring belong to the monitor(s), who disciplines himself because he is the residual claimant. According to Alchian and Demsetz (1972: 79), the essence of the classical firm is: "a contractual structure with 1) joint input production 2) several input owners 3) one party who is common to all the contracts of the joint inputs 4) who has the right to renegotiate any input's contract independently of contracts with other input owners 5) who holds the residual claims and who has the right to sell his central contractual residual status."

The ability of the classical firm to efficiently manage team production derives from the rights and responsibilities of the central agent, who is the firm's owner and residual claimant, as described above. Given these rights, all members of the team can be induced to work efficiently (that is, with a minimum of residual loss) toward consequent increases in the value of team production.

The extended analysis of residual claimants provided in Fama and Jensen (1983a, 1983b) is extremely insightful in its explanation of different organizational forms. Two related and central aspects of the contract structures of different organizational forms relates to how uncertainty is borne, and the nature of residual claims. The risks of most of the parties in a nexus of contracts can be limited by specifying fixed payoffs in exchange for their contributions. The residual risk is the risk of the stochastic cash flows less the promised payment to agents; this is borne by the residual claimant(s), who are the owner(s) of the firm. Essentially, say

Fama and Jensen, the residual claimants bear most of the uncertainty associated with the operations of the firm.

This suggests an important tension between the benefits and costs of concentrated ownership, which must be balanced in considering optimal ownership structure. As described above, ownership concentrated in the hands of a single residual claimant has the important advantage that the costs of monitoring are willingly borne by that individual, who has the incentive to bear these costs because he derives the benefits from monitoring. When ownership is shared between two or more parties, there is the obvious disadvantage that each owner has the incentive to shirk, because he alone realizes benefits from shirking but the costs of it are borne by all owners in proportion to their ownership stake. Nonetheless, there are important benefits to shared or diffused ownership. For example, the common stock of open corporations allows residual risk to be spread over many residual claimants, lowering the cost of risk-bearing services. Having many claimants thus has beneficial risk-sharing properties. However, when ownership is diffused it becomes inefficient for each owner to participate in the ratification and monitoring of all decisions. This gives rise to an optimal separation of the risk-bearing and decision management functions.

Agency Theory and Joint Ventures

We suggest, following agency theory, that JVs can be considered as market-organized team activities where the liability and residual cash flows are shared between the JV partners in proportion to their investments. These organizational forms come into being as a result of the advantages of team production by two firms that own diverse inputs, each set of inputs being necessary to pursue the productive opportunity. If the asset owned by a potential JV partner cannot be separated from the other activities of the firm (as when it has strong complementarities with a range of the firm's activities), then the costs of acquiring that asset by another firm may be prohibitive. A potential buyer would need to compensate the seller for not only the stand-alone value of the asset but the value of the lost complementarities. Thus, agency theory makes the same prediction as does the property rights approach:

PROPOSITION A1: All else being equal, an investment opportunity is more likely to be pursued as a shared investment (as in a JV) than as a wholly owned investment when the critical inputs required to pursue the opportunity are owned by different parties, and when these inputs are inseparable from the other assets of the owner firms.

In their discussion of the determinants of ownership structure, Demsetz and Lehn (1985: 1158) propose that under conditions of high "control potential," relatively concentrated ownership is preferable. Control potential is "the wealth gain achievable through more effective monitoring of managerial performance by a firm's owners." One important condition under which control potential is valuable is firm-specific uncertainty. Under conditions of rapidly changing technology, prices, market share, and so on, there exist higher costs of monitoring as well as higher payoffs to it. If, under uncertainty, the additional benefits exceed the additional costs, the firm's control potential is associated with the noisiness of the firm's environment: noisier environments represent greater payoffs to tight control, and should accordingly give rise to more concentrated ownership. We note that the following two propositions are also predicted (although using different reasoning) by the property rights perspective:

PROPOSITION A2: All else being equal, JVs are more likely to be formed in industry sectors that represent considerable technological uncertainty (such as the high-tech sector) or demand uncertainty (such as airlines) than in industry sectors with stable cash flows.

PROPOSITION A3: All else being equal, JVs are more likely to be formed in periods of economic and competitive volatility than in periods of stability.

Although control potential is valuable under conditions of firm-specific uncertainty, its value is reduced when even a high level of monitoring by a partner cannot assign the responsibility for negative outcomes to another partner's actions and take appropriate corrective action. In the international context, this condition may arise in a nation characterized by high political risk. Political risk arises if the operating climate of an international firm will deteriorate because of changes in the political climate; there may be uncertainty regarding changes in rules, takeover of property, and so on. In this climate, it may be especially difficult to disentangle whether negative outcomes result from a lack of effort on the part of the local JV partner or from political changes. In addition, a JV partner may have little ability to take corrective action. Therefore:

PROPOSITION A4: All else being equal, IJVs are less likely to be formed with partners from countries that present a high level of politiical risk than a low level of political risk.

The agency explanation also suggests that systematic regulation to monitor and control the activities of firms reduces control potential, because it restricts the options open to owners (Demsetz and Lehn 1985). Given this, ownership concentration should be reduced. In and of itself, this implies a lower incidence of IJVs in countries subject to strict regulations (even if the regulations don't completely prohibit foreign ownership). Therefore:

PROPOSITION A5: All else being equal, relative to wholly owned investments, IJVs are less likely to be formed with partners from countries that have a high level of governmental regulations rather than a low level of governmental regulations.

Demsetz and Lehn (1985) also suggest that the larger the competitively viable size of the firm, the higher its need for large capital resources and the greater the price of a given fraction of the firm. Thus, even under conditions of risk neutrality, larger firms are likely to be associated with more diffused ownership. This argument can be applied in a relatively straightforward manner to JVs. The higher the amount of capital required to pursue an investment opportunity, the more necessary is the requirement for shared investment. Therefore:

PROPOSITION A6: All else being equal, the higher the required initial investment, the more likely that the investment opportunity will be pursued as a shared investment (as in a JV) rather than as a wholly owned investment.

The above six propositions explain why JVs are formed. The agency perspective is also instructive about the factors that influence the nature of the JV relationship. Risk aversion reinforces the effect described in Proposition A6: if a single firm that is relatively undiversified commits a relatively sizable amount of capital to a large firm, it must be compensated for the high risk it bears, implying a higher cost of capital relative to smaller levels of capital contributed by a larger number of owners. JVs bring no financial diversification benefits to parents who are themselves owned by a group of well-diversified individual claimants, but may do so for parents with highly concentrated ownership when the owners themselves are not well diversified. For the latter category of firms, because the risks associated with an investment are shared by a group of residual claimants rather than a single residual claimant, the cost of capital for the JV would decrease. Therefore:

PROPOSITION A7: All else being equal, JVs are more likely to be formed between partners of whom at least one is characterized by relatively concentrated ownership.

Agency theory suggests that an important means of aligning interests is via joint ownership wherein residual risk and residual claims are shared by co-owners. An equity JV, by inducing both partner and agent to commit themselves through equity investments, provides a powerful incentive for cooperation to align their interests. Not only does sharing residual claims suggest that each partner has strong incentives to desist from taking actions that detract from the value of the residual claims, it also provides incentives for each partner to monitor the employees of the JV as well as each other. The relative amount of equity that the partners invest in the JV is conceptually similar to posting a performance bond. Furthermore, as sharing residual claims provides the incentive to voluntarily control the degree of shirking on the part of the owners and the incentive for mutual monitoring, the fewer owners, the greater the incentive. Thus:

PROPOSITION A8: All else being equal, the higher the investment in the JV relative to the size of the parent company, the greater the commitment to the objectives of the JV and the greater the extent of mutual monitoring.

PROPOSITION A9: All else being equal, JVs are more likely to be formed between two partners than between multiple partners.

Further, the alignment of incentives is more perfect to the extent that the partners in the JV have approximately equivalent ownership stakes. This suggests that trust is a function of the structure of the equity arrangement between JV partners. Previous researchers have argued that extant research on IJVs "does not adequately recognize the inseparability of the outcome from the process" (Madhok 1995: 117); we go one step beyond: previous work also does not adequately recognize the inseparability of the process from the structure of the IJV partnership. We suggest that the nature of the contractual agreement between IJV partners itself defines the process, and ultimately the outcome of the IJV. This leads to the following proposition:

PROPOSITION A10: All else being equal, a higher degree of cooperation and mutual trust will be exhibited in JVs with equivalent ownership by the parents, relative to JVs where ownership is relatively unequal.

With regard to this proposition, we note that share ownership captures only one of a range of possible incentive alignment mechanisms, which may act as substitutes in generating trust and cooperation (Rediker and Seth 1995). In addition, the proposition does not account for the possibility of trilateral governance, where a third party monitors the commitments of two firms that they cannot get out of (Roehl 1983).

In summary, agency theory represents a fruitful theoretical perspective for understanding numerous issues associated with JVs and usefully complements the TC perspective. We note again that there are many similarities between the two views; however, there is one key dissimilarity that underlies the added value of the agency perspective. As stated by Fama and Jensen (1983b: 327; emphasis ours), "*Absent fiat,* the form of organization that survives in an activity is the one that delivers the product demanded by customers while covering costs." However, as stated by Williamson (1991: 276; emphasis ours), "*firms do and can exercise fiat* that markets cannot." This seemingly small difference gives rise to the greater relative emphasis placed by agency theory on specific aspects of contracts such as residual claims, and thereby provides the means for rich theorizing. It is also useful to note that the agency view predicts that JVs are as likely to be formed to carry out short-lived as long-lived activities. The JV, like any other firm, is a nexus of contracts, and the duration of these contracts depends upon the specific nature of the team production activities the JV engages in, as well as specific conditions that influence the efficacy of the contracts to achieve the objectives of the contracting agents.

Prospect Theory and Framing Risky Alternatives

Unlike the transactions costs, property rights, agency, and options perspectives on JVs, prospect theory by itself does not identify key exogenous factors that govern the choice of organizational form. It does, however, describe the processes that frame a decision, such as the one to form a JV. The TC perspective explicitly assumes risk neutrality. In contrast, prospect theory finds that decision makers are risk-seeking or risk-averse depending upon the framing of the decision, and that choices among risky prospects exhibit several pervasive effects that violate the tenets of expected utility theory. This finding leads to an important incommensurability of prospect theory not only with the TC view but also the property rights perspective and agency theory, as all these theories assume that decision making is rational (that is, it observes the axioms of expected utility theory).

The parameters of a decision problem include the acts among which one must choose, the possible outcomes of those acts, and the expected relationships between the acts and their outcomes. Tversky and Kahneman (1981) use the term *decision frame* to refer to the decision maker's conception of the acts, outcomes, and contingencies associated with a particular choice. Whereas expected utility theory suggests that all decision makers frame their decision problems in an identical manner, prospect theory suggests that the decision frame varies among decision makers. In making a decision, risky alternatives are characterized by their possible outcomes and the probabilities of those outcomes. The same option, however, can be framed or described in different ways. Rational choice requires that the preference between options in a choice set not be altered with changes of frame. However, because of imperfections in human decision making, changes of perspective often alter the relative desirability of options and lead to choices very different from those predicted by expected utility theory. These imperfections may stem from the use of decision-making heuristics, or may have to do with whether the decision problem is framed as representing a loss-avoidance or a gain-seeking option.

In prospect theory, outcomes are expressed as positive or negative deviations (gains or losses) from a neutral reference outcome. Variations of the reference point can determine whether a given outcome is evaluated as a gain or a loss. Although subjective values differ among individuals and attributes, Tversky and Kahneman (1981) propose that because the value function is generally concave for gains, convex for losses, and steeper for losses than gains, shifts of reference can change the value of outcomes and thereby reverse the preference order between options. Of particular interest for the purposes of this chapter is the "certainty effect." Prospect theory suggests that the decision maker is either risk-averse or risk-seeking, depending on whether the outcome of a decision presents sure gains or sure losses. The certainty effect posits that there is a risk-averse preference for a sure gain over a larger gain that is merely probable. Similarly, there is a risk-seeking preference for a loss that is merely probable over a smaller loss that is certain.

Prospect Theory and Joint Ventures

As to whether or not a firm should enter into a IJV, prospect theory suggests that the choice is contingent on how the decision is framed. In other words, is the IJV seen as a gain-seeking device or a loss-avoidance device? Consider JVs in the context of investment in a particular international market. Two alternatives to a JV are the wholly owned subsidiary (WOS) and doing nothing. If returns to the WOS are seen as relatively certain and the returns to IJVs as relatively uncertain, even though the expected value of both options is the same, the choice is framed as gain seeking and the firm elects the WOS alternative. However, if the choice between WOS and IJV is framed as loss avoidance, with the WOS or doing nothing representing a sure loss and the IJV representing a higher loss that is merely probable, prospect theory suggests that the firm will choose the IJV entry mode even if the expected value of the investment under the choices is the same. But under what conditions will choices be framed as seeking gain or avoiding loss?

We suggest that the conditions prevailing in the 1960s were seen as a more certain environment in which the choice of entry mode into a particular market was framed in a gain-seeking mode, whereas the 1970s to the present are a more troubled environment in which problems became framed much more in a loss-awareness or loss-avoidance mode. To see why this might be the case, it is instructive to refer to Vernon's product cycle model (1966). As recognized by Caves (1982), although the product cycle model is primarily concerned with explaining international shifts in trade and production, it also explains stages in the evolution of the MNE. The model proposes that innovations are usually concentrated in high-income countries, because the value of people's time is highest there relative to the user cost of capital—in other words, there are strong incentives to innovate. Not only innovation but also early production is tied to the high-income geographical market where the innovation has the greatest potential. Eventually, rising real wages in other countries and the declining real costs of the innovation create a demand that is met by exports from high-income areas. Increasing price elasticities of demand, as users grow more familiar with the innovation and product-market competition becomes sharper, create a pull toward the displacement of exports by expanding production in other industrial countries. Finally, as the innovation matures, there may be a shifting pattern of production and use toward less-developed countries. The parallel evolution of MNEs, starting with innovation and home country investment, progressing from export to foreign direct investment (FDI), then to JVs, and finally to licensing has been documented by Vernon and Davidson (1979).

However, Vernon subsequently repudiated his product cycle model (Vernon, 1979). In his view, the well-defined, stable international environment (within which the early product cycle model was built) was more or less valid until the mid-1970s. The new international economic environment is marked by a much greater parity that has both decreased the concentration of innovation in any location (particularly the previously dominant U.S.) and severed the relation between the origin of the innovation and the process of its commercialization. Competitive parity and volatility are almost undisputed attributes of the changed economic environment.

We suggest that during the stable international environment that existed until the mid-1970s, governance choices were more likely to be framed between the more risky prospect of gains to be achieved by IJVs and the surer prospect of gains from FDI. In contrast, in today's highly competitive and turbulent environment these choices are more likely to be framed between the probable losses that would be incurred if a JV breaks down, and the much surer prospect of perceived losses arising from not doing anything, or from going it alone. As described by prospect theory, the tendency to frame the situation as choices between seemingly negative outcomes induces a greater tolerance for the ambiguity and risk in JVs.

It is again interesting that perspectives with different theoretical rationales discussed here make similar empirical predictions. Our discussion of prospect theory leads to two of the same propositions as predicted by the property rights perspective and agency theory with regard to the question, "Why are JVs formed?"

PROPOSITION P1: All else being equal, relative to wholly owned investments, JVs are more likely to be formed in industry sectors that represent considerable technological uncertainty (such as the high-tech sector) or demand uncertainty (such as airlines) than in industry sectors with stable cash flows.

PROPOSITION P2: All else being equal, relative to wholly owned investments, JVs are more likely to be formed in periods of economic and competitive volatility than in periods of stability.

However, there also are differential predictions. Prospect theory highlights the importance of the cognitive frame in which the decision to form a JV is embedded. This implies that the importance of JVs lies in the eyes of the decision maker. Prospect theory suggests that firms are risk-averse in the context of sure gains, but risk-seeking in the context of sure losses. If JVs are considered to result in possible losses relative to the surer losses of doing nothing or going it alone, this suggests:

PROPOSITION P3: All else being equal, industries with high mortality rates are also characterized by a significant number of JV formations.

PROPOSITION P4: All else being equal, firms that have been performing poorly will be more likely to form JVs than firms that are performing well.

Note, however, that an alternative explanation for the conclusion drawn by Proposition P4 is that high-performance firms have resources to enter a market through direct investment, whereas poor-performing firms do not, and so have to share entry costs with others.

Conclusion

We have briefly discussed transaction costs economics, property rights, agency theory, and prospect theory to highlight some possible directions for research on JVs. We have demonstrated that looking at JVs through multiple lenses gives us a sense of the limits and strengths of any single approach. As Hennart (1988: 373) points out, "JVs are often the product of multiple factors, and any (single) theory must necessarily abstract from some of them." In this chapter we have attempted to show how different perspectives shed light on various aspects of JVs. Table 3.2 summarizes the propositions we derive, and shows how different theories make similar predictions (although, as we have seen above, different assumptions and logical arguments underlie these predictions). The table also indicates whether the propositions based on each theory are consistent with those from other theories, and identifies inconsistencies. We submit that these propositions represent useful avenues for future research into JVs.

The differences among the theories, as highlighted in the table, suggest that we carefully reconsider the important question: is any single theory more powerful in explaining all JVs, or are there different kinds of JVs calling for different theoretical explanations? We could view a JV as one animal, but it might be more reasonable to view it as a species. This implies that different theoretical lenses may be operative for different types of JVs. For instance, JVs formed to optimally utilize idiosyncratic assets may be best explained in terms of reducing transaction costs, and JVs formed for financial diversification benefits may be best explained by agency theory. If different theoretical perspectives are needed to explain different types of JVs, then propositions such as the ones discussed earlier will prove to be true or false depending on the type of JV that forms the basis for empirical tests. We consider that, in addition to attempting to judge the predictive precision of a theory over the entire range of JVs, it is also appropriate to conduct a more finely grained analysis of the differential predictive and explanatory power of various theories across JV types (see Seth and Zinkhan 1991).

Another avenue for future research is to examine the implications of each of the theories we have presented here in much more detail. For example, the property rights perspective suggests that the specific obligations as well as the rights contained in the JV contract would be interesting to examine in detail. Such an examination for the case of franchises is contained in Leblebici and Shalley (1995), which describes how the microcontractual aspects of franchises (that is, the specification of rights and

Proposition	TC Theory	Property Rights	Agency Theory	Prospect Theory
Why are JVs formed?				
All else being equal, an investment opportunity is more likely to be pursued as a shared investment (as in a JV) than as a wholly owned investment when the critical inputs required to pursue the opportunity are owned by different parties and when these inputs are inseparable from the other assets of the owner firms.	C	P	P	—
All else being equal, JVs are more likely to be formed in industry sectors that present considerable technological uncertainty (such as the high-tech sector) or demand uncertainty (such as airlines) than in industry sectors with stable cash flows.	I	P	P	P
All else being equal, JVs are more likely to be formed in periods of economic and competitive volatility than in periods of stability.	I	P	P	P
All else being equal, IJVs are less likely to be formed with partners from countries that present a high level of political risk than a low level of political risk.	—	—	P	—
All else being equal, relative to wholly owned investments, IJVs are less likely to be formed with partners from countries that have a high level of governmental regulations rather than a low level of governmental regulations.	—	—	P	—
All else being equal, the higher the required initial investment, the more likely that the investment opportunity will be pursued as a shared investment (as in a JV) rather than as a wholly owned investment.	—	C	P	—

Table 3.2. Joint Ventures: Propositions from Alternative Theoretical Perspectives.

Note: P = predicted by, C = consistent with, I = inconsistent with, — = not addressed

Proposition	TC Theory	Property Rights	Agency Theory	Prospect Theory
All else being equal, industries with high mortality rates are also characterized by a significant number of JV formations.	—	—	—	P
All else being equal, firms that have been performing poorly will be more likely to form JVs than firms that are performing well.	—	—	—	P
What factors influence the nature of the JV partnership?				
All else being equal, JVs are more likely to be formed between partners of whom at least one is characterized by relatively concentrated ownership.	—	—	P	—
All else being equal, the higher the investment in the JV relative to the size of the parent company, the greater the commitment to the objectives of the JV and the greater the extent of mutual monitoring.	—	C	P	—
All else being equal, JVs are more likely to be formed between two partners than between multiple partners.	C	C	P	—
All else being equal, a higher degree of cooperation and mutual trust will be exhibited in JVs with equivalent ownership by the parents, relative to JVs where ownership is relatively unequal.	—	C	P	—

Table 3.2. Joint Ventures: Propositions from Alternative Theoretical Perspectives. (*continued*)
Note: P = predicted by, C = consistent with, I = inconsistent with, — = not addressed

obligations among contracting parties) relate to the governance structures and performance outcomes of alternative forms of organizing.

We identified a select group of theories for discussion based on their differential discussions of risk and uncertainty, which we believe represents an underresearched JV issue. However, there clearly exist other theoretical perspectives that merit continued investigation. For example, an extremely interesting application of the insights of the Austrian school of economics to develop an entrepreneurial model of cooperative strategy is contained in Chapter Five. In addition, signaling and game theory perspectives highlight that a firm's decision making may be thought of as a strategic response to the competitor's behavior. A firm may be influenced by its competitors' actions or by the possible effect of its actions on competitors. This could imply that in the absence of competitors the focal firm may favor greenfield entry rather than outright acquisition. However, the presence of competition may signal the need for a quick entry to a particular industry segment. In such cases, there is insufficient time for greenfield entry and a JV may be the best compromise. Similarly, options theory offers interesting potential insights, as JVs may be considered as real options that provide the important benefit of flexibility in making investment decisions under uncertainty.

The above are only some illustrations of promising areas that merit continuing inquiry. In summary, we would recommend that researchers continue in the spirit of theoretical pluralism to understand in greater depth the complex phenomenon of JVs and, in particular, IJVs.

NOTES

1. Many of the authors cited in this section have, in fact, made eclectic contributions to the theory of joint ventures that go beyond or diverge from the traditional (or Williamsonian) transactions cost perspective. Some of Hennart's arguments (1988) may be considered as closer to an agency theory or property rights perspective than to traditional transactions cost theory.

2. Six kinds of asset specificity have been identified: site specificity, physical asset specificity, human asset specificity, brand name capital, dedicated assets, and temporal specificity (Masten, Meehan, and Snyder 1991).

3. Although each of our propositions highlights one specific antecedent condition for the formation or structure of JVs, we recognize that a number of these antecedent conditions might coexist in a complex manner. To the extent that antecedent conditions with opposing predictions coexist, in order to make a general prediction it would be necessary to identify the relative importance of each condition. The relative importance question is outside the scope of this chapter.

4. In this section, we do not employ the "principal-agent" terminology that is often used to describe the relationship between shareholders and managers and that is an important area of investigation for agency theory. Rather, we use language consistent with that branch of agency theory that describes optimal organization forms.

BIBLIOGRAPHY

Alchian, A., and H. Demsetz. 1972. Production, information costs, and economic organization. *American Economic Review,* 62: 777–795.

Beamish, P., and J. C. Banks. 1987. Equity joint ventures and the theory of the multinational enterprise. *Journal of International Business Studies,* 18(2): 1–16.

Buckley, P. J., and M. Casson. 1988. A theory of cooperation in international business. In F. J. Contractor and P. Lorange, editors, *Cooperative Strategies in International Business,* 31–54. San Francisco: New Lexington Press.

Caves, R. E. 1982. *Multinational Enterprise and Economic Analysis.* New York: Cambridge University Press.

Caves, R. E. 1994. Stasis and flux in multinational enterprises: Equilibrium models and turnover processes. Discussion paper number 1692, Harvard Institute of Economic Research, Harvard University, Cambridge, Mass.

Child, J., Y. Yan, and Y. Lu. 1997. Ownership and control in Sino-foreign joint ventures. In P. W. Beamish and J. P. Killing, editors, *Cooperative Strategies: Asian Pacific Perspectives.* San Francisco: New Lexington Press.

Coase, R. H. 1937. The nature of the firm. *Economica,* 4: 386–405.

Coase, R. H. 1960. The problem of social cost. *Journal of Law and Economics,* 3: 1–44.

Commons, J. R. 1934. *Institutional Economics.* Madison: University of Wisconsin Press.

Demsetz, H., and K. Lehn. 1985. The structure of corporate ownership: Causes and consequences. *Journal of Political Economy,* 93(6): 1155–1177.

DiMaggio, P. J., and W. W. Powell. 1983. The iron cage revisited: Institutional isomorphism and collective rationality in organizational fields. *American Sociological Review,* 48: 147–160.

Dunning, J. H. 1995. Reappraising the eclectic paradigm in an age of alliance capitalism. *Journal of International Business Studies,* 26(3): 461–491.

Fama, E. F. 1980. Agency problems and the theory of the firm. *Journal of Political Economy,* 88(2): 288–305.

Fama, E. F., and M. C. Jensen. 1983a. Separation of ownership and control. *Journal of Law and Economics,* 26: 301–325.

Fama, E. F., and M. C. Jensen. 1983b. Agency problems and residual claims. *Journal of Law and Economics,* 26: 327–349.

Franko, L. G. 1971. *Joint Venture Survival in Multinational Corporations.* New York: Praeger.

Furubotn, E. G., and S. Pejovich. 1974. Introduction: The new property rights literature. In E. G. Furubotn and S. Pejovich, editors, *The Economics of Property Rights.* New York: Ballinger.

Gatignon, H., and E. Anderson. 1988. The multinational corporation's degree of control over foreign subsidiaries: An empirical test of a transaction cost explanation. *Journal of Law, Economics and Organization,* 4(2): 305–336.

Ghoshal, S., and P. Moran. 1996. Bad for practice: A critique of the transactions cost theory. *The Academy of Management Review,* 21(1): 13–47.

Gomes-Casseres, B. 1989. Ownership structures of foreign subsidiaries: Theory and evidence. *Journal of Economic Behavior and Organization,* 1: 1–25.

Grossman, S., and O. Hart. 1986. The costs and benefits of ownership: A theory of vertical and lateral integration. *Journal of Political Economy,* 94: 691–719.

Hart, O. 1995. *Firms, Contracts and Financial Structure.* Oxford, England: Clarendon Press.

Hennart, J.-F. 1988. A transaction costs theory of equity joint ventures. *Strategic Management Journal,* 9: 361–374.

Hennart, J.-F. 1989. The transaction-cost rationale for countertrade. *Journal of Law, Economics and Organization,* 51: 127–153.

Hennart, J.-F., and S. Reddy. 1994. The choice between mergers/acquisitions and joint ventures: The case of Japanese investors in the United States. CIBER working paper, University of Illinois at Urbana-Champaign.

Jarillo, J. C. 1988. On strategic networks. *Strategic Management Journal,* 9: 31–41.

Jensen, M. C., and W. H. Meckling. 1976. Theory of the firm: Managerial behavior, agency costs and ownership structure. *Journal of Financial Economics,* 34: 305–360.

Kogut, B. 1988. Joint ventures: Theoretical and empirical perspectives. *Strategic Management Journal,* 94 (Winter): 319–332.

Leblebici, H., and C. Shalley. 1995. The organization of relational contracts: The allocation of rights in franchising. Working paper, University of Illinois at Urbana-Champaign.

Libecap, G. D. 1986. Property rights in economic history: Implications for research. *Explorations in Economic History,* 23: 227–252.

Madhok, A. 1995. Revisiting multinational firms' tolerance for joint ventures: A trust-based approach. *Journal of International Business Studies,* 26(1): 117–137.

Masten, S., J. Meehan, and E. Snyder. 1991. The costs of organization. *Journal of Law, Economics and Organization,* 7: 1–25.

Milgrom, P., and J. Roberts. 1992. *Economics, Organization and Management.* Englewood Cliffs, N.J.: Prentice Hall.

Morgan, G. 1986. *Images of Organization.* Thousand Oaks, Calif.: Sage.

Parkhe, A. 1991. Interfirm diversity, organizational learning, and longevity in global strategic alliances. *Journal of International Business Studies,* 22(4): 579–601.

Rediker, K., and A. Seth. 1995. Boards of directors and substitution effects of alternative governance mechanisms. *Strategic Management Journal,* 16(2): 85–99.

Roehl, T. 1983. A transactions cost approach to international trading structures: The case of the Japanese general trading companies. *Hitotsubashi Journal of Economics,* 24: 119–135.

Seth, A., and H. Thomas. 1994. Theories of the firm: Implications for strategy research. *Journal of Management Studies,* 31(2): 165–191.

Seth, A., and G. M. Zinkhan. 1991. Strategy and the research process: A comment. *Strategic Management Journal,* 12(1): 75–83.

Shenkar, O., and Y. Zeira. 1987. Human resources management in international joint ventures: Directions for research. *Academy of Management Review,* 12(3): 546–557.

Stopford, J. M., and L. T. Wells Jr. 1972. *Managing the Multinational Enterprise.* New York: Basic Books.

Tallman, S. B., and O. Shenkar. 1994. A managerial decision model of international cooperative venture formation. *Journal of International Business Studies,* 25(1): 91–113.

Thorelli, H. B. 1986. Networks: Between markets and hierarchies. *Strategic Management Journal,* 7: 37–51.

Tversky, A., and D. Kahneman. 1981. The framing of decisions and the psychology of choice. *Science,* 211(30): 453–458.

Vernon, R. 1966. International investment and international trade in the product cycle. *Quarterly Journal of Economics,* 80: 190–207.

Vernon, R. 1979. The product cycle hypothesis in a new international environ-ment. *Oxford Bulletin of Economics and Statistics,* 41: 255–267.

Vernon, R., and W. R. Davidson. 1979. Foreign production of technology-intensive products by U.S. based multinational enterprises. Working paper, Graduate School of Business Administration, Harvard University, Cam-bridge, Mass.

Whetten, D. A. 1989. What constitutes a theoretical contribution? *Academy of Management Review,* 14(4): 490–495.

Williamson, O. E. 1975. *Markets and Hierarchies.* New York: Free Press.

Williamson, O. E. 1985. *The Economic Institutions of Capitalism: Firms, Mar-kets, Relational Contracting.* New York: Free Press.

Williamson, O. E. 1991. Comparative economic organization: The analysis of discrete structural alternatives. *Administrative Science Quarterly,* 36: 269–296.

PART TWO

FORMATION OF COOPERATIVE ALLIANCES

4

ON DEVELOPING A CONTINGENCY MODEL OF TECHNOLOGY ALLIANCE FORMATION

Veronica Horton and Brenda Richey

DESPITE CONSIDERABLE *discussion about international cooperative ventures, it is not certain when it is advantageous to undertake technology development within a cooperative format. Focusing on the issues of opportunism, trust, and reciprocity, this chapter develops a prescriptive model arguing that a firm's incentive to form a technology alliance is contingent on three sets of factors: firm factors, project factors, and environmental factors.*

IN HIS SEMINAL PAPER on the "messy" state of research on collaborative alliances, Parkhe (1993) called for an effort to combine the four core issues of collaboration—trust, opportunism, reciprocity,[1] and mutual forbearance—into a unifying whole. He noted that although current research efforts have brought advances in our understanding of alliances, the understanding is incomplete because the research is fragmented. There is no overriding work that links the frequently disparate efforts into a unifying theory. His suggestion is that the four core issues provide the missing link

The authors wish to thank Paul Beamish, three anonymous reviewers, and the participants of the North American Conference on Global Perspectives on Cooperative Strategies for their helpful comments and suggestions on earlier drafts of this chapter.

between the various studies, and therefore must be brought together to act as a unifying base for research in the area.

In this chapter, we clean up some of the mess discussed by Parkhe by developing a model that suggests when technology collaboration will occur. The model incorporates Parkhe's core issues and brings together ideas from diverse streams of research, including discussions of transaction costs, resource dependency and strategic intent, organizational behavior theory, and the process of innovation. By moving beyond the traditional transaction costs analysis, we are able to focus not just on the reduction of transaction costs (that is, questions related to opportunism), but also on how cooperative ventures can be used to build value through increased alliance reciprocity (see Chapter Three). Although we do not suggest that our model acts as a unifying base for all alliances, it brings together the core issues related to determining when a firm will choose to form a technology alliance. We have chosen to focus on technology alliances because, although there has arguably been an increase in the number of all types of alliances (Horton 1992; Beamish and Delios 1997), technology alliances sit at the nexus of two important issues for managers and management scholars—when an alliance makes sense, and how to harness technology to achieve firm success (Brown and Eisenhardt 1995). Our model (see Figure 4.1) proposes that a firm's incentive to form a technology alliance is contingent on factors related to individual firm characteristics (firm factors), factors related to the technology project at hand (project factors), and factors related to the operating environment of the firm (environmental factors).

Each set of factors is affected by, or affects in some manner, at least one of the four issues noted by Parkhe. However, the principal emphasis of the factors is on issues of opportunism, reciprocity, and trust, as mutual forbearance is more closely connected to issues of partner selection, governance mode, and the relationships developed between partners following the decision to collaborate. It is also important to recognize that though discussed separately, the factors are not only interrelated but interdependent. For example, a firm's position toward project factors may be tempered by its position toward environmental factors, or vice versa. Moreover, we do not claim that a positive decision to proceed in an alliance format is a final one. The initial "yes" decision predicted by this model may be revisited after the firm reviews the selection of available partners or after the relationship formation process is undertaken (see Chapter Eleven).

Though our model brings together several streams of scientifically tested research, it is not intended to be a basis for rigorous empirical testing, nor do we pretend to use it in such a manner. Rather, we propose that our model be seen as a framework within which firms can assess their situations and

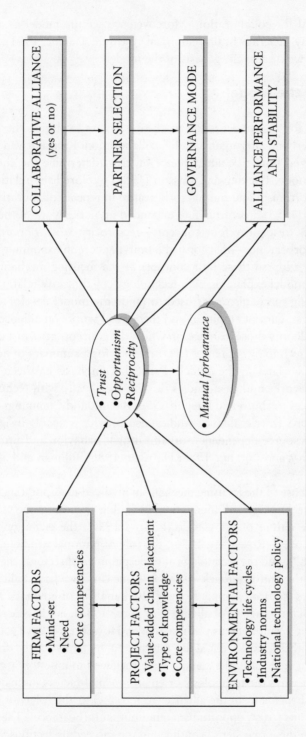

Figure 4.1. A Contingency Model of Technology Alliance Formation.

their potential for collaboration. Moreover, we see the model as a think piece that may generate future empirical research (Daniels 1991). In the next section, we discuss the genesis of the model.

Genesis of the Model

The linchpin for the model is the work of scholars exploring the central concepts underlying interorganizational collaboration. Ring and Van de Ven (1992) analyzed how risk and reliance on trust determine the choice of governance mode. Buckley and Casson (1988) explored the relationship between opportunism and mutual forbearance in repeat collaborative ventures. Parkhe (1993) drew from and expanded upon the work of these and other scholars to identify four concepts—reciprocity, trust, opportunism, and mutual forbearance—that formed a unifying core in examining alliances. We have adopted these four concepts as the focusing mechanism for developing a model explaining high-technology collaborative relationships.

The focusing mechanism was used to guide the model development in two ways. First, current empirical and theoretical works on alliances were reviewed to identify those instances in which the concepts arise in a context applicable to technology alliances (see Table 4.1 for a summary of how relevant research relates to the model). Particular emphasis has been placed on empirical works and case studies dealing specifically with technology-related alliances (Osborn and Baughn 1990; Bidault and Cummings 1994), but many more generic alliance studies also provide valuable insights on the roles of resource dependency, organizational behavior, and firm strategy (Contractor and Lorange 1988; Harrigan 1988; Tallman and Shenkar 1994).

The second use of the focusing mechanism involved incorporating broader works on technology and innovation, including classics on the tacit versus encodable nature of knowledge (Polanyi 1967), the evolution of the innovation process (Rosenberg 1976), the role of national technology policy (Ergas 1987), and the technological underpinnings of sectoral characteristics (Abernathy and Utterback 1978). In some cases we have built on the work of others (see for example Kogut's 1988 analysis of how tacit knowledge may explain some use of alliances, or Teece 1988), but in general, alliances have not been the focus of these works. However, we have sought to explain how these works could be interpreted in terms of the focusing mechanism. In each case, the classics were reviewed in an effort to understand in what ways the technology or environmental factors discussed will influence the benefits from the alliance (reciprocity) or the behavior of alliance participants (trust, opportunism, and mutual forbearance). The model resulting from these two steps is outlined in the succeeding sections.

Factor	*Author(s)*	*Research Type*
Firm	Beamish and Banks 1987	Empirical
• Mind-set	Buckley and Casson 1988	Conceptual
• Need	Contractor and Lorange 1988	Conceptual
• Core competencies	Doz 1988	Conceptual
	Hamel 1991	Case study
	Harrigan 1988	Conceptual
	Kanter 1994	Empirical
	Madhok 1995	Empirical
	Osborn and Baughn 1990	Empirical
	Parkhe 1993	Conceptual
	Ring and Van de Ven 1992	Conceptual
	Spekman and Sawhney 1990	Conceptual
	Tallman and Shenkar 1994	Conceptual
	Tyler and Steensma 1995	Empirical
Project	Badaracco 1991	Case study
• Value-added chain	Bidault and Cummings 1994	Case study
placement	Kogut 1988	Conceptual
• Type of knowledge	Tiemessen, Lane, Crossan	
• Core competencies	and Inkpen 1997	Conceptual
	Tyler and Steensma 1995	Empirical
Environmental	Demers, Hafsi, Jorgensen	
• Technology life cycle	and Molz 1997	Case study
• Industry norms	Evan and Olk 1990	Empirical
• National technology	Fusfeld and Haklisch 1985	Empirical
policy	Gulati 1995	Empirical
	Hagedoorn 1993	Empirical
	Hagedoorn and	
	Schakenraad 1994	Empirical
	Håkansson, Kjellber and	
	Lundgren 1993	Empirical
	Mytelka and Delapierre 1987	Empirical
	Osborn and Baughn 1990	Empirical
	Perry and Sandholtz 1988	Conceptual

Table 4.1. Literature Related to the Three Dimensions of the Model.

The Model

We will begin initially with a discussion of the firm factors, followed by a discussion of project factors, and finally a discussion of environmental factors. Our underlying premise is that a firm will only form an alliance when the three sets of factors indicate that it is favorable to do so.

Firm Factors

We propose that in every firm there will be a certain alliance culture or predisposition toward the use of collaborative alliances.

MIND-SET. In some firms, the alliance culture is such that alliances are seen as an effective and efficient way of improving the firm's competitive position; in others, collaboration is viewed with suspicion, and may be avoided when possible. Various factors contribute to this mind-set for or against the use of alliances, including a firm's past experiences either operating within alliances or independently outside of alliances, and its attitude toward control, risk, and interdependence.

Underlying much of the discussion about mind-set is the question of uncertainty. If future events were predictable, much of the risk associated with collaboration would become a nonissue; firms could agree to map out all necessary contingencies *ex ante*. However, because a firm's decision-making capabilities are in reality limited by an unpredictable and uncertain environment, the potential for opportunistic behavior on the part of a partner firm must be considered (Spekman and Sawhney 1990). Yet suppose a firm does not believe that a potential partner would act opportunistically in the face of uncertainty and could in fact be trusted (Parkhe 1993; Beamish and Banks 1987): then collaboration may represent a viable strategic alternative.

Contributing to a firm's mind-set or predisposition toward alliances is its past experience with collaboration. Several researchers (Tyler and Steensma 1995; Kanter 1994; Ring and Van de Ven 1992; Buckley and Casson 1988) have suggested that trust between partners may motivate future collaboration, and that a shared history of successful collaboration lowers the transaction costs of future cooperative efforts. If firms develop reputations with each other for acting fairly and nonopportunistically, the resulting trust between them may make collaboration appropriate even when there is a high level of *ex ante* transaction risk. Indeed, it has been argued (Ring and Van de Ven 1992: 489) that "the prospect of repeat business discourages attempts to seek a narrow, short-term advantage." Even in situations in which firms have not had a previous relationship, collaboration may occur when a firm's general reputation for trustworthiness acts as a proxy for a shared collaborative history (Parkhe 1993). Buckley and Casson (1988: 49) propose that when there is mutual forbearance between partners, more alliances are likely to follow, "perhaps in the same grouping or perhaps in other groupings involving other parties with whom the original participants have established a reputation."

It has been suggested that the social dimension of an alliance focusing on the value that may be created through the management of a relationship is also an important consideration in the decision to collaborate (Madhok 1995). From this perspective, the initial decision to form an alliance may center around an opportunism-avoidance mentality. In such cases, trust between firms then becomes a part of the value created as a result of collaboration and is seen as an asset that may be nurtured over time.

There have been recent suggestions that because a firm's national culture may affect its attitude toward uncertainty, those from some cultures may be more comfortable operating within the uncertain environment of a collaborative alliance than others (Richey and Horton 1995). In fact, the impact of a firm's national culture on its mind-set toward alliances may make it possible for some firms to achieve greater benefits from collaboration than others (Hamel 1991).

A firm's predisposition toward the use of collaborative alliances may also be affected by its attitude toward control. Most firms are likely to prefer an organizational structure that affords them the most control over their destinies, namely a wholly owned operation. Yet, collaboration by definition involves some loss of control. Thus, we argue that tightly controlled firms are less likely to be inclined to pursue collaborative projects than firms that are comfortable operating in a less controlled atmosphere. Parkhe (1993) has suggested that there is indeed a strong preference toward wholly owned structures among managers who have worked in highly bureaucratic organizations; only when firms see their future payoff as large enough to offset the uncertainty and mutual interdependence associated with the loss of control inherent in an alliance will they turn to collaboration as a first-best strategy.

In some cases, alliances may be seen as a means of gaining control over or managing a firm's dependencies (Spekman and Sawhney 1990: 14). That is to say, firms that have a high resource dependency position become very vulnerable to outsiders, and in the process lose some control over their decision making. In such situations, firms may find that collaboration provides them with greater control over their destinies. But in other situations, firms contemplating entering alliances may be concerned about being taken over by, or becoming dependent on, the partner. Firms that are extremely risk-averse may consequently hesitate to utilize alliances because of these issues. However, Contractor and Lorange (1988) note that the problem of being taken over by a partner depends on the duration of the agreement in question, whether a partner has the ability to go it alone, and whether partners keep up with changes (either technical or market-related) in the industry. They suggested that it was important to determine whether an agreement would leave its participants mutually interdependent, and thus more vulnerable in the future.

In conclusion, it is important to recognize that firms, like people, are creatures of habit, frequently preferring the safe and comfortable way of doing things to the challenges of the unknown. We suggest that firms that are comfortable operating within the context of collaborative alliances are likely to continue to do so, but firms that have had little experience cooperating with other firms are likely to be hesitant about collaboration and may shy away from opportunities to form alliances. A firm's choice of strategies will reflect its previous strategic moves, as it usually applies "familiar solutions to problems and [is] reluctant to change [its] approach" (Spekman and Sawhney 1990: 20).

NEED. According to the strategic intent framework, firms will be motivated to form alliances when they further their own interests (Spekman and Sawhney 1990)—in other words, when they need alliances (and the associated tangible or intangible assets) to become more competitive. Several factors affect a firm's need, including its mind-set toward collaboration (see previous section), its size, its ability to acquire necessary resources elsewhere, its managerial capabilities, its reputation, and whether the alliance would involve core competencies (see following section).

Larger firms may have an advantage over smaller firms when it comes to the question of need because they often have the resources, both capital and managerial, to simply buy the assets they require. Smaller firms may be forced to collaborate with other, frequently larger, firms in order to acquire necessary assets (Osborn and Baughn 1990). Thus, larger firms may have more choices than smaller firms. Whether larger firms choose to acquire needed assets by purchase or through alliance probably depends on the relative efficiency of each alternative. If the assets in question are not tacit, acquisition of the information in the open market is more likely. To obtain tacit information, however, one firm may consider forming an alliance with, or simply purchasing outright, a second firm that has it. Collaboration may represent the more efficient alternative, though, because it would not involve the acquisition of unwanted assets.

Smaller firms, on the other hand, frequently devote large amounts of resources to the development of new technologies, but lack the assets or resources necessary to properly disseminate them (Contractor and Lorange 1988). In such circumstances they often turn to larger firms as a source of market access (Doz 1988). However, there is some concern in the literature that small firms may be at a disadvantage when it comes to trusting larger firms to behave fairly. Doz, for example, notes that the future of a particular alliance may not be as important to a larger firm (where the alliance is one of many) as it is to a smaller firm (where it may be of critical importance). Therefore, smaller firms may have an incentive to preserve the advantage arising from proprietary technology.

In some cases, the lack of alternatives to collaboration, rather than firm size, is the real problem. When there are few alternative sources for the assets in question, firms may find that collaboration is actually an attractive option because alliance participants are essentially tied into the relationship, not only because of the small numbers involved but because of the specialized assets that may be required (Spekman and Sawhney 1990). Parkhe (1993: 16) notes that "anticipated future gains from a partnership may promote reciprocity of cooperation, thereby holding in check proclivity toward agreement violations." Moreover, the decision to form an alliance may be affected by a firm's reputation and experience with other firms. Firms contemplating the formation of alliances in small numbers situations may find that reputation (for trustworthy behavior) plays a major role in the decision to collaborate because of the limited strategic alternatives available.

CORE COMPETENCIES. The final factor that may affect a firm's decision to form a collaborative alliance is its core competencies. Firms may be hesitant to form collaborative agreements involving these because of the risk of opportunistic behavior by proposed partners. Harrigan (1988: 155) notes that "technology leaders will not readily share the appropriable kernels of knowledge that are central to their sources of competitive advantage unless they must do so." Yet collaboration may provide firms with the ability to exploit their core competencies in a manner they could not achieve alone.

Alliances involving technology may be particularly difficult because of the public goods nature of the technology (Doz 1988). Technology agreements necessarily have some uncertainty, as some of the elements cannot be disclosed until after the alliance has been formed; consequently, the potential for opportunism is present. Teece (1988: 77) suggests that internalizing a technology transaction is not optimal "when the innovator's appropriability regime is tight and the complementary assets are more available in competitive supply." In other words, collaboration is risky for firms that cannot adequately protect their innovations.

Finally, it should be noted that a firm may view collaboration involving core competencies from different perspectives depending on the current stage of market evolution. In both early and late market stages, when firms face uncertain transition periods, they may see the formation of alliances as a means of shaping their environment to some degree (Spekman and Sawhney 1990). Technology firms in particular may form alliances as a proactive means of dealing with an uncertain future.

In sum, the degree to which collaboration involves a firm's core competencies will affect its inclination toward the use of alliances. Typically, firms will be reluctant to share their proprietary assets with outsiders. This factor will be discussed in greater depth in the following section.

Project Factors

The complex relationships between activities in the technology value-added chain limit the benefits to be derived from different ways of organizing technology projects. In this section, we briefly outline how our understanding of these relationships has changed over time, and what this means for alliance reciprocity.

TECHNOLOGY VALUE-ADDED CHAIN. Traditionally, the process of new product development has been conceptualized as a sequence of distinct activities that we call the technology value-added chain (Blackwell and Eilon 1991). Activities that are part of the chain include basic research, applied research, experimental development, product design and testing, production, and sales and marketing. Firms that view the process of new product development in this manner may have a tendency to use the stages as a guide for determining whether a particular activity should be organized inside or outside the firm. This tendency may be augmented by the current focus on downsizing and reengineering; managers may feel pressured to strip the firm of all functions considered nonessential, particularly if these functions can be supplied more cheaply on the outside. Because managers may view the stages of the value-added chain as separable, only essential activities will be maintained in-house, and technology may be purchased outside the firm, possibly even after initial exploratory development. At subsequent stages, manufacturing may also be farmed out, with the firm primarily being responsible for coordinating the outside activities and providing strategic guidance to the outside firms. However, this strategy may not be optimal.

Despite the breakdown of the process of product development into separable activities, the loss of interplay between the stages may limit the overall benefits from moving the activities outside the firm. In other words, the complexity of the interaction affects the reciprocity aspects of collaborative alliances. Product development does not occur in a linear progression along the technology value-added chain. Although these stages must all occur, the idea of a sequential progression across these stages is challenged by scholars of both marketing and technology. Marketing scholars suggest that it is market pull rather than technology push that leads to successful product development, and thus argue that the process must start, or at least be contemporaneous with, firm strategy and market analysis, rather than with basic research (Blackwell and Eilon 1991; Monroe 1989).

Technology scholars, on the other hand, argue that the process of innovation is one of iterative cycles among the stages that may, at times, result in relationships that appear counterintuitive (Rosenberg 1976). Applied research or product development may precede and even focus the search of pure science. For example, new alloys developed in the field of metallurgy raised questions and led to research that only later provided the basic science necessary to understand the properties found in the new metals (Rosenberg 1976, 1982). At later stages of the product development process, the results of learning by doing (in the production stages) and learning by using are incorporated to refine product design and production processes.

The complex relationships along the technology value-added chain suggest that any organizing mode that restricts the necessary interplay between the different activity stages along the chain reduces the benefits to be achieved on a technology project. Whether or not an alliance form would have this effect depends, in part, on how the activities had been organized in the past. Moving an activity outside the firm that had previously been undertaken within the firm might severely disrupt these ties. However, employing an alliance rather than relying completely on the market might lessen this disruption somewhat. Even so, at least one study has concluded that using collaborative alliances to undertake product development may have a negative impact on certain managerial roles, such as that of sponsor and internal champion (Bidault and Cummings 1994). These roles are necessary to guide development projects through the stages of the value-added chain. Where the value-added chain is already divided among a number of separate firms, undertaking a development project through an alliance involving all the firms will serve to reconnect the chain. The benefits gained from securing access to the entire technology value-added chain may explain the growing interest in joint development alliances between formerly independent customers and suppliers.

TYPE OF KNOWLEDGE. We propose that collaborative alliance reciprocity is also affected by the type of knowledge that forms the basis for the technology project. The extent of this impact is determined both by whether the knowledge is tacit and by the extent to which this knowledge is embedded in a system.

Knowledge is considered tacit when it is not easily encoded (Polanyi 1967). Thus, technological advances that can be completely incorporated into a set of drawings or into a chemical formulation are not considered highly tacit, while information such as skills learned through experience that cannot be easily incorporated into written form is considered highly tacit. In his discussion of collaborative alliance motivation, Kogut (1988) gives a cogent analysis of how tacit knowledge explains why firms may engage in collaborative alliances in lieu of purchasing technology. In effect, the tacit nature of the technology being sought requires a closer association between the transferring firms than would be possible in a market transaction. In other words, the tacit nature of the technology demands a higher degree of interaction between parties to the development process and thus increases the potential benefits from an alliance.

Although the relationship between the tacit nature of knowledge and the benefits from collaborative alliances has been recognized, as by Kogut, (1988), the shape of the relationship is not clear. Taken to an extreme, it could be argued that highly tacit knowledge might be so difficult to transfer that technology projects at that level should only be undertaken in-house. We suggest that although there may be some level at which knowledge is too tacit to be transferred from a collaborative alliance, these problems can be handled by changes in the alliance governance mode or in the organization of communication between an alliance and its parent firms. In other words, alliance structure and organization learning skills may improve the chance of a firm's being able to harvest knowledge from a cooperative venture (see Chapter Fourteen).

Another dimension of knowledge that affects technology alliance reciprocity is the extent to which knowledge is incorporated as part of an integrated system. When a firm is involved in a technology project dealing with knowledge embedded as part of a system, an alliance with firms engaged to work on other parts of the system would appear to be particularly beneficial. An example of this was seen in the European efforts to develop high-definition television. A radical shift in television technology involved a variety of industries including broadcasters, manufacturers of transmission equipment, consumer electronics firms, and the makers of television programs. A firm grounding in computer and telecommunications was also required. An attempt at a radical shift of technology by a single firm would encounter substantially greater risk than a shift that was coordinated across all the firms and industries that make up the system. Thus, the benefits of some form of alliance or cooperation among members of these industries is greatly enhanced. This situation is seen with increasing frequency as firms pursue technologies that reflect the convergence of once-separate industries (Freeman 1991).

CORE COMPETENCIES. A final factor that may affect the choice of whether to enter a collaborative alliance is the relevance of the technology project to the firm's core competencies and its strategic plans for developing these competencies. In the previous section, core competencies were discussed as they related to firm factors. Here we focus on how core competencies affect decisions related to the project at hand, and in particular on the manner in which the distance between the project and the firm's core competencies influences issues related to reciprocity and opportunism.

Distance appears to affect reciprocity is several ways. For example, the greater the distance between a firm's core competencies and the subject matter of the project at hand, the greater the gap between a firm's knowledge base and the project. This should increase the possibility that a well-selected partner, with distinctly different resources in terms of knowledge base, assets, and skills, will have valuable contributions to bring to an alliance (Tyler and Steensma 1995). The danger, however, is that if the partner's skills are unrelated to any part of the firm's knowledge base, the firm will lack the resources to absorb and apply the new technology.

The relationship between the project and the firm's core competency also influences the firm's need and ability to coordinate the alliance and its outcomes with firm strategy. One key to successful technology development is the extent to which the development process is tied to firm strategy (Monroe 1989; Nevens, Summe, and Uttal 1990). This is particularly crucial when the alliance involves core competencies. Failure to coordinate alliance operations could reduce the value of alliance outcomes to the firm. Alternatively, if the choice is made to closely tie the alliance to overall firm strategy, the firm runs the risk of hampering alliance activities, which by definition must at some level meet the needs of at least two firms (Harrigan 1984). These strategic issues would appear to present fewer problems for projects that are distant from the firm's core competencies.

Finally, the distance between a project and a firm's core competencies is a factor in determining the exposure a firm faces when it develops a project outside, through a collaborative alliance. Though opportunistic behavior by a partner may be just as likely when the project is far removed from the firm's core competencies as when it is not, there is less potential for damage to the firm in the former situation compared to the latter. For example, partner learning is a topic of interest to researchers; Hamel (1991) has expressed concern that a firm's alliance partners may learn its skills so rapidly that the firm loses its value to the alliance. Another pertinent issue involves the danger of unintended learning by alliance partners, by which information and skills not originally intended as part of the contribution are exposed to a firm's alliance partners (Reich and Mankin 1986). The greatest potential damage to the firm occurs when the knowledge and skills exposed in this manner are closely related to the core activities of the firm. Thus, the greater the distance between the project and the firm's core competencies, the smaller the potential damage from opportunistic behavior.

Together these factors suggest that greater distance between the firm's core competence and the project may both increase the benefits of the alliance and reduce the dangers of opportunism. This may not, however, represent a linear relationship: the firm's ability to use the new technology may depend on the existence of at least some knowledge base within the firm (Cohen and Levinthal 1990). Nor is it an unwaivable rule. It is easy to contemplate examples in which the collaborative alliance format makes sense even for projects closely connected to a firm's core competencies. For example, a firm wishing to make major changes in its strategic directions may need to shift or expand its core competencies. In doing so, the firm may find that it needs access to a knowledge base and skills that are unavailable internally (Badaracco 1991). In cases where the needed knowledge is tacit in nature, or is part of an embedded system, cooperation with another firm may be the only viable option.

Environmental Factors

Among environmental factors affecting firms' willingness to enter alliances, the concept of the technology life cycle has been explored by a number of technology scholars.

TECHNOLOGY LIFE CYCLE. Abernathy and Utterback (1978) proposed that industry changes can be explained by an analysis of the changes in technology. Technology can be traced through a fluid stage during which the design is open, manufacturing is loosely organized, and major changes in product and process can be expected; to a dominant design stage during which uncertainty is reduced, industry standards for design are set, manufacturing methods become routine, and incremental improvements are the norm; and finally to a mature stage in which the design is fixed, manufacturing methods are standardized, and process improvements for cost reduction purposes are the only advances sought by dominant firms that by this point are reluctant to make other changes.

Technology life cycle, interacting with firm and project factors, will have a major impact on the issue of reciprocity. For example, Teece (1988), in his study of EMI, suggests that during the fluid stage of the life cycle, a large innovative firm may be able to go it alone, but a small innovative firm may need to form an alliance with a partner that offers complementary production and marketing skills to avoid losing first-mover advantages. In the fluid stage of the life cycle, a firm might need research consortia to keep abreast of the variety of technology changes being explored, or might need to join consortia that are seeking to influence the establishment of industry standards (Richey 1994).

Alliances may offer fewer attractions in the dominant design phase, at least for firms in a position of industry leadership. An exception to this rule might apply for those with strong production skills but weak technology skills. Mowery and Rosenberg (1989) suggest that at least in the case of Japanese firms, research consortia have not produced cutting-edge technology, but have been successful in allowing firms to play technology catch-up. Knowledge gained in these venues can then be combined with the firm's prowess in manufacturing to capture a formerly closed market. Exceptions may also exist for niche players in an industry (see Chapter Five). In the mature stage of the technology life cycle, major benefits of alliances include the ability to monitor technological advances and opportunities to explore radical technological alternatives. Perry and Sandholtz (1988) have suggested that a firm that is good at making incremental and process improvements may not be good at making more radical technology changes. This trait, combined with the "strong resistance to change" seen in dominant industry firms (Martin 1994: 37), suggests that the dominant firm in a mature industry might find technology alliances beneficial.

NATIONAL TECHNOLOGY POLICY. A second environmental factor that may impact the decision to form an alliance involves the role of national or regional policies. These may be considered a subset of national or regional science and technology systems. The differences in technology systems around the world (Ergas 1987; Davidson 1989; Peterson 1993) have a substantial influence on firm needs (see the second firm factor). For example, in Europe the combination of small firms serving small, possibly protected, national markets and closed economic systems that have discouraged the interchange of ideas and personnel between industry and research institutes, or between large and small firms, has had a strong negative impact on the technological capabilities of European firms (de Woot 1990). In contrast, in the U.S. active venture capital markets and government support for big science projects combined with an interchange between industry and academe have, in the past, met many firm needs (Ergas 1987; Porter 1992). Although it is important to recognize the effects of national policies on firms, the full impact of macroeconomic systems on firms is too broad for this chapter. Instead, we will focus on policy specifically aimed at technology alliances, which, we argue, impacts the reciprocity aspect of alliances.

Prior to 1980, national policies toward research alliances might have been conceived of as clearly divided between the U.S. approach, in which coordination between firms was viewed with a great deal of suspicion, and the Japanese model, in which the government actively promoted meetings between industry leaders both to set technical standards and to coordinate joint research projects (Davidson 1989). The distinction between these policies is no longer as clear cut. Japanese firms are reported to be reluctant at times to participate fully in industrywide consortia, or at least to contribute their best people to the effort (Mowery and Rosenberg 1989). In the U.S., restrictions on "precompetitive" associations between firms have been loosened with the passage of the National Cooperative Research Act (1984), and in some cases (SEMATECH, for one) such associations have been actively promoted. However, there are still concerns about the possibility of antitrust laws inhibiting interfirm cooperation (Evan and Olk 1990).

In Europe, programs actively promoting interfirm alliances have been included as part of the technology policies adopted by the European Union and the even more broadly based European Research Cooperation Agency (EUREKA). In response to the perceived deficiencies in technology efforts of European firms discussed above, these programs aim to increase European alliance participation. ESPRIT, for example, provides funds for precompetitive research for alliances representing firms from different EU member states. It has also arguably allowed the development of networks of relationships between industry leaders that might otherwise have been considered oligopolistic (Mytelka and Delapierre 1987). Although it may be argued that programs such as ESPRIT assure funding to established national champions that may have received the funds under any circumstances, EUREKA may also provide easier access to national science funding for smaller firms choosing to participate in technology alliances that have received the official EUREKA designation (Peterson 1991). These, combined with other forces, may have increased the incidence of technology alliances and changed alliance characteristics in Europe (Richey 1994).

In sum, these varying technology policies have the effect of increasing the benefits that firms can anticipate receiving when they enter technology alliances. We propose that this increases alliance reciprocity even though the benefits come from a third party, not directly from the alliance partner. In Europe, alliance participation may increase access to government science funds and possibly avoid antitrust scrutiny. In Japan, participation represents compliance with established government policy. In the U.S., national policy toward alliances has shifted somewhat, but many firms are said to be actively discouraged from entering collaborative alliances by the possibility of antitrust actions (Evan and Olk 1990).

INDUSTRY NORMS. A final environmental factor is the institutional environment of the industry. We propose that just as national macroeconomic and technology policies influence a firm's inclination to pursue collaborative arrangements, the industry may also be an institutional force (Scott 1987), and that industry patterns may encourage alliances by reducing uncertainty and chances of opportunistic behavior and by increasing levels of trust.

We suggest that in some industries, alliances have become routine on an industrywide basis. Economics may be partly responsible for this phenomenon. Transaction costs, for example, may explain the high incidence of alliances in natural resources industries. The formation of such alliances becomes self-reinforcing, creating a situation in which the existence of multiple collaborative alliances is routine. The net result is the establishment of industry norms of appropriate firm behavior in an alliance setting. The industry shares an increased understanding of how alliances work and how partners are expected to behave, thus reducing uncertainty. An increase in alliance frequency also provides greater opportunities for repeat alliances, enhancing the role of reputation in restraining opportunistic behavior and promoting trust. In their study of SEMATECH, Browning, Beyer, and Shelter (1995) discuss how the process of establishing the relationships among the firms involved led to the establishment of a "moral community" that changed behavior in the highly competitive semiconductor industry. Participation in the alliance was preceded by factors such as a threatened industry and national policies that promoted participation, but in Browning, Beyer, and Shelter's estimation, it was the actions of a few leading firms that served as the catalyst to create an "emerging norm of reciprocity" within the industry.

Although the SEMATECH example involves a single cooperative entity, it is probably too much to suggest that a single alliance would have the same effect. SEMATECH was exceptional in that it brought together substantial portions of one industry with strong support from its leaders. It does suggest, however, that where multiple collaborative connections become the industry norm, the pattern of cooperative behavior may become institutionalized and reduce opportunistic behavior.

Conclusion

In this chapter, we have developed a contingency model of technology alliance formation that brings together the four core issues of collaboration, namely trust, opportunism, reciprocity, and mutual forbearance (Parkhe 1993). The model is a prescriptive one that suggests that a firm's incentive to form a technology alliance is contingent on three sets of factors: firm factors, project factors, and environmental factors. According to the model, firms should only form an alliance when the factors indicate that it is favorable to do so. Each of the primary factors is influenced by, and has an impact on, the core issues of trust, opportunism, and reciprocity. As shown in the model (see Figure 4.1), mutual forbearance affects issues related to alliance stability and performance rather than the decision to form an alliance in the first place. As this chapter is devoted to increasing our understanding of when it is appropriate to form a technology alliance, the issue of mutual forbearance has not been discussed in great depth, nor has the fact that the choice of governance mode could affect alliance performance and stability. The model is intended to be not only a guide for managers that are considering whether to initiate a technology project within an alliance format, but also a framework for further discussion and research.

In developing this model, we have drawn upon the findings of many studies exploring issues related to specific aspects of technology alliances, and combined them with related works on strategy, management, and innovation. Our goal here is to produce a comprehensive model explaining when technology alliances make sense. The need for this type of model is great. Bidault and Cummings's 1994 study exploring fundamental problems in conducting new product development and Hagedoorn and Schakenraad's findings of "no straight-forward relations between strategic technology partnering and company performance" (1994: 300) have suggested a need for a greater understanding of technology alliances. The authors suggest that despite mixed performance results, alliances generally compare favorably to the results observed arising from mergers, and may have longer-term benefits that are not being measured. We propose that a model such as the one developed here is a first step in determining the benefits of technology alliances, and under what circumstances alliances represent an optimal governance mode. As mentioned previously, this effort is a think piece that we hope will generate future empirical research. In particular, we see the model as a framework by which a group of case studies exploring the relationship between firms and technology alliances may be conducted.

NOTE

1. For the purposes of the overall discussion, the concept of reciprocity in this chapter encompasses both the elements of equity suggested by Ring and Van de Ven (1992) (the giving of something in exchange for something received) and Parkhe's suggestion (1993) that the concept reflects the reasons for entering into a collaborative alliance. Thus, reciprocity is influenced both by the choice of partner (choosing partners capable of contributing elements valued by the corporation) and by the firm's own needs and ability to take value. For example, Hamel (1991), in his study of learning in collaborative alliances, noted that the learning accomplished by a partner is dependent not just on the provision of learning opportunities by the other parties (the extent to which they were open), but also by the partner's ability as a receptor.

BIBLIOGRAPHY

Abernathy, W. J., and J. M. Utterback. 1978. Patterns of industrial innovation. *Research Policy,* 14: 3–22.

Badaracco, J. L. Jr. 1991. *The Knowledge Link: How Firms Compete Through Strategic Alliances.* Boston: Harvard Business School Press.

Beamish, P. W., and J. C. Banks. 1987. Equity joint ventures and the theory of the multinational enterprise. *Journal of International Business Studies,* 19(2): 1–16.

Beamish, P. W., and A. Delios. 1997. Incidence and propensity and alliance formation by U.S., Japanese and European MNEs. In P. Beamish and J. P. Killing, editors, *Global Strategies: Asian Pacific Perspectives.* San Francisco: New Lexington Press.

Bidault, F., and T. Cummings. 1994. Innovating through alliances: Expectations and limitations. *R&D Management,* 24(1): 33–45.

Blackwell, B., and S. Eilon. 1991. *The Global Challenge of Innovation.* Oxford, England: Butterworth, Heinemann.

Brahm, R. 1995. National targeting policies, high-technology industries, and excessive competition. *Strategic Management Journal,* 16: 71–91.

Brown, S. L., and K. M. Eisenhardt. 1995. Product development: Past research, present findings, and future directions. *Academy of Management Review,* 20(2): 343–378.

Browning, L. D., J. M. Beyer, and J. C. Shelter. 1995. Building cooperation in a competitive industry: SEMATECH and the semiconductor industry. *Academy of Management Journal,* 36(1): 113–151.

Buckley, P. J., and M. Casson. 1988. A theory of cooperation in international business. In F. J. Contractor and P. Lorange, editors, *Cooperative Strategies in International Business,* 31–54. San Francisco: New Lexington Press.

Cohen, W. M., and D. A. Levinthal. 1990. Absorptive capacity: A new perspective on learning and innovation. *Administrative Science Quarterly,* 35: 128–152.

Contractor, F. J., and P. Lorange. 1988. Why should firms cooperate? The strategy and economics basis for cooperative ventures. In F. J. Contractor and P. Lorange, editors, *Cooperative Strategies in International Business,* 3–30. San Francisco: New Lexington Press.

Daniels, J. 1991. Relevance in international business research: A need for more linkages. *Journal of International Business Studies,* 22(2): 177–186.

Davidson, W. H. 1989. Ecostructures and international competitiveness. In A. R. Negandi, editor, *International Strategic Management.* San Francisco: New Lexington Press.

de Woot, P. 1990. *High Technology Europe: Strategic Issues for Global Competitiveness.* Oxford: Blackwell.

Demers, C., T. Hafsi, J. Jørgensen, and R. Molz. 1997. The industry dynamics of cooperative strategy: Dominant and peripheral games. In P. W. Beamish and J. P. Killing, editors, *Cooperative Strategies: North American Perspectives.* San Francisco: New Lexington Press.

Doz, Y. L. 1988. Technology partnerships between larger and smaller firms: Some critical issues. In F. J. Contractor and P. Lorange, editors, *Cooperative Strategies in International Business,* 317–338. San Francisco: New Lexington Press.

Ergas, H. 1987. Does technology policy matter? In B. R. Guild and H. Brooks, editors, *Technology and Global Industry: Companies and Nations in the World Economy.* Washington, D.C.: National Academy Press.

Evan, W. M. and P. Olk. 1990. R&D consortia: A new U.S. organizational form. *Sloan Management Review,* 31(3): 37–45.

Freeman, C. 1991. The challenge of new technologies. In H. Vernon-Wortzel and L. H. Wortzel, editors, *Global Strategic Management: The Essentials,* 2nd ed. New York: Wiley.

Fusfeld, H. I., and C. S. Haklisch. 1985. Cooperative R & D for competitors. *Harvard Business Review,* No. 6: 60–76.

Gulati, R. 1995. Does familiarity breed trust? The implications of repeated ties for contractual choice in alliances. *Academy of Management Journal,* 38(1): 85–112.

Hagedoorn, J. 1993. Understanding the rationale of strategic technology partnering: Interorganizational modes of cooperation and sectoral differences. *Strategic Management Journal,* 14(5): 371–385.

Hagedoorn, J., and J. Schakenraad. 1994. The effect of strategic technology alliances on company performance. *Strategic Management Journal,* 15: 291–309.

Håkansson, P., H. Kjellber, and A. Lundgren. 1993. Strategic alliances in global biotechnology—A network approach. *International Business Review,* 2(1): 65–82.

Hamel, G. 1991. Competition and inter-partner learning within international strategic alliances. *Strategic Management Journal,* 12 (Special Issue): 83–103.

Harrigan, K. R. 1984. Joint ventures and global strategies. *Columbia Journal of World Business,* 19: 7–16.

Harrigan, K. R. 1988. Joint ventures and competitive strategy. *Strategic Management Journal,* 9: 141–158.

Horton, V. 1992. Strategic alliances: An exploration of their incidence, configuration and transformation in the Pacific Rim, Europe and North America from 1985 to 1991. Unpublished doctoral dissertation, Ohio State University, Columbus.

Kanter, R. M. 1994. Collaborative advantage: The art of alliances. *Harvard Business Review,* No. 4: 96–108.

Kogut, B. 1988. Joint ventures: Theoretical and empirical perspective. *Strategic Management Journal,* 9(4): 319–332.

Madhok, A. 1995. Opportunism and trust in joint venture relationships: An exploratory study and a model. *Scandinavian Journal of Management,* 11(1): 57–74.

Martin, M.J.C. 1994. *Managing Innovation and Entrepreneurship in Technology-Based Firms.* New York: Wiley.

Monroe, J. 1989. Strategic use of technology. *California Management Review,* 31(4): 911–1010.

Mowery, D. C., and N. Rosenberg. 1989. *Technology and the Pursuit of Economic Growth.* Cambridge University Press.

Mytelka, L. K., and M. Delapierre. 1987. The alliance strategies of European firms in the information technology industry and the role of ESPRIT. *Journal of Common Market Studies,* 26(2): 239–253.

Nevens, M., G. L. Summe, and B. Uttal. 1990. Commercializing technology: What the best companies do. *Harvard Business Review,* 68 (May-June): 154–163.

Osborn, R. N., and C. C. Baughn. 1990. Forms of interorganizational governance for multinational alliances. *Academy of Management Journal,* 33(3): 503–519.

Parkhe, A. 1993. "Messy" research, methodological predispositions, and theory development in international joint ventures. *Academy of Management Review,* 18(2): 227–268.

Perry, L. T., and K. W. Sandholtz. 1988. A "liberating form" for radical product innovation. In U. E. Gattiker and L. Larwood, editors, *Managing Technological Development.* Berlin: de Gruyter.

Peterson, J. 1991. Technology policy in Europe: Explaining the framework programme and eureka in theory and practice. *Journal of Common Market Studies,* 29(3): 269–289.

Peterson, J. 1993. *High Technology and the Competition State: An Analysis of the Eureka Initiative.* London: Routledge.

Polanyi, M. 1967. *The Tacit Dimension.* New York: Doubleday.

Porter, M. 1992. Capital disadvantage: America's failing capital investment system. *Harvard Business Review,* 70 (September-October): 65–82.

Reich, R. B., and E. D. Mankin. 1986. Joint ventures with Japan give away our future. *Harvard Business Review,* 64 (March-April): 78–86.

Richey, B. 1994. EUREKA's first years: A study of alliances formed under the auspices of the European research cooperation agency. Unpublished doctoral dissertation, Ohio State University, Columbus.

Richey, B., and V. Horton. 1995. Feeling our way in the dark: How the lack of "good" data shapes our understanding of international strategic alliances. Paper presented at the 1995 Academy of Management Meeting, Vancouver, BC.

Ring, P. S., and A. H. Van de Ven. 1992. Structuring cooperative relationships between organizations. *Strategic Management Journal,* 13: 483–498.

Rosenberg, N. 1976. *Perspectives on Technology.* Cambridge University Press.

Rosenberg, N. 1982. *Inside the Black Box.* Cambridge University Press.

Scott, W. R. 1987. The adolescence of institutional theory. *Administrative Science Quarterly,* 32: 493–511.

Spekman, R. E., and K. Sawhney. 1990. Toward a conceptual understanding of the antecedents of strategic alliances. *Marketing Science Institute,* Report No. 90–114.

Tallman, S. B., and O. Shenkar. 1994. A managerial decision model of international cooperative venture formation. *Journal of International Business Studies,* 25(1): 91–114.

Teece, D. J. 1988. Capturing value from technological innovation: Integration, strategic partnering, and licensing decisions. *Interfaces,* 19 (May-June): 65–94.

Tiemessen, I., H. W. Lane, M. M. Crossan, and A. Inkpen. 1997. Knowledge management in international joint ventures. In P. W. Beamish and J. P. Killing, editors, *Cooperative Strategies: North American Perspectives.* San Francisco: New Lexington Press.

Tyler, B. B., and H. K. Steensma. 1995. Evaluating technological collaborative opportunities: A cognitive modeling perspective. *Strategic Management Journal,* 16: 43–70.

5

INDUSTRY DYNAMICS OF COOPERATIVE STRATEGY

Dominant and Peripheral Games

*Christiane Demers, Taïeb Hafsi,
Jan Jørgensen, and Richard Molz*

COOPERATIVE STRATEGY IS *often viewed as a transitory or
second-best strategy in policy and international business. The
role of cooperative strategy can best be understood within a contextual framework. Much of the strategy literature focuses on
dominant games involving leading firms in mature industries. A
dynamic view of industry demonstrates the relative importance of
dominant and peripheral games over space and time. The dominant games are often associated with national models of competition in stable, mature industries. The peripheral games are often
associated with a firm-level virtual diamond in emerging industries or industries being reconfigured. Globalization is driving an
increasing number of industries and segments into a reconfiguration phase where cooperative strategies are essential.*

We thank Paul Beamish and two anonymous reviewers for their thoughtful comments and suggestions on earlier drafts. We acknowledge the assistance of Line
Bonneau, Henry Adobor, Lise Céré, and Vincent Pelade for data collection, and
of Christophe Vessier for his ideas. Financial support for the research was provided by the Social Sciences and Humanities Research Council of Canada.

ANY EXAMINATION OF THE daily business press demonstrates a fact that has long occupied management scholars: the myriad combinations of competitive and cooperative strategies used by successful firms throughout the world. Porter (1990a, 1990b) has admonished firms to compete rather than collaborate to develop world-class advantage, but Ohmae (1989) has identified cooperation and collaboration as the means to global success. Other authors have taken an intermediate view, in which cooperative and competitive strategies involve trade-offs depending on a firm's position within a global industry (Prahalad and Doz 1987; Contractor and Lorange 1988; Jorde and Teece 1989; Nohria and Garcia-Pont 1991; Yoshino and Rangan 1995; Dunning 1995). What has been lacking is a framework for analyzing cooperative strategy within the context of industry dynamics.[1]

A first step in this direction is distinguishing between *dominant* and *peripheral games,* so as to weigh their relative importance in industry evolution and globalization. We argue that dominant games are based mostly on strategies requiring integration and control (Porter 1990b; Ghoshal 1987; Doz, Prahalad, and Hamel 1987), and peripheral games are characterized by strategies requiring flexibility and collaboration. Forces leading to globalization—rapid technological change, deregulation, and emergence of trading blocs and global markets—are pushing more and more industries into a reconfiguration phase where dominance is challenged and peripheral games become more important. Yet most of the literature in strategy and international business has focused on dominant games.

A good example in the international business literature is Porter's national diamond model. Porter (1990a) argued that global advantage depended on a tightly coupled national diamond that combined sophisticated home demand, rich supporting and related industries, favorable domestic factors, and vigorous domestic rivalry to enable a firm to dominate internationally without having to rely on foreign or domestic collaboration. Based on our study of the effects of globalization on the Canadian clothing, engineering, telecommunications, and forest industries, we propose an alternative path to success at the firm level: the *virtual diamond.* We argue that the international success of firms in peripheral games depends on an evolving network of partnerships constructed by firms according to their needs and opportunities. The contribution of this chapter is to contextualize international cooperative strategies and to suggest how collaborative patterns differ in dominant and peripheral games.

In the following section, we describe dominant and peripheral games. Then the temporal context of peripheral games is discussed using an industry evolution framework. Next, to complement Porter's national diamond, we develop implications of peripheral games by fleshing out the virtual diamond concept and the cooperative strategy that it entails. The virtual diamond explains the success of individual *firms* where success would not be expected at the *industry level* according to the national diamond.

Finally, we synthesize our research findings as propositions to guide further research on the context of collaborative strategies.

The National Diamond: Dominant and Peripheral Games

We believe that cooperative strategy can be systematically understood better within the context of industry dynamics. Much of the strategy literature has focused on dominant games where cooperative strategy is less important. For example, in Porter's national diamond model, the global competitiveness of an industry (or firm) depends on the characteristics of its home base. Even though Porter (1991a) approvingly cited Schumpeter (1942) on the dynamic role of innovation in eroding equilibrium, innovation in Porter's model was fostered within a strong diamond in the home nation. Hence the national diamond functioned as a *mobility barrier* in relation to firms less favorably located: "While disadvantages in one or two determinants do not necessarily prevent a nation from gaining competitive advantage, the most robust competitive advantage tends strongly to be associated with widespread and self-reinforcing advantage in many determinants.... The entire system is difficult and time-consuming to duplicate ... and the system is hard to penetrate from another home base" (Porter 1990a: 147).

Advantage thus rests on a tightly coupled national diamond that combines sophisticated home demand, rich supporting and related industries, favorable domestic factors, and vigorous domestic rivalry to allow a firm to dominate internationally. According to Porter, the home nation is important even in cases where global competitors disperse activities in the value chain outside the home nation: "The home base is where strategy is set, core product and process development takes place, and the essential and proprietary skills reside" (1990a: 69).

Critics such as Rugman and D'Cruz (1993a) and Penttinen (1994) maintained that the national diamond model does not fit small, open economies whose industries are dependent on the diamonds of other countries. Porter himself dealt in passing with small economies and with industries whose activities tend to be geographically dispersed. For example, he noted that the Swiss pharmaceutical industry successfully sources foreign technology and relies on demanding foreign customers more than on a large domestic market. Similarly, the recent history of Taiwan (Daleu-Diabé and Hafsi

1993) shows that an economy composed primarily of small and medium-sized firms, in which peripheral games are prevalent, can be highly competitive in international markets. Even Porter (1990a: 321) acknowledged that selective factor disadvantages such as a small home market, labor shortages, and a lack of natural resources serve as "an essential motive force behind innovation and upgrading in Swiss industry" to compete in a remarkably diverse set of specialized global segments. For example, Cerberus, a leader in fire detection equipment, succeeded internationally in the absence of domestic rivalry. Yet Porter avoided pursuing the full implications of these Swiss anomalies. Instead, he argued that such cases were comparatively rare: "More generally, compensating for a missing determinant is most likely once a nation's firms have achieved international leadership. Here, global strategies may be employed to tap selectively into advantages in other nations, and firms can command the attention and support of foreign buyers and suppliers" (Porter 1990a: 146).

Hence the main focus in Porter's work on international competitiveness, as in earlier work on competitive strategy, rests on what we label *dominant games:* tightly integrated competitive strategies of leading firms operating within a stable industry that has clear boundaries. Dominant games are linked to competitive strategies derived from industrial organization research in economics. Certain firm-level strategies are thought to yield above-average returns by creating and manipulating mobility barriers, such as scale and scope economies, and by using product differentiation (Barney 1986b; Porter 1991a). In dominant games, success is based on observable, measurable strategic factors (Shamsie 1991). Examples of such measurable strategic factors are those used in the PIMS studies: relative market share, prices of products and services relative to competitors, research and development as a percentage of sales, and others (Buzzell and Gale 1987). The spirit of dominant games is captured in Jack Welch's 1981 declaration of strategy that General Electric be number one or number two globally in each of its markets (Tichy and Charan 1989).

By contrast, what we term *peripheral games* are based on entrepreneurial discovery in processes analogous to those described by the Austrian school of economics (Jacobson 1992). Here the goal is to outpace or side-step the competition by doing new things or doing things differently. The choice of entrepreneurial strategy varies widely: simple arbitrage of differences in market conditions across space; segmenting markets in new ways; extensions of existing products, technology, or markets; occupying niches ignored by dominant firms; inventions whose marketability is uncertain; and complex innovations to "create the future" (Mascarenhas 1986; Hamel and Prahalad 1994). Success is often based on the skillful employment of intangible and difficult-to-imitate strategic factors (Barney 1991), such as corporate culture (Barney 1986a), or unique management skill or accumulated technology (Itami and Roehl 1987). It is the very nature of peripheral games that these inimitable strategic factors are ones that are marginal in dominant games.

Industry Evolution: Dominant and Peripheral Games over Time

From an industry evolution perspective, the relative importance of dominant and peripheral games varies in relation to the phase of industry evolution, from industry formation through maturity and into industry reconfiguration, as Figure 5.1 suggests. Although collaborative strategies are

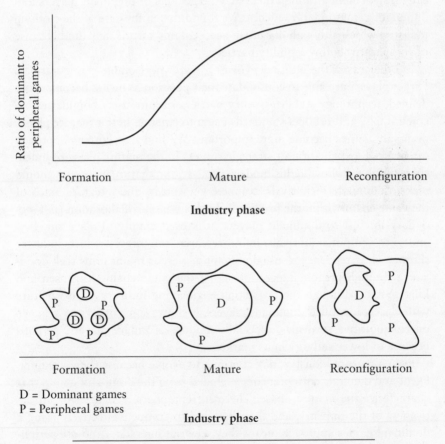

Figure 5.1. Industry Dynamics: Dominant and Peripheral Games.

found in both dominant and peripheral games, their importance is greater in peripheral games. There are parallels between our industry evolution framework and the technology life cycle explanation of alliances (Horton and Richey 1997).

In the industry formation phase, peripheral games are prevalent because there are not yet dominant players or even stable, well-defined industry boundaries. In this phase, there is greater scope for collaboration (Romanelli 1991). Porter (1980) himself noted that cooperation among firms could help promote a new industry and accelerate its growth. The dynamics of this phase are so fluid that a firm would be foolhardy to expend resources on a dominant game approach. The key to success in the industry formation phase is collaboration to gain needed resources and reduce the downside risk of heavy resource commitment (see Chapter Two; Bell, Barkema, and Verbeke 1997). Sometimes an industry remains basically fragmented, although there may be pockets of dominant players and dominant games in larger niches. We found this in the case of the clothing industry, which although mature in age, remains surprisingly fluid because of comparatively low mobility barriers.

In other cases, the industry evolves toward more stable configurations. Larger players are able to consolidate their position as niches become more defined, technology stabilizes, entry barriers rise, industry boundaries become stable, and product standards begin to emerge. In this mature phase, dominant games become more important. We find that Porter's approach offers a rich explanation of strategic success in the mature phase of industry evolution. Following his models, firms within mature industries should seek to dominate their rivals, compete vigorously, and integrate much of the value chain within the firm itself. In this phase, collaboration is of secondary interest to dominant players; it is used mainly to place side-bets and to co-opt potential rivals. In our research, the forest products industry shows a clear tendency to use dominant games, as major firms seek dominance through greater integration along the value chain (Jørgensen and Lilja 1995). Although the consulting engineering industry is also mature with clearly identified dominant players, it shows signs of greater reliance on collaborative strategies, especially among secondary players, perhaps because of lower stability in its markets.

Even a mature industry may continue to evolve because there are intelligent and dynamic entrepreneurs excluded from the dominant games that characterize the mature phase. These entrepreneurs recognize the attractiveness of the industry, and their inability to compete effectively using a dominant games approach means they seek out interstices and use peripheral games to penetrate or reconceive the industry. These firms may move an industry toward market disequilibrium and reconfiguration through entrepreneurial discovery and the use of cooperative strategies.

As disequilibrium increases, the industry enters the reconfiguration phase. Dominant games continue, but the boundaries of the industry are eroding, reforming, or being permeated through the successful attacks of peripheral players. Survival in the industry becomes dependent on employing cooperative strategy in peripheral games, as dominant games can no longer be sustained and thus become less relevant.

We argue that the forces that drive globalization—technological innovation, deregulation, and the emergence of regional trading blocs and global market segments—are shifting many industries from the mature to the reconfiguration phase. Even dominant players begin to engage in peripheral games through the use of cooperative strategies. For example, the erosion of dominance and the consequent increase in the use of peripheral games in industries such as telecommunications (Smith 1995) and automobiles (Rosegger 1991; Yoshino and Rangan 1995) is linked to an increase in collaborative strategies. The need for innovation and flexibility outweighs the short-term need for integration. Our study leads us to suggest that there might be different types of collaboration for players in different games.

Cooperative Strategies in Dominant and Peripheral Games

Dominant games assume that competitive advantage requires internal integration. Thus an important competitive advantage is the firm's ability to coordinate and perform activities along a value chain (Porter 1985). For Porter (1990a), global competitive advantage arises from integrating activities on a worldwide basis. Similarly, for Doz, Prahalad, and Hamel (1990), cooperative strategy is a means to fill gaps in the firm's strategic infrastructure but carries significant coordination costs. From Porter's national diamond view (1990a: 66–67), there are severe difficulties associated with alliances and other cooperative strategies: (1) they require strategic and organizational coordination with a partner with different goals, who may be a rival; (2) they are temporary devices in industries beset by transition or uncertainty; (3) they are tools for second-tier competitors trying to catch up; and (4) they are poor substitutes for developing capabilities internally. In short, in dominant games the use of cooperative strategy is limited to the equivalent of side-bets and short-term tactics by leading firms, or catch-up strategies by trailing firms. As Jarillo (1988: 31) notes, "the construct of networks is difficult to fit within the basic paradigm of competitive strategy."

In contrast, peripheral games require flexibility to permit entrepreneurial discovery and response to changing market conditions. There may be a need for coordination within the firm or within its network, often through "soft" mechanisms (Jarillo 1988; Martinez and Jarillo 1989; Geringer and Hébert 1989; Ghoshal and Bartlett 1988), but coordination is assumed to be less important than flexibility for entrepreneurial innovation. Cooperative strategy thus plays a larger role in peripheral games. It can enhance the firm's flexibility in responding to local conditions (Prahalad and Doz 1987) or can enable it to enter global markets rapidly (Contractor and Lorange 1988; Kogut and Singh 1988). It can facilitate innovation by followers (Contractor and Lorange 1988). It can reduce uncertainty in industries and segments in disequilibrium (Nohria and Garcia-Pont 1991). Jarillo (1988: 39) links networks (cooperative strategy) directly to entrepreneurial strategy: "It is an essential characteristic of entrepreneurs to end up using more resources than they control." For players in peripheral games, cooperative strategies are necessary for survival, but collaboration also facilitates redefining the game, creating new segments, and reconfiguring existing ones.

Peripheral games assume that advantage lies in economies of deintegration whereby the firm internalizes only those key components in the value chain that are most crucial for developing the capabilities needed for innovation (Jarillo 1988; Quinn 1992; Normann and Ramirez 1993). Other activities may be outsourced according to transaction and factor costs. More radically, the firm may deintegrate core activities by engaging in cooperative ventures to develop needed capabilities. For example, in their study of outsourcing as a form of collaboration in financial services, McLellan and Beamish (1995) found that outsourcing of information technology was growing more rapidly in the fragmented U.S. financial sector than in the highly concentrated Canadian financial sector. Similarly, firms engaged in technological innovation may seek entrepreneurial advantage by designing modularly upgradable systems to obtain "economies of substitution" either within the firm or across firms (Garud and Kumaraswamy 1995). In his study of large European and North American manufacturing firms, Madhok (1993) discovered that flexibility for global presence and development of organizational capabilities for innovation were becoming more important than transaction costs in determining modes of international entry.

Based on our research on the impact of globalization in the Canadian engineering and clothing industries, we propose an alternative to the national diamond: the virtual diamond. We argue that the international success of firms in peripheral games depends on a continually evolving network of partnerships constructed by firms according to their needs and opportunities.

The Virtual Diamond: A Framework for Peripheral Game Cooperative Strategies

Using his national diamond model, Porter examined the competitiveness of Canadian industries (Porter 1991b). The results suggested serious trouble, in that most of the examined industries were in a poor competitive position. A few industries, such as mining and forestry, had a credible chance to compete globally but were still weak contenders.

Yet Canada was one of the richest nations in the world, and one of the most successful among the OECD nations. What could explain this discrepancy? We suggest the reason is that Porter's model focuses on mature, stable industries where dominant games prevail and firms seek domination by integrating and controlling elements in the value chain.

Thus we propose the virtual diamond to complement Porter's national diamond. The virtual diamond offers a collaborative approach to competition, whereby a firm creates a network of value chain elements to compete globally. The virtual diamond may or may not be characterized by formal contracts, joint ventures, or legal arrangements.

The virtual diamond differs from Porter's national diamond in several ways. First, the diamond is not nation-specific; elements of the value chain and other points from the national diamond may be located anywhere in the world. Second, the virtual diamond is a creation of a firm, reflecting its competitive strategy; it is not a result of a country's endogenous characteristics. Each firm taps into various countries' stock of endowments and specific social, political, cultural, and historical contexts for demand conditions, factor conditions, competitive structure, and supporting industries. Third, the virtual diamond requires collaboration among firms, where the national diamond disdains collaboration. Table 5.1 summarizes the key elements of both the national and virtual diamonds.

The following examples draw on successful Quebec firms in consulting engineering and clothing manufacturing, two industries that do not fit the predictions of Porter's diamond of national competitive advantage. The virtual diamond is a useful analytical tool for understanding the performance of firms in these industries.

The Virtual Diamond of Consulting Engineering Firms in Canada

Numerous authors have written about the development of consulting engineering firms in Canada and have tried to explain their international success (Niosi 1990; Hammes 1988; Verreault and Polèse 1989). Their explanations tend to confirm the thesis of the national diamond (Porter

	National Diamond **Dominant Game**	**Virtual Diamond** **Peripheral Game**
Basis of advantage	Domestic	International:
	Preexistent industry factors	Industry factors tapped or constructed anywhere by the firm
	Home-country cluster	Enacted cluster
Global strategy focus	Economies of scale and scope	Focus, innovation, flexibility
Organizational type	Tight coupling	Loose coupling
Role of cooperative strategy	Epiphenomenal: limited to side-bets and also-rans, viewed as burden on strategic integration	Essential: used to add resources, for flexibility and for learning and innovation

Table 5.1. Comparison of the National and Virtual Diamonds.

1990a). Yet, as we shall see, Quebec engineering firms also pose interesting anomalies.

According to these authors, Quebec firms attained international-caliber expertise in consulting engineering primarily due to governmental policies that favored the development of a strong local diamond (Niosi 1990).

Demand was provided by a sophisticated and very demanding client: Hydro-Quebec, the provincial electric utility. Geography and difficult climatic conditions forced local engineers to develop a unique expertise that could be applied elsewhere in the world. Furthermore, Hydro-Quebec attracted bright young employees. In part because of the needs of Hydro-Quebec, University of Montreal's School of Engineering (École Polytechnique) grew into a center of expertise in electrical engineering capable of training high-caliber engineers, who could then be recruited by local engineering firms or directed by Hydro-Quebec.

In supporting industries, important firms such as Asea Brown Boveri and GEC-Alsthom established operations in Quebec. Hydro-Quebec also founded l'IREQ (Institut de la recherche en électricité du Québec), a research institute focusing on research and development in electricity, which is credited with numerous important technological innovations. Finally, because of Hydro-Quebec's decision not to favor one consulting engineering firm, a strong rivalry emerged between a number of firms that developed the necessary skills to be competitive on the international market. Throughout the 1960s, Quebec encouraged a strong, well-integrated diamond to emerge. This explains the success local engineering firms enjoy internationally.

Up to this point, the consulting engineering case is a good illustration of Porter's national diamond. But looking at another characteristic of this mature service industry, the important role played by collaboration in consortia and other types of alliances reveals another facet of the emergence of world-class consulting engineering in Quebec, which the Porter model neglects through its emphasis on tight integration.

The use of collaboration was even more important for Quebec's firms, which, despite their position among the world leaders, were only one-quarter to one-tenth the size of their major rivals. For example, SNC-Lavalin's yearly revenues for 1994 totaled $795 million compared with $7.7 billion for Fluor Daniel, a leading U.S. firm with headquarters in Irvine, California. In part this occurred because the Quebec firms were traditionally free-standing consulting engineering firms, whereas their major competitors were either integrated construction groups, such as Bechtel, or part of large manufacturing or financial groups, such as GEC-Alsthom.

Free-standing consulting engineering firms have always worked with subcontractors. But since the late 1970s it has become common practice for these firms to form consortia and alliances for major projects, especially those where competition was global. Such collaboration with other engineering firms and manufacturers, both domestic and foreign, allowed consulting engineering firms with a weaker capital base to participate in large international projects, such as the BOT (build-operate-transfer) projects. With their partners, these firms obtained the starting capital required (for the main contractor was frequently responsible for financing the venture). According to Verreault and Polèse (1989), a part of the recent international success of Quebec's engineering firms can be attributed to the experience and know-how they have acquired in the design and management of such partnerships. For Niosi (1990: 30), the existence of this collaboration allowing minor partners to acquire part of their major partner's know-how also explained why engineering was a sector where dominance was hard to maintain.

The Virtual Diamonds of Two Clothing Firms

A second example is the Canadian clothing industry, which was particularly insignificant in Porter's analysis (1991b). Clearly, Canada not only was in deep trouble, but the clothing situation was so weak that nobody would even think about entering such an industry. The Porter study did not deem that industry worthy of consideration.

In many respects, Porter was right. The Canadian clothing industry was small and fragmented, compared to major competitor countries. Apparently, there were no basic advantages on which to base a competitive business. Canadians were not known for their clothing know-how. Canada was not an attractive base for production, design, or marketing. For example, costs were generally high, and in particular costs of labor were much higher than those of competitors from Southeast Asia. Clothing design was dominated by large and well-established European, American, and some Japanese designers. Marketing required extensive networks and highly sophisticated world-class firms. Consequently the industry was dominated by American and European firms. In the early 1990s even the government had started giving up on the industry, and to secure the passage of the North American Free Trade Agreement in the U.S. it agreed to eliminate progressively all traditional protective measures, despite the industry's outcry. Yet, this dismal picture also shows intriguing spots that deserve a closer look.

Our study of the industry reveals a surprisingly large number of small firms that successfully compete internationally. It is interesting to note that Canadian firms whose center of gravity[2] is production appear to be doing better than others. That is a clear surprise. One would have expected that given their labor cost disadvantage Canadian firms would have concentrated on marketing or design services, for which labor costs are less important. Yet many firms in clothing and other production areas compete successfully in a global industry.

Peerless Clothing is an old Montreal clothing firm, created in 1919. Today, Peerless Clothing operates the world's largest single plant for men's suit manufacturing. It was the largest exporter of high-quality wool suits to the U.S., in 1995, competing successfully with major European suit manufacturers such as the German Hugo Boss or the Italian Armani in the CAN $300 to $600 retail price range. It exports 80 to 90 percent of its production, with revenues around CAN $150 million.

Three contingencies favor Peerless: (1) a high demand in the U.S. market for quality private-label products, (2) a North American Free Trade Agreement (NAFTA) quota arrangement by which Peerless is able to import wool fabrics without paying customs duties, provided that these fabrics are used in manufacturing products for export, and (3) the sophistication of the labor force. In particular, local universities provide high-quality graduates that are available at a reasonable cost. In addition, there is a large pool of new immigrants with, according to managers interviewed, a higher level of education and qualifications than in the past.

In contrast to traditional industry practice, Peerless Clothing acts as part of its customers' value chain by producing to inventory, enabling customers to buy only those items and quantities that they currently need, which reduces their inventory costs and losses. The availability of products in inventory allows also a highly valued rapid response rate, which other competitors do not seem able to match. The know-how base is twofold: (1) a technologically advanced and highly flexible production sys-tem, and (2) a highly sophisticated planning system. What Peerless does appears easy, but it involves a difficult-to-imitate set of skills. Competi-tors would have to invest significantly in equipment and inventory (over CAN$40 million) and in continual training. More importantly, they would have to develop the capacity to forecast the demand that retailers face, which is a time-consuming, experience-based type of know-how. Peerless's well-targeted customers, most of them small chains, are generally unwilling to take any risk, least of all inventory risk. They are, as a consequence, willing to pay for the value provided.

Because of its production orientation, marketing is less well developed at Peerless. To compensate for that, the company has made alliances with small firms or talented individuals that take care of sales and promotion of suits in the U.S. These arrangements allow more flexibility and a large measure of entrepreneurial behavior on the part of both Peerless and its partners. Peerless, however, provides all the organizational and infrastructural support that is needed by the partners. For example, a large distribution center has been set up in Vermont to ensure fast response to customer needs. According to the managers interviewed (Alvin Segal, Peerless president and CEO, and Michael Costello, March and April 1995), customer service quality is among the best in their target segment. The acid test is provided by Peerless's market penetration; the company has captured close to 20 percent of the U.S. market for medium-priced men's wool suits.

Another Quebec firm is Paris Star, which benefits from the same advantages. It is able to provide higher value to its customers than they may receive from manufacturers in Europe or Asia, according to George Guttman, president and CEO (interview with the authors, March 31, 1995). Contrary to Peerless, Paris Star is a small conglomerate, able to produce a large array of products for any customer in North America. Recently Paris Star has started to serve Europe. It is recognized for manufacturing high-quality knits, children's wear, women's sportswear, underwear, dresses, skirts, and embroideries.

Paris Star's strategy is to stick with a large number of "interstice" markets. Leslie Guttman, its former president and founder, said, "In the USA, they are looking for big opportunities. We look for enough small niches of, say, $10 million in the USA, and if we succeed we are in good shape." Paris

Star's strategy resembles a project strategy. They are constantly looking for small markets or contracts. They have built a highly automated and technologically sophisticated system, using advanced information technology, in a rich labor market of highly qualified and enthusiastic professionals. Combined with a highly decentralized, entrepreneurial marketing organization, Paris Star is able to respond fast and flexibly, and at reasonable costs. Paris Star's formula provided a better compromise of cost and responsiveness (such as flexibility for product changes and delivery time), even for large firms. Recently, such firms as Liz Claiborne have started contracting with the company, and with similar ones in Canada.

Paris Star's philosophy is to penetrate markets in various kinds of alliances with other firms and individuals. The alliances are made either through acquisitions and mergers or through contractual arrangements. For example, Paris Star is allied with such large firms as Baird Textile in Britain and with Koret and Junior Gallery in the U.S.

Firms such as Peerless and Paris Star have developed an uncanny ability to thrive within the changing conditions and high degree of uncertainty that characterize clothing markets. They believe that what they control today is not going to be there tomorrow, so they are constantly working to improve competitiveness and to discover new opportunities, especially in foreign markets, that are consistent with the strengths of the local factors. Even though they consciously avoid competing head-on with the dominant firms, their degree of technological sophistication plus their marketing, design, and organizational skills are easily comparable to the best firms, which makes them somewhat secure. It is very hard even for the large and powerful firms in this industry to compete with such firms as Peerless or Paris Star in their niche markets, especially because these smaller firms are nimble, able to retreat and come back.

Even more interesting is the fact that these firms' cooperative agreements are not stereotypical. They look for all kinds of possible arrangements with other partners in order to thrive or simply survive. The nature of the cooperative arrangements changes constantly and is the subject of constant creative innovation. It is an integral part of the "creative destruction" process that nibbles at the power of dominant firms. These patterns suggest that collaborative characteristics may be related to the nature of the games and the phase in the industry evolution.

We find the consulting engineering and clothing industries interesting because dominance cannot be sustained easily. This suggests that different types of industries (for example, service industries [Segal-Horn 1993] and fragmented industries [Porter 1980]) where peripheral games are more prevalent give rise to more varied patterns of collaboration. Peripheral actors may be able to attack the most solid advantages of dominant firms, leading to a constant state of flux and shifting destinies. No competitors, not even those that seem well entrenched, may take their advantages for granted, nor their positions to be secure. Therefore, associations, alliances and collaborations, where possible, are an effective way to reduce the risk of being brushed aside by a luckier rival.

Because they are not tied to a particular dominant firm, the successful peripheral games of the firms in our study differ from the dedicated "key suppliers" in the flagship-partners model of D'Cruz and Rugman (1993). Their situation is also quite different from what Porter (1990a) describes in his national diamond, where the four basic dimensions (factors, demand, support industries, and industry structure) constitute a tightly knit configuration. Because no national platform can be foolproof, the best strategy is to search constantly for better practices and better ideas and to move fast (Jacobson 1992; Alvin Segal and George Guttman, interviews with the authors, March 1995). Successful actors such as Peerless Clothing are those willing to design a complex system, in which advantages of various countries are pulled together to build a firm's own competitive advantage. Through the combination of internal strengths and strengths borrowed through alliances, successful firms design a "virtual" diamond that facilitates survival today. More importantly, these firms continuously update their diamond to enhance its competitiveness. However, virtual diamond configurations may differ by industry type. Similarly, some patterns of collaboration may be more appropriate for interstice competition and virtual diamond configurations, whereas others may be more appropriate for dominant games.

Canadian firms have been able to experiment with a virtual diamond partly because NAFTA provides them with a chance to construct an initial diamond based on assets located in both Canada and the United States, as suggested by Rugman and D'Cruz (1993b) via their double-diamond concept. More generally, it seems that the forces that drive globalization are eroding dominance and making peripheral games and the virtual diamond more pertinent.

Conclusion

This chapter has argued that cooperative strategies can be understood best if we analyze them in the context of relevant industry dynamics. Our analysis has centered on the distinction between dominant and peripheral games and the relative importance of collaboration in an industry evolution framework. We propose the virtual diamond as a way to represent the continuously evolving network of international and domestic partnerships of players in peripheral games, as a complement to Porter's national diamond. We maintain that collaboration plays a different role for players in dominant and peripheral games. Our discussion also suggests that both industry type and phase of evolution affect the relative importance of dominant and peripheral games and, consequently, the prevalence of collaboration. We discuss and synthesize the findings emerging from our research and summarize them in the form of propositions, which can provide the basis for further research.

PROPOSITION 1: The importance of collaborative strategies is related to industry types. specifically, the less an industry allows dominance, the more it fosters collaboration.

We find in our study of the Canadian consulting engineering industry more collaboration, even by major players, than would be expected by Porter (1990a), and agree with Niosi (1990) that this finding was related to the difficulty of maintaining dominance in that sector. These findings suggest that industry type is related to collaboration. Further, we think that because there seem to be fewer strategic incentives for vertical integration in the service industries, the distinction between manufacturing and services could be an interesting one. For example, in response to a recent article by Normann and Ramirez (1993) suggesting that firms should think in terms of a value constellation rather than a value chain to emphasize the creation of dynamic strategic partnerships, Hama (1993), of the Mitsubishi Research Institute, suggested that this approach was more appropriate for light industries as opposed to heavy manufacturing industries. Similarly, Buckley and Casson (1997) maintained that high-technology industries of the 1990s such as information and biotechnology offered greater incentives for joint venture collaboration than the heavy industries of the 1960s. Segal-Horn (1993) argued that in service industries, economies of scope and scale were difficult to achieve (or were not a relevant strategic advantage), which made vertical integration a less appropriate strategy and collaboration more likely.

But with globalization, even in heavy manufacturing industries, we see more and more collaboration, which brings us to our second proposition.

PROPOSITION 2: The importance of collaborative strategies is related to the phase of the industry cycle. in phases with less dominance there is more collaboration.

An interesting illustration of this proposition is provided by our engineering study. At the end of the 1980s, the emergence of regional trading blocs, among other factors, pushed this industry into the reconfiguration stage and led to many partnerships among large and small players wishing to position themselves in these markets. SNC, for example, made international alliances one of the main focuses of its strategy for the 1990s. Yet in 1995, when the situation had somewhat stabilized and the rules were clearer, SNC-Lavalin engaged in mergers and acquisitions to solidify its position in the main international markets and had reduced its dependence on cooperation.

PROPOSITION 3: In dominant games, collaboration is conceived as a side-bet and a short-term response to competitive dynamics. in peripheral games collaboration is the name of the game, necessary for survival, and instrumental in the redefinition of the nature of the game.

In his study of the American automobile industry, Rosegger (1991) concluded that the international strategic partnering of the Big Three could be understood "in terms of some well-defined short-term and medium-term gains" (p. 97). He added "It would be difficult to argue that . . . the existence of strategic partnerships has changed the underlying pattern of rivalry" (p. 99). Similarly, in the consulting engineering industry, Canadian firms like SNC and Lavalin entered into partnerships with very large players. For example, SNC engaged in an alliance with Fluor Daniel in 1990 and with Bouygues in 1991, and Lavalin formed a joint venture with Bechtel in 1989. However, these were unstable, and not strategically significant for the firms, according to M. St-Pierre, CEO of SNC-Lavalin (in answer to a participant's question during the Revue Gestion Yearly Colloquium at École des Hautes Études Commerciales, September 1995). On the other hand, smaller Quebec firms like Roche International, which opened a Singapore office with a number of partners, depend on partnerships for their success in international markets. Our findings from the clothing industry also yielded examples where timely alliances could change the rules of the game and allow small firms to become successful major players. We argue that different types of industries and different phases will lead to different patterns of collaboration.

Therefore, an interesting area of study suggested by our model is of the different patterns of international collaboration represented in the virtual diamond. For example, the configuration of the diamond itself could vary in terms of the nature of its elements and the links among them. The study of the configurations of the virtual diamond in different types of industries and in different phases of industry evolution could help us better understand the nature of cooperative strategies. Thus the virtual diamond framework could help in understanding the strategies underlying alliances between two dominant firms, between a dominant and a peripheral firm, or between two peripheral firms in different industry contexts.

The dynamic nature of the virtual diamond suggests another area of research concentrating on the different paths followed by firms. For example, there may be a transition from either a virtual diamond to a formal diamond in the case where a firm is becoming dominant, or to a succession of virtual diamonds in the case of a firm specializing in niche strategies.

Finally, this chapter was intended to provide a contextualized view of collaboration. In attempting this, we have drawn on different literatures and theories in strategy, economics, and international business. We recognize that our approach is not the only way to contextualize collaborative strategy; for example, Yeung (1997) has developed a power and cultural contextual framework for studying Asian business networks. We have proposed the virtual diamond as a complement to Porter's national diamond, which is an industry-level explanation of international success. The virtual diamond is a way to conceptualize and represent the myriad of collaborative partnerships in which individual firms engage in the process of creating and re-creating an international strategy. This framework suggests a number of interesting avenues for future research.

NOTES

1. This chapter takes a different approach than others in this volume. The authors did not set out to study strategic alliances or international joint ventures. Instead, we wished to compare organizational responses to globalization across four industries (textiles, consulting engineering, telecommunications, and pulp and paper). The main research questions were grouped under four broad themes. What is the pattern and meaning of globalization in each industry? Within each, how have firms responded to globalization? How have government policies affected and responded to globalization? And how do patterns of organizational response vary by industry, nation, and firm? In this chapter, the patterns of response to globalization are discussed along three overlapping dimensions: dominant versus peripheral games, competitive versus cooperative strategies; and national versus virtual diamonds.

2. The idea of center of gravity has been introduced by Galbraith (1985) to suggest where, in the firm value chain, lie the principal core competencies. The idea of center of gravity suggests also that core competencies evolve

and may change over time, thus changing the overall balance of the firm and its center of gravity.

BIBLIOGRAPHY

Barney, J. B. 1986a. Organizational culture: Can it be a source of competitive advantage? *Academy of Management Review,* 11: 656–665.

Barney, J. B. 1986b. Types of competition and the theory of strategy: Toward an integrative framework. *Academy of Management Review,* 11(4): 491–500.

Barney, J. B. 1991. Firm resources and sustained competitive advantage. *Journal of Management Review,* 17: 99–120.

Bell, J.H.J., H. G. Barkema, and A. Verbeke. 1997. An eclectic model of the choice between wholly owned subsidiaries and joint ventures as modes of foreign entry. In P. W. Beamish and J. P. Killing, editors, *Cooperative Strategies: European Perspectives.* San Francisco: New Lexington Press.

Buckley, P. J., and M. Casson. 1997. An economic model of international joint venture strategy. In P. W. Beamish and J. P. Killing, editors, *Cooperative Strategies: European Perspectives.* San Francisco: New Lexington Press.

Buzzell, R. D., and B. T. Gale. 1987. *The PIMS Principles.* New York: Free Press.

Contractor, F. J., and P. Lorange. 1988. Why should firms cooperate? The strategy and economics basis for cooperative ventures. In F. J. Contractor and P. Lorange, editors, *Cooperative Strategies in International Business,* pp. 4–28. San Francisco: New Lexington Press.

Daleu-Diabé, M., and T. Hafsi. 1993. *La stratégie nationale de Taiwan de 1895 à 1990* [The national strategy of Taiwan from 1895 to 1990]. Montreal: Monographies du CÉTAI, 93–01.

D'Cruz, J., and A. M. Rugman. 1993. Developing international competitiveness: The five partners model. *Business Quarterly,* 58 (Winter): 60–72.

Doz, Y., C. K. Prahalad, and G. Hamel. 1990. Control, change, and flexibility: The dilemma of transnational collaboration. In C. Bartlett, Y. Doz, and G. Hedlund, editors, *Managing the Global Firm.* New York: Routledge.

Dunning, J. H. 1995. Reappraising the eclectic paradigm in an age of alliance capitalism. *Journal of International Business Studies,* 26(3): 461–491.

Galbraith, J. 1985. Types of strategic change. Research paper presented to the McGill Policy Colloquium, Montreal, October 1985.

Garud, R., and A. Kumaraswamy. 1995. Technological and organizational designs for realizing economies of substitution. *Strategic Management Journal,* 16: 93–109.

Geringer, J. M., and L. Hébert. 1989. Control and performance of international joint ventures. *Journal of International Business Studies,* 20(2): 235–254.

Ghoshal, S. 1987. Global strategy: An organizing framework. *Strategic Management Journal,* 8: 425–440.

Ghoshal, S., and C. A. Bartlett. 1988. Creation, adoption, and diffusion of innovations by subsidiaries of multinational corporations. *Journal of International Business Studies,* 19(3): 365–388.

Hama, N. 1993. Perspectives. *Harvard Business Review,* 71 (September–October): 39–53.

Hamel, G., and C. K. Prahalad. 1994. *Competing for the Future.* Boston: Harvard Business School Press.

Hammes, D. L. 1988. *An Economic Analysis of Canada's Consulting Engineers.* Vancouver: Fraser Institute.

Horton, V., and B. Richey. 1997. On developing a contingency model of technology alliance formation. In P. W. Beamish and J. P. Killing, editors, *Cooperative Strategies: European Perspectives.* San Francisco: New Lexington Press.

Itami, H., and T. W. Roehl. 1987. *Mobilizing Invisible Assets.* Cambridge, Mass.: Harvard University Press.

Jacobson, R. 1992. The "Austrian" school of strategy. *Academy of Management Review,* 17(4): 782–807.

Jarillo, J. C. 1988. On strategic networks. *Strategic Management Journal,* 9: 31–41.

Jorde, T. M., and D. J. Teece. 1989. Competition and cooperation: Striking the right balance. *California Management Review,* (Spring): 25–37.

Jørgensen, J., and K. Lilja. 1995. Managerial agency and its sectoral embeddedness: A process model of strategic moves in the pulp and paper industry. In *Strategic Management Society of Finland Yearbook,* 18–22. Helsinki: Strategic Management Society of Finland.

Kogut, B., and H. Singh. 1988. The effect of national culture on the choice of entry mode. *Journal of International Business Studies,* 19(3): 411–432.

Madhok, A. 1993. Mode of foreign market entry: An integrative study. Unpublished doctoral thesis, Faculty of Management, McGill University, Montreal.

Martinez, J. I., and J. C. Jarillo. 1989. The evolution of research on coordination mechanisms in multinational corporations. *Journal of International Business Studies,* 20(3): 489–514.

Mascarenhas, B. 1986. International strategies of non-dominant firms. *Journal of International Business Studies,* 17(1): 1–25.

McLellan, K., and P. Beamish. 1995. The new frontier for information technology outsourcing: International banking. *European Management Journal,* 12(2): 210–215.

Niosi, J. 1990. *La montée de l'ingénierie canadienne* [The rise of Canadian engineering]. University of Montreal Press.

Nohria, N., and C. Garcia-Pont. 1991. Global strategic linkages and industry structure. *Strategic Management Journal,* 12: 105–124.

Normann, R., and R. Ramirez. 1993. From value chain to value constellation: Designing interactive strategy. *Harvard Business Review,* 71 (July-August): 65–77.

Ohmae, K. 1989. The global logic of strategic alliances. *Harvard Business Review,* 89(2): 143–154.

Penttinen, R. 1994. Summary of the critique on Porter's diamond model. Discussion paper no. 462. Helsinki: Research Institute of the Finnish Economy.

Porter, M. E. 1980. *Competitive Strategy.* New York: Free Press.

Porter, M. E. 1985. *Competitive Advantage.* New York: Free Press.

Porter, M. E. 1990a. *Competitive Advantage of Nations.* New York: Free Press. Copyright © 1990 by Michael E. Porter. Reprinted with permission of The Free Press, a division of Simon & Schuster.

Porter, M. E. 1990b. Compete, don't collaborate. *The Economist,* June 9, 17–19.

Porter, M. E. 1991a. Towards a dynamic theory of strategy. *Strategic Management Journal,* 12: 95–117.

Porter, M. E. 1991b. *Canada at the Crossroads.* Ottawa: Business Council on National Issues.

Prahalad, C. K., and Y. L. Doz. 1987. *The Multinational Mission.* New York: Free Press.

Quinn, J. B. 1992. *Intelligent Enterprise: A Knowledge and Service-Based Paradigm.* New York: Free Press.

Romanelli, E. 1991. The evolution of new organizational forms. *Annual Review of Sociology,* 17: 79–103.

Rosegger, G. 1991. Diffusion through interfirm cooperation. *Technological Forecasting and Social Change,* 39: 81–101.

Rugman, A. M., and J. R. D'Cruz. 1993a. The "double diamond" model of international competitiveness: The Canadian experience. *Management International Review,* 33(2): 17–39.

Rugman, A. M., and J. R. D'Cruz. 1993b. Strategic management, networks and international competitiveness. In J. Kantor, editor, *International Business: Business Practice and Research,* 14(8): 146–154. Administrative Sciences Association of Canada.

Schumpeter, J. A. 1942. *Capitalism, Socialism, and Democracy.* New York: HarperCollins.

Segal-Horn, S. 1993. The internationalization of service firms. *Advances in Strategic Management,* 9: 31–55.

Shamsie, J. 1991. The context of dominance: A cross-sectional study. Unpublished doctoral thesis, Faculty of Management, McGill University, Montreal.

Smith, A. 1995. Going global: The international expansion of the seven regional Bell operating companies, 1984–1991. Unpublished doctoral dissertation in Strategic Management, Kenan-Flager School of Business, University of North Carolina.

Tichy, N., and R. Charan. 1989. Speed, simplicity, self-confidence: An interview with Jack Welch. *Harvard Business Review,* 67 (September-October): 112–120.

Verreault, R., and M. Polèse. 1989. L'exportation de services par les firmes Canadiennes de génie-conseil: Évolution récente et avantages concurrentiels [Exportation of services by Canadian consulting engineering firms: Recent evolution and competitive advantages]. Montreal: Institute for Research in Public Policy.

Yeung, H. W.-C. 1997. Cooperative strategies and Chinese business networks: A study of Hong Kong transnational corporations in the ASEAN region. In P. W. Beamish and J. P. Killing, editors, *Cooperative Strategies: Asian Pacific Perspectives.* San Francisco: New Lexington Press.

Yoshino, M. Y., and U. S. Rangan. 1995. *Strategic Alliances.* Boston: Harvard Business School Press.

6

THE EFFECT OF PARTNER DIFFERENCES ON THE PERFORMANCE OF R&D CONSORTIA

Paul Olk

THIS CHAPTER INVESTIGATES *two explanations for inconsistent findings on the relationship between partner differences and joint venture performance. The first attributes the problem to multiple dimensions of differences, the second to variations in performance definition. Analysis of U.S.-based R&D consortia supports both explanations. Dissimilarity on one dimension (nationality) was positively related to performance; for another (research location) it was negative. For the performance explanation, the predictors of consortium-level performance were not the same as those of member organization–level performance. The chapter concludes with implications for IJV research.*

CENTRAL TO THE MANAGEMENT of and research into an international joint venture (IJV) is understanding the role of differences between partners. Numerous studies have addressed the issue of member diversity in terms of

Funding for this project was granted by Lehigh University's Center for Innovation Management Studies and University of California-Irvine's Committee on Research and University of California-Irvine's Junior Faculty Career Development Award. The author appreciates the comments on earlier versions of this chapter made by the conference participants, the anonymous reviewers, and the editors.

strategic interest in the venture (such as Osborn and Baughn 1990), national culture (such as Lane and Beamish 1990), and operating styles (such as Baird, Lyles, and Wharton 1990). Typically these differences have been considered problematic, and, if not overcome, were thought to lead to inter-partner conflict and eventual poor performance of the IJV. Writing from this perspective, researchers have recommended how to minimize these sources of disagreement through a variety of mechanisms including partner selection (Geringer 1988), negotiation (Contractor 1984), and joint venture structure (Killing 1983). Other researchers, however, have noted that the strategic contribution of an IJV may stem from partner heterogeneity (Hamel 1991). A joint venture with a partner who has unique attributes represents an opportunity to gain access to a dissimilar set of skills or resources. Variance among the partners, then, may represent an important source of success for an international joint venture.

Parkhe (1991) attempted to resolve these competing perspectives by contrasting Type I and Type II differences. Type I are similar to those described by Hamel (1991). When members contribute dissimilar resources, it may create a synergy that leads to alliance success. Parkhe (1991) argued that an international joint venture requires a minimum level of Type I differences in order to make an alliance viable, and any erosion of the differences will likely result in termination of the relationship. Type II differences, on the other hand, are those associated with creating conflict in the alliance. Parkhe included in this group divergence in the companies' national culture, industrial and regulatory context, and corporation-specific characteristics. To ensure an IJV's survival, partners must reduce the impact of any such differences. Although Parkhe recommended that researchers look at the degree and type of interfirm diversity that exists, the influence of these differences on performance remains untested.

Besides this conceptual explanation, an empirical reason may account for the findings: researchers have not consistently used the same measures of IJV performance. Much of the research on IJVs has measured performance at the venture level (for example, Gomes-Casseres 1987; Blodgett 1992). That is, the performance indicator, typically termination or stability in membership, reflects the venture's status rather than a member organization's evaluation. This misspecification is problematic because it does not necessarily reflect each partner's criteria for performance. This is because, first, observers often assume that termination or instability represents failure; studies, however, have found that termination may indicate joint venture success (Kogut 1991). Second, using a joint venture–level measure assumes that all members use this same evaluation of performance. For some organizations, however, termination of a joint venture may mean success even though for others it signals failure. Consequently, studies using performance measures at the venture level may find differences creating instability and assume the performance is bad, while other studies using performance at the member organization–level may consider the instability a sign of success.

This chapter tests these two explanations by examining the relationship between differences among member organizations and the performance of an R&D consortium. The R&D consortium structure (two or more companies pooling resources to conduct collaborative research and development) has emerged in the U.S. over the last ten years to facilitate technological innovation. Although designed primarily to improve the competitive positions of U.S. companies against global competitors, in practice many consortia have involved foreign participants. By examining consortia, this chapter makes three contributions to our understanding of IJVs. First, it investigates simultaneously the importance of various types of differences among member organizations on their evaluation of alliance performance. Second, it provides a more refined evaluation of the performance of the alliance, one derived from the members' perspective and composed of multiple dimensions of performance. Finally, the chapter presents the first empirical evaluation of the sources of effective R&D consortium performance. Although this structure has received much attention and commentary in the popular press, data on effective consortia have been lacking.

The chapter begins by first examining four types of differences that may exist among member organizations within a consortium and the problem of level of analysis in performance evaluation. After presentation of the data on R&D consortia, the results reveal no support for a simple explanation of the influence of member characteristics on performance. One difference (research location) was negatively related to performance and another (nationality) was associated with better performance. The findings also show that some, but certainly not all, of the divergent findings in the research stem from the level of analysis of the performance measures. The discussion addresses the significance of understanding partner differences for researchers and managers of IJVs.

Differences Among Member Organizations

International joint venture researchers have identified several dimensions by which member organizations may vary, but disagree about whether these differences are a source of opportunity and competitive advantage or of conflict and poor performance. To evaluate the importance of these differences, we simultaneously examine separate dimensions on which member organizations may vary. We do so by focusing on differences in terms of inputs, transformation, and outputs, an approach used by other researchers to evaluate joint venture activities and explain performance (for example, Anderson 1990; Thomas and Trevino 1993). This perspective is particularly relevant for analyzing R&D consortia, where knowledge development and transfer represent primary reasons for their existence. Consequently, the four dimensions we examine indicate different dimensions of the knowledge creation process. Technological linkage is related to the inputs received from the member organizations, research location to where the transformation process occurs, industry to the ability of member organizations to use the findings from the research, and nationality to the overall organizing approaches toward this knowledge creation used by the member organizations. Additionally, these four were chosen because some of their expected relationships to effectiveness may be a function of the measures of performance used.

Technological Linkage

One of the primary considerations in developing an R&D consortium is the nature of the technology. Ouchi and Bolton (1988) contend that research consortia exist to control "leaky intellectual property," information applicable to too many companies in an industry to be controlled by any one company through a patent, but not as widespread as public intellectual property. Hennart (1988) also provided a technology-based explanation for alliances by distinguishing between scale and link joint ventures. Scale joint ventures entail partners combining comparable resources to achieve the necessary economies of scale unattainable by one member. Alternatively, link joint ventures bring together partners with distinct resources for a transaction that is either too risky or too complex to combine internally or in a market transaction. The degree of differences in expertise that may lead to the formation of the collaboration is likely to change over time (Gray and Yan 1992). Although some members may acquire the skills and abilities of the other members, thereby reducing any differences, others may develop new ones that they contribute to the venture, and increase the differences. The ability to maintain a minimum level of these differences has been cited as the primary determinant of joint venture survival (Hamel 1991). Differences in members' contributions are likely to affect performance throughout the duration of the IJV.

Research on the performance of research units underscores the importance of the scale versus link distinction. Dailey (1980), in a study of the management of research teams, found a negative relationship between task interdependence and performance. He concluded that the extra time and assets devoted toward coordinating the work leads to the lower performance of each person and, as a consequence, of the team in total. The present study extends the relationship to the consortium and advances the idea that the more member organizations provide like skills and know-how, the easier the coordination and management of the consortium. When consortium members provide unique contributions, more effort and attention will be required toward integration. Consequently, we propose a negative relationship between difference in contributions and consortium performance.

HYPOTHESIS 1: Members' providing different skills and know-how is negatively associated with a member organization's evaluation of the performance of the consortium.

Research Location

Studies of collaborative research provide conflicting recommendations on the decision of where to locate research. One approach stresses the importance of a central location. The common research site is argued to be advantageous because it increases the level and frequency of communication among researchers, especially face-to-face interactions. This facilitates the development of innovation not only because of greater accumulation of knowledge in one site, but because it also increases the frequency of interpersonal interactions that are generally associated with greater levels of researcher learning in R&D consortia (Smilor and Gibson 1992). Grindley, Mowery, and Silverman (1994) noted another benefit from a centralized structure in their review of the U.S. consortium SEMATECH. They observed that the consortium was able to revise its research agenda in part because the centralized structure increased both its autonomy from member organizations and its corresponding ability to adapt rapidly to changing conditions. Browning, Beyer, and Shelter (1995), also looking at SEMATECH, argued that the centralized structure had the effect of refining the cooperative practices and helped to develop stronger norms against free-riding. Such congruency in objectives and practices has been linked to better joint venture performance (Beamish and Delios 1997). Thus, this perspective leads to the conclusion that success in a collaborative research arrangement comes from a critical mass of the research occurring in a central location. The second approach advances the importance of transferring the research to the member organizations and the adoption of the research findings by the member organization. For example, Aldrich and Sasaki (1995) regarded technology transfer as the primary purpose of R&D consortia. They noted that Japanese consortia conduct a greater percentage of the research in member organizations, giving them more control over the appropriability of their research, and thus expend less energy on technology transfer. In this view, success stems from a member successfully absorbing the technology, which is more likely to occur when the research is conducted within the member organization.

A parallel debate has occurred among researchers studying international joint venture control. In one of the first studies on the issue of control, Killing (1983) argued that independent joint ventures are preferable to single-partner dominant IJVs, which in turn are superior to shared-control IJVs; the source of poor performance in a shared-control IJV is interference by the partners, which limits the ability of joint venture managers to adapt to changing market conditions. Likewise, Parkhe (1991) stated that the likelihood of longevity of a global alliance increases with the development of a single management process and structure. For these researchers, centralization of activities was associated with better performance. Other studies have questioned this relationship, both conceptually (for example, Geringer and Hebért 1989) and empirically (Beamish 1985). Yan and Gray (1994a), for example, found that alliances with shared control reported higher levels of performance than those that did not. When both members had input into the operations of the venture, rather than just one, both considered the venture a success. They attributed this dissonant finding to be, in part, a function of the samples studied.

These discrepant relationships may also be due to the types of criteria used by the researchers, with studies finding support for centralized activities using consortium indicators and those finding superior results with decentralized operations using member organization criteria. Although this possible explanation will be discussed later, because there are compelling arguments for both directions we propose competing hypotheses on the relationship between research location and performance. The first draws from the importance of centrality of activity and contends that the greater the percentage of activities included in a common location, the better the performance of the consortium. The second emphasizes the importance of transferring the information to the member organizations and stipulates that the smaller the percentage of research conducted in a common area and the more of it that is conducted within the member organization, the better the performance.

HYPOTHESIS 2A: The percentage of research conducted in a common site is positively associated with amember organization's evaluation of the performance of the consortium.

HYPOTHESIS 2B: The percentage of research conducted in a common site is negatively associated with a member organization's evaluation of the performance of the consortium.

Industry

A strategic choice perspective regards industry structure as the primary determinant of the occurrence of a joint venture (Harrigan 1985). A company creates a joint venture in order to improve or sustain its competitive position. For R&D consortia in the U.S., which in order for member organizations to receive antitrust protection have a precompetitive focus, industry also represents a company's familiarity with and ability to use the developed technology. Industry membership, rather than firm characteristics such as size, has been found to be the primary determinant of the R&D spending levels of companies (Cohen, Levin, and Mowery 1987). Variations in efforts expended on R&D by a company, in turn, influence its absorptive capacity (Cohen and Levinthal 1990). This capacity represents the ability of the organization to appropriate externally developed knowledge. Companies coming from industries with dissimilar R&D levels should therefore have varying capacities for absorbing new technologies. Differences in these capacities, we argue, will lead to problems in the management of the consortium and to lower levels of performance.

A clear example of this relationship occurred in Microelectronics and Computer Technology Corporation (MCC). One of the first consortia in the United States, the original members came primarily from three industries—computers, semiconductors, and aerospace (Gibson and Rogers 1994). The initial structure consisted of four separate research programs, one of which was software development. As this program matured, observers commented that participants began to see a constant problem stemming from difference in the companies' internal capabilities (personal communication). The computer and semiconductor companies had maintained strong in-house software programming departments, and considered the consortium as a source of basic knowledge to facilitate their in-house research. The aerospace companies, however, had less-developed in-house departments; they required more turnkey software programs because they could not easily develop the software internally. This tension led to problems within the consortium and hindered its development.

Consequently, we believe that a consortium composed of members from the same industry, with similar levels of absorptive capacity and a more common understanding of the relevant technology, will have a higher level of performance. We propose a positive relationship between the percentage of members coming from the same industry and consortium performance.

HYPOTHESIS 3: A higher percentage of members of a consortium from different industries is negatively associated with a member organization's evaluation of the performance of the consortium.

Nationality

Researchers on joint ventures have frequently commented on the difficulties associated with international arrangements (for example, Schaan and Beamish 1988; Gomes-Casseres 1989). Cultural differences create challenges for companies managing international joint ventures not found in domestic ones (Gray and Yan 1992). For example, Olson and Singsuwan (1997) noted that managers from Thailand and the U.S. have differences in their evaluations of the factors important for a successful strategic alliance. In IJVs, managers will have to spend additional time on communication, on designing compatible work routines, and on developing common managerial approaches. Even though cross-cultural challenges are well known, there have been few empirical comparisons of the performance of international versus domestic joint ventures. Consequently, based on the argument that crossing national boundaries increases the difficulty of management, we propose that a higher percentage of international members in a consortium is associated with lower performance.

HYPOTHESIS 4: The percentage of foreign members in a consortium is negatively associated with a member organization's evaluation of the performance of the consortium.

Performance Measures

The preceding hypotheses examined several dimensions of member organization differences and their influence on consortium performance. An alternative explanation for the discordant findings in the research is that they are due to the performance measure specified. In many studies of IJVs, performance has been conceptualized at the joint venture level (for example, Geringer and Hebért 1991). This has led several authors to provide suggestions on how to establish a strong and independent joint venture (for example, Lorange and Probst 1987). Using measures at this level, an effective joint venture is one that can function independently from the member organizations and that endures. Although less common, other researchers have measured performance at the member level (Hamel 1991; Parkhe 1993). This distinction shifts the emphasis from building a strong IJV organization to ensuring that the partners are satisfied with the IJV's activities. In this case, even if a venture no longer exists, so long as it provided valuable resources to the member organization it might be considered a success. Given the possible discrepancy between the two sets of criteria, the factors that lead to an effective joint venture may not be the same as those that lead to effective membership. To test this possibility, we formally propose that no significant difference exists between the relationship of the indepen-dent variables with consortium-level performance measures and the relationship of these same independent variables with member organization–level measures.

HYPOTHESIS 5: The relationship of the independent variables to member organizations' evaluation of the consortium using consortium-level performance measures is the same as when using member organization–level performance measures.

Methods

This section explains the research bases on which the hypotheses in this chapter are based.

Sample

The population for this study is members of ongoing research and development consortia registered with the U.S. Department of Justice under the National Cooperative Research Act of 1984 and listed in the federal register during the period January 1985 through January 1992. Firms registered under the act in order to receive the antitrust protection it provides. Although 242 consortia were filed under the act during this period, many of them were not relevant for this study. Some were informal research agreements between two individual researchers from separate organizations, which do not, in the words of one manager, represent a "strategic alliance"; others were add-on projects for previously filed consortia and essentially were repetitive. We also eliminated those listings reporting only two members or those that were confirmed prior to our survey to have ceased operations. The final targeted sample was 110 consortia.

Through listings in *The Million Dollar Directory* and *The Reference Book of Corporations,* and through telephone calls, we were able to identify addresses for U.S. organizations representing 915 memberships in the 110 consortia. A questionnaire was sent to the executive within each company who was identified as the primary liaison between the consortium and the member organization. (When a company was a member of more than one consortium, we sent questionnaires for each to an executive able to forward them to the appropriate liaisons.) Following the initial mailing and follow-up phone calls, we received 253 responses. Of these, 164, representing 81 of the 110 consortia (74 percent), were usable. Although some were eliminated because the respondents were not knowledgeable about membership in the consortium, the primary reason some responses were not used is because of missing data.

The final response rate for this study (17.9 percent) is somewhat low, though not atypical of surveys of this type. We tested for nonresponse bias in two ways. First, we compared the respondents to nonrespondents in terms of reliably known data, including company sales, number of employees, industry SIC code, consortium size, and number of consortia in which a company was a member. Company information was collected from the directories identified above, and consortia information was obtained from federal register filings. We found no variation in terms of the industries and consortia represented, consortium size, or number of consortia in which a company was a member. A *t*-test did indicate that responding companies were slightly, yet significantly, larger than nonrespondents.

Second, we used the successive waves extrapolation method described by Armstrong and Overton (1977). This method assumes that information received from companies who respond only after repeated contacts resembles that of nonrespondents. In a comparison across all the variables used in this study, we found that early and late respondents diverged significantly only on the age of the consortium. Early responses tended to come from members of slightly older consortia. These analyses suggest that although our sample appears overall to be representative, the findings may be somewhat biased toward larger members and toward members of older consortia.

An additional limitation to this sample is that we rely upon a single key informant for all the information about each member. The key informant method has been widely used in IJV survey research (for example, Geringer and Hébert 1991; Parkhe 1993), and is preferable to reliance upon multiple respondents with varying familiarity about the phenomena in question (Brown and Lusch 1992). It nonetheless requires some examination of the reliability of the data obtained. We conducted three tests on the reliability of the data, none of which provides strong evidence of unreliability.[1] We therefore conclude that our reliance upon key informants has not introduced any substantial bias to our study.

Dependent Variables: Performance

To derive our measure of performance, we drew upon recent research that has examined joint venture performance from the members' perspective. In this research (Parkhe 1993; Yan and Gray 1994b), member companies were asked to weigh various criteria and evaluate the joint venture on them. The weighted values were summed to derive a single measure of performance. In our study, the informants were asked to evaluate on a seven-point scale the importance of each of thirty-one criteria for evaluating consortium performance (1 = not important, 7 = very important). A list of the measures appears in Table 6.1. These items, consisting of objective and subjective measures of input, throughput, and output, and at varying levels of analysis (including member organization and consortium), were derived from previous research and pretested with joint venture managers. Space was provided for respondents to supply additional measures, but rarely were any offered. We also asked informants to evaluate consortium performance on each measure the member organization used. For subjective criteria, this was a seven-point scale (1 = very poor, 7 = very good). For objective evaluations (for example, patents and return on investment) we asked for the actual value. To combine subjective and objective evaluations into a single composite measure, we normalized the objective measures on a seven-point scale (lowest = 1 and highest = 7). A weakness of this approach is that it may inappropriately scale the data. For example, a member organization may be as satisfied with a consortium that produces a single patent as another member is with a consortium that produces five, but the rescaling will assign the first a lower value. This classification, however, is not expected to be a significant factor. The generally lower weighting of the objective measures led to many of these indicators not being used in calculating performance. In passing, it should be noted that the average correlation between the importance of a criterion and the actual performance was quite low ($r = .13$), with only a few being significantly related. Respondents do not appear to have a preference for criteria by which the consortium excels.

We used these data to develop a single composite measure of performance. Before combining them, we first accounted for the fact that many of these thirty-one measures may not be important to the consortium members; including them would incorporate unnecessary information into the

LEVEL OF ANALYSIS

Measures	Consortium	Member Organization	Other
Percentage changes in consortium's annual budget	x		
Annual percentage of consortium research project completed	x		
Annual number of papers consortium researchers present at conferences or publish	x		
Annual number of new products developed by consortium	x		
Annual number of patents from consortium research	x		
Annual number of licensing arrangements from consortium patents	x		
Annual profitability of consortium—return on investment	x		
Planned versus actual costs of consortium research	x		
Annual number of member organizations retained	x		
Annual number of new member organizations attracted	x		
Annual number of contacts between consortium and your organization		x	x
Annual amount of time consortium research saves your organization		x	
Annual return on your organization's investment		x	
Annual percentage of consortium research results adopted by your organization		x	
Number of spinoff companies created from consortium research			x
Probability of commercial success of consortium research findings	x		
Technical quality of consortium research	x		

External reputation of consortium

Responsiveness of consortium to your organization's needs

Improvement in consortium researchers' skills and knowledge

Consortium's contribution to improvement in skills and knowledge of your organization's researchers

Consortium's contribution to improvement in your organization's competitive position

Level of cooperation among member organizations

Value of information obtained on the internal research of other member organizations

Perceived benefits to U.S. competitiveness

Perceived benefits to member organizations versus nonmembers

Equitable distribution of benefits among member organizations

Planned versus actual progress of consortium research

Planned versus actual outcomes from consortium research

Value of consortium research in comparison to your organization's internal research

Value of consortium research in comparison to your organization's other cooperative research activities

Table 6.1. R&D Consortium Performance Measures.

composite measure. Consequently, we eliminated those criteria for which the respondent did not rate above the theoretical mean (four on the seven-point scale).[2] Next, to weight the remaining criteria we multiplied the performance evaluation by the importance assigned to the criterion (either by five, six, or seven). Finally, we calculated the mean of these scores and divided by seven to rescale the measure from 1 to 7. This variable had a mean of 3.68 and a range from 1.67 to 6.7. A check on the validity of this weighted measure found that it was quite significantly correlated with a straight summing of the thirty-one performance evaluations and with the informants' responses to each of three summary measures of consortium performance (Overall, how effective is the consortium? Has it met your expectations for its research and development activities? To what degree would you change the consortium?).

Independent Variables

Our research considered several of these.

TECHNOLOGICAL LINKAGE. The technological linkage among the member organizations was derived by asking respondents whether the members generally supplied similar or different skills and know-how to the consortium. This was evaluated on a scale where 1 = similar and 7 = different. Although this was a single-item measure, an ANOVA found high within-consortium agreement on this item.

RESEARCH LOCATION. Research location was measured by asking respondents the percentage of research occurring in several possible sites: member organization, other member organizations, a consortium-owned facility, or another site. The last two represented locations where researchers from the member organizations could work together on the research. The scores for these two categories were combined to develop a measure of the percentage of research conducted in common facilities. An ANOVA showed that respondents involved in the same consortium had high agreement on the amount of research conducted in the common location.

INDUSTRY. Industry membership information came from a second survey questionnaire administered to consortium managers. For each consortium, we mailed to the highest-ranking manager a questionnaire that inquired about the consortium's management and operations. Included was an item asking about the percentage of member organizations coming from the primary industry. Of the 110 questionnaires mailed out, we received 35 usable responses (31.8 percent response rate). These provided industry membership information for 54 of the 164 consortia members. Data for the remaining consortia were derived from federal register filings. Where there were overlapping data, a significant correlation between the questionnaire measures and the archival measures confirmed the validity of the measure.

INTERNATIONAL MEMBERSHIP. A consortium's international membership was defined by the percentage of members, at the time of the survey, that came from outside the United States. This information came from federal register filings.[3]

Control Variables

The study controlled for age and size of the consortium. Prior research has found that performance may vary with the age of a venture (Anderson 1990). Size was evaluated because it has been associated with problems in formulating joint venture policies and coordinating activities (Zeira and Shenkar 1990).

AGE. Age was defined as the time since the consortium's first filing under the National Cooperative Research Act, except for consortia filed immediately after passage of the act. For these, data from archival and earlier research were used. Prior experience with this population found these to be reliable sources. This value was converted to the logarithmic value.

SIZE. Size was determined by counting the number of members listed under the NCRA at the time of the survey. The logarithmic value of this number was used in the analysis.

Results

Means, standard deviations, and correlations among the variables appear in Table 6.2.[4]

Table 6.3 reports the findings from regressing performance on the control and independent variables. Model 1 included only the control variables. The model was significant, and size had a significantly negative relationship with performance. Members of smaller consortia reported higher performance than those of larger consortia. Model 2 added the independent variables with the control variables. In this model, age was not related to performance, but consortium size remained significant. The findings for the independent variables revealed mixed support for the hypotheses.

Variable	Mean	SD	2	3	4	5	6	7
Performance (1 = Poor, 7 = Good)	3.80	0.88						
Age (Log of years since start of consortium)	1.25	0.76	1.00					
Size (Log of number of members)	3.05	1.12	.23	1.00				
Technological Linkage (1 = Similar, 7 = Different)	3.88	1.59	.03	.03	1.00			
Common Research Location (Percentage of research at one site)	60	38	.21	.09	−.08	1.00		
Industry (Percentage of members from same industry)	85	24	−.12	−.22	−.02	−.14	1.00	
International Members (Percentage of members from outside the U.S.)	10	14	−.17	.13	−.13	−.05	−.20	1.00

Table 6.2. Means, Standard Deviations (SDs), and Correlations.
Note: N = 164. Correlations of .15 and larger are significant at p < .05.

Hypothesis 1 predicts that different contributions of skills and know-how would be associated with poorer performance. However, the scale versus link relationship among the member organizations was not significantly related to performance. Hypotheses 2a and 2b address the relationship between a common research location and performance. The findings confirmed 2a, which proposes a positive relationship (the greater the percentage of research conducted in a common location, the higher the performance). The model also revealed no evidence for Hypothesis 3. The percentage of members coming from a single industry did not affect the performance of the consortium. For Hypothesis 4, in which an international consortium is predicted to be related to poorer performance, the opposite relationship was found. The more a consortium had non-U.S. partners, the higher the rating given by U.S. members.[5]

To test Hypothesis 5 and determine whether the findings were influenced by consortium- or member organization–level performance measures, we separated the thirty-one performance measures into three categories: consortium-level, member organization–level, and other. The last category included members versus nonmembers items and societal measures. Table 6.1 reports the classification of the various items. We reestimated the models using consortium-level measures and then member organization–level items. These results also appear in Table 6.3. Model 3 in the table reports the findings for consortium-level indicators. Similar to Model 2, size, location of research, and international members remained significant, but industry and technology linkage did not. For Model 4, which used performance measures only at the member organization–level and because of missing performance data had three fewer cases, when compared to Model 2 location was no longer important, but size, industry, and international members were. A multivariate comparison of the parameter estimates in Model 3 versus Model 4 revealed that the two equations were significantly different ($F = 2.95$, $p < .01$), leading to a rejection of Hypothesis 5. Consortium and member organization criteria have distinct relationships with the independent variables. An item-by-item test revealed that the primary source of the significance came from the estimates for age and industry. Older consortia and those with a lower percentage of members from the industry were evaluated higher on consortium–level criteria than on member organization-level criteria.

Conclusion

This study investigated two explanations for reconciling conflicting accounts of how member organizations' differences affect the performance

Variable	Overall Performance, Model 1	Overall Performance, Model 2	Consortium-Level Performance, Model 3	Member Organization-Level Performance, Model 4
Intercept	4.34***	3.69***	3.74***	3.58***
	(0.21)	(0.43)	(0.47)	(0.55)
Age	−0.05	−0.02	0.14	−0.15
	(0.09)	(0.09)	(0.10)	(0.12)
Size	−0.16**	−0.18***	−0.16**	−0.21**
	(0.06)	(0.06)	(0.07)	(0.08)
Technological Linkage		−0.01	−0.02	0.002
		(0.002)	(0.05)	(0.05)
Common Research Location		0.004**	0.004**	0.002
		(0.002)	(0.002)	(0.002)
Industry		0.004	0.001	0.007*
		(0.003)	(0.003)	(0.004)
International Members		1.33***	1.49***	1.33**
		(0.49)	(0.53)	(0.63)
	df = 2, 161	df = 6, 157	df = 6, 157	df^a = 6, 154
	F = 3.92	F = 3.38	F = 2.44	F = 2.98
	R^2 = .03	R^2 = .11	R^2 = .12	R^2 = .08
	p = .02	p = .004	p = .002	p = .004

Table 6.3. Regression Equations Predicting Performance
Overall and at the Consortium and Member Organization Levels.
Note: Coefficients are unstandardized. Standard errors are in parentheses.
$* p < .10$ $** p < .05$ $*** p < .01$
^{a} *Three member organizations did not use company-level measures and were not included in this analysis.*

of a joint venture. The first examined member differences (in terms of the knowledge transformation process of the consortium) and their relationship to poor performance. The second suggested that the differences are due to varying definitions of performance. The results revealed support for both explanations. Specifically, Hypothesis 1 proposed that the more a consortium receives dissimilar skills and know-how from member organizations, the poorer the performance. Failure to confirm this hypothesis suggests that any additional efforts required to integrate the distinct contributions did not adversely affect performance. For location of research, two competing hypotheses were offered. The results found evidence for 2a, which proposed a positive relationship between common research location and performance. This is consistent with the claim that a similar location provides for greater researcher interactions, more innovation, greater adaptability, and a minimization of partner conflict, leading to better performance. It did not support the alternative argument that the transformation process positively affects performance when more research is conducted in member organizations. Hypothesis 3 advanced a negative relationship between the percentage of consortium members coming from different industries and performance. The evidence did not support the idea that having more member organizations from the same industry, with comparable internal capabilities, leads to better performance.

We explored this finding in more detail because recent research (for example, Hagedoorn and Narula 1996) has shown that the relative use of joint ventures and contractual partnerships varies with industry sector and partner nationality. The measure of industry similarity does not distinguish among the various industrial sectors represented. To test whether there was variation by sector, we categorized the consortia into eleven different sectors: microelectronics, software, semiconductors, telecommunications, new materials, automotive, industrial manufacturing, steel, energy, chemicals, and other. We developed a measure of concentration of members within the sector by multiplying the percentage of members coming from the same industry by the sector. We then inserted, one at a time, each sector concentration variable into Model 2 in place of the industry measure. In almost all cases, the sector variable was not associated with performance, and its inclusion did not affect the significance of the other variables. An exception to this was for chemical-related consortia. The chemicals sector variable was positively related to performance, although it did not change the significance levels of the other predictors. This indicates that members of a consortium with a higher percentage of companies coming from the chemicals sector reported better performance. However, in general, performance does not appear to be dependent upon the sector to which the member organizations belong.

For the final dimension of similarity studied, nationality, the results contradicted the hypothesized relationship that domestic consortia would perform better than international consortia. Even though the performance evaluation came from U.S. managers, membership in a consortium consisting of only U.S. organizations was rated lower than membership in a consortium with non-U.S. members.

This unusual result runs counter to much of the literature on international joint ventures that documents the difficulty of cross-border management. One possible explanation is that with non-U.S. organizations involved in a consortium, U.S. members may act differently compared to consortia composed only of domestic members. The U.S. Congress passed the National Cooperative Research Act because of concerns over the long-term competitiveness of domestic companies, relative to their foreign counterparts. The U.S. companies may also have these concerns, even though they permit a non-U.S. organization to join, and may manage their involvement in a consortium more cautiously. However, nonreported correlations between the presence of international members with variables indicating U.S. members' activities—assets contributed, level of trust in the consortium, level of communication, commitment to the consortium—were not significant. Another explanation is that international consortia may vary in terms of the type of research conducted. Correlations between variables measuring nature of technology and nationality, however, were not significant. Although international membership was related to age (younger), it was not related to any perceivable differences in research agenda. The findings also do not appear to be an artifact of the cross-sectional nature of the data. Foreign participants were almost always members of a consortium from the beginning and were not joining already successful U.S. consortia. Finally, coding consortia by industry revealed no distinctive relationship between international membership and performance.

Finding that the performance differences do not stem from characteristics of the consortium nor from the behavior of the U.S. members suggests that the source may be the foreign participants. These members may provide unique contributions not supplied by domestic members. As noted earlier, nationality represents the approach to organizing. With joint ventures, this includes the experience or knowledge of how to cooperate. The U.S. has less experience with R&D consortia than either Japan (Ouchi and Bolton 1988) or Europe (Jorde and Teece 1988). Further, the U.S. consortium approach varies from the approach used in Japan (Aldrich and Sasaki 1995), where some of the foreign members in this sample originate. The better performance may stem from non-U.S. members contributing technical or organizational skills that lead to a more effective consortium.

To investigate this explanation, we categorized the foreign members by regions, noting whether they came from North America, Europe, Japan, or elsewhere. Because a consortium could have member organizations from more than one region, we calculated the relationship with performance for each region separately and in conjunction with the other regions. The results revealed performance was positively related to the presence of European member organizations, when no other regions were represented. The presence of member organizations from Japan, North America, or other regions was not associated with performance. One explanation for this finding suggests an interactive relationship may exist between collaborative experience and cultural distance. Although Japanese companies have been cited for their propensity to form strategic alliances (Parkhe 1991), and have been noted for taking unique approaches toward organizing joint ventures (Cullen, Johnson, and Sakano 1995), the cultural distance between Japan and the U.S. may be too great for this experience to be of value to the U.S. party. The cultural distance between Europe and the U.S. is generally considered to be smaller, and has been associated with the tendency to rely on more informal control arrangements in U.S.-European alliances than U.S.-Japan (Hagedoorn and Narula 1996). For consortia, which are all equity arrangements, cultural distance may influence the nature of knowledge exchange, with the greater proximity of European members increasing the likelihood of transferring consortium organizing skills to the U.S. members.

Hypothesis 5 proposed that these relationships would remain constant for both consortium-level variables and member organization–level measures, yet this study found a significant variation between the two models. The consortium level of performance was significantly predicted by size, common location, and international membership, while for the member-organization level of performance the significant indicators were size, industry, and international membership. The evidence confirms the assertion that factors leading to an effective joint venture organization are not necessarily the same as those leading to effective membership in the joint venture. In the present study, the difference appears to be due to age of the consortium and industry. The finding for age is consistent with life cycle explanations that argue that as an IJV matures, it develops routines and experiences that further facilitate its development (Lyles 1988). For industry, the data suggest that members may receive greater benefits from working with others from within the industry, although this does not necessarily translate into a more effective consortium. That is, a consortium consisting of members from the same industry may leverage the contributions of others. Although the leveraging does not improve the effectiveness at the consortium level, individual consortium members may benefit from the contributions of others. Additional research should explore the nature of this interaction to better understand this relationship.

Future research should also investigate these issues by going beyond some of the limitations of the current data. The data came from U.S. managers of U.S.-based R&D consortia. Consortia represent a unique type of alliance, characterized by multiple members and a focus on precompetitive activity. For IJVs pursuing other activities, issues of location, industry representation, and nationality may have another relationship with performance. Non-U.S. managers may also evaluate a consortium in a distinct manner. Additionally, other variables on the input-output continuum beyond those used in this study should be considered. Even with these limitations, this chapter makes several significant contributions to our understanding of the management of international joint ventures. The first is that member organization differences affect performance in a far more complex manner than has generally been considered. By providing the first test of multiple dimensions of member differences, the study demonstrated that these differences do not act in a uniform manner. A smaller difference in the research location, a measure of throughput similarity, was associated with better performance, but so was a larger difference in nationality among member organizations. Meanwhile, technological linkage and similar industry, indicators of input and output similarity, had no relationship.

The second contribution is that by using criteria representing multiple dimensions of performance and by restricting the evaluation to those measures respondents believed were important, this study provides a much more detailed measure of performance of international joint ventures than has been generally used. In doing so, this is the first study to distinguish between performance at the consortium level and at the member-organization level. It also revealed that although some predictors significantly relate to measures at both levels, others did not, offering evidence that IJV researchers need to be careful in defining performance.

Finally, this study provides the first empirical evaluation of the effectiveness of R&D consortia and its relationship to member characteristics. In selecting potential members, this study's findings suggest that organizers need to consider the location of the research and members' nationalities. Particularly interesting is that for nationality, the findings run counter to the practice advocated by some managers and government officials of restricting membership to domestic organizations. Opening up membership to foreign organizations, especially European members, may lead to better performance for the U.S. members. The foreign member may be a source of technical and organizational skills that lead to improved consortium and member performance.

In addition to the aforementioned issues, future efforts should extend this research by exploring further the behavioral interactions among the member organizations. This study, using a combination of archival and survey data, investigated how differences in the characteristics of the members related to performance. The next step is to examine how these characteristics translate into member interactions and how these subsequently affect IJV performance. By pursuing these issues, researchers will help to develop a deeper theoretical understanding of the significance of partner differences for an IJV and the practical implications of these differences on performance.

NOTES

1. Consistent with research on evaluating the reliability of a single informant (Kumar, Stern, and Anderson 1993), we examined respondents' knowledge on multiple global indicators. First, we examined whether there was any influence due to inadequate knowledge about the company's membership in the consortium. To test this, we reran the analyses using only those informants who had been involved in the consortium for more than a year. The findings are identical to those we report. Second, we examined whether respondents' position in the consortium or the organization might influence the knowledge about membership. We separated respondents based on their self-reported position in their own organization and on their affiliation with the consortium. The positions were collapsed into upper management, middle management, and lower management. Most respondents (78 percent) reported coming from middle management in their organization, but held an upper-management position in the consortium (81 percent). Comparisons across these three levels on the measures used in this study found no significant differences. Third, for consortia with more than one respondent, we compared informants' responses on the survey questions requesting consortium-level information. The items included the nature of the consortium's research. Separate ANOVAs found intraconsortium consensus significantly higher than consensus across-consortium ($p < .05$).

2. As a precaution, we reran the results using criteria weighted above a value of 3, on a 7-point scale, and again with criteria weighted above a value of 5. The direction and significance of the coefficients of the variables were

identical to those reported in Model 2 of Table 6.3. These findings indicate that the relationships reported are not an artifact of the weighting scheme. An attempt to analyze the relationship using only those criteria weighted with a 7 resulted in a loss of half of the sample. Many respondents did not rate at least one criterion a 7, which led to there being no performance measure.

3. Although in most cases it was not difficult to distinguish between foreign and domestic members, there was ambiguity in a few instances. For these cases, unless there was compelling reason for believing the members were foreign, they were coded as domestic. We also conducted the analyses using a simple dichotomous variable of a 1 if at least one member was from outside the U.S. and a 0 if none were foreign. Because most of the ambiguous cases occurred in consortia with other foreign companies, this coding was more reliable. The direction and significance level for the international variable when using this more conservative coding scheme were identical to those reported in Tables 6.2 and 6.3.

4. The significant correlations among some of the independent variables suggest multicollinearity may influence the findings. To test this, we reran the analyses inserting each of the correlated variables one at a time. The results do not differ from those reported.

5. As one participant at the conference noted, member organization differences may be compensated for by intensive integration efforts. Including frequency of communication—both for among member organizations and for between the consortium and the member organization—as an additional control in the regression equations did not affect the findings reported in Table 6.3.

BIBLIOGRAPHY

Aldrich, H., and T. Sasaki. 1995. R&D consortia in the United States and Japan. *Research Policy,* 24(2): 301–326.

Anderson, E. 1990. Two firms, one frontier: On assessing joint venture performance. *Sloan Management Review,* Winter: 19–30.

Armstrong, J. S., and T. S. Overton. 1977. Estimating nonresponse bias in mail surveys. *Journal of Marketing Research,* 51: 71–86.

Baird, I., M. Lyles, and R. Wharton. 1990. Attitudinal differences between American and Chinese managers regarding joint venture management. *Management International Review,* 30: 53–68.

Beamish, P. W. 1985. The characteristics of joint ventures in developed and developing countries. *Columbia Journal of World Business,* Fall: 13–19.

Beamish, P. W., and A. Delios. 1997. Improving joint venture performance through congruent measures of success. In P. W. Beamish and J. P. Killing, editors, *Cooperative Strategies: European Perspectives*. San Francisco: New Lexington Press.

Blodgett, L. 1992. Factors in the instability of international joint ventures. *Strategic Management Journal*, 13: 475–481.

Brown, J., and R. Lusch. 1992. Using key informants in marketing channels research: A critique and some preliminary guidelines. In G. Frazier, editor, *Advances in Distribution Channel Research*. Greenwich, Conn.: JAI Press.

Browning, L., J. Beyer, and J. Shelter. 1995. Building cooperation in a competitive industry: SEMATECH and the semiconductor industry. *Academy of Management Journal*, 38: 113–151.

Cohen, W., R. Levin, and D. Mowery. 1987. Firm size and R&D intensity: A re-examination. *The Journal of Industrial Economics*, 35: 543–565.

Cohen, W., and D. Levinthal. 1990. Absorptive capacity: A new perspective on learning and innovation. *Administrative Science Quarterly*, 35(1): 128–152.

Contractor, F. 1984. Strategies for structuring joint ventures: A negotiation planning paradigm. *Columbia Journal of World Business*, 19 (Summer): 30–39.

Cullen, J., J. Johnson, and T. Sakano. 1995. Japanese and local partner commitment to IJVs: Psychological consequences of outcomes and investments in the IJV relationship. *Journal of International Business Studies*, 26(1): 91–115.

Dailey, R. C. 1980. A path analysis of R&D team coordination and performance. *Decision Sciences*, 11: 357–369.

Geringer, J. M. 1988. *Joint Venture Partner Selection: Strategies for Developed Countries*. New York: Quorum Books.

Geringer, J. M., and L. Hébert. 1989. Control and performance of international joint ventures. *Journal of International Business Studies*, 20(2): 235–254.

Geringer, J. M., and L. Hébert. 1991. Measuring performance of international joint ventures. *Journal of International Business Studies*, 22(2): 249–263.

Gibson, D., and E. Rogers. 1994. *R&D Collaboration on Trial*. Boston: Harvard Business School Press.

Gomes-Casseres, B. 1987. Joint venture instability: Is it a problem? *Columbia Journal of World Business*, Summer: 71–77.

Gomes-Casseres, B. 1989. Joint ventures in the face of global competition. *Sloan Management Review*, Spring: 17–26.

Gray, B., and A. Yan. 1992. A negotiations model of joint venture formation, structure and performance: Implications for global management. *Advances in International Comparative Management,* 7: 41–75.

Grindley, P., D. Mowery, and B. Silverman. 1994. SEMATECH and collaborative research: Lessons in the design of high-technology consortia. *Journal of Policy Analysis and Management,* 13: 723–758.

Hagedoorn, J., and R. Narula. 1996. Choosing organizational modes of strategic technology partnering: International and sectoral differences. *Journal of International Business Studies,* 27(2): 265–284.

Hamel, G. 1991. Competition for competence and inter-partner learning within international strategic alliances. *Strategic Management Journal,* 12: 83–103.

Harrigan, K. 1985. *Strategies for Joint Ventures.* San Francisco: New Lexington Press.

Hennart, J.-F. 1988. A transaction cost theory of equity joint ventures. *Strategic Management Journal,* 9: 361–374.

Jorde, T., and D. Teece. 1988. *Innovation, Cooperation and Antitrust.* Monograph. University of California, Berkeley.

Killing, J. P. 1983. *Strategies for Joint Venture Success.* New York: Praeger.

Kogut, B. 1991. Joint ventures and the option to expand and acquire. *Management Science,* 37(1): 19–33.

Kumar, N., L. Stern, and J. Anderson. 1993. Conducting interorganizational research using key informants. *Academy of Management Journal,* 36: 1633–1651.

Lane, H., and P. Beamish. 1990. Cross-cultural cooperative behavior in joint ventures in LDCs. *Management International Review,* 30: 87–102.

Lorange, P., and G. Probst. 1987. Joint ventures as self-organizing systems: A key to successful joint venture design and implementation. *Columbia Journal of World Business,* Summer: 71–77.

Lyles, M. 1988. Learning among joint venture sophisticated firms. In F. J. Contractor and P. Lorange, editors, *Cooperative Strategies in International Business,* 301–316. San Francisco: New Lexington Press.

Olson, L. B., and K. Singsuwan. 1997. The effect of partnership, communication, and conflict resolution behaviors on performance success of strategic alliances: American and Thai perspectives. In P. W. Beamish and J. P. Killing, editors, *Cooperative Strategies: Asian Pacific Perspectives.* San Francisco: New Lexington Press.

Osborn, R., and C. C. Baughn. 1990. Forms of interorganizational governance for multinational alliances. *Academy of Management Journal,* 33: 503–519.

Ouchi, W., and M. Bolton. 1988. The logic of joint research and development. *California Management Review,* Spring: 9–33.

Parkhe, A. 1991. Interfirm diversity, organizational learning, and longevity in global strategic alliances. *Journal of International Business Studies,* 22: 579–601.

Parkhe, A. 1993. Partner nationality and the structure-performance relationship in strategic alliances. *Organization Science,* 4: 301–324.

Schaan, J.-L., and P. Beamish. 1988. Joint venture general managers in LDCs. In F. J. Contractor and P. Lorange, editors, *Cooperative Strategies in International Business,* 297–300. San Francisco: New Lexington Press.

Smilor, R., and D. Gibson. 1992. Building a technology transfer infrastructure. In D. Gibson and R. Smilor, editors, *Technology Transfer in Consortia and Strategic Alliances,* 129–149. Lanham, Md.: Rowman and Littlefield.

Thomas, J., and L. K. Trevino. 1993. Information processing in strategic alliance building: A multiple-case approach. *Journal of Management Studies,* 30(5): 779–814.

Yan, A., and B. Gray. 1994a. Bargaining power, management control, and performance in United States–China joint ventures: A comparative case study. *Academy of Management Review,* 37: 1478–1517.

Yan, A., and B. Gray. 1994b. The determinants of management control and performance in international joint ventures: An empirical test. Paper presented at the Academy of Management Annual Meeting, Dallas.

Zeira, Y., and O. Shenkar. 1990. Interactive and specific parent characteristics: Implications for management and human resources in international joint ventures. *Management International Review,* 30: 7–22.

PART THREE

DYNAMICS OF PARTNER RELATIONSHIPS

7

TRUST AND PERFORMANCE IN CROSS-BORDER MARKETING PARTNERSHIPS

A Behavioral Approach

Preet S. Aulakh, Masaaki Kotabe, and Arvind Sahay

EXISTING RESEARCH ON *international partnerships focuses primarily on the* ex ante *structuring of interorganizational relationships. This chapter departs from that by taking a behavioral approach to understanding the* ex post *maintenance of cross-border marketing partnerships. A conceptual model is developed by identifying the antecedents of trust and performance in such partnerships; it is then empirically tested on a sample of U.S. firms having distributor and licensing relationships with firms from Asia, Europe, and Central and South America. The findings support the importance of bilateral relational norms and informal monitoring mechanisms in building interorganizational trust and improving market performance of international partnerships.*

The authors thank the editors, three anonymous reviewers, and participants at the Global Cooperative Strategies Conference held at London, Ontario, for their valuable suggestions on earlier versions of this chapter. Partial support for this project was provided through the Associates Fund at Memorial University of Newfoundland and the Center for International Business Education and Research at the University of Texas at Austin.

THE GLOBALIZATION OF THE business environment and the need to compete simultaneously in multiple markets have led to the proliferation of interfirm marketing partnerships across national borders. For instance, manufacturing firms are using distribution or licensing partnerships with foreign companies to access complementary marketing skills, make quick entry into foreign markets, reduce risks and costs of doing business in foreign markets, and circumvent tariff and nontariff barriers, among other things (Contractor and Lorange 1988; Kotabe and Swan 1995). In these partnerships, the manufacturing firm (hereafter referred to as the focal firm) depends upon the foreign distributor or licensee to penetrate the market and achieve adequate sales growth and market share for its products. Given that the focal firm's success in a given foreign market is intertwined with the performance of the partnership, a major challenge for its management is to ensure that the partner firm conforms to its contractual obligations to optimize partnership performance.

The importance of managing cross-border interorganizational partnerships is reflected in the extensive literature on this topic, which has focused primarily on the *ex ante* structuring of cross-border partnerships (see Parkhe 1993a for a review). For instance, a number of studies have examined the rationale for international partnerships, including joint ventures (such as Contractor and Lorange 1988; Hagedoorn 1993), partner selection and characteristics (such as Geringer 1991; Parkhe 1993c), and performance effects of ownership control in such partnerships (such as Beamish 1985; Geringer and Hébert 1989). The underlying premise of these studies is that choosing the appropriate partner, aligning strategic and economic incentives of the partner firms, and using ownership control are critical determinants of partnership success, and mitigate the risk of opportunistic behavior inherent in interorganizational relationships. Though this research stream provides important insights into the structuring of cross-border partnerships, it sheds little light on the appropriate maintenance of existing relationships. It is assumed that a firm may choose from among many prospective foreign partners and that it has the scanning capability to make the optimal choice. However, evidence indicates that the choice is sometimes mandated by the host government, or that the optimal partner may not be selected because, as the partnership is being initiated, information asymmetries exist about long-term partner objectives. In these cases, the critical determinant of partnership success becomes the *ex post* maintenance of the partnership.

A second stream of research on cross-border partnerships complements the structural approach described above by explicitly considering the behavioral dimensions of maintaining interorganizational partnerships (such as Beamish and Banks 1987; Bradach and Eccles 1989; Casson 1992; Hill 1990; Madhok 1995). The behavioral element of importance in these studies is trust, for according to Casson (p. 11), "in a high-trust environment the true nature of economic relations cannot be inferred from the ownership structure because the relations that really matter exist in the social fabric beneath." Thus, trust has the potential of enhancing our understanding of the dynamics and performance of interorganizational relationships.

The purpose of this chapter is to extend this behavioral approach by identifying the antecedents of trust in cross-border marketing partnerships and examining the relationship between trust and performance. The choices for a firm in organizing its foreign marketing activities can be viewed along a continuum of markets and hierarchies (Heide and John 1992; Webster 1992). Between the extremes of one-time spot transactions and vertically integrated hierarchies, there exist various intermediate forms, including repeated transactions, strategic alliances or joint ventures, and networks. All these intermediate forms share one fundamental property: long-term relationships with one or more foreign firms (Thorelli 1986; Webster 1992). We define partnership in this chapter to mean any long-term relationship that exists between two firms. In particular, the focus is on two specific types of marketing partnerships: manufacturer–foreign distributor and licensor–foreign licensee.

This chapter builds on previous research on four aspects. First, it explicitly examines the behavioral determinants of interfirm trust, which has been identified as an important alternative to hierarchical exchanges (that is, ownership-based control). Second, it explores the different types of monitoring mechanisms available to the focal firm that are functional substitutes of control and enforcement, normally considered to be achieved through ownership in vertically integrated hierarchies (Grossman and Hart 1986; Noordewier, John, and Nevin 1990). Third, the chapter examines the effects of trust on partnership performance. Fourth, the conceptual model is empirically tested on a sample of U.S. firms' partnerships with foreign firms in Asia, Europe, and Central and South America.

The rest of the chapter is organized as follows. In the next section, the conceptual model is introduced through a survey of the relevant literature. This is followed by the development of specific research hypotheses to be empirically tested. Next, after reviewing the research method used, we report the results of the empirical tests. The last section discusses the implications of the findings along with our study's limitations and directions for future research.

Conceptual Model and Research Hypotheses

The Role of Trust in Interorganizational Partnerships

Trust has been examined in a wide variety of organizational and social settings and, accordingly, conceptualized in different ways (see Hosmer 1995 for a review). For instance, trust in interpersonal relations is defined as the willingness of one person to increase his or her vulnerability to the actions of another person (for example, Zand 1972); in economic exchanges as the expectation that parties will make a good faith effort to behave in accordance with any commitments, be honest in negotiations, and not take advantage of the other, even when the opportunity is available (Hosmer 1995); and in society as a collective attribute based upon the relationships in a social system (Lewis and Weigert 1985). A review of the literature examining trust points to two issues relevant to this discussion. First, just as trust can exist between individuals, with expectations of behavior on both sides, it can also exist between organizations because individuals manage interorganizational relationships (see, for example, Bradach and Eccles 1989; Hosmer 1995). Thus, as suggested by Madhok (1995) and Thorelli (1986), trust in interfirm relationships includes a set of expectations between partners about the behavior of each and about the anticipation that each will fulfill its perceived obligations. Second, the literature suggests that the "expectations of behavior" between exchange partners has two components: structural and behavioral (Hosmer 1995; Madhok 1995). The structural component refers to trust fostered by mutual "hostages" and the complementarity contributed by the partners (Madhok 1995). As suggested by Madhok, this structural dimension may be essential for the creation of the relationship but is not sufficient for its continuation, as one partner may become more vulnerable in the relationship because of unequal dependence.

The behavioral component of trust in exchange relationships has to do with confidence. Moorman, Deshpande, and Zaltman (1993: 82), for instance, define trust as "a willingness to rely on an exchange partner in whom one has confidence." Similarly, Anderson and Narus (1990: 45) focus on this aspect of trust by defining it as a "firm's belief that another company will perform actions that will result in positive outcomes for the firm as well as not take unexpected actions that result in negative outcomes." This is especially critical in maintaining ongoing relationships, as cooperation is achieved not through structural vulnerability but through the partners' confidence in the integrity of each other. Thus, following Morgan and Hunt (1994), we focus on the behavioral dimension by conceptualizing trust in a partnership as the degree of confidence the individual partners have on the reliability and integrity of each other.

Existing literature identifies three interrelated roles of trust in interorganizational exchanges. First, trust is an important deterrent to opportunistic behavior (Bradach and Eccles 1989). Because interorganizational partnerships involve two or more firms that try to balance individual gains with joint partnership performance, without trust there is a strong probability that a partner would sacrifice joint goals in favor of individual benefits, especially when such behavior is not transparent to the other firm. But if trust is in place, such opportunistic behavior is unlikely; partners will pass up short-term individual gains in favor of the long-term interests of the partnership (Axelrod 1986; Beamish and Banks 1987; Stinchcombe 1986). It should be noted that other factors also reduce opportunistic behavior: partners will likely forbear in a mutual hostage situation (Buckley and Casson 1988), or if one fears the other will also become opportunistic—the "tit for tat" possibility in game theory (Parkhe 1993b). However, unlike the structural approach where the *ability* of partner firms to behave opportunistically is curbed, in a trust-based approach the *motivation* for opportunistic behavior is minimized because "behavioral repertoires are biased toward cooperation, rather than opportunism" (Hill 1990: 511).

Second, trust can substitute for hierarchical governance, thus accomplishing interfirm organizational objectives when ownership-based control is not strategically viable or economically feasible. Unlike hierarchical exchanges, where formal authority structures based on ownership are used to enforce contractual obligations, trust-based exchanges rely on mutuality of interests between partner firms (Bradach and Eccles 1989; Dwyer, Schurr, and Oh 1987). Trust allows for bilateral governance that achieves the individual goals of independent firms by way of a partnership's joint accomplishments, shared beliefs, and mutual concern for long-term benefits (Heide 1994; Ouchi 1980).

Third, besides deterring opportunism and giving an alternative to ownership control, partnership trust has important market performance and efficiency implications, according to some research (Bleeke and Ernst 1991; Parkhe 1993b; Wilkins and Ouchi 1983).

All the literature cited above strongly points to the importance of trust in achieving behavioral and market performance objectives in interorganizational partnerships, especially across borders where hierarchical control may not be a viable alternative. However, little systematic research attention has been given to identifying the determinants of interorganizational trust. The purpose of this chapter is to fill this important gap in the literature by simultaneously identifying the antecedents of trust in cross-border

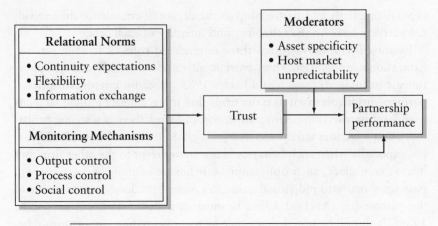

Figure 7.1. Conceptual Model of Interorganizational Trust.

marketing partnerships and formally examining the trust-performance relationship that has been implicit in previous research. The proposed conceptual model is provided in Figure 7.1.

Research Hypotheses

Building trust in cross-border partnerships can generally be accomplished over time. As trust involves expectations about future behavior, it is necessarily guided by the past behavior of exchange partners. Partner firms have to learn about each other's ways of doing business and to interpret each other's acts (Håkansson and Johanson 1988). It is proposed that bilateral relational norms between partner firms as well as the unilateral monitoring mechanisms used by the focal firm are both representations of past interactions and therefore are important determinants of trust and performance in cross-border partnerships.[1]

Relational norms are defined as expectations about behavior shared by a group of decision makers (Thibaut and Kelley 1959; Heide and John 1992) that "provide guidelines for the initial probes that potential exchange partners may make towards each other" (Scanzoni 1979: 68). According to Dwyer, Schurr, and Oh (1987: 17), "by adopting norms and establishing standards of conduct, emerging exchange partners start setting the ground rules for future exchange." Thus relational norms prescribe acceptable behavior at the onset of partnerships; if considered equitable by the partner firms, they eventually lead to future expectations of trust (Ring and Van de

Ven 1992). Although a number of different overlapping relational norms have been identified in various disciplines, in marketing partnerships the three norms of continuity expectations, flexibility, and information exchange are particularly important (Heide and John 1992; Kumar, Scheer, and Steenkamp 1995) and are therefore considered in this chapter.

The norm of continuity expectations is the mutual recognition that the relationship will continue. As such a norm develops, exchange partners achieve a level of satisfaction with the relationship and thus do not look for alternative partners (Anderson and Weitz 1989; Dwyer, Schurr, and Oh 1987). Continuity expectation is analogous to the behavioral commitment in cross-border partnerships suggested by Cullen, Johnson, and Sakano (1995). It has the effect of encouraging partner firms to "perceive cooperation not as a means but an end in itself" (Buckley and Casson 1988: 39). The expectation of continuity is hypothesized to be positively related to trust because it extends the time in which mutual benefits will be received, and this leads partners to pass up short-term gains in the interest of the long-term viability of the relationship. Furthermore, it allows for long-term scenario planning by both partners. Thus, as suggested by Buckley and Casson (1988), commitment in the relationship leads to higher market performance of the partnership.[2] Based on the above arguments, the following hypotheses are proposed:

HYPOTHESIS 1A: A bilateral norm of continuity expectations is positively related to the trust in the partnership.

HYPOTHESIS 1B: A bilateral norm of continuity expectations is positively related to the market performance of the partnership.

The norm of flexibility in a partnership is defined as the willingness to make adjustments as circumstances change (Heide and John 1992). Flexibility is particularly important in cross-border relationships because partner firms often operate in diverse political, cultural, and economic environments, thus making relationship adjustments imperative to deal with different and changing environmental conditions. Furthermore, partner firms are often called upon to react to unforeseen changes. Bleeke and Ernst (1991), in their study of forty-nine cross-border partnerships, found that alliances characterized by a high degree of flexibility evolved better in the face of unexpected contingencies arising from changes in strategies, skills, and resources of partner firms. Thus, it is proposed that a norm of flexibility is positively related to trust because it creates a stock of goodwill (Madhok

1995), as well as enhance market performance by allowing the firms to better respond to changing operating conditions. Accordingly:

HYPOTHESIS 2A: A bilateral norm of flexibility is positively related to the trust in the partnership.

HYPOTHESIS 2B: A bilateral norm of flexibility is positively related to the market performance of the partnership.

The norm of information exchange in interorganizational partnerships is defined as the "formal and informal sharing of meaningful and timely information between firms" (Anderson and Narus 1990: 44). Such exchanges foster trust (Morgan and Hunt 1994; Moorman, Deshpande, and Zaltman 1993) because communication helps to resolve disputes and align perceptions and expectations. Furthermore, the expectation of getting all information on an ongoing basis enables the partner firms to cope better with internal processes and external market conditions (Heide and John 1992). Based on these arguments, the following two hypotheses are proposed:

HYPOTHESIS 3A: A bilateral norm of information exchange is positively related to the trust in the partnership.

HYPOTHESIS 3B: A bilateral norm of information exchange is positively related to the market performance of the partnership.

Monitoring Mechanisms

Besides developing bilateral relational norms to build trust and enhance market performance in cross-border partnerships, the focal firm can also use appropriate unilateral monitoring mechanisms to achieve the same objectives.[3] Conceptually, monitoring of the foreign partner involves establishing the extent to which contractual compliance has taken place (Heide 1994). Most research based on transaction cost economics has assumed that the ability to monitor and control is dependent on the degree of ownership of the focal firm, but there is growing evidence that various types of monitoring mechanisms with fundamentally different properties, independent of ownership, can also be put into place (for examples, see Gencturk and Aulakh 1995; Heide 1994). These mechanisms provide the enforcement function normally achieved in hierarchical exchanges (Noordewier, John, and Nevin 1990) and have both behavioral and performance consequences (Anderson and Oliver 1987; Jaworski 1988).

Organizational theory research suggests that monitoring by the focal firm can be accomplished externally by explicitly measuring outputs or behavior of the partner, or internally by aligning the incentives of decision makers to reduce the performance measurement altogether (Heide 1994). In particular, three types of monitoring mechanisms are identified: output control, process control, and social control. Output and process controls are considered different types of formal controls, as they represent focal firm–initiated mechanisms generally linked to specific economic and behavioral outcomes, respectively (Anderson and Oliver 1987). Output control is in place when the focal firm monitors the results or outcomes produced by the foreign partner; process control is in place when the focal firm monitors the partner's behavior—that is, what means the partner uses to achieve the desired ends. Social control is the establishment of an organizational context that encourages self-control by the partner firm. Thus, instead of prescribing specific outcomes, social control involves building a common organizational culture (Ouchi 1979) and performance is viewed as a social obligation maintained via mechanisms of social pressure (Jaeger 1983).

With an output-based monitoring mechanism, the focal firm shifts the risk to the foreign partner by prescribing specific performance goals for it (Bergen, Dutta, and Walker 1992; Eisenhardt 1989). But this encourages the partner to assume a loner attitude, because such control does not offer protection against downside risk (Anderson and Oliver 1987). Hopwood (1972) suggests that heavy reliance by the focal firm on quantitative measures of performance tends to increase the agent's tension, leading to poorer behavioral relations with the focal firm. Output controls may encourage foreign partners to seek immediate payoffs at the expense of the partnership's long-term goals; thus:

HYPOTHESIS 4A: The use of output control by the focal firm to monitor the foreign partner is negatively related to the trust in the partnership.

HYPOTHESIS 4B: The use of output control by the focal firm to monitor the foreign partner is negatively related to the market performance of the partnership.

Process-controlled relationships require active involvement by the focal firm management, which provides the inputs the foreign partner needs to achieve partnership goals. As the focal firm prescribes specific behaviors, it assumes all the risk. Such acceptance of risk sends a positive signal to the partner and diminishes motivations for opportunistic behavior. Furthermore, process control tends to result in supportive, yet more bureaucratic and formalized, relationships than output controls, thus reducing the uncertainty faced by the partner. Process control is also expected to enhance the market performance of the partnership, because such behavioral monitoring mechanisms reward long-term outlook by removing pressures and incentives to sacrifice long-term results for immediate results (Anderson and Oliver 1987). Accordingly, the following hypotheses are proposed:

HYPOTHESIS 5A: The use of process control by the focal firm to monitor the foreign partner is positively related to the trust in the partnership.

HYPOTHESIS 5B: The use of process control by the focal firm to monitor the foreign partner is positively related to the market performance of the partnership.

Social control is an informal control mechanism that operates by establishing an organizational context or culture wherein the need for formal measurement of outcomes or behaviors is greatly reduced (Ouchi 1979). Dalton (1971) suggests that informal controls can provide both the implicit rules and supportive structures needed to facilitate role understanding in organizational exchanges. The social identity theory further posits that social control is conducive to shared beliefs and mutual identification by the partner firms (Ashforth and Miles 1989). Accordingly, in socially controlled partnerships, monitoring occurs through interpersonal interactions, and these repeated interactions over time lead to systematized and shared organizational values that help build trust between the partners. The achievement of long-term economic performance is also enhanced through social control. Through the process of socialization and indoctrination, the focal firm allows wide latitude to the partner firm, enabling the latter to respond to conditions quickly and in a manner consistent with the goals and objectives of the partnership. Therefore:

HYPOTHESIS 6A: The use of social control by the focal firm to monitor the foreign partner is positively related to the trust in the partnership.

HYPOTHESIS 6B: The use of social control by the focal firm to monitor the foreign partner is positively related to the market performance of the partnership.

Relationship Between Trust and Performance

As discussed earlier, partnership trust is likely to be positively related to market performance. This has been empirically supported in a variety of intra- and interorganizational contexts (such as Crosby, Evans, and Cowles 1990; Robicheaux and Coleman 1994) and also suggested in cross-border partnerships (such as Madhok 1995; Parkhe 1993a). Similar to these studies, we propose:

HYPOTHESIS 7: Trust is positively related to the partnership's market performance.

Trust has generally been conceptualized as the opposite of opportunism (Morgan and Hunt 1994; Parkhe 1993b), but Bradach and Eccles (1989) propose that the risk of it must nevertheless be present for trust to have meaningful consequences—in other words, trust becomes important only when there is risk of opportunistic behavior by the partners. In particular, from the focal firm's perspective its investment in idiosyncratic assets specific to its relationship with the foreign partner creates a dependence that can be exploited by the partner (Heide and John 1992). Similarly, as stated by Madhok (1995: 120), "trust is especially important in situations of uncertainty since, in its presence, less stringent contracting can occur in the expectation that social dimensions of the relationship will occasion mutually desirable behavior." Noordewier, John, and Nevin (1990) found that having shared beliefs in times of external uncertainty improves performance in buyer-vendor relationships. In view of these studies, the moderator effects of two variables—asset specificity and host market unpredictability—are proposed to influence the trust-performance relationship in cross-border partnerships:

HYPOTHESIS 8: The positive relationship between trust and market performance is stronger when there is high asset specificity from the perspective of the focal firm.

HYPOTHESIS 9: The positive relationship between trust and market performance is stronger when there is high host market unpredictability.

Method

Research Setting and Data Collection

The data for our study were collected by a mail survey of Fortune 500 U.S. industrial firms and their major affiliates. This target sample was considered appropriate because it consists of multinational firms that are actively involved internationally and thus likely to have distribution or licensing partnerships with foreign firms. Data were collected in two stages. During the first, introductory participation request letters, along with a summary of the proposed research and a promise to share the findings and provide comparative benchmark results tailored to individual firms, were sent to the presidents or CEOs of the Fortune 500 firms and their major affiliates. They were asked to provide the names and addresses of managers directly responsible for international operations. As a result, 652 potential informants were identified.[4]

In the second stage, a questionnaire was mailed to the 652 managers, along with a personalized cover letter explaining the nature of the study and informing them that their names had been provided by their company heads. The managers were asked to choose either a distributor or a licensee in a foreign country with which their respective firm has an ongoing relationship, and to respond to several questions about that relationship. After two follow-up letters, 257 completed questionnaires were received, a response rate of 39.4 percent. The respondents held upper-management positions (six presidents, seventy-two directors, eighty-four vice presidents, and ninety-five area or general managers), and had an average of 11.7 years of experience with the current firm and 8.2 years of experience making decisions in the foreign country they had selected. These characteristics suggest that the respondents are likely to be familiar with their firm's foreign operations and would be involved in making decisions about the selected foreign partnerships.

Two important issues have been raised concerning survey research methodology: first, nonresponse bias could lead to a systematic exclusion of firms from the population, and second, common method variance (Podsakoff and Organ 1986). Nonresponse bias was assessed in two ways. First, following the procedure suggested by Armstrong and Overton (1977), *t*-tests were performed comparing early and late respondents on key variables. No significant differences were found between early and late respondents on the international experience of the firms and firm size. Second, industry representation of firms in the sample was similar to the Fortune 500 sample. Harman's one-factor test was used to address the common method variance issue. If common method variance were a serious problem in the study, we would expect a single factor to emerge from a factor analysis or one general factor to account for most of the covariance in the independent and criterion variables (Podsakoff and Organ 1986). We performed factor analysis on items related to the six independent variables and two dependent measures, extracting eight factors with eigenvalues greater than one. Furthermore, no general factor was apparent in the unrotated factor structure, with Factor One accounting for only 22 percent of the variance.

The primary interest of this study was to examine interorganizational distribution and licensing partnerships of U.S. firms in three regions: Asia, Europe, and Central and South America. Thus only the 181 marketing partnerships that belong to these three regions were considered (99 in Asia, 51 in Europe, and 31 in Central and South America). The characteristics of the sample are summarized in Table 7.1. Subsequent data analyses are performed on this reduced sample of 181.

Measures and Psychometric Considerations

Multi-item scales were used to operationalize the independent and dependent variables. The response format and specific items used for each variable are described in the chapter appendix.

RELATIONAL NORMS. The three bilateral norms considered in this study are continuity expectation, flexibility, and information exchange. *Continuity expectation* is the degree to which partner firms expect that the relationship will continue in the future. Based on this definition, a four-item scale was adapted from Noordewier, John, and Nevin (1990). Coefficient alpha for this scale is 0.83. *Flexibility* is the bilateral expectation of willingness to make adaptations in the relationship as circumstances change. A three-item scale used by Heide and John (1992) was adapted, with a coefficient alpha of 0.68. *Information exchange* is the bilateral expectation that parties will proactively provide market information useful to the partner (Heide and John 1992). Accordingly, a two-item scale was used, with a coefficient alpha of 0.86.

MONITORING MECHANISMS. *Output control* is based on specific performance measures; the focal firm evaluates the partner's realized outcomes. Accordingly, a four-item scale was used, with each item relating to the focal firm's specification of goals for the foreign partner. *Process control* is the monitoring of behavior or means used to achieve the desired ends. In exercising process control, the focal firm spends considerable time and effort in monitoring the partner's activities, as it needs to be constantly aware of what and how things are being done. Accordingly, a four-item scale is used to measure the extent of process control used by the focal firm. *Social control* is an informal control mechanism based on prevailing social perspectives and patterns of interpersonal interactions. The focal firm hopes to establish an organizational context for the foreign partner

COUNTRIES REPRESENTED IN THE SAMPLE
(COUNTRY OF FOREIGN PARTNER)

Asia (n = 99)	*Europe (n = 51)*	*Central and South America (n = 31)*
Japan	Italy	Argentina
China	Germany	Chile
Indonesia	Netherlands	Venezuela
Saudi Arabia	France	Mexico
India	Greece	Brazil
Oman	England	Colombia
Israel	Spain	Costa Rica
Thailand	Turkey	Puerto Rico
Taiwan	Switzerland	Panama
Singapore		
Philippines		
S. Korea		
Malaysia		

EQUITY STRUCTURE OF PARTNERSHIPS IN THE SAMPLE

Number of partnerships involving no equity = 136

Number of partnerships involving shared equity = 45 (Range 1–80 percent)

TYPE OF PARTNERSHIPS REPRESENTED IN THE SAMPLE

Distribution partnerships (U.S. manufacturer with foreign distributor) $n = 87$

Licensing partnerships (U.S. licensor with foreign licensee) $n = 94$

INDUSTRIES REPRESENTED IN THE SAMPLE

Aerospace (13)	Apparel (5)	Beverages (4)
Building Materials (2)	Chemicals (22)	Computers (5)
Electronics (21)	Food (8)	Forest Products (7)
Furniture (1)	Industrial & Farm Equip. (8)	Metals & Metal Products (11)
Mining, Crude Oil Prod. (6)	Motor Vehicles & Parts (11)	Petroleum Refining (10)
Pharmaceuticals (9)	Publishing, Printing (5)	Rubber & Plastic Products (10)
Scientific & Photog. Equip. (3)	Soaps, Cosmetics (2)	Textiles (4)
Tobacco (1)	Toys, Sporting Goods (8)	Transportation Equipment (2)

Table 7.1. Sample Characteristics.

to achieve its objectives through shared beliefs. Based on this, a three-item scale was used to measure social control. The output, process, and social control measures show reasonable internal consistency, with coefficient alphas of 0.75, 0.79, and 0.76, respectively.

RELATIONSHIP CONSEQUENCES. *Trust* is measured on a three-item scale adapted from Moorman, Deshpande, and Zaltman (1993). The first item (our business relationship with this foreign partner is characterized by high levels of trust) gets at the aggregate nature of confidence in the partnership. Items two and three (our firm and the partner firm generally trust each other that each will stay within the terms of the contract; we and our partner firm are generally skeptical of the information provided to each other) are more specific to the reliability and integrity aspects of trust.[5] Coefficient alpha for the three-item scale is 0.77. *Partnership performance* is measured on a two-item scale that includes market performance (relative to competitors) in terms of sales growth and market share. Coefficient alpha for the two-item scale is 0.80.

MODERATOR VARIABLES. *Asset specificity* for the focal firm is the extent to which it has invested in assets specific to its relationship with the foreign partner. A three-item scale was used; its coefficient alpha is 0.70. *Host market unpredictability* is the perceived discontinuity in the operating macro-environment in the foreign country. A six-item scale was used that measures the degree of predictability of the foreign country on general economic conditions as well as the regulations governing foreign firms. Coefficient alpha for this scale is 0.88.

CONTROL VARIABLES. Although no specific hypotheses were developed for the effects of ownership level, type of partnership, the industry of the firms, and the geographical home base of the foreign partner, these were incorporated in the analysis as control variables. Dummy variables were used for equity (0 = no ownership; 1 = shared ownership), partnership type (0 = distribution partnership; 1 = licensing partnership), and industry (0 = raw materials and intermediate goods; 1 = finished goods). Two dummy variables were used (Region 1 and Region 2) to control for differences across the three regions (Central and South America (0, 0), Europe (0, 1), Asia (1, 0)).

All the multi-item scales show reasonable internal consistency. To further assess the construct validity of the six independent variables, the items across the scales were subjected to a factor analysis. Results of the oblimin rotated factor analysis are provided in Table 7.2. The pre-specified six-factor solution accounted for 68.9 percent of the variance and represented all the derived factors with eigenvalues greater than one. The pattern of observed loadings indicate that the scales represent independent measures of the underlying construct, thus further supporting unidimensionality and discriminant validity of the scales.

Data Analyses

The data analyses for testing the hypotheses proposed in this study were carried out in three stages. In the first, H1a, H2a, H3a, H4a, H5a, and H6a, on the associations between the six independent variables and trust, were evaluated with multiple regression analysis. In the second stage, H1b, H2b, H3b, H4b, H5b, H6b, and H7, on the impact of six independent variables and trust on partnership performance, were tested using hierarchical multiple regression (HMR) analysis.[6] The basic principle underlying this analysis is the entry of predictor variables in some prespecified hierarchy where R^2 is determined at each stage. Therefore, partnership performance was regressed on the six relational norm and monitoring mechanism variables in step one to estimate their collective effect. In step two, trust was entered; the incremental increase in R^2 obtained here has to do with the unique contribution of trust to the explained variance beyond that accounted for by the previously entered variables. The significance of the hypothesized relationships was then tested based on an F-test for the increase in R^2 at each stage as described by Cohen and Cohen (1983: 145–146). In the third stage, the moderator hypotheses (H8 and H9) were tested using split-group analysis. Accordingly, partnership performance was regressed on trust with subgroups consisting of low and high asset specificity and host market unpredictability. Subsequently, Chow tests were performed to assess the statistical significance of the differences in regression coefficients across low and high groups.

Preliminary Considerations

In the absence of contrary evidence, a first-order additive model with linear parameters is used to represent the functional form of all the regression models. In using the ordinary least squares (OLS) procedure to estimate the parameters, the aptness of the hypothesized model for the data was tested through an analysis of residuals. The assumptions of equality of variance, independence of error, and normality of the distribution of residuals were met for all the analyses. Furthermore, because the sample consists of

	Factor 1	Factor 2	Factor 3	Factor 4	Factor 5	Factor 6
CONEXP1	**.67**	−.01	−.19	.22	−.12	.02
CONEXP2	**.73**	−.12	.01	−.01	.16	−.01
CONEXP3	**.80**	.05	−.01	.03	.11	−.08
CONEXP4	**.86**	.03	.06	−.04	−.03	.07
FLXBIL1	.08	−.01	−.03	**.73**	−.05	.07
FLXBIL2	.23	.04	.09	**.80**	−.04	.01
FLXBIL3	−.19	−.02	−.02	**.72**	.20	−.07
INFOEX1	.03	.04	−.03	.04	**.91**	.04
INFOEX2	.18	−.04	−.04	.08	**.82**	.03
OUTCON1	.10	**.83**	.18	−.07	.03	.08
OUTCON2	.11	**.84**	−.16	−.07	.01	−.12
OUTCON3	−.18	**.77**	.07	.03	.11	.02
OUTCON4	−.09	**.57**	−.04	.13	−.18	.05
PROCON1	.01	.25	−.11	.08	.14	**.64**
PROCON2	.10	.32	−.32	.02	.03	**.40**
PROCON3	.02	−.05	−.18	.04	−.04	**.78**
PROCON4	−.03	−.09	.12	−.06	.01	**.91**
SOCCON1	.23	−.10	**−.59**	.25	−.11	.04
SOCCON2	−.03	−.07	**−.87**	−.01	.17	−.04
SOCCON3	−.04	.09	**−.83**	−.12	−.05	.15
Eigen value	5.0	3.3	1.8	1.3	1.3	1.0
Percent of variance	25.2	16.6	9.1	6.6	6.4	5.0
Cumulative percent of variance	25.2	41.8	50.9	57.5	63.9	68.9

Table 7.2. Rotated Factor Matrix for Multi-Item Contextual Variables.

both equity and nonequity as well as distribution and licensing partnerships, it was deemed important to test the appropriateness of pooling the data. This test involves a comparison of residual sum of squares of regression equations across the subsamples with potential source of heterogeneity in the pooled data (Johnston 1984). Accordingly, Chow tests were performed for the equity structures and partnership types. The F-values for these tests were not statistically significant (at $p = .10$), suggesting that the relationships considered in this study are homogenous in equity structure and type of partnership, and therefore the data can be pooled. A correlation analysis was also performed to assess the degree of multicollinearity present in the sample data, the result of which is provided in Table 7.3. As the table shows, the bivariate associations between the independent variables suggest that any impact of multicollinearity on the parameter estimates should not be substantial.

Research Findings

Table 7.4 shows the effect of the independent variables on trust in the partnership. The regression equation is significant at the .01 level; 47 percent of the variance in trust is explained by the variables considered in the study. Individual beta coefficients support H1a ($b = .47, p < .01$) and H3a ($b = .17, p < .01$), and moderately support H2a ($b = .12, p < .10$). As hypothesized, these findings indicate that the existence of bilateral norms of continuity expectations, flexibility, and information exchange in cross-border market partnerships leads to greater trust in these partnerships. Mixed support is found for the effect of monitoring mechanisms used by the focal firm on trust. As hypothesized, the use of social control is positively related to trust ($b = 19, p < .05$), thus supporting H6a. However, the beta coefficients for output ($b = -.02, p > .10$) and process control ($b = -.05, p > .10$) are not statistically significant. Therefore, H4a and H5a are not supported.

Interestingly, the results in Table 7.4 also suggest that U.S. firms' partnerships with Asian and European firms ($b = .24, p < .01$) are characterized by higher levels of trust than those with Central and South American firms. This has important managerial and theoretical implications, which will be discussed in the next section. However, no ownership (equity) or industry effects were observed.

The hierarchical multiple regression (HMR) results with partnership performance as the dependent variable are provided in Table 7.5. In step one of this HMR analysis, only the six independent variables and the five control variables are entered to examine the direct effects of relational norms and

Variables	Mean	SD	1	2	3	4	5	6	7	8	9	10
1. CONEXP	3.97	0.86	1.00									
2. FLXBIL	3.76	0.71	.47***	1.00								
3. INFOEX	3.26	1.08	.43***	.35***	1.00							
4. OUTCON	2.12	0.86	−.04	.01	−.05	1.00						
5. PROCON	2.85	0.90	.22***	.14*	.14*	.39***	1.00					
6. SOCCON	2.90	0.86	.38***	.28***	.23***	.09	.51***	1.00				
7. TRUST	3.97	0.75	.63***	.41***	.43***	−.07	.16**	.37***	1.00			
8. PARTPER	3.54	0.87	.48***	.39***	.22***	−.13*	.10	.33***	.43***	1.00		
9. ASSET	3.09	0.97	.32***	.15**	.19**	.08	.35***	.33***	.19***	.32***	1.00	
10. HMKUPR	2.63	0.73	−.01	.05	.02	−.01	−.16**	.01	−.03	.03	.24***	1.00

Table 7.3. Correlation Matrix.
*$p < .10$ **$p < .05$ ***$p < .01$

Predictors	Coefficients (t-value)
Relational Norms	
Continuity expectations (H1a)	.47 (6.58)***
Flexibility (H2a)	.12 (1.85)*
Information exchange (H3a)	.17 (2.62)***
Monitoring Mechanisms	
Output control (H4a)	−.04 (−0.61)
Process control (H5a)	−.07 (−0.88)
Social control (H6a)	.19 (2.56)**
Control Variables	
Equity	−.02 (−0.37)
Partnership type	.02 (0.39)
Industry	.01 (0.06)
Region1	.24 (2.97)***
Region2	.14 (1.60)
R^2 adjusted	.47
F-value	14.61***

Table 7.4. Multiple Regression Results for Trust.
$*p < .10$ $**p < .05$ $***p < .01$

monitoring mechanisms on the market performance of the partnership. As shown in Table 7.5, the regression model is significant at the .01 level, with the set of independent variables explaining 24 percent of the variance. The norms of continuity expectations and flexibility are positively related to partnership performance ($b = .33, p < .01$ and $b = .17, p < .05$, respectively), thus supporting H1b and H2b. H3b is not supported, as the beta coefficient for the norm of information exchange is not statistically significant ($b = −.05, p > .10$). Two of the three hypotheses linking the monitoring mechanisms to partnership performance are supported. As expected, output control is weakly but negatively related ($b = −.13, p < .10$), and social control is positively related ($b = .18, p < .05$) to market performance, thus supporting H4b and H6b. However, H5b is not supported, as the beta coefficient for process control ($b = −.02, p > .10$) is not statistically significant.

Predictors	Step 1	Step 2
Relational norms		
Continuity expectations (H1b)	.33 (4.08)***	.26 (2.84)***
Flexibility (H2b)	.17 (2.28)**	.16 (2.07)**
Information exchange (H3b)	−.05 (−0.64)	−.07 (−0.97)
Monitoring mechanisms		
Output control (H4b)	−.13 (−1.67)*	−.12 (−1.61)
Process control (H5b)	−.02 (−0.19)	−.01 (−0.11)
Social control (H6b)	.18 (2.15)**	.16 (1.84)*
Control variables		
Equity	−.01 (−0.07)	−.01 (−0.04)
Industry	−.04 (−0.56)	−.04 (−0.57)
Region1	.07 (0.76)	.03 (0.37)
Region2	−.02 (−0.23)	−.04 (−0.44)
Trust		
Trust (H7)		.08 (0.73)
R^2 adjusted	.24	.25
F-value	6.29***	6.05***
ΔR^2		.01
ΔF-value		2.67

**Table 7.5. Hierarchical Multiple Regression Results
for Partnership Performance (PARTPER).**
Note: t-values are in parentheses.
$^*p < .10$ $^{**}p < .05$ $^{***}p < .01$

Furthermore, no significant effects of equity, industry, and the geographical region were observed. Contrary to the widely accepted assumption in the hierarchical control literature, the lack of significant association between the ownership level and partnership performance should be noted.

To test H7, trust was entered into the regression equation in step two along with all the variables entered in step one. The results show that the beta coefficients for the six independent variables are stable even when trust

Moderator Variable	Criterion Variable	R^2	Moderator Level	Predictor Variable = Trust, Beta Coefficient	Chow Test
Asset specificity (H8)	Partnership performance	.05	Low	.23, n.s.	
		.16	High	.40, $p < .01$	$F(2,69) = 5.83, p < .01$
Host market unpredictability (H9)	Partnership performance	.29	Low	.53, $p < .01$	
		.24	High	.49, $p < .01$	$F(2,71) = 0.39, $ n.s.

Table 7.6. Trust-Performance Relationship: Moderated Regression Results Using Subgroup Analysis.

Note: n.s. = not statistically significant, $p > .10$

is included in the equation, thus reaffirming the direct effects of relational norms and monitoring mechanisms on partnership performance. However, trust is not significantly related to performance ($b = .08$, $p > .10$), thus failing to support H7. Also the incremental change in R^2 is not significant ($F = 2.67$, $p > .10$). These findings, along with a strong bivariate correlation ($r = 0.43$, $p < .01$) between trust and performance (Table 7.3), suggest that although trust and performance are positively related, trust does not uniquely explain variance in partnership performance above and beyond that explained by the relational norms and monitoring mechanisms.

Moderator effects of asset specificity and host market unpredictability on the trust-performance relationship were assessed through separate regressions using subgroups, the results of which are provided in Table 7.6. The results support the moderator effects of asset specificity, thus supporting H8. The beta coefficient for trust is not statistically significant under a low level of asset specificity ($b = .23$, $p > .10$), but it is significant for high asset specificity ($b = .40$, $p < .01$). Furthermore, a significant Chow test ($F = 5.83$, $p < .01$) also points to differences in the beta coefficients for low and high asset specificity. However, the positive relationship between trust and performance is consistent under both low and high host market unpredictability ($F = 0.39$, $p > .10$). Thus, H9 is not supported.

Conclusion

Recent research in international business has stressed a need for understanding behavioral and social dynamics in cross-border partnerships. One such dimension is the degree of trust that exists between partner firms, which becomes a functional substitute for hierarchical control, especially when such ownership-based control is not feasible in structuring interfirm relationships. This study builds on the behavioral approach of interorganizational governance by examining the role of trust on the performance of cross-border marketing partnerships, and by identifying the specific mechanisms that help firms build trusting relationships. Thus, the model proposed in this study, based on behavioral determinants of partnership trust and performance and emphasizing the *maintenance* of such partnerships, complements the structural approach of interfirm cooperation.

The empirical findings support the importance of both bilateral relational norms and monitoring mechanisms initiated by the focal firm as determinants of trust and performance in cross-border partnerships, although with differential effects. Initiating and fostering norms of continuity expectations, flexibility, and information exchange between the partner firms are positively related to trust in the partnership. Furthermore, continuity expectations and flexibility are found to enhance the partnership's market performance. These findings lend credence to the recently developed theoretical arguments based on relational exchanges where interfirm obligations are enforced by minimizing the motivation of partners to forgo individual gains in the interests of the partnership, and where the relationship is characterized by cooperation rather than competition. This argument is further reinforced by the effects on trust and performance of the three monitoring mechanisms initiated by the focal firm. In particular, use of social control by the focal firm has positive effects on building trust and market performance. Social control, although initiated by the focal firm, is bilateral; it requires interpersonal interactions to inculcate shared organizational beliefs. Output and process control, on the other hand, are formal mechanisms initiated by the focal firm to specify the outcomes and monitor the behavior of the partner firm, respectively. The results show that neither has significant effects on relationship trust. This suggests that although formal monitoring mechanisms may be put in place by the focal firm to reduce its own ambiguity about the actions of the partner firm, imposing specific goals in the form of output control is actually detrimental to partnership performance. Thus, focal firm management needs to be cognizant of the behavioral and economic consequences in designing monitoring mechanisms for its partners.

This study has also empirically examined the direct association between trust and performance, as well as contingency effects. The results support the notion that trust in cross-border partnerships becomes particularly important in explaining market performance when conditions exist for opportunism by the partner firm. In particular, when the focal firm has invested in substantial assets specific to its relationship with the foreign partner, trust in the relationship counterbalances the possibility of opportunism, and thus has positive implications for partnership performance. However, the lack of a significant direct relationship between trust and performance should not trivialize the role of trust-building. Trust may have other consequences, such as efficiency and longevity of the partnership, which were not explicitly considered in this study.

Two additional findings relate to the international business aspect of interorganizational partnerships. First, differences in partnership trust were observed in the three geographical regions considered in this study; U.S. firms' partnerships in Asia and Europe incorporated a higher level of trust than those in Central and South America. Although no hypotheses were proposed regarding region-specific effects and the size of the sample precluded a systematic analysis of them, it seems that the role of trust in partnerships and its underlying dynamics may vary according to the internal organizational cultures of the partner firms (Parkhe 1993c) as well as the macrocultural environment that surrounds them. Therefore, future research is encouraged to examine the different aspects and types of trust as they apply to cross-border partnerships, especially by incorporating the cultural differences that exist across countries. For theory development to have external validity, it must incorporate idiosyncratic characteristics specific to organizational behavior in individual countries.

Second, our study has found that ownership level and partnership performance are not statistically related. This finding contradicts a widely held assumption in the international business literature that suggests ownership is necessary for effective control of a firm's partners, implying that their performance depends on the focal company's ownership control. This finding appears to further support our thesis that effective control of partners can be achieved by nonownership means, as presented in our conceptual model.

Managerial Implications

There are three significant managerial implications of the study's findings. First, because firms are finding it increasingly difficult to perform all activities along the value chain internally, it is becoming important for them to forge long-term partnerships with other firms in different countries. The findings suggest that these partnerships can be based on cooperative aspects that achieve joint objectives. Thus, forging bilateralism through symbiotic commitment to each other, maintaining flexibility, and allowing for open information exchange have a positive effect on the trust between firms, and also enhance partnership performance, which is eventually beneficial to both firms.

Second, the results suggest that individual firm objectives in a partnership can be achieved without ownership control. In fact, even attempts at formal monitoring of partner activities may have an adverse impact on partnership performance. Thus firms should rely more on bilateralism and social interactions rather than formal monitoring mechanisms to maintain their partnerships.

The third implication is that the dynamics of partnerships in different regions or countries are guided by local and regional cultural practices. Therefore, management needs to be cognizant of this so as to avoid the pitfall of trying to find a partnership management formula that can be transferred across countries.

Limitations and Future Research Directions

Though this study addressed behavioral issues in cross-border partnerships and complements the research based on the structural approach by identifying the antecedents and performance consequences of interfirm trust, the findings should be evaluated in light of the following limitations. First, the study used cross-sectional data, thus precluding an examination of the dynamic effects of interorganizational trust and performance. This becomes particularly crucial because two-way causal linkages have been suggested in the literature between relational norms and trust. Similarly, the trust-performance relationship could be reciprocal; that is, trust leads to performance, but improved performance may also build trust. Second, our results were based on information obtained from one side of the partnership. We attempted to obtain information from both partners, but many U.S. firms were unwilling to identify their partners for confidentiality and strategic reasons. As some variables in the study were bilateral, data collection from only one partner did not capture all aspects of the relationship, and the findings should be interpreted accordingly. Future research is encouraged that uses responses from both the focal and foreign agents to understand the social dynamics of such partnerships. Third, we only considered the behavioral dimension of trust. As described earlier, trust is a multidimensional concept with distinct meanings across different levels of analysis. Thus, our use of a three-item scale did not capture the many facets of trust. Finally, only one type of partnership performance (sales growth and market share) was considered in this study. Firms may determine the success of partnerships in other ways as well, and these need to be examined. Furthermore, we encourage future research to systematically examine the trust-performance relationship by incorporating the different dimensions of trust and performance.

Appendix: Measurement

Questionnaire respondents were asked to respond to the following items with respect to their firm's relationship with a foreign distributor or licensee. Except as noted for certain items, respondents used a scale of 1 to 5 where 1 = strongly disagree, 5 = strongly agree. The notation (R) means the item was reverse coded.

Relational Norms

CONTINUITY EXPECTATIONS. Coefficient alpha is .83.

- Our firm and our partner firm are very committed to each other. (CONEXP1)
- If our firm could find another partners in this country, we are likely to switch to a new partner. (R) (CONEXP2)

- There is a high level of uncertainty in this partnership. (R) (CONEXP3)
- We and our partner firm are not sure how long our relationship will last. (R) (CONEXP4)

FLEXIBILITY. Coefficient alpha is .68.

- In this partnership, our firm and our foreign partner expect to be able to make adjustments in the ongoing relationship to cope with changing circumstances. (FLXBIL1)
- Flexibility in response to requests for changes is a strong characteristic in this partnership. (FLXBIL2)
- Whenever some unexpected situation arises, we would rather work out a new deal with our foreign partner than hold each other to original terms. (FLXBIL3)

INFORMATION EXCHANGE. Coefficient alpha is .86.

- We hesitate to give our partner information that is not part of the contract. (R) (INFOEX1)
- Our partner firm hesitates to give us information that is not part of the contract. (R) (INFOEX2)

Monitoring Mechanisms

OUTPUT CONTROL. Coefficient alpha is .75.

- Established sales targets for this foreign partner are specified in the contract. (OUTCON1)
- The terms of our agreement require this foreign partner to attain a certain market share for our products. (OUTCON2)
- The extent of territorial coverage that this foreign partner needs to attain for our products is clearly specified in the contract. (OUTCON3)
- Our future relationship with this foreign partner is contingent on how it achieves the specified goals. (OUTCON4)

PROCESS CONTROL. Coefficient alpha is .79.

- Our firm regularly monitors the quality control maintained by this foreign partner. (PROCON1)

- Our firm frequently monitors the marketing activities performed by this foreign partner. (PROCON2)
- Our firm closely monitors the extent to which the partner firm follows established procedures. (PROCON3)
- We have developed specific procedures for this foreign partner firm to follow. (PROCON4)

SOCIAL CONTROL. Coefficient alpha is .76.

- This foreign partner fully understands the philosophy of our firm. (SOCCON1)
- This foreign partner has tried to incorporate our management philosophy into its own organization. (SOCCON2)
- We have made concerted efforts to instill our business philosophy in this foreign partner's managers. (SOCCON3)

Relationship Consequences

TRUST. Coefficient alpha is .77.

- Our business relationship with this foreign partner is characterized by high levels of trust. (TRUST1)
- Our firm and the partner firm generally trust each other that each will stay within the terms of the contract. (TRUST2)
- We and our partner firm are generally skeptical of the information provided to each other. (R) (TRUST3)

PARTNERSHIP PERFORMANCE. Coefficient alpha is .80. Relative to competitors in the foreign market, rate the performance of the partnership on the following dimensions:

- Sales growth (1 = very low, 5 = very high)
- Market share (1 = very low, 5 = very high)

Moderator Variables

ASSET SPECIFICITY. Coefficient alpha is .70.

- Our firm has made significant investments that are specific to our relationship with this foreign partner.

- Our firm's products or technologies are tailored to meet the requirements of this foreign partner.
- It will be very costly for us to replace this foreign partner.

HOST MARKET UNPREDICTABILITY. Cronbach coefficient alpha is .88. Scale: 1 = very predictable, 5 = very unpredictable.

- Import regulations
- Export regulations
- Economic conditions
- Remittances and repatriation regulations
- Inflation rates
- Exchange rate fluctuations

Control Variables

- Equity. Values: 0 = no ownership, 1 = shared ownership
- Industry. Values: 0 = raw materials and intermediate goods, 1 = finished goods
- Region 1 and Region 2: These are two dummy variables for the three regions: Central and South America, Europe, and Asia.
- Partnership type. Values: 0 = distribution, 1 = licensing.

NOTES

1. Noordewier, John, and Nevin (1990) consider monitoring mechanisms as one of the elements of relational norms. However, the important characteristic of relational norms is the bilateralism between the exchange partners. Monitoring mechanisms are generally initiated by one partner (usually the focal firm in agency relationships) to enforce compliance (Gencturk and Aulakh 1995; Jaworski 1988). Keeping this distinction in perspective, we consider the monitoring mechanisms as distinct from relational norms. As discussed later in the section, one of the monitoring mechanisms, social control, may eventually lead to a bilateral relational element, although it is still initiated by one firm as a monitoring tool.

2. There is some ambiguity about the causal linkage between commitment and performance (Cullen, Johnson, and Sakano 1995). For instance, in commitment theory, it is argued that commitment in exchange partnerships develops only if the partnerships are successful. On the other hand, Buckley and

Casson (1988) suggest commitment to be a precursor of performance. In fact, reciprocal causal linkages could be argued for the relationships between the three norms and trust and performance. Because we test the hypotheses on cross-sectional data related to a specific point in time, the exact causal directions cannot be empirically verified. Our premise is that as the objectives in interorganizational partnerships are to develop trust and enhance market performance, the presence of relational norms allows firms to achieve these objectives. However, we do not discount a feedback loop from the consequences to the relational norms.

3. Because this study focuses on cross-border partnerships from the perspective of U.S. manufacturing firms and the data were collected from only that side, the different controls are examined from the perspective of the focal firm. This does not imply that the focal firm is always the one that can impose its will on partners. Rather, in interorganizational partnerships, both firms attempt to influence each other's decisions through different monitoring mechanisms.

4. The 652 potential informants represented 249 of the Fortune 500 firms and affiliates. This is because some firms provided names of more than one manager, and multiple affiliates of the same parent provided names of managers dealing with their specific international operations. The 257 respondents who actually filled out survey questionnaires represented 137 Fortune 500 firms. Thus, we received more than one questionnaire from some firms. However, for these firms, respondents were from different affiliates and therefore are considered as separate data points.

5. Given that trust has been conceptualized at various levels (such as interpersonal, organizational, and societal [Hosmer 1995]) and incorporates both behavioral (such as confidence and behavioral intention [Anderson and Narus 1990; Moorman, Deshpande and Zaltman 1993]) and structural (such as vulnerability and dependence [Madhok 1995]) aspects, the three-item scale used in this study does not capture the different dimensions of trust. We thank the reviewers for bringing this to our attention, and we explicitly acknowledge this limitation in the conclusions section.

6. We attempted to test moderating hypotheses (H8 and H9) by entering the interaction terms (trust $\times$ asset specificity and trust $\times$ host market unpredictability) into the HMR analysis in step three. However, despite the rescaling of the interaction terms through a mean centering approach suggested by Darlington (1990), parameter estimates were very unstable because of high multicollinearity (correlations between the original and interaction variables of 0.85). Thus the moderator effects of asset specificity and host market unpredictability on the trust-performance relationship were tested by using subgroup analysis.

Bibliography

Anderson, E., and R. D. Oliver. 1987. Perspectives on behavior-based versus outcome-based sales force control systems. *Journal of Marketing,* 51 (October): 76–88.

Anderson, E., and B. A. Weitz. 1989. Determinants of continuity in conventional industrial channel dyads. *Marketing Science,* 8 (Fall): 310–323.

Anderson, J. C., and J. A. Narus. 1990. A model of distributor firm and manufacturer firm working partnerships. *Journal of Marketing,* 54(1): 42–58.

Armstrong, J. S., and T. Overton. 1977. Estimating nonresponse bias in mail surveys. *Journal of Marketing Research,* 14 (August): 396–402.

Ashforth, B. E., and F. Miles. 1989. Social identity theory and the organization. *Academy of Management Review,* 14(1): 20–39.

Axelrod, R. 1986. An evolutionary approach to norms. *American Political Science Review,* 80(4): 1095–1111.

Beamish, P. W. 1985. *Joint venture performance in developing countries.* Unpublished Ph.D. dissertation, University of Western Ontario.

Beamish, P. W., and J. C. Banks. 1987. Equity joint ventures and the theory of the multinational enterprise. *Journal of International Business Studies,* 18(2): 1–16.

Bergen, M., S. Dutta, and O. C. Walker. 1992. Agency relationships in marketing: A review of the implications and applications of agency and related theories. *Journal of Marketing,* 56 (July): 1–24.

Bleeke, J., and D. Ernst. 1991. The way to win in cross-border alliances. *Harvard Business Review,* November-December: 127–135.

Bradach, J. L., and R. G. Eccles. 1989. Price, authority, and trust: From ideal types to plural forms. *American Review of Sociology,* 15: 97–118.

Buckley, P. J., and M. Casson. 1988. A theory of cooperation in joint ventures. In F. J. Contractor and P. Lorange, editors, *Cooperative Strategies in International Business,* 31–54. San Francisco: New Lexington Press.

Casson, M. 1992. Internalization theory and beyond. In P. J. Buckley, editor, *New Directions in International Business: Research Priorities for the 1990s,* 4–27. Brookfield, Vt.: Edward Elgar.

Cohen, J., and P. Cohen. 1983. *Applied Multiple Regression/Correlation Analysis for Behavioral Science.* Hillsdale, N.J.: Lawrence Erlbaum.

Contractor, F. J., and P. Lorange. 1988. Why should firms cooperate? The strategy and economics basis for cooperative ventures. In F. J. Contractor and P. Lorange, editors, *Cooperative Strategies in International Business,* 3–30. San Francisco: New Lexington Press.

Crosby, L. A., K. R. Evans, and D. Cowles. 1990. Relationship quality in services selling: An interpersonal perspective. *Journal of Marketing,* 54 (July): 60–81.

Cullen, J. B., J. L. Johnson, and T. Sakano. 1995. Japanese and local partner commitment to IJVs: Psychological consequences of outcomes and investments in the IJV relationship. *Journal of International Business Studies,* 26(1): 91–115.

Dalton, G. W. 1971. Motivation and control in organizations. In G.W. Dalton and P. R. Lawrence, editors, *Motivation and Control in Organizations,* 1–35. Homewood, Ill: Irwin.

Darlington, R. B. 1990. *Regression and Linear Models.* New York: McGraw-Hill.

Dwyer, F. R., P. H. Schurr, and S. Oh. 1987. Developing buyer-seller relationships. *Journal of Marketing,* 51 (April): 11–27.

Eisenhardt, K. M. 1989. Agency theory: An assessment and review. *Academy of Management Review,* 14(1): 57–74.

Gencturk, E. F., and P. S. Aulakh. 1995. The use of process and output controls in foreign markets. *Journal of International Business Studies,* 26(4): 755–786.

Geringer, J. M. 1991. Strategic determinants of partner selection criteria in international joint ventures. *Journal of International Business Studies,* 22(1): 41–62.

Geringer, J. M., and L. Hébert. 1989. Control and performance in international joint ventures. *Journal of International Business Studies,* 20(2): 235–254.

Grossman, S., and O. D. Hart. 1986. The costs and benefits of ownership: A theory of vertical and lateral integration. *Journal of Political Economy,* 94(4): 691–719.

Hagedoorn, J. 1993. Understanding the rationale of strategic technology partnering: Interorganizational modes of cooperation and sectoral differences. *Strategic Management Journal,* 14: 371–385.

Häkansson, H., and J. Johanson. 1988. Formal and informal cooperation strategies in international industrial networks. In F. J. Contractor and P. Lorange, editors, *Cooperative Strategies in International Business,* 369–380. San Francisco: New Lexington Press.

Heide, J. B. 1994. Interorganizational governance in marketing channels. *Journal of Marketing,* 58 (January): 71–85.

Heide, J. B., and G. John. 1992. Do norms matter in marketing relationships? *Journal of Marketing,* 56 (April): 32–44.

Hill, C. W. 1990. Cooperation, opportunism, and the invisible hand: Implications for transaction cost theory. *Academy of Management Review,* 15(3): 500–513.

Hopwood, A. 1972. An empirical study of the role of accounting data in performance evaluation. *Empirical Research in Accounting,* 10 (Summer): 156–182.

Hosmer, L. T. 1995. Trust: The connecting link between organizational theory and philosophical ethics. *Academy of Management Review,* 20(2): 379–403.

Jaeger, A. M. 1983. The transfer of organizational culture overseas: An approach to control in the multinational corporation. *Journal of International Business Studies,* (Fall): 91–114.

Jaworski, B. J. 1988. Toward a theory of marketing control: Environmental context, control types, and consequences. *Journal of Marketing,* 52 (July): 23–39.

Johnston, J. 1984. *Econometric Methods.* Singapore: McGraw-Hill.

Kotabe, M., and K. S. Swan. 1995. The role of strategic alliances in high-technology new product development. *Strategic Management Journal,* 16: 621–636.

Kumar, N., L. K. Scheer, and J.-B. E.M. Steenkamp. 1995. The effects of supplier fairness on vulnerable resellers. *Journal of Marketing Research,* 32 (February): 54–65.

Lewis, J. D., and A. Weigert. 1985. Trust as social reality. *Social Forces,* 63: 967–985.

Madhok, A. 1995. Revisiting multinational firms' tolerance for joint ventures: A trust-based approach. *Journal of International Business Studies,* 26(1): 117–137.

Moorman, C., R. Deshpande, and G. Zaltman. 1993. Factors affecting trust in market research relationships. *Journal of Marketing Research,* 57 (January): 81–101.

Morgan, R. M., and S. D. Hunt. 1994. The commitment-trust theory of relationship marketing. *Journal of Marketing,* 58 (July): 20–38.

Noordewier, T. G., G. John, and J. R. Nevin. 1990. Performance outcomes of purchasing arrangements in industrial buyer-vendor relationships. *Journal of Marketing,* 54(4): 80–93.

Ouchi, W. G. 1979. The relationship between organizational structure and organizational control. *Management Science,* 25(9): 833–848.

Ouchi, W. G. 1980. Markets, bureaucracies, and clans. *Administrative Science Quarterly,* 25 (March): 129–143.

Parkhe, A. 1993a. "Messy" research, methodological predispositions, and theory development in international joint ventures. *Academy of Management Review,* 18(2): 227–268.

Parkhe, A. 1993b. Strategic alliance structuring: A game theoretic and transaction cost examination of interfirm cooperation. *Academy of Management Journal,* 36(4): 794–829.

Parkhe, A. 1993c. Partner nationality and the structure-performance relationship in strategic alliances. *Organization Science,* 4(2): 301–324.

Podsakoff, P. M., and D. W. Organ. 1986. Self-reports in organizational research: Problems and prospects. *Journal of Management,* 12(4): 531–544.

Ring, P. S., and A. H. Van De Ven. 1992. Structuring cooperative relationships between organizations. *Strategic Management Journal,* 13: 483–498.

Robicheaux, R. A., and J. E. Coleman. 1994. The structure of marketing channel relationships. *Journal of the Academy of Marketing Science,* 22(1): 38–51.

Scanzoni, J. 1979. Social exchange and behavioral interdependence. In R. L. Burgess and T. L. Huston, editors, *Social Exchange in Developing Relationships.* New York: Academic Press.

Stinchcombe, A. L. 1986. Norms of exchange. In A. L. Stinchcombe, editor, *Stratification and Organization: Selected Papers,* 231–267. Cambridge University Press.

Thibaut, J. W., and H. H. Kelley. 1959. *The Social Psychology of Groups.* New York: Wiley.

Thorelli, H. B. 1986. Between markets and hierarchies. *Strategic Management Journal,* 7: 35–51.

Webster, F. E. 1992. The changing role of marketing in the corporation. *Journal of Marketing,* 56: 1–17.

Wilkins, A. L., and W. G. Ouchi. 1983. Efficient cultures: Exploring the relationship between culture and organizational performance. *Administrative Science Quarterly,* 28: 468–481.

Zand, D. E. 1972. Trust and managerial problem solving. *Administrative Science Quarterly,* 17: 229–239.

8

PROCEDURAL JUSTICE PERCEPTIONS AMONG INTERNATIONAL JOINT VENTURE MANAGERS

Their Impact on Organizational Commitment

James P. Johnson

INTERNATIONAL JOINT VENTURES (IJVs) *have been identified as a difficult form of alliance to manage because they involve shared ownership of assets and, often, joint control. This chapter reports the results of a study that suggests that the joint venture managers' perceptions of the procedural justice of strategic decision making may have an impact on several aspects of organizational commitment: to the IJV and its parents, to the IJV top management team, and to implementing the IJV's current strategy.*

INTERNATIONAL COOPERATIVE STRATEGIES are of many kinds. They include technical training agreements, assembly and buyback agreements, licensing, franchising, exploration, research and development partnerships, and equity joint ventures (Contractor and Lorange 1988). The motivations

The author is indebted to the following for their help and encouragement: the Center for International Business Education and Research at the University of South Carolina; the participants at the Global Perspectives on International Cooperative Alliances conference, University of Western Ontario, March 1996; and three anonymous reviewers.

for international cooperative strategies are also varied; they include risk-sharing, gaining access to resources, overcoming political barriers, pooling complementary technologies, and seeking economies of scale (Contractor and Lorange 1988; Harrigan 1985). The focus of this chapter is the management of international equity joint ventures (IJVs); an IJV is defined here as a legal entity created by two or more parent organizations headquartered in two or more countries.

The IJV has been accused of being a form of alliance that is difficult to manage because it involves shared asset ownership and joint control, which creates ambiguity for the IJV management team that is expected to satisfy the often conflicting demands of its parent organizations (Beamish 1988; Killing 1983; Kogut 1988; Schaan 1983). Multiple ownership also creates problems in assessing IJV performance, as partners' goals for the venture may differ (Harrigan 1985) and either or both partners may have a hidden agenda in setting up the alliance (Hamel 1991). Furthermore, some studies (for example, Franko 1971; Harrigan 1985) have suggested that IJVs are an inherently unstable organizational form, which begs the questions of why firms would choose to use an IJV and whether stability and longevity are appropriate measures of IJV performance. These are important to international business researchers and managers, because the number of international alliances, including IJVs, has increased sharply in the past two decades (Hergert and Morris 1988) and because the strategic importance of IJVs is expected to continue in the near future (Geringer and Hébert 1991).

Several studies of IJVs (such as Beamish 1988; Buckley and Casson 1988; Peterson and Shimada 1978; Sullivan and Peterson 1982) have found the establishment of trust and commitment between IJV partners to be an important determinant of perceived IJV success. Yet successful IJV performance may also depend on the establishment of commitment between the partners and the IJV management team, as well as on the trust and commitment developed within the IJV management team itself. Another important aspect of commitment in a strategic management context is the IJV managers' commitment to carrying out the strategy that has been set for the venture (Guth and MacMillan 1986). Thus, the dual aspects of commitment—organizational and strategic—should be examined when assessing the role of commitment in contributing to the effective management of the IJV.

In recent years, organizational justice theory has been applied to an increasing number of organizational contexts. Organizational justice is the term used to describe the role of fairness[1] as it directly relates to the workplace (Moorman 1991). Three aspects of organizational justice are distributive justice (Adams 1963, 1965; Homans 1961; Blau 1968), which relates to the perceived fairness of the outcomes that an individual receives; procedural justice (Thibaut and Walker 1975; Lind and Tyler 1988), which relates to the perceived fairness of the processes used to determine those outcomes; and interactional justice (Greenberg 1990), which relates to how the manner in which information about a decision or event is presented to individuals influences their reaction to the decision or event. Recent studies have extended organizational justice theory to multinational subsidiaries (Kim and Mauborgne 1991, 1993a, 1993b, 1993c, 1995) and to the dynamics of top management teams (Korsgaard, Schweiger, and Sapienza 1995). Organizational justice theory can therefore be applied to the management of international joint ventures to further our understanding of the relationship between strategic decision making and the commitment of IJV managers to implementing strategic decisions, as well as their organizational commitment to the IJV.

This chapter reports the preliminary results of a study that examined how IJV managers perceive and respond to the way strategic decisions are made for their unit. As the way strategic decisions are made and the roles and responsibilities of the decision makers can vary widely from one organization to another, the focus of procedural justice is the decision-making process, not the specific decision inputs or the decision outcomes. The conceptual and theoretical foundation for the study draws on three streams of literature that are reviewed in the following sections: organizational commitment, procedural justice, and control and decision making in IJVs.

Commitment in IJVs

The antecedents of commitment are diverse (Steers 1977), but two major views of commitment have emerged from the literature (Eisenberger, Huntington, Hutchison, and Sowa 1986): calculative or continuance commitment, and affective attachment (Allen and Meyer 1990; Buchanan 1974; Eisenberger, Fasolo, and Davis-LaMastro 1990; Etzioni 1961; Gould 1979; Meyer and Allen 1984; Mowday, Steers, and Porter 1979). Both types of commitment have been investigated at the organizational level, or macrolevel, focusing on commitment to the organization as a whole. Because an IJV is a hybrid organizational form, commitment to the organization as a whole is multidimensional; on the one hand, IJV managers can be expected to exhibit some level of commitment to the IJV itself, since it is the focal organization of their daily activities; on the other hand, they can also be expected to exhibit some level of commitment to the IJV's parent companies, to which they are ultimately responsible and for which, as is often the case, they may have given many years of previous service. Therefore, organizational commitment at the macrolevel should consider IJV managers' commitment to the IJV itself and to both parent organizations.

However, commitment can also occur at the suborganizational level, or microlevel, of analysis, focusing on commitment to a group or a strategy. Several studies (for example, Guth and MacMillan 1986; Schweiger, Sandberg, and Rechner 1989) have examined the strategic decision-making process and the effect of managers' participation in decision making on their acceptance of and commitment to strategic decisions. Thus, both macrolevel and microlevel perspectives are relevant to an investigation of commitment within work organizations.

Mowday, Steers, and Porter (1979) and Mowday, Porter, and Steers (1982) defined macrolevel commitment in terms of attitudinal commitment, consisting of both attitudes and behaviors; they defined commitment as a belief in and acceptance of organizational goals and values, a willingness to exert effort toward organizational goal accomplishment, and a strong desire to maintain organizational membership. Steers (1977) distinguished between passive and active commitment; passive commitment is reflected in an attitude of loyalty to the organization and characterized by compliance, or in-role behavior (O'Reilly and Chatman 1986), a form of calculative attachment in which attitudes and behaviors are adopted in exchange for rewards. However, compliance does not result in active commitment, which is prosocial behavior above and beyond the call of duty or high levels of effort to achieve organizational goals. Active commitment is often expected by an organization, especially from its top management; passive commitment is generally taken for granted as a *quid pro quo* of organizational membership, yet it is active commitment that most people have in mind when they refer to commitment to an organization.

Socialization is recognized as an important way to foster active commitment. Buchanan (1974) argued that during the first few years of organizational membership, social interaction with peers and superiors who have a positive attitude toward the organization helps to promote individuals' identification with the goals and values of the organization. Edstrom and Galbraith (1977) found that the socialization of managers in multinational corporations is an important means of creating organizational commitment because their frequent intracompany transfers resulted in the organization becoming the most constant and consistent part of their life. Ouchi (1980) noted the importance of socialization in creating and maintaining organizational commitment in organizations with "clan" cultures. We would therefore expect to find high levels of active commitment in organizations that strongly promote team spirit and group membership.

Kim and Mauborgne (1993c), in examining commitment among multinational enterprise (MNE) subdsidiary managers, made a similar distinction between compulsory execution and voluntary execution of strategic decisions; the latter occurs when managers exert an effort beyond what is required in order to execute decisions to the best of their ability. Therefore, it can be expected that IJV managers who exhibit active or voluntary commitment are prepared to do their utmost to implement strategic decisions effectively.

Individuals vary in their level of commitment to the goals and values of the organization (Buchanan 1974); although the literature on commitment to the organization emphasizes the antecedents and consequences of high commitment, it neglects the antecedents and consequences of low commitment, which can have a detrimental effect on strategy implementation. Guth and MacMillan (1986) addressed the issue of low organizational commitment at a different level of analysis: the need to secure middle managers' commitment to a selected strategy.

IJV managers whose responsibility is the implementation of strategic decisions can be viewed as midlevel managers. Guth and MacMillan (1986) argued that, when middle managers feel that their self-interest is threatened, they can redirect the strategy, delay or reduce the quality of its implementation, or even totally sabotage it. Conversely, when their self-interest is aligned with that of the organization and, in the case of IJVs, with the interests of the parents, it can be expected that IJV managers will exert greater effort to implement the strategy effectively. It is assumed that, provided the strategy is a good one, successful implementation will result in superior performance; if the managers recognize that the strategy is not a good one, or that its implementation may harm their own interests, they are less likely to work for its successful implementation. Thus, securing the commitment of managers to the strategy set for the IJV may be crucial to its effective implementation. A fundamental way of securing managers' commitment to a strategy is to include them in the decision-making process, and recent studies of procedural justice have examined this issue.

Procedural Justice

In many exchange situations, the parties are concerned as much about the procedures used—the rules of the game—as they are about outcomes. In sports, for example, players are concerned that their opponents play according to the rules and that the rules be applied fairly by the umpire or referee, because "procedural justice in games is meant to ensure distributive justice, to ensure that the best man will win" (Homans 1976: 239). Thibaut and Walker (1975) made a clear distinction between distributive justice, which is concerned with the principles by which outcomes of an exchange are allocated among individuals or groups, and procedural justice, which is concerned with the procedures used to determine the outcomes. In their experimental studies of methods of resolving disputes, they concluded that a dispute resolution process is perceived as fairer if control of it is kept in the hands of the disputants and decision control is exercised by an unbiased third party. This conclusion was generally supported by Folger's experimental study (1977), which found that subjects who were given voice (that is, the opportunity to influence allocations) perceived outcomes as fairer than those who had received the same outcomes but were given no voice. The parallel with the arguments in favor of participation in organizational decision-making (Guth and MacMillan 1986; Miller and Monge 1986) is striking, suggesting that the way strategic decisions are made may affect the acceptance of the decisions by those who are to implement them.

Folger and Greenberg (1985) were the first to apply procedural justice to organizational settings and to establish the importance of procedural justice in the context of work organizations. Procedural justice in work organizations is concerned with how individuals view the process used to make the decisions that affect them and, especially, whether they perceive the process to be fair. A fair process is assumed to be one in which the procedures used to determine allocations are perceived to be consistent, accurate, correctable, representative, and ethical, and to suppress bias on the part of the decision maker (Leventhal 1980; Leventhal, Karuza Jr., and Fry 1980). Procedural justice has been applied to performance appraisals (for example, Folger and Greenberg 1985; Greenberg 1986), pay raise decisions (Folger and Konovsky 1989), layoffs (Brockner and Greenberg 1990; Brockner, Tyler, and Cooper-Schneider 1992), compensation plans (Miceli, Jung, Near, and Greenberger 1991), drug-testing in the workplace (Konovsky and Cropanzano 1991), commitment, group attachment, and trust in management teams (Korsgaard, Schweiger, and Sapienza 1995), and formulating and implementing corporate strategies in MNE subsidiaries (Kim and Mauborgne 1991, 1993a, 1993b, 1993c, 1995).

Procedural Justice and Organizational Commitment

Two models of procedural justice explain why individuals view procedures as important (Lind and Tyler 1988). The first is the self-interest model, in which parties to an exchange seek to control the decision-making process in order to maximize their own outcomes. However, the self-interest model does not account for why individuals would perceive as fair an allocation procedure that fails to provide them with the desired level of outcomes, a phenomenon that often occurs in judicial and work settings. A complementary perspective is offered by the group-value model of social behavior, which emphasizes the importance of group identification and group procedures as determinants of individual behavior. According to the group-value model, individuals in groups are less likely to pursue their individual self-interest, because group identification and group procedures are important determinants of individual behavior. Group procedures are viewed as the norms for treatment and decision making within the group; socialization plays an important role in instilling group values, and when group procedures are congruent with the values of the group and individuals, a sense of procedural justice results. It is important to note that the outcomes need not be favorable to an individual for procedural justice to be perceived, as long as the individual has had the opportunity to affirm group membership and status through the voice effect, and provided that the individual's views are considered by the decision maker.

Because procedures are viewed as important features of social life, and because of the close link between procedural justice and group values in the group-value model, procedural justice perceptions can strongly affect group loyalty and group commitment. Within IJVs, group commitment can be manifested by senior managers both at the macrolevel, in terms of commitment to the values and goals of IJV itself and to those of its parent organizations, and at the microlevel, in terms of commitment (or attachment) to the IJV management team and managers' commitment to implementing the IJV's strategy.

Korsgaard, Schweiger, and Sapienza (1995), in an experimental study of decision making in intact teams of managers of a Fortune 500 firm, found a strong relationship between managers' perceptions of the procedural justice of decision making and their attachment to the team. They also found a "frustration effect" when managers believed that their input had been ignored by the team leader; their frustration was reflected in significantly lower feelings of team attachment and trust in the leader. This suggests that managers not only expect to have some input into important decisions (the voice effect), but that they also expect their input to be given proper consideration. The experimental study also concluded that decision quality need not be harmed by the adoption of procedures that foster perceptions of fairness and that result in more positive group affect. Thus, where there is a strong perception of procedural justice in organizational decision making, the effect can be to strengthen both attachment to the management team and commitment to the organization. In the case of an IJV, which may be viewed both as an independent organization and as an affiliate of the parents, the effect may be to strengthen not only group attachment within the IJV management team but also organizational commitment to the IJV as a whole, and to its parents.

HYPOTHESIS 1A: High levels of perceived procedural justice in strategic decision making are associated with high levels of attachment to the IJV top management team.

HYPOTHESIS 1B: High levels of perceived procedural justice in strategic decision making are associated with high levels of organizational commitment to the IJV.

HYPOTHESIS 1C: High levels of perceived procedural justice in strategic decision making are associated with high levels of organizational commitment to the IJV's parent organizations.

Procedural Justice and Commitment to IJV Strategy

The works of Kim and Mauborgne and of Korsgaard, Schweiger, and Sapienza (1995) are particularly relevant to IJVs because they focus on procedural justice, decision making, and top management teams. Kim and Mauborgne (1993a, 1993b) found that the exercise of procedural justice has a positive effect on subsidiary top management compliance, leading to improved implementation of global strategies, and that procedural justice perceptions are positively associated with a subsidiary's ability to gather, interpret, and synthesize the types of information necessary for implementing global strategies. More importantly, perhaps, they found that MNE subsidiary managers are prepared to accept and implement global decisions that are not in their own best interests, provided that they believe they have been treated fairly in the decision-making process. They noted that subsidiary managers in global industries face a dual-allegiance dilemma: subsidiary units are often expected to make sacrifices at the national level or to forgo short-term gains for the sake of long-term priorities to help the parent company leverage its global assets. Procedural justice, then, acts as a countervailing mechanism to give subsidiary managers a sense of ownership of the parent's global strategy. This finding has direct relevance for IJV managers, who may find themselves facing a "tri-allegiance" dilemma: do what is best for Parent A, what is best for Parent B, or what is best for the

IJV and themselves. IJV managers' positive perceptions of procedural justice may result in greater acceptance of and commitment to implementing decisions made for the IJV.

Korsgaard, Schweiger, and Sapienza (1995) also found a positive relationship between managers' perceptions of the procedural justice of strategy making and their commitment to the strategy. This evidence, supported by the group-value model of procedural justice, suggests that perceptions of the procedural justice of strategic decision making may have a direct effect on managers' commitment to implementing strategy.

HYPOTHESIS 1D: High levels of perceived procedural justice in strategic decision making are associated with high levels of commitment to implementing the IJV's strategy.

Korsgaard and her colleagues also noted that as individuals' influence over decisions that affect them decreases, the perceived fairness of the decision-making procedures assumes greater importance. Thus, in an IJV context, the extent to which the venture's parents exert control over strategic decision making in IJVs is expected to affect the relationship between procedural justice and commitment to the IJV strategy. This relationship is examined further in the following section.

Control and Decision Making in IJVs

When a firm enters a joint venture, it gives up some control of the venture's activities. If it has insufficient control over activities it deems important to corporate strategy, its ability to coordinate corporate activities, use resources efficiently, or implement strategy can be impaired (Geringer and Hébert 1989). Thus, a firm may be expected to seek control over those aspects of the IJV's activities it deems essential to its own interests.

Control

Schaan (1983: 57) defined control as "the process through which a parent company ensures that the way a JV is managed conforms to its own interest." He found that control could be exercised through many more mechanisms than had been identified in previous studies, and concluded that control is a complex and multidimensional concept with structural and informal dimensions that offer important mechanisms for its exercise. Just as importantly, Schaan found that firms did not seek to exercise control over all IJV activities, only those strategically important ones crucial to furthering its interests. This conclusion was supported by Geringer's study (1986) of ninety JVs in developed countries. This suggests that a mode of split control may exist in which one parent exercises dominant control over specific JV activities and the other (or the IJV management) exercises dominant control over other activities.

Ownership and control are not synonymous (Geringer and Woodcock 1989); control over an IJV can be exerted in a minority-ownership situation through contractual arrangements such as royalty agreements, patent rights, component supply, and buyback agreements (Contractor 1985). Geringer and Hébert (1989) identified three parameters of control: focus, extent, and mechanisms. Focus of control is the scope of "strategically important" activities (Schaan 1983) over which parents choose to exercise control; extent of control is the relative amount of control a parent exercises over each activity (Killing 1983); and mechanisms of control are the ways control is exercised (Schaan 1983). In a later study, Hébert and Beamish (1994) argued that the division of control is a reflection of each parent's respective bargaining power (Blodgett 1987), and they identified three types of activities that parents seek to control: operations, technology, and strategy. Operational control involves day-to-day decisions in areas such as manufacturing, pricing, marketing, and personnel; technological control relates to decisions over the use of technology, patents, and R&D; and strategic control relates to decisions in four strategic areas: financing, capital expenditures, location of the JV, and nomination of the JV general manager.

Procedural Justice and Parental Control of Strategic Decision Making in IJVs

Of the three types of parental control, strategic control is most in line with the topic of this chapter. We examine here the extent to which parental control of the strategic decision-making process affects IJV managers' perceptions of the fairness of that process.

In an IJV context, strategic decision making can be viewed as a crucial group process, whose outcomes will affect all members of the IJV management team. The primary group for IJV managers is the IJV itself, but *group* here can be viewed in a wider context to include the IJV parents. According to the group-value model, positive perceptions of procedural justice serve to reinforce group norms and strengthen the individual's identification with the group, as well as strengthen the group members' compliance with the decision. In contrast, negative perceptions of procedural justice are likely to weaken the individual's identification with and commitment to the group, and to weaken members' compliance with the decision. Thus, IJV managers' perceptions of the fairness of the decision-making process can have a direct impact on their commitment to the IJV and to implementing its strategy; additionally, depending on the extent to which the parents are involved in the strategic decision-making process, fairness perceptions may also strengthen or weaken their commitment to one or both parents.

The group-value model is reinforced by commitment theory and socialization theory. Identification and internalization have been identified as bases for psychological attachment to organizations (O'Reilly and Chatman 1986). Both identification, which is involvement with a group or organization based on a desire for affiliation, and internalization, which is involvement based on the congruence of personal and organizational values, are attributes of the group-value model of procedural justice (Lind and Tyler 1988). Thus, identification and internalization are strong foundations for establishing group or organizational commitment. Socialization theory (for example, Buchanan 1974; Edstrom and Galbraith 1977) provides additional theoretical support for the group-value model, suggesting that the experience of group membership strengthens group identification and reinforces the acceptance of group norms.

From a group-value model perspective, it is expected that positive perceptions of the procedural justice of the strategic decision-making process will lead to higher levels of organizational commitment and an increased effort to implement strategic decisions. As Korsgaard, Schweiger, and Sapienza (1995) observed, as individuals' influence over decisions that affect them decreases, the perceived fairness of the decision-making procedures assumes greater importance. Therefore, the effect of procedural justice on organizational commitment is expected to be moderated by the extent of the parents' control of the strategic decision-making process.

HYPOTHESIS 2: The impact of IJV managers' procedural justice perceptions on organizational commitment varies according to whether the level of parental control of strategic decision making is high or low. specifically, when parental control of the process is high, a high level of perceived procedural justice is associated with higher levels of organizational commitment and higher levels of commitment to implementing the IJV strategy than when parental control of decision making is low.

Methodology

Research Design and Sample Frame

To test the hypotheses, a survey questionnaire was sent to senior managers of manufacturing IJVs in the U. S. and Canada. As no comprehensive roster of IJVs exists, the following sources were used to select the sampling frame: The *Wall Street Journal Index, Mergers and Acquisitions,* the *Directory of Corporate Affiliations,* the *F&S Index of Corporate Change,* the *Yearbook on Corporate Mergers, Joint Ventures and Corporate Policy,* and *Foreign Direct Investment in the U.S.,* published by the U.S. Department of Commerce. Because of considerations of time and cost, the sampling frame was limited to IJVs with only two parents, at least one of which is headquartered outside the U. S. or Canada. Because commitment to both parents were variables of the study, the sampling frame was further limited to those IJVs in which both parents were represented on the management board.

The unit of study was the IJV top management team. The general manager was asked to distribute the survey to members of the top management team who were not also members of the IJV's board of directors; this was done to avoid a positive bias in the responses, as those closely involved in setting strategic goals would be less likely to be critical of the process and its outcomes. One hundred twenty-eight IJVs were identified that met these criteria; multiple surveys were sent to each of these IJVs between April and September 1995.

Independent Variables

Procedural justice (JVPJ) is the main independent variable of interest for this study. Therefore, we asked about IJV managers' perceptions of the procedural justice of the decision-making process that resulted in establishing the major strategic goals currently facing the IJV. To measure this construct, a five-item measure developed by Kim and Mauborgne (1991) was used. (See the appendix at the end of this chapter for all multiple-scale items and their anchor ratings.) Following Leventhal and his colleagues (Leventhal 1980; Leventhal, Karuza Jr., and Fry 1980), a sixth item was added to assess whether respondents perceived that decision makers always treated them with respect and courtesy, and two final items were added as a global assessment of the fairness of the strategy-making process and respondents' satisfaction with it.

Parental control of the strategic decision-making process (JVPC) was measured by three items on a five-point Likert-type scale that asked respondents the extent to which the parent companies controlled the procedures for making strategic decisions affecting the IJV and to what extent the parent determined when and how changes could be made in the process.

Dependent Variables

Group attachment, or commitment to the IJV top management team (TCOM), was measured by four items on a five-point Likert-type scale, using four items from the Organizational Commitment Questionnaire (OCQ) (Mowday, Steers, and Porter 1979; Mowday, Porter and Steers 1982) that capture identification with the group and internalization of its values (O'Reilly and Chatman 1986). This scale yielded a Cronbach's alpha of .71, the lowest of the multi-item scales but still an acceptable level of internal consistency reliability for field research (Nunnally 1978).

Commitment to the IJV (CMJV) was measured on a five-point Likert-type scale by eleven items from the OCQ. Commitment to Parent A (the foreign parent) (CMPARA) and Commitment to Parent B (usually the local parent) (CMPARB) used the same items as those used to measure commitment to the IJV, with a few minor word changes. In cases where both parents were headquartered overseas, Parent B was also a foreign parent.

Commitment to implementation (COMIMP) of the IJV's strategy was measured with an instrument adapted from that used by Earley and Lind (1987) in order to capture respondents' commitment to a particular course of action. To ensure that respondents within each IJV focused on the same set of strategic decisions, they were asked to address the strategic direction, goals, and responsibilities facing the IJV on January 1.

Control Variables

Many variables may affect organizational commitment, not all of which can be included in a single study. However, several important control variables were identified that might confound the analyses: the age of the venture; its industry, grouped by four-digit SIC code; its size, measured by both number of employees and annual revenue; the number of years of experience that respondents had in the IJV and in either parent; the size of the IJV top management team; and respondents' perceptions of the favorability of the strategic decision outcome, a measure of distributive justice that is not viewed as a design criterion in assessing the impact of procedural justice on compliance with strategic decisions (Kim and Mauborgne 1993a).

Analyses and Results

Of the 128 IJVs identified in the sample frame, responses were received from 54 (42 percent); of these, multiple responses were received from 45 firms and single responses from 9. The majority of responding firms were Japanese-U.S. joint ventures (n = 35, 60 percent), followed by European-U.S. (n = 11, 20 percent) and Canadian-U.S. (n = 4, 7 percent). The industries they represented ranged from automotive (n = 16) and metals (n = 11) to glassmaking (n = 2) and aircraft engines (n = 1). The average number of responses per IJV was 3.1. Table 8.1 shows the means, standard deviations, and Pearson correlations for the main variables in the study. As expected, there was a strong positive correlation ($p < .001$) between the procedural justice variable (JVPJ) and the five commitment variables. The correlation between the parental control variable (JVPC) and the commitment variables was negative, as expected, indicating that a low level of parental control was associated with greater organizational commitment, but the relationships between parental control of decision making and commitment to implementing the IJV strategy (COMIMP), commitment to Parent A (CMPARA), and commitment to Parent B (CMPARB) were not statistically significant.

As the unit of analysis for the study was the IJV top management team, scores for each variable were aggregated across the responses from each firm to yield a single representative score for each IJV management team. An important issue in aggregating data at the organizational level is assessing the reliability of the mean scores—that is, the degree to which respondents within each organization agree with one another (Glick 1985; James 1982; Jones and James 1979; Jones, Johnson, Butler, and Main 1983), but there is considerable disagreement in the literature over which indices are the most appropriate. Two commonly used indices of interrater agreement are the intraclass correlation (ICC) calculated from the mean squares provided by a one-way ANOVA (James 1982), and the average pairwise correlation (Jones, Johnson, Butler, and Main 1983), obtained by calculating a Pearson correlation across all pairs of individuals rating the same object. In this case, average pairwise correlations were used. An initial analysis of the data indicated that in several cases there was considerable disagreement among respondents; these cases were deleted and the resulting analysis yielded an average pairwise correlation of .62, which suggests a moderately high level of agreement among respondents.

Hypotheses 1 and 2 were tested by regression analysis. A multiple regression model was used to test Hypothesis 1, which predicted positive association between procedural justice perceptions and the five commitment variables. Procedural justice (JVPJ) was the main independent variable, and control variables were included in the model; none of the control variables had a significant effect at the $p < .05$ level. The results are shown in Table 8.2. In all cases, the regression model was significant, with F values ranging

	Mean	SD	1	2	3	4	5	6	7
TCOM	4.3544	.5003	1.00						
JVPJ	3.8140	.6441	.5666**	1.00					
COMIMP	4.0409	.5438	.5068**	.5238**	1.00				
JVPC	2.5796	.8419	−.4391**	−.4556**	−.3072	1.00			
CMJV	4.2333	.3799	.4869**	.5824**	.4972**	−.3648*	1.00		
CMPARA	3.7956	.5610	.1400	.4635**	.3389*	−.0027	.5303**	1.00	
CMPARB	3.8212	.6654	.5282**	.6022**	.5155**	−.2000	.5209**	.4210*	1.00

Table 8.1. Descriptive Statistics and Correlations.
$N = 51$ 1-tailed significance: * −.01 ** −.001

Hypothesis 1a: Dependent Variable TCOM

Multiple R	.62795
R^2	.39433
Adjusted R^2	.38171
Standard Error	.32458

ANALYSIS OF VARIANCE

	df	Sum of Squares	Mean Square
Regression	1	3.29242	3.29242
Residual	48	5.05705	.10536

$F = 31.25069$ Signif $F = .0000$

VARIABLES IN THE EQUATION

Variable	B	SE B	Beta	T	Sig T
JVPJ	.40030	.07161	.62795	5.590	.0000
(Constant)	2.86452	.27756		10.320	.0000

Hypothesis 1b: Dependent Variable CMJV

Multiple R	.58241
R^2	.33920
Adjusted R^2	.32571
Standard Error	.31195

ANALYSIS OF VARIANCE

	df	Sum of Squares	Mean Square
Regression	1	2.44762	2.44762
Residual	49	4.76826	.09731

$F = 25.15247$ Signif $F = .0000$

VARIABLES IN THE EQUATION

Variable	B	SE B	Beta	T	Sig T
JVPJ	.34350	.06849	.58241	5.015	.0000
(Constant)	2.92317	.26486		11.037	.0000

Hypothesis 1c: Dependent Variable CMPARA

Multiple R   .46347

R²   .21480

Adjusted R²   .19878

Standard Error .50220

ANALYSIS OF VARIANCE

	df	Sum of Squares	Mean Square
Regression	1	3.38069	3.38069
Residual	49	12.35791	.25220

F = 13.40469   Signif F = .0006

VARIABLES IN THE EQUATION

Variable	B	SE B	Beta	T	Sig T
JVPJ	.40370	.11026	.46347	3.661	.0006
(Constant)	2.25589	.42639		5.291	.0000

Hypothesis 1c: Dependent Variable CMPARB

Multiple R   .60224

R²   .36269

Adjusted R²   .34969

Standard Error .53661

ANALYSIS OF VARIANCE

	df	Sum of Squares	Mean Square
Regression	1	8.02997	8.02997
Residual	49	14.10981	.28796

F = 27.88616   Signif F = .0000

Table 8.2. Regression Model for Hypotheses 1a–1d.

VARIABLES IN THE EQUATION

Variable	B	SE B	Beta	T	Sig T
JVPJ	.62218	.11782	.60224	5.281	.0000
(Constant)	1.44824	.45561		3.179	.0026

Hypothesis 1d: Dependent Variable COMIMP

Multiple R	.52385
R^2	.27441
Adjusted R^2	.25961
Standard Error	.46794

ANALYSIS OF VARIANCE

	df	Sum of Squares	Mean Square
Regression	1	4.05775	4.05775
Residual	49	10.72925	.21896

$F = 18.53158$ Signif $F = .0001$

VARIABLES IN THE EQUATION

Variable	B	SE B	Beta	T	Sig T
JVPJ	.44228	.10274	.52385	4.305	.0001
(Constant)	2.35404	.39730		5.925	.0000

Table 8.2. Regression Model for Hypotheses 1a–1d. (*continued*)

from 13.4 (CMPARA) to 31.25 (TCOM), and R^2 from .21 (CMPARA) to .39 (TCOM). Hypotheses 1a to 1d are therefore supported.

To test the second hypothesis, parental control of the strategic decision-making process (JVPC) was added to the regressions used to test Hypothesis 1. Hypothesis 2 predicts that parental control would have a moderating effect on the relationship between procedural justice and the commitment variables. However, in all cases the introduction of the parental control variable resulted in only a slight increase in R^2, ranging from .01 to .05, but the regression coefficient for the parental control variable was not significantly different from zero. An interaction term (XPJPC) was added to each equation, but again no significant effect occurred at the $p < .05$ level. In the case of commitment to the IJV management team, parental control clearly had some effect on the dependent variable at the $p < .10$ level, but the effect was not sufficiently large to support the hypothesis. However, when the regression criterion was changed to allow the interaction term to enter at the $p < .10$ level, a noticeable change occurred; there was a significant interactive effect ($p = .097$) and a model R^2 of .48 (see Table 8.3).

In conclusion, as predicted in Hypothesis 1, IJV managers' organizational commitment—to the IJV management team, to the IJV itself, to its parents, and to implementing strategic decisions—varies according to their perception of procedural justice. When procedural justice is perceived to be high, organizational commitment is high. Hypothesis 2 predicts that when the control of the strategy-making process is out of the hands of the IJV management team—associated with the negative regression coefficient for JVPC—procedural justice perceptions assume greater importance. However, the support for this hypothesis is weak; there is only partial support for the moderating effect of parental control on the relationship between procedural justice and commitment to the IJV management team ($p < .10$), but no support for a similar relationship holding for the other commitment variables.

Conclusion

The results of the analyses show strong support for the view that IJV managers' perceptions of procedural justice have an important and sizable impact on their attachment to the management team, their commitment to the IJV and its parent organizations, and their commitment to the effective implementation of the IJV strategy. The review of the literature suggests that commitment to implementing a decision or a strategy may be a distinct dimension of organizational commitment, a dimension that is supported by the evidence in this study.

Hypothesis 2a: Dependent Variable TCOM

Multiple R	.69241
R^2	.47943
Adjusted R^2	.44548
Standard Error	.30739

ANALYSIS OF VARIANCE

	df	Sum of Squares	Mean Square
Regression	3	4.00297	1.33432
Residual	46	4.34650	.09449

$F = 14.12142$ Signif $F = .0000$

VARIABLES IN THE EQUATION

Variable	B	SE B	Beta	T	Sig T
XPJPC	.11521	.06804	.77716	1.693	.0971
JVPJ	.04579	.18221	.07183	.251	.8027
JVPC	−.53634	.24965	−1.10220	−2.148	.0370
(Constant)	4.49435	.71693		6.269	.0000

Hypotheses 2b, 2c, 2d

No significant interaction between procedural justice (JVPJ) and parental control of the strategic decision-making process ($p < .10$).

Table 8.3. Regression Model for Hypothesis 2.

Earlier studies of the effect of procedural justice on strategic decision making (for example, Kim and Mauborgne 1993a, 1993b, 1993c, 1995; Korsgaard, Schweiger, and Sapienza 1995) focused on individual outcomes; the focus of this study has been the IJV management team rather than individuals, and the results show that procedural justice in decision making is associated with significantly higher levels of group attachment and group commitment. Group attachment, a sense of identity with the group and its values, is a powerful influence on individuals to pursue group goals rather than their own self-interest (Janis 1982), and procedural justice can be viewed as a mechanism to promote the pursuit of organizational rather than individual goals. In the context of MNE subsidiaries in global industries, Kim and Mauborgne (1993a) discuss the role of procedural justice as a countervailing mechanism that helps compensate for the decline in fiat, monitoring, and auditing capabilities in MNEs. This study suggests that procedural justice may also play an important role in fostering organizational commitment not only to the local parent, but to the distant one; the perceived fairness of the decision-making procedures demonstrates that the foreign parent is concerned about its managers and wants them to feel part of its corporate team. Thus, positive procedural justice perceptions on the part of senior IJV managers may be a means for the distant parent to exert an additional element of control over the subsidiary from a distance.

Parental control of the strategic decision-making process was not found to have an overall significant impact on IJV managers' levels of commitment, contrary to predictions. There are several possible explanations for this. The first is that parental control may not have been well operationalized, and that the construct should have measured parental inputs into strategic decisions rather than control of the decision-making process itself. This approach was considered and rejected, as procedural justice is concerned not with the volume or provenance of inputs but with the process itself and how it is managed. A second explanation is that parental control of the process was not a major issue for managers of the IJVs sampled. Of all the variables studied, parental control had the lowest mean (mean = 2.6, s.d. = .84), which indicates that, for most of the IJVs studied, control of the strategy-making process was not in the hands of the parents but was at least a shared activity. However, there was some support for parental control having an impact on IJV managers' commitment to the management team, such that when IJV managers had less control over how strategic decisions were made, the perceived fairness of the process assumed much greater importance and contributed to a higher degree of commitment to the team.

This study has clear implications for both managers and researchers. For managers of IJVs and their parent organizations, the results indicate that positive procedural justice perceptions on the part of senior IJV managers can mitigate the negative effects of dual allegiance or tri-allegiance by strengthening their commitment to the goals of the IJV and its parent companies and, more specifically, their commitment to implementing the IJV strategy resulting from the strategic decisions that were made. As Kim and Mauborgne indicated in their studies, subsidiary (or here, IJV) managers' compliance with directives from their parent organizations may be crucial to the effective implementation of global strategies, where the roles and responsibilities assigned to a subsidiary may not be optimal from the perspective of subsidiary managers but play a crucial role in the execution of a global strategy. Although the present study examined manufacturing IJVs, there are also clear implications for the managers of service IJVs, especially when the distant parent organization seeks to have the IJV managers exhibit a high degree of commitment and loyalty to its brand, image, and values. At the microlevel, too, positive perceptions of procedural justice result in greater commitment by IJV managers to the IJV management team, fostering a desire to satisfy group interests and goals rather than individual self-interest (Janis 1982) and making it less likely that individual managers will seek to delay or obstruct the implementation of strategic decisions.

For international management researchers, the present study extends procedural justice research to examine its impact on organizational commitment in a more complex organizational form—international joint ventures—than hitherto, one in which managers are expected to exhibit multiple allegiances. The study indicates the need to examine organizational commitment at multiple levels in IJVs: managers' commitment to the IJV and its parents, commitment to the IJV management team, and commitment to implementing the IJV's current strategy. Also, the study furthers our understanding of strategic decision making in IJVs by focusing on the decision-making process, rather than its inputs or outcomes, and suggests that IJV managers' perceptions of the fairness of that process affect their acceptance of and commitment to implementing the strategic decisions that result. Future research should examine the relationship between organizational commitment and IJV performance, and between procedural justice and performance, in order to assess the overall impact of procedural justice perceptions on IJV performance. Also, as suggested earlier, the scope of this research should be extended to include IJVs in service industries.

Finally, some of the limitations of this study should be mentioned. Because the focus of the study was the IJV management team, the overall sample size is relatively low ($N = 51$), which does not permit the use of more sophisticated analyses. Second, the question of causality is an important limitation here because correlations do not necessarily imply causal direction. The results of this study should therefore be treated with caution. Third, all responses were self-reported and may be affected by personal bias and misperceptions. However, for most of the variables, respondents were asked to indicate the management team's assessment, rather than their own personal assessment, in order to avoid personal bias. Also, because multiple responses were aggregated across firms, individual response biases are likely to have been mitigated. Fourth, in survey research there may be a possibility of common method variance; to reduce this possibility, several items were reverse-scored. Fifth, as is common in studies that examine organizational commitment, there was significant correlation among the commitment variables, which raises a potential problem of multicollinearity. In this case, the correlations ranged from .14 to .53, levels that do not appear to be problematic. Furthermore, there is a sufficiently strong conceptual and theoretical foundation to justify the use of multiple indicators of organizational commitment. Finally, to reduce the possibility of social response bias, all respondents were given the standard assurances of anonymity.

Appendix: Measures

The notation (R) means reverse scored. The scale for all items is 1 = not at all, 5 = to a very great extent.

Procedural Justice

Cronbach's alpha = .92. Respondents were asked to indicate "the extent to which the following statements are characteristic of the process used to determine the major strategic direction, goals, and responsibilities of your subsidiary."

1. There was two-way communication in the decision-making process.

2. Decision-making procedures were applied consistently.

3. I was given the opportunity to challenge and refute the views of the decision makers.

4. The decision makers were familiar with and well informed about the situation(s) facing this subsidiary.

5. I was provided with a full account of the final decisions that affected this subsidiary.

6. Decision makers always treated me with respect and courtesy.

Parental Control of Strategic Decision Making

Cronbach's alpha = .83. Respondents were asked to indicate the extent to which

1. The way strategic decisions are made for this subsidiary is determined by the parent corporations.
2. The subsidiary has control over the strategic planning process. (R)
3. The subsidiary's parent corporations decide when and how changes should be made in the strategic planning process.

Group Attachment

Cronbach's alpha = .71. Respondents were asked to indicate "the extent to which you agree with the following statements as they apply to your membership of the subsidiary's management team."

1. My values and those of the other members of the management team are very similar.
2. I'm proud to consider myself a member of this team.
3. I feel that I'm not really a part of this team. (R)

Commitment to IJV Strategy

Cronbach's alpha = .74. Respondents were asked to indicate "the extent to which the following statements currently apply to the subsidiary's management team."

1. We always try to implement strategic decisions as directed.
2. Our spending extra time and energy won't help to achieve this subsidiary's strategic goals. (R)
3. We put in a great deal of effort beyond what is normally required in order to implement the strategic decisions that have been made for this subsidiary.
4. We don't make a special effort to implement those strategic goals or deadlines with which we disagree. (R)
5. Overall, we are committed to achieving the strategic goals that have been made for this subsidiary.

Organizational Commitment: IJV

Cronbach's alpha = .82. Respondents were asked, "With respect to *the management team's* feelings about your subsidiary, please indicate the extent to which you agree with each statement."

1. Our team is willing to put in a great deal of effort beyond that normally expected in order to help this organization be successful.
2. The management team talks up this organization to our friends as a great one to work for.
3. The management team feels very little loyalty to this organization. (R)
4. We are proud to tell others that we work for this organization.
5. Deciding to work for this organization was a definite mistake on our part. (R)
6. Often, we find it difficult to agree with this organization's policies on important matters relating to its employees. (R)
7. We really care about the fate of this organization.
8. There's not much to be gained by sticking out with this organization indefinitely. (R)
9. For us, this is the best of all organizations to be associated with.

Note: Similar items were used to assess Commitment to Parent A and Commitment to Parent B, with minor word changes. Cronbach's alpha was .90 and .91, respectively.

NOTE

1. The terms *fairness* and *justice* are often used interchangeably in the organizational justice literature. When referring to the procedures used, this is acceptable. However, a just outcome may not be perceived as a fair one, so care should be taken not to confuse the two when discussing outcomes rather than procedures. I thank Peter Ring and Jean Johnson for raising this issue.

BIBLIOGRAPHY

Adams, J. S. 1963. Toward an understanding of inequity. *Journal of Abnormal and Social Psychology*, 67: 422–436.

Adams, J. S. 1965. Inequity in social exchange. In L. Berkowitz, editor, *Advances in Experimental Social Psychology*, Vol. 2: 267–299. New York: Academic Press.

Alexander, S., and M. Ruderman. 1987. The role of procedural and distributive justice in organizational behavior. *Social Justice Research,* 1: 177–198.

Allen, N. J., and J. P. Meyer. 1990. The measurement and antecedents of affective, continuance, and normative commitment to the organization. *Journal of Applied Psychology,* 63: 1–18.

Beamish, P. W. 1984. Joint venture performance in developing countries. Unpublished doctoral dissertation, University of Western Ontario, London.

Beamish, P. W. 1988. *Multinational Joint Ventures in Developing Countries.* New York: Routledge.

Blau, P. M. 1968. Interaction: Social exchange. In D. L. Sills, editor, *International Encyclopedia of the Social Sciences,* Vol. 7: 452–458. New York: Macmillan and Free Press.

Blodgett, L. L. 1987. A resource-based study of bargaining power in U.S.-foreign equity joint ventures. Unpublished doctoral dissertation, University of Michigan.

Brockner, J., and J. Greenberg. 1990. The impact of layoffs on survivors: An organizational justice perspective. In J. S. Carroll, editor, *Applied Social Psychology in Organizational Settings.* Hillsdale, N.J.: Lawrence Erlbaum.

Brockner, J., T. Tyler, and R. Cooper-Schneider. 1992. The influence of prior commitment to an institution on reactions to perceived unfairness: The higher they are, the harder they fall. *Administrative Science Quarterly,* 37: 241–261.

Buchanan, B. 1974. Building organizational commitment: The socialization of managers to work organizations. *Administrative Science Quarterly,* 19: 533–546.

Buckley, P. J., and M. Casson. 1988. A theory of cooperation in international business. In F. Contractor and P. Lorange, editors, *Cooperative Strategies in International Business,* 31–54. San Francisco: New Lexington Press.

Contractor, F. 1985. A generalized theorem for joint venture and licensing negotiations. *Journal of International Business Studies,* 16(2): 23–50.

Contractor, F., and P. Lorange. 1988. Why should firms cooperate? The strategy and economics basis for cooperative ventures. In F. Contractor and P. Lorange, editors, *Cooperative Strategies in International Business,* 3–30. San Francisco: New Lexington Press.

Earley, P. C., and E. A. Lind. 1987. Procedural justice and participation in task selection: The role of control in mediating justice judgments. *Journal of Personality and Social Psychology,* 52: 1148–1160.

Edstrom, A., and J. Galbraith. 1977. Transfer of managers as a coordination and control strategy in multinational organizations. *Administrative Science Quarterly,* 22: 248–263.

Eisenberger, R., P. Fasolo, and V. Davis-LaMastro. 1990. Perceived organizational support and employee diligence, commitment, and innovation. *Journal of Applied Psychology,* 75(1): 51–59.

Eisenberger, R., R. Huntington, S. Hutchison, and D. Sowa. 1986. Perceived organizational support. *Journal of Applied Psychology,* 71(3): 500–507.

Etzioni, A. 1961. *A Comparative Analysis of Complex Organizations.* New York: Free Press.

Folger, R. 1977. Distributive and procedural justice: Combined impact of "voice" and improvement on experienced inequity. *Journal of Personality and Social Psychology,* 35: 108–119.

Folger, R., and J. Greenberg. 1985. Procedural justice: An interpretative analysis of personnel systems. In K. Rowland and G. Ferris, editors, *Research in Personnel and Human Resources Management,* Vol. 3, 145–164. Greenwich, Conn.: JAI Press.

Folger, R., and M. A. Konovsky. 1989. Effects of procedural and distributive justice on reactions to pay raise decisions. *Academy of Management Journal,* 32(1): 115–130.

Franko, L. G. 1971. *Joint Venture Survival in Multinational Corporations.* New York: Praeger.

Geringer, J. M. 1986. Criteria for selecting partners for joint ventures in industrialized market economies. Unpublished doctoral dissertation, University of Washington, Seattle.

Geringer, J. M., and L. Hébert. 1989. Control and performance of international joint ventures. *Journal of International Business Studies,* 20(2): 235–254.

Geringer, J. M., and L. Hébert. 1991. Measuring performance of international joint ventures. *Journal of International Business Studies,* 22(2): 249–263.

Geringer, J. M., and C. P. Woodcock. 1989. Ownership and control of Canadian joint ventures. *Business Quarterly,* 54(1): 97–101.

Glick, W. H. 1985. Conceptualizing and measuring organizational and psychological climate: Pitfalls in multilevel research. *Academy of Management Review,* 10: 601–616.

Gould, S. 1979. An equity-exchange model of organizational involvement. *Academy of Management Review,* 4: 53–62.

Greenberg, J. 1986. Organizational performance appraisal procedures: What makes them fair? In R. J. Lewicki, B. H. Sheppard, and M. Bazerman, editors, *Research on Negotiation in Organizations,* Vol. 1: 25–41. Greenwich, Conn.: JAI Press.

Greenberg, J. 1990. Organizational justice: Yesterday, today, and tomorrow. *Journal of Management,* 16(2): 399–432.

Guth, W. D., and I. C. MacMillan. 1986. Strategy implementation versus middle management self-interest. *Strategic Management Journal,* 7: 313–327.

Hamel, G. 1991. Competition for competence and inter-partner learning within international strategic alliances. *Strategic Management Journal,* 12: 83–104.

Harrigan, K. R. 1985. *Strategies for Joint Ventures.* San Francisco: New Lexington Press.

Hébert, L., and P. W. Beamish. 1994. The control-performance relationship in international versus domestic joint ventures. Paper presented at the Academy of Management Meeting, Dallas.

Hergert, M., and D. Morris. 1988. Trends in international collaborative agreements. In F. Contractor and P. Lorange, editors, *Cooperative Strategies in International Business,* 99–111. San Francisco: New Lexington Press.

Homans, G. C. 1961. *Social Behavior: Its Elementary Forms.* London: Routledge.

Homans, G. C. 1976. Commentary on equity theory. In L. Berkowitz and E. Walster, editors, *Advances in Experimental Social Psychology,* Vol. 9: 231–244. New York: Academic Press.

James, L. R. 1982. Aggregation bias in estimates of perceptual agreement. *Journal of Applied Psychology,* 67: 219–229.

Janis, I. L. 1982. *Groupthink: Psychological Studies of Foreign Policy Decisions and Fiascoes.* Boston: Houghton-Mifflin.

Jones, A. P., and L. R. James. 1979. Psychological climate: Dimensions and relationships of individual and aggregated work environment perceptions. *Organizational Behavior & Human Performance,* 23(2): 201–250.

Jones, A. P., L. A. Johnson, M. C. Butler, and D. S. Main. 1983. Apples and oranges: An empirical comparison of commonly used indices of interrater agreement. *Academy of Management Journal,* 26(3): 507–519.

Killing, P. 1983. *Strategies for Joint Venture Success.* New York: Praeger.

Kim, W. C., and R. A. Mauborgne. 1991. Implementing global strategies: The role of procedural justice. *Strategic Management Journal,* 12: 125–143.

Kim, W. C., and R. A. Mauborgne. 1993a. Procedural justice, attitudes, and subsidiary top management compliance with multinationals' corporate strategic decisions. *Academy of Management Journal,* 36(3): 502–526.

Kim, W. C., and R. A. Mauborgne. 1993b. Effectively conceiving and executing multinationals' worldwide strategies. *Journal of International Business Studies,* 24(3): 419–448.

Kim, W. C., and R. A. Mauborgne. 1993c. Making global strategies work. *Sloan Management Review,* Spring: 11–27.

Kim, W. C., and R. A. Mauborgne. 1995. A procedural justice model of strategic decision making: Strategy content implications in the multinational. *Organization Science,* 6(1): 44–61.

Kogut, B. 1988. A study of the life cycle of joint ventures. In F. Contractor and P. Lorange, editors, *Cooperative Strategies in International Business.* San Francisco: New Lexington Press.

Konovsky, M. A., and R. Cropanzano. 1991. Perceived fairness of employee drug testing as a predictor of employee attitudes and job performance. *Journal of Applied Psychology,* 76(5): 698–707.

Korsgaard, M. A., D. M. Schweiger, and H. J. Sapienza. 1995. Building commitment, attachment, and trust in top management teams: The role of procedural justice. *Academy of Management Journal,* 38(1): 60–84.

Leventhal, G. S. 1980. What should be done with equity theory? New approaches to the study of fairness in social relationships. In K. Gerger, M. Greenberg, and R. Willis, editors, *Social Exchange: Advances in Theory and Research,* 27–55. New York: Plenum.

Leventhal, G. S., J. Karuza Jr., and W. R. Fry. 1980. Beyond fairness: A theory of allocation preferences. In G. Mikula, editor, *Justice and Social Interaction.* Bern, Switzerland: Hans Huber.

Lind, E. A., and T. R. Tyler. 1988. *The Social Psychology of Procedural Justice.* New York: Plenum.

Meyer, J. P., and N. J. Allen. 1984. Testing the "side-bet theory" of organizational commitment: Some methodological considerations. *Journal of Applied Psychology,* 69: 372–378.

Miceli, M. P., I. Jung, J. P. Near, and D. B. Greenberger. 1991. Predictors and outcomes of reactions to pay-for-performance plans. *Journal of Applied Psychology,* 76(4): 508–521.

Miller, K. I., and P. R. Monge. 1986. Participation, satisfaction, and productivity: A meta-analytic review. *Academy of Management Journal,* 29(4): 727–753.

Moorman, R. H. 1991. Relationship between organizational justice and organizational citizenship behaviors: Do fairness perceptions influence employee citizenship? *Journal of Applied Psychology,* 76(6): 845–855.

Mowday, R. T., L. W. Porter, and R. M. Steers. 1982. *Employee-Organizational Linkages: The Psychology of Commitment, Absenteeism, and Turnover.* New York: Academic Press.

Mowday, R. T., R. M. Steers, and L. W. Porter. 1979. The measurement of organizational commitment. *Journal of Vocational Behavior,* 14: 224–247.

Nunnally, J. C. 1978. *Psychometric Methods.* New York: McGraw-Hill.

O'Reilly, C. III, and J. Chatman. 1986. Organizational commitment and psychological attachment: The effects of compliance, identification, and internalization on prosocial behavior. *Journal of Applied Psychology,* 71(3): 492–499.

Ouchi, W. G. 1980. Markets, bureaucracies, and clans. *Administrative Science Quarterly,* 25: 129–141.

Peterson, R. B., and J. Y. Shimada. 1978. Sources of management problems in Japanese-American joint ventures. *Academy of Management Review,* 3(3): 796–804.

Schaan, J.-L. 1983. Parent control and joint venture success: The case of Mexico. Unpublished doctoral dissertation, University of Western Ontario, London.

Schweiger, D. M., W. R. Sandberg, and P. L. Rechner. 1989. Experimental effects of dialectal inquiry, devil's advocacy, and consensus approaches to strategic decision making. *Academy of Management Journal,* 32: 745–772.

Steers, R. M. 1977. Antecedents and outcomes of organizational commitment. *Administrative Science Quarterly,* 22: 46–56.

Sullivan, J., and R. Peterson. 1982. Factors associated with trust in Japanese-American joint ventures. *Management International Review,* 22(2): 30–40.

Thibaut, J. W., and L. Walker. 1975. *Procedural Justice: A Psychological Analysis.* Hillsdale, N.J.: Lawrence Erlbaum.

9

SETTING THE STAGE FOR TRUST AND STRATEGIC INTEGRATION IN JAPANESE-U.S. COOPERATIVE ALLIANCES

Jean L. Johnson, John B. Cullen,
Tomoaki Sakano, and Hideyuki Takenouchi

THIS CHAPTER INVESTIGATES *the formation and outcomes of*
trust between partners in a specific form of strategic alliance not
often studied: the nonequity-based international cooperative alli-
ance (ICA). Because a component of the investigation involved
the reciprocal effects of trust in the ICA relationship, dyadic data
were gathered from Japanese and U.S. partners in 101 ICAs
based in Japan. Results showed that partner cultural sensitivity is
an important contributor to trust building for both sides of the
dyad. Complementarity with the partner contributed to trust for
the U.S. but not for the Japanese. Similarity between ICA part-
ners led to trust for the Japanese but not for the U.S. partner.
The results also show strong reciprocal effects of trust in the rela-
tionship, and that trust of the ICA partner leads the individual
firm to integrate the ICA into its own strategic framework.

INTERNATIONAL JOINT VENTURES (IJVs) are perhaps the most widely
studied form of strategic alliance. However, a significant number of international strategic alliances do not involve the creation of separate legal

entities as with the IJV. These alliances involve agreements to cooperate in joint activities such as codevelopment of a new product or technology, or marketing a new product or an existing product to a new market. They span national boundaries and are most often based in one of the partner's home countries. Though not as observable as the IJV, international cooperative alliances (ICAs) also offer an important means of doing business in the global economy.

Despite the frequency with which the ICA occurs and its potential strategic value ("Making Global Alliances Work," 1990), researchers often neglect the study of ICAs. Most of our understanding of international strategic alliances comes indirectly from the study of IJVs (for example, Beamish 1984; Hébert 1994; Killing 1983). However, the ICA differs in a variety of ways. It offers a number of advantages and disadvantages, such as more flexibility, easier dissolution, a lower public profile and, therefore, a veil of competitive secrecy, reduced legal encumbrances, easier negotiation, and a more transient and less institutionalized relationship between partners, to name just a few. Although IJV research provides many insights into ICAs, the uniqueness of the ICA demands additional research.

To understand ICAs more thoroughly, we draw on the IJV and interfirm relationship literature as a starting point for investigating ICA relationships. Given the oft-cited importance of trust (for example, Madhok 1995), we explore trust and its antecedents, along with the extent to which participant firms strategically integrate the ICA. Specifically, we investigate how similarity and complementarity between ICA partners result in the partners trusting each other. We also test the effects of a firm's sensitivity to its partner's culture in building ICA partner trust. An important advance offered in this chapter involves the often suggested but yet unverified reciprocal effects of trust in the ICA relationship. We investigate how a firm's trust in the partner leads that partner to trust it in return. Finally, we investigate how trusting the ICA partner leads the firm to integrate the ICA relationship into its own strategic framework.

In this chapter, we focus on ICAs between U.S. and Japanese firms. All ICAs included were based in Japan. The investigation of the reciprocal effects of trust dictated a dyadic study. Though ICAs can involve more than two firms, we included only those with two partners. Thus, information from key informants in both the Japanese and U.S. firms allowed us to capture fully the reciprocal dynamics of trust in the ICA relationship. Further, the dyadic approach allowed us to investigate our research questions from the perspective of both the U.S. and the Japanese partner firms. In other words, we tested the relationships once with the U.S. partner as the focal firm (that is, from the U.S. partner's perspective), and once with the Japanese partner as the focal firm (that is, from the Japanese partner's perspective).

Building Trust in International Cooperative Alliances

Blau (1964) suggested that one of the most important outcomes of exchange is the creation of trust within and between firms. In the interfirm relationship, trust is essential for the development of enduring partnerships (Morgan and Hunt 1994; Williamson 1985) because it facilitates constructive dialogue and cooperative problem solving (Pruitt 1981). Because trust plays such a central role in interfirm relationships, some researchers argue that trust is the major factor in the formation of strategic partnerships between firms (Madhok 1995).

Definitions of trust abound. For example, Rotter (1967) defines trust as the extent to which the word or promise of another can be believed. Similarly, Blau (1964) holds that trust means that a party's (for example, a firm's) word or promise is reliable and that the party will fulfill obligations in a relationship. Thorelli (1986) contends that trust is the assumption that partners will fulfill their transactional obligations. Most conceptualizations of trust, regardless of their source, pivot on two major factors: a cognitive component derived from confidence in the reliability of a partner, and a behavioral component derived from confidence in the intentions, motivations, or benevolence of a partner (Moorman, Deshpande, and Zaltman 1993; Ring and Van de Ven 1992).

Following from these and other similar conceptualizations, researchers have tended to adopt a multidimensional approach to trust in interfirm relationships. In the marketing interfirm literature, for example, trust exists when both the cognitive component—confidence in the exchange partner's reliability—and the behavioral component—confidence that the exchange partner will behave with benevolence or integrity—are present (Morgan and Hunt 1994). Consistent with recent treatments, in this chapter we conceptualize trust between ICA partners on two dimensions, credibility (the cognitive component) and benevolence (the behavioral component). Credibility connotes the extent to which a firm in the ICA believes that its partner has the required expertise and resources to meet expectations in the ICA and is willing to use them appropriately in the ICA relationship. Benevolence is the extent to which a firm in the ICA believes that the partner has good intentions and will behave in a fashion beneficial to both the ICA and

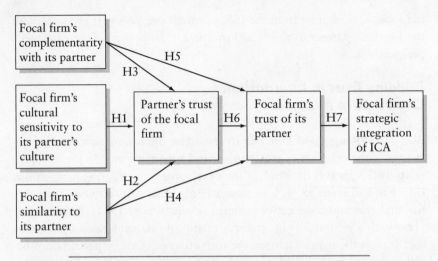

Figure 9.1. Conceptual Model for Trust and the Strategic Integration of a Focal Firm and Its Partner in an ICA.

to it. These intentions and behaviors remain even when new conditions arise (Ganesan 1994).

Given that trust provides a major foundation for the ICA relationship (McLellan 1993), it becomes important to understand the factors in the ICA relationship that facilitate trust. To address this, we isolate several constructs central for trust development between ICA partners, including cultural sensitivity and partner similarity and complementarity. We then develop the relationships between them and trust in the ICA. Figure 9.1 depicts these relationships.

Cultural Sensitivity

When transactions cross cultural boundaries, the effects of cultural differences pervade the relationship. Researchers have demonstrated this in distribution relationships (Johnson, Sakano, Cote, and Onzo 1993) and in IJVs (for example, Cullen, Johnson, and Sakano 1995). Indeed, authors (for example, Lorange and Roos 1993) have linked international strategic alliance success at least in part to firms' ability to tailor their approach to the cultures involved. This tailoring entails what we refer to as cultural sensitivity. Cultural sensitivity begins with the firm's awareness of cultural differences between it and its partners. It also involves dealing with and managing these differences.

To achieve cultural sensitivity and successfully manage cultural differences, members of the firm must develop a fairly deep understanding of the partner's culture. This requires investment of money, managerial effort, and time, specifically in the form of comprehensive cultural training programs. The culturally sensitive firm uses the understanding of partner culture acquired in training to span the cultural gap between ICA partners. It also looks for ways to adapt to cultural differences in its partner's business and relevant social practices. Culturally sensitive managers appreciate the foreign partner's culture and behave accordingly.

Despite the logic of cultural sensitivity in cross-cultural interfirm relationships, with few exceptions (for example, Kraft and Chung 1992) it has not been investigated in this context. However, the international human resources management literature provides compelling evidence for the role of cultural sensitivity in ICAs. Studies indicate that expatriate success in foreign assignments derives largely from what amounts to cultural sensitivity (for example, Dowling and Schuler 1990; Lolla and Davis 1991; Tung 1981). Researchers cite factors such as the ability to relate to cultural counterparts and colleagues, understanding of the other culture, ability to adapt, sensitivity training, and willingness to communicate and make relationships in the other culture. Indeed, studies cite expatriate managers' lack of cultural adjustment as a major reason for failed foreign assignments.

Cultural sensitivity provides a foundation for trust development in the ICA because it strengthens communication effectiveness in it. A lack of cultural sensitivity can easily lead to misunderstandings in cross-cultural interfirm relationships (Datta and Rasheed 1993). When a firm understands and bridges cultural differences in the ICA, the ability to communicate effectively increases substantially. With effective communication, problems are solved, decision making is shared, and expectations are clarified. Good communication contributes to trust building and neutralizes the deleterious effects of conflict and misunderstandings. The firm's sensitivity to its partner's culture removes a significant barrier to communication and, therefore, to trust building.

Further, cultural sensitivity enhances ICA partner trust from a broader perspective. Cultural understanding and adapting require a substantial investment. When the firm makes this investment, it signals commitment to the ICA and suggests that the firm cares about the ICA partner. When the ICA partner feels valued, it will come quickly to trust its counterpart. Thus, we hypothesize:

HYPOTHESIS 1: Greater cultural sensitivity in the focal firm results in higher levels of partner trust of the focal firm.

Similarity

Similarity between ICA partners connotes the extent to which partners overlap on dimensions relevant to ICA success. Doz (1988) suggests that similarity should be at both the strategic and operational levels. Gray and Yan (1992) suggest partners should overlap in broad expertise bases that each brings to the relationship. Geringer (1988) cautions managers regarding partnerships with dissimilar companies. Differences in size, organizational culture, policies, and management styles can affect the quality of a partnership (Bucklin and Sengupta 1993).

Similarity also prepares the common ground for successful relationship management. It provides the basis of cooperation, communication, and effective signaling between the partner firms (Geringer 1988). If partners have similar corporate values, cultures, managerial styles, and processes, the relationship is more viable (Bucklin and Sengupta 1993; Doz 1988; Dymsza 1988). Similarity suggests that partners have similar approaches to problems, or at least are tolerant of each other's approaches. In addition, similarity facilitates the transfer of individual partner strengths, knowledge, and resources to the alliance (Wallets, Peters, and Dess 1994). Without similarity, alliances may fail due to a lack of commonality in strategic fit, managerial processes and styles, and corporate cultures (Dymsza 1988).

Doz (1988) suggests that similarity between ICA partner firms results in an affinity that he refers to as convergence, which facilitates mutual understanding and combats competitive tendencies, strategic conflict, and damaging hidden agendas in the relationship. Convergence involves a deepening in the ICA relationship and a clear shared focus. Because similarity results in a general affinity between partner firms, trust thrives. Thus, we offer:

HYPOTHESIS 2: Greater similarity between focal firm and partner results in higher levels of partner trust of the focal firm.

Complementarity

Complementarity in an ICA suggests that each firm contributes unique strengths and resources valued by the partners (Dymsza 1988). For example, one firm may contribute market knowledge, while a partner firm contributes technical expertise. Harrigan (1985) sees complementarity in terms of strategic symmetry, that is, an interdependence between partners where each contributes a balanced share of unique strengths. Thus, complementarity involves both the uniqueness and symmetry dimensions of partners' resource contributions to the ICA.

Complementarity comprises one important factor in strategic alliance formation (Lorange and Roos 1993). Firms seek partners who provide contributions that work in tandem with their own to produce an enhanced competitive viability for the ICA (Doz 1988). The right combination of competencies and resources results in synergy where total ICA results exceed the sum of the individual partner contributions (Dymsza 1988). In contrast, a lack of strategic symmetry destabilizes the relationship. Researchers (for example, Dymsza 1988) have cited partner perceptions of unequal contribution in strategic alliances as a reason for failure. With complementarity, firms can jointly optimize the unique and respective resources each ICA partner brings. These combined efforts produce more competitive results than either firm could alone (Contractor and Lorange 1988).

Complementarity encourages trust by fostering mutual dependence. Firms rely on each other for enhanced outputs they are unable to accomplish alone. Each partner requires, or at least is better off with, the competencies and resources that the other brings. However, resources and competencies contributed by the firms cannot be used to advantage without trust (Johanson and Mattson 1987). Without trust, the complementary resources and competencies do not produce beyond the sum of their parts and, perhaps, produce even less. With trust, firms can parlay complementary resources and competencies into much more than the sum of their parts. As the potential for such enhanced advantage serves to encourage trust, we offer the following hypothesis:

HYPOTHESIS 3: Greater complementarity between the focal firm and its partner results in higher levels of partner trust of the focal firm.

For the same reasons that apply to partner trust of the focal firm, similarity and complementarity should result in focal firm trust of the partner. Thus, we posit the following:

HYPOTHESIS 4: Greater similarity between the focal firm and its partner results in higher levels of focal firm trust of its partner.

HYPOTHESIS 5: Greater complementarity between the focal firm and its partner results in higher levels of focal firm trust of its partner.

The Reciprocal Effects of Trust

Researchers suggest that trust in the interfirm relationship possesses a self-fulfilling quality. The firm's trust of a partner motivates and encourages that partner to trust in return (Bradach and Eccles 1989). Likewise in the ICA relationship, we expect that trust is contagious. In the ICA, trust begets trust. Despite the logical appeal, these reciprocal effects of trust remain largely conjectural. The major conceptualization of reciprocal trust is set within the firm between managers, and focuses on mistrust. Zand's reciprocal model of mistrust (1981) involves the manager signaling mistrust through behaviors. These signals of mistrust include, for example, withholding information, imposing controls, and surveillance or monitoring. These lead the other manager to perceive and expect mistrust and engage in similar mistrusting behaviors.

The reciprocal effects of trust in the ICA operate in fundamentally the same way. The firm behaves in a fashion that signals trust to its partner. These signals include, for example, meeting obligations and expectations, performing relevant ICA tasks competently and reliably, sharing information, consistently delivering expertise and resources, and generally nurturing the relationship. A firm's trust-signaling behaviors motivate the ICA partner to feel and expect trust. The partner firm then engages in similar behaviors, which signals its trust back to the original firm. In essence, when a firm trusts, that trust manifests itself in behaviors that communicate its trust to partners and encourage the partners to trust in return. On this basis, we offer the following:

HYPOTHESIS 6: Greater trust by one partner firm leads to greater trust by the other partner firm.

Strategic Integration of the ICA by Partner Firms

The literature has shown that close interfirm arrangements benefit participants (for example, Morgan and Hunt 1994; Neupert 1994). In ICAs, as with other interfirm arrangements, trusting relationships offer advantages. Compelling questions derive from the relationship evolution processes in the interfirm alliance. Where does the deepening in the ICA relationship lead? Here, we build on extant interfirm research and the notion of strategic networks (for example, Borys and Jamison 1989; Larson 1992; McLellan 1993) to investigate strategic integration between ICA partners.

Strategic integration occurs when the interfirm relationship moves beyond being simply important—that is, when the relationship is core, rather than peripheral, in either the firm's input or output sector. For example, when a manufacturer and its supplier form an ICA to develop a new product (Neupert 1994), the relationship with the supplier is core in the manufacturer's input sector. The principle of being core in the input or output sector holds regardless of whether the firms are vertically (for example, supplier) or horizontally (for example, potential competitor) aligned.

The strategically integrated relationship offers symbiotic benefits. Each player in the relationship has a stake in the other's success. For the ICA firm, when strategic integration occurs, the partner plays a role in the firm's strategic position. The firm explicitly includes the partner and ICA in its strategic plans. Partners acknowledge and rely, in a strategic sense, on coming together to create value that the individual firms alone could not (Larson 1992; Neupert 1994).

The foundation of strategic integration involves dependence on partner firms. Porter (1986) advises that to achieve internal goals, a firm should avoid depending on trade partners—a view generally shared by many scholars. Unfortunately, this advice ignores the substantial gains derived when firms integrate strategically. Buchanan (1992), for example, found that dependence under the right conditions enhances performance.

Strategic integration can leave the ICA firm vulnerable. The firm assumes a significant level of risk in relying on the ICA as part of its strategy or in putting the ICA in a strategically central role. This presents even more of a problem given the easy dissolution and transient nature of ICAs as compared to other alliance forms. Linking competitive positions to an ICA requires that it have a strong foundation with a strong relationship between the partners. One critical element in such relationships is trust. When the firm trusts its partner, it knows that the partner is reliable and competent. The firm has confidence that the partner will meet obligations and that it can be relied on to protect the ICA relationship. Thus, trust allows the firm to incorporate the ICA into its own strategic framework and optimize an important strategic asset. Hence, we posit:

HYPOTHESIS 7: Greater focal firm trust of its partner results in the focal firm's strategic integration of the ica.

Methods

The study discussed in this chapter involved nonequity cooperative alliances based in Japan and involving Japanese and U.S. firms in the electronics industry in areas such as consumer electronics, computers, and power supplies. They consist of parts supply, original equipment manufacture, technology exchange and development, and sales and marketing types of alliances.

Unlike other types of equity-based international strategic alliances (such as IJVs), the nonequity-based cooperative alliances investigated here did not exist as separate legal entities. This makes data collection on nonequity-based alliances unique and challenging. We began by reviewing public sources of information such as Japanese business periodicals and the *Nikkei Telecom* to identify Japanese firms that were forming or had formed ICAs with Western firms. This procedure is consistent with literature-based alliance counting procedures used in strategic alliance database development (for example, Hagedoorn 1993). We developed a list of fifteen Japanese firms that tended to form ICAs. We personally contacted these firms to enlist their participation and identify the appropriate alliances within the firm. Six of the fifteen declined to participate because of the competitive sensitivity of ICAs. In each of the nine consenting firms, we identified approximately fifteen ICAs, for a total of 135.

Once we gained access and identified appropriate alliances within the firms, we identified qualified key informants. Through personal contact with the ICA, we identified the senior Japanese and U.S. managers based in Japan for each ICA as key informants. We contacted these individuals directly to enlist their participation in the study. We then hand-delivered the research instrument to each with verbal and written instructions to complete the questionnaire independently. We provided self-addressed stamped envelopes to each informant for returning the questionnaire. Follow-up required more personal visits and telephone contact.

Data collection yielded responses from 101 alliances. Ninety-eight of these consisted of matched dyads, with a response from the leading Japanese manager and the leading U.S. manager in the ICA. No sampling frames exist for ICAs other than nonobligatory press announcements; therefore we had no information regarding population size. This precluded any direct calculation of response rate. In addition, our field research suggested that firms often considered even the existence of these nonequity-based alliances as proprietary information. However, assuming each of the fifteen firms contacted participated in fifteen qualified ICAs, that gives an initial sample of 225 ICAs and an estimated response rate of 45 percent.

Instrument Development and Pretest

Our study required new measures for complementarity, similarity, cultural sensitivity, and strategic integration. To do this, we reviewed relevant literature to delimit construct domains and develop operational definitions, and we generated item pools for each construct and assembled them into a preliminary questionnaire draft. A panel of Japanese experts on strategic alliances reviewed this preliminary questionnaire. At this stage, we eliminated several items and reworded several others. Our concern at this stage, especially about trust, was to ensure construct equivalence between the two cultures and the validity of measurement approaches across cultures (Douglas and Craig 1983). Within Japanese culture are concepts related to trust such as *amae* (indulgent dependency) and *giri-ninjo*, (obligation to show compassion to those who show it to you). These are really not consistent with Western ideas of trust, and they apply only to Japanese-Japanese interaction. Thus, the sharp distinction between in-group and out-group interaction made by the Japanese (Alpert and others 1995; Wiersema and Bird 1993) comes into play here. Our preliminary field interviews with Japanese managers indicated strongly that, when interacting with out-groups (for example, foreign partners), the Japanese use partner credibility and benevolence similar to Western cultural perspectives on trust. These managers spoke of whether partners would behave opportunistically, and whether the partner would behave beneficially or detrimentally to them in the ICA relationship.

We developed a Japanese version of the questionnaire with items to parallel the U.S. version. For cultural sensitivity, the items had to refer to an awareness of U.S. and Japanese cultural differences and focus on how the Japanese adapted. A panel of Japanese academics and graduate students translated the questionnaire, which involved several iterations of translation and back translation until the entire panel reached consensus (Douglas and Craig 1983).

The questionnaire was pretested on a pool of four Japanese managers and four U.S. managers with extensive experience in Japanese-U.S. ICAs. We debriefed the pretest subjects at length in personal interviews. Refinement of instructions and individual items resulted.

Measures

To tap the strategic integration between two ICA firms, we developed an eight-item measure. Each queried the ICA managers about ICAs' importance in their firms' strategic plans, the effects on their strategic objectives, and about whether their competitive positions are coupled with ICAs. A sample item: "Our strategic plans relate closely to the relationship with our partner firm." Respondents indicated the extent to which each statement was true on a scale of 1 (strongly disagree) to 7 (strongly agree). See the chapter appendix for details.

We operationalized trust with four items for each dimension (Ganesan 1994). The credibility measure consisted of statements such as: "Our partner is very knowledgeable about everything relevant to our alliance." A benevolence sample item was "We feel that our ICA partner is on our side." Again, managers responded on a 1 (strongly disagree) to 7 (strongly agree) scale.

The measure of cultural sensitivity pivoted on elements isolated for cultural adaptation as identified by Mendenhall and Oddou (1988) for effective cross-cultural training programs. We constructed a set of ten statements addressing the extent to which managers understand and adapt to differences in their partner firms' cultures. Statements such as "In this relationship, we are fully aware that, compared to us, the Japanese need to have much more lengthy discussions before they are comfortable with a course of action" comprised the measure of Western partner cultural sensitivity. We constructed items with parallel logic for the Japanese respondent. Managers indicated their responses on the same 1 to 7 scale.

To measure similarity we developed a set of eleven attributes cited by researchers as important dimensions of ICA partner similarity (Geringer 1988), including size, product lines, organizational cultures (apart from national cultures), goals and objectives, long-term versus short-term orientation, and innovativeness, as examples. Based on these attributes, we constructed statements suggesting similarity (or dissimilarity, which we then reverse coded). Respondents indicated the extent of their agreement on the 1 to 7 scale.

For complementarity, we assessed the unique and balanced contribution of resources brought by each partner to the ICA. We provided a list of seven resources, among them technical skills, market knowledge, access to raw materials, and access to labor pools. For each resource, respondents indicated which side of the ICA dyad contributed most, based on a seven-point scale anchored by "Mostly the Japanese partner" (coded +3) and "Mostly the foreign partner" (coded −3). The two neutral categories (coded 1 and −1) were labeled "about equal." We assumed that if each side made a balanced contribution to the ICA the scale would sum to 0. Thus, for example, if the Japanese partner contributed most of the technical skills and the foreign partner contributed most of the local market knowledge, a 0 would indicate perfectly balanced resource contribution. To measure the balance component of complementarity, we used the following equation: Balance = 21 − ABS ($\sum$ items 1 . . . 7), where subtracting 21 reverse coded the score so that higher scores indicated more balanced resource contribution.

Complementarity, however, implies more than balanced resource contribution. Each partner must contribute unique resources that the other partner needs. For example, without unique contributions, two firms could contribute about equally in terms of technical skills and local knowledge (scored +1 and −1 in our initial coding) and have balanced yet overlapping resource contributions. To obtain information on the uniqueness of contribution from our measure, we recoded the response categories of all seven items to 3, 2, 1, 1, 2, and 3, eliminating negative numbers. Here, a 3 represents resource contributions that are either "mostly the Japanese partner" or "mostly the foreign partner." Summing this information for the scale shows the total unique resource contributions of the partners to the ICA. For example, if the Japanese partner contributed most of the technical skills (scored +3) and the foreign partner contributed most of the local market knowledge (scored +3), a 6 would indicate the maximum unique contributions of resources complementarity. To capture uniqueness in our measure we used the following equation: *Uniqueness* = $\sum$ *(items 1 ... 7)* where the maximum possible score is 21 and higher scores indicate that resources were contributed more by a given partner. To capture both uniqueness and balance in our measure, we combined the estimation of balance with uniqueness in the following equation: *Complementarity = Balance * Uniqueness*, with higher scores indicating greater complementarity.

Data Analysis

Before hypotheses testing, we validated the measures. Exploratory factor analyses revealed strong single-factor solutions for the trust and strategic integration measures on both sides of the dyad. The variance explained by the first factor was over 74 percent for strategic integration and 70 percent for trust. All factor loadings for individual items were at or above .70. The Cronbach's alphas exceeding .90 for strategic integration and trust for both Japanese and U.S. responses (see Table 9.1) surpassed recommended benchmarks for reliability (Nunnally 1978). The factor and reliability analyses revealed one problematic item in the cultural sensitivity measure; deletion of that item resulted in a single factor and Cronbach's alphas of approximately .90.

Combined factor analyses performed separately for the Japanese and U.S. responses assessed discriminant validity. With few exceptions, the factors emerged consistent with the *a priori* operationalizations. Nearly all the items loaded greater than .60 on their respective factors. In the few cross-loading instances, the item still loaded at .4 or greater on its correct factor. The overall pattern of results suggested the cross-loadings did not pose a threat to validity.

Our understanding of the complementarity and similarity constructs from preliminary field interviews, pretesting, the literature, and our conceptualizations suggested formative measurement approaches. In a practical sense, formative measures involve a checklist approach, where each

	U.S. PARTNER					JAPANESE PARTNER				
	Cultural Sensitivity	Comple-mentarity	Similarity	Trust	Strategic Integra-tion	Cultural Sensitivity	Comple-mentarity	Similarity	Trust	Strategic Integra-tion
Cultural Sensitivity	.91					.89				
Comple-mentarity	-.01	—				.18	—			
Similarity	.14	-.06	—			.18	.09	—		
Trust	.66	.01	.24	.94		.54	.04	.22	.92	
Strategic Integration	.74	-.01	.32	.74	.95	.31	-.03	.10	.49	.94
# of items	9	7	14	8	8	9	7	14	8	8
Means	32.72	177.71	53.73	31.71	32.72	38.82	176.42	49.92	31.51	28.89
SD	7.98	41.16	9.60	8.09	7.97	7.93	42.37	9.21	7.29	8.25

Table 9.1. Correlations, Means, and Standard Deviations (SDs).
Note: Cronbach's alphas on diagonal.

item embodies a single dimension of the construct. With formative measures, traditional associational validation procedures do not apply (Bollen and Lennox 1991). Validation rests largely on the thoroughness with which the construct domain is established and tapped—that is, content validity. In the complementarity and similarity scales, based on the literature, expert panel review, and pretesting we developed a set of similarity and complementarity dimensions. These scale development procedures and a visual inspection of the items suggest content validity. Except for the complementarity composite above, we summed the items to form scales for data analysis.

We tested hypotheses for the U.S. and Japan separately in a series of OLS regressions (Table 9.2). Although no formal hypotheses were involved, we also investigated the differences between Japanese and U.S. ICA partner results. To explore these differences, we compared each OLS parameter estimate for the Japanese and U.S partners. We followed procedures outlined by Cohen and Cohen (1983) to calculate a test statistic that conforms to the t-distribution (Table 9.3).

Results

The first three hypotheses concern the antecedents of partner trust of the focal firm, in this case, the Japanese partner's trust of the U.S. (focal) firm.

U.S. ICA Firm

Overall, the equation testing H1–H3 was significant, with an F statistic of 36.27 ($p < .000$). The three antecedent variables explained 54 percent of the variance in Japanese partner trust. In H1, we hypothesized that U.S. cultural sensitivity enhances Japanese partner trust. The statistically significant standardized parameter estimate of .70 ($p < .01$) indicated support for H1. We expected that similarity and complementarity, H2 and H3, would increase partner trust. The estimate of .12 ($p < .10$) suggested support for H2. However, the statistically nonsignificant estimate of $-.11$ for complementarity indicated no support for H3.

H4 through H6 concern the antecedents of the U.S. (focal) firm's trust of the Japanese partner. The equation testing H4–H6 was significant ($F = 90.83$, $p < .000$), with Japanese partner trust, similarity, and complementarity explaining nearly 74 percent of the variance in U.S. firm trust. In H4 and H5, we expected similarity and complementarity to increase U.S. firm trust. The results indicated no support for similarity (H4). The estimate of .12 ($p < .05$) for complementarity indicates support for H5. H6

Dependent Variable	Independent Variable	Standardized Estimate	t-value
Estimates from U.S. firm perspective			
Japanese partner trust of U.S. firm	U.S. firm cultural sensitivity	.700	9.87***
	Similarity	.117	1.64*
	Complementarity	−.111	1.58
$F = 11.99, p < .000; R^2 = .49$			
U.S. firm trust of Japanese partner	Similarity	.055	1.03
	Complementarity	.120	2.26**
	Japanese partner trust of U.S. firm	.810	15.90***
$F = 90.83, p < .000, R^2 = .74$			
Strategic integration	U.S. firm trust of Japanese partner	.750	11.07***
$F = 122.50, p < .000, R^2 = .56$			
Estimates from Japanese firm perspective			
U.S. partner trust of Japanese firm	Japanese firm cultural sensitivity	.447	4.70***
	Similarity	.062	.66
	Complementarity	−.063	.67
$F = 8.16, p < .000; R^2 = .21$			
Japanese firm trust of U.S. partner	Similarity	.101	1.88*
	Complementarity	−.027	.51
	U.S. partner trust of Japanese firm	.840	15.71***
$F = 87.95, p < .000, R^2 = .74$			
Strategic integration	Japanese firm trust of U.S. partner	.489	5.46***
$F = 29.85, p < .000, R^2 = .24$			

Table 9.2. OLS Regression Estimates for
U.S. and Japanese Firms in ICAs.
$*p < .10$ $**p < .05$ $***p < .01$

Hypothesis	U.S. Firms	Japanese Firms	Comparison
1. Focal cultural sensitivity → Partner trust	Support	Support	Japanese lower**
2. Focal similarity → Partner trust	Support	No support	No difference
3. Focal complementarity → Partner trust	No support	No support	No difference
4. Focal similarity → Focal trust	No support	Support	No difference
5. Focal complementarity → Focal trust	Support	No support	Japanese lower***
6. Partner trust → Focal trust	Support	Support	Japanese higher***
7. Focal trust → Focal strategic integration	Support	Support	Japanese lower***

Table 9.3. Summary of Hypothesis Tests for U.S. and
Japanese Partners and *Post Hoc* Comparison of Differences.
*$p < .10$ **$p < .05$ ***$p < .01$

addresses the reciprocal effects of trust. Specifically, we expected that trust on the part of the Japanese partner leads to trust on the part of the U.S. firm. The statistically significant parameter estimate of .810 ($p < .000$) indicated strong support for H6.

H7 addressed the effects of U.S. firm trust of the Japanese partner on the extent of U.S. firm strategic integration. The standardized parameter estimate of .75 ($p < .001$) shows support of H7. Trust explained 56 percent of the variance in strategic integration.

Japanese ICA Firm

For this set of results, interpretation takes the perspective of the Japanese firm, that is, the Japanese firm becomes the focal firm. H1 through H3 explore how the factors on the Japanese firms' side of the ICA result in their U.S. partners trusting them. The equation testing H1–H3 was significant overall, with an F statistic of 8.16 ($p < .001$). The antecedent variables explained 21 percent of the variance in U.S. partner trust for the Japanese firm. The statistically significant parameter estimate of .45 ($p < .001$)

showed support for H1, that Japanese firm cultural sensitivity results in U.S. partner trust. The results for similarity and complementarity suggested no support for H2 and H3.

The next three hypotheses address the antecedents the Japanese firms' own trust of their U.S. partner. Overall, the equation was significant ($F = 87.95, p < .000$), and these variables explained nearly 74 percent of the variance in Japanese firm trust of the U.S. counterpart. With a parameter estimate of .101 ($p < .10$), H4, that Japanese similarity to the U.S. partner results in a greater tendency to trust that U.S. partner, was supported. The nonsignificant estimate indicated no support for H5, that Japanese complementarity resulted in trust of the U.S. partner. In H6, we again expected reciprocal effects of trust. From the Japanese perspective, U.S. partner trust leads to the Japanese firm's trust in return. The results confirmed our expectations with a parameter estimate of .84 ($p < .01$).

In H7 we expected that the Japanese firms' trust of their U.S. partners enhances the Japanese firms' tendency to incorporate the ICA into their strategic frameworks (that is, strategically integrate). The statistically significant estimate of .489 ($p < .01$) supports H7. Trust of the U.S. partner explained 24 percent of the variance in the Japanese firms' strategic integration of this ICA.

U.S.-Japanese ICA Partner Differences

The results revealed several noteworthy differences between the Japanese and U.S. partners. In equations involving antecedents of partner trust, the U.S. firm factors explained 54 percent of the variance in Japanese trust of the U.S. firm, while Japanese partner factors explained 21 percent of the variance in U.S. trust of the Japanese firm. For the equation testing the antecedents of the focal firm's trust of its partner, results indicated similar amounts of explained variance in focal firm trust for the partner for both the Japanese and U.S. The explained variance in strategic integration by focal firms of their ICA partner was greater for the U.S. (56 percent) than for the Japanese (24 percent).

A direct comparison of the specific parameter estimates (see Table 9.3) shows that, in four hypotheses, U.S. and Japanese results were significantly different. In H1, the effects of cultural sensitivity on partner firm trust was significantly greater for building Japanese partner trust than U.S. partner trust. That is, U.S. firms' cultural sensitivity contributed more to Japanese trust of U.S. firms than the Japanese firms' cultural sensitivity contributed to U.S. partners' trust of the Japanese. The comparison for H5 suggested that complementarity is more important in building U.S.

trust of the Japanese than it is for building Japanese trust of U.S. firms. The comparison for H6 indicated that the reciprocal effects of trust were stronger for the Japanese than for the U.S. That is, a U.S. firm's trust in their Japanese partner resulted in greater trust by the Japanese than when the positions were reversed. For H7, U.S. trust of the Japanese resulted in more strategic integration of the relationship than did the Japanese firms' trust of their U.S. partners.

Conclusion

Cooperative alliances succeed when partners merge firm-specific assets for mutual advantage. This cooperative behavior may have various motivations (Kogut 1988). It may reduce transaction costs without the costs of internalization (McLellan 1993), or provide competitive advantage (Neupert 1994), or gain organizational knowledge (Inkpen 1992). Regardless of the motivation, however, most experts attribute the success of cooperative arrangements to how well the partners get along (for example, Beamish 1984; Cullen, Johnson, and Sakano 1995). Cooperation works when the relationship "generates the largest possible amount of *mutual* trust" (Buckley and Casson 1988: 24, emphasis added). Because of the potential benefits of trust in cooperative relationships, we investigated its reciprocal effects in Japanese-U.S. ICAs. Our findings of reciprocal trust between Japanese and U.S. partners suggest the presence of a trust cycle where trust begets trust. From the focal firm's perspective, when your partner trusts you, you trust your partner. Importantly, because our data come from self-reports of trust by each partner they avoid the cognitive consistency biases. These biases would exist had we asked the firms whether they trusted their partners and whether they perceived that their partners trusted them.

We found that reciprocal trust was greater for the Japanese than for the U.S., suggesting that reciprocity (Gouldner 1960) and pressure to seek win-win solutions (Axelrod 1984) may be more prevalent with the Japanese. Conversely, should the Japanese perceive a violation of their trust by partners, they will cycle quickly into distrust (Brown, Rugman, and Verbeke 1989).

From a broad perspective, our treatment of trust has its roots in the classic social psychological theories of liking behavior. Similarity and complementarity predict liking, and if partners like each other, trusting is more likely. Further, we drew on the literature that prescribes how to choose alliance partners and how to prepare managers for international cooperation. Good partner selection and good preparation leads to trust and its benefits (Geringer 1988). However, in spite of the recommendations that similarity and complementarity contribute to the development of the ICA relationship, neither had major effects on trust. Apparently, although complementarity no doubt offers advantages, it may also introduce asymmetries in relationship dependence structures. These dependence imbalances result from variances in the importance of contributions by the individual partners. Partner tolerances for dependence and the risks it brings may differ. Thus, the possible dependence introduced by complementarity, and a firm's possible aversion to it, may diminish the positive effects of complementarity in relationship building. Likewise, although similarity may bring benefits, it can also introduce competition in the relationship. If partners are similar on too many dimensions, they may find themselves actually competing rather than cooperating. This could diminish the positive effects of similarity.

In further consideration of complementarity and similarity, it seems unlikely that both would occur in the same relationship. Perhaps more likely, partners are either similar or complementary. We explored this in a *post hoc* investigation of whether a trade-off in similarity and complementarity occurs in these relationships. We checked whether similarity assumes a larger role when complementarity is not present, and vice versa. We found that this trade-off existed for the U.S. partners but not for the Japanese. That is, for the U.S. partner, trust of the Japanese partner developed when either similarity or complementarity existed, but not when both were present.

From a social psychological perspective, another important factor in relationship building is sensitivity to the needs of another. This takes the more specific form of cultural sensitivity in cross-culture interfirm alliances. Scholars have recommended cross-cultural preparation before entering international alliances (Geringer 1988). Indeed, a failure to break from culture-bound views of business can lead to trouble in Japanese-Western alliances (Pucik 1988). Our findings supported this notion. For both Japanese and U.S. partners, cultural sensitivity predicted increased trust in their partners. Apparently, cultural sensitivity provides a foundation on which trust builds. We suspect that cultural sensitivity creates a benevolent interorganizational climate (Cullen, Victor, and Stephens 1989) that provides fertile ground for the development of mutual trust. Cultural sensitivity of the U.S. partner was more important for Japanese trust than the reverse. This suggests that sensitivity to interpersonal interaction on the U.S. side was key in generating trust from the Japanese. Given that Japanese culture is high context, culturally sensitive behaviors may communicate to the Japanese an aura of trustworthiness that goes beyond verbal communication.

Relationships between firms can range from those with minimal importance to those that are crucial for organizational survival. We view the degree of strategic integration as a progressive involvement of two firms in a relationship that has strategic consequences for the individual firms and their success. A successful ICA may not require high levels of strategic integration. However, higher levels of strategic integration may provide value-added benefits that lead to the most successful ICA (Larson 1992). Because strategic integration increases vulnerability and creates the potential for opportunism, a firm's trust of its partner is crucial for strategic integration. Our findings clearly supported this. Surprisingly, considering the Japanese use of personal relationships in business, trust increased strategic integration less for the Japanese than for their U.S. partners.

There are several limitations to our study. First, we examined existing ICAs at one point in time and with major Japanese companies. Studying ICAs from birth to death would provide a more dynamic view of how mutual trust develops and the impact of trust on strategic integration and the relationship. Second, we suspect that the relationships were successful and that partners had experience in cooperative alliances. In addition, although there was considerable variance in strategic integration, the fact that U.S. firms were actively involved with Japanese firms in Japan suggests the firms were inherently more strategically integrated. Third, our treatment of complementarity did not consider the importance of the unique partner contributions. Investigating the importance of contributions may help in understanding the role of complementarity in alliances. However, our study addressed the important and neglected question of conditions in the ICA that set the stage for trust and strategic integration. Other questions about the role of cultural sensitivity, trust, and strategic integration in relation to variables such as commitment, communication processes, investment of resources, and performance, still remain and should be addressed in future research.

In summary, trust is key to a cooperative relationship. However, the marriage of firms from different cultures creates a potential for opportunism, conflict, and mistrust. Without cultural sensitivity to each other, partners fail to work out problems. Instead, they retreat to their own companies or cultures, leaving issues unresolved and feeling that the venture is not worth the effort. Managerial implications of our study suggest that companies should invest heavily in cross-cultural training for managers, technicians, and workers who participate in ICAs. Subjective cultural factors related to social interaction may be as important as the more objective economic and strategic compatibility of firms. That is, even if the relationship is logical from a business point of view, it may not work without cultural sensitivity and the eventual resulting trust. A relationship without trust makes partners tentative in their involvement and reluctant to reveal their true motives or share knowledge. Without trust, partners hold back information or take unfair advantage if given the opportunity (McLellan 1993). When this happens, the ICA seldom evolves to offer the benefits of a strategically integrated relationship.

Appendix: Measures

Japanese and U.S. managers were given the following questionnaire items (adapted by nationality).

Strategic Integration

Scale anchors: 1 = strongly disagree, 7 = strongly agree.

1. Our firm's strategic plans link closely to the relationship with our partner firm.

2. If our partner went out of business, we would immediately have to make major changes in our strategic plans.

3. We would not be able to achieve our strategic goals and objectives without this relationship with our partner.

4. This relationship provides our firm with many strategic benefits.

5. When we develop our strategic plans, our partner firm is a large part of the picture.

6. We must maintain a strong, healthy relationship with our partner to be able to implement our strategic plan.

7. Our competitive position is closely coupled to our relationship with our partner firm.

8. The relationship with our partner is strategically very important to our firm.

Trust

Items 1 through 4 address credibility; 5 through 8 address benevolence. Scale anchors: 1 = strongly disagree, 7 = strongly agree.

1. We can always rely on our Japanese partner to do their part in our alliance.

2. We know that our Japanese partner is capable and competent.

3. Our Japanese partner is always frank and truthful in its dealings with us.

4. Our Japanese partner is very knowledgeable about everything relevant to our alliance.

5. Our Japanese partner would go out of its way to make sure our firm is not damaged or harmed in this relationship.

6. In this relationship, we feel like our Japanese partner cares what happens to us.

7. Our Japanese partner always looks out for our interests in this alliance.

8. We feel like our Japanese partner is on our side.

Cultural Sensitivity

Item 6 deleted in scale purification. Scale anchors: 1 = strongly disagree, 7 = strongly agree.

1. In our firm, we know that business is done very differently in Japan.

2. In this relationship, we always try to show our willingness to adapt to the Japanese way of doing things.

3. Our managers and representatives are aware that the norms for business communication are different in Japan.

4. In our firm, we have worked very hard to familiarize ourselves with the Japanese legal and economic environment.

5. We appreciate the nature of Japanese decision making and management techniques.

6. Our managers are sensitive to the amount of time it takes Japanese managers to decide on an action.

7. Our managers and representatives know not to press individual Japanese managers for immediate decisions.

8. We are fully aware and understand that, compared to us, the Japanese need to have much more lengthy and detained discussions before they are comfortable committing to a course of action.

9. No one in our firm seems to know anything about the Japanese culture and way of doing business.

10. A number of our representatives and managers speak Japanese or are spending much time learning Japanese.

Similarity

Scale anchors: 1 = strongly disagree, 7 = strongly agree.

1. Our partner's firm is approximately the same size (that is, number of employees) as ours.
2. We have a very similar product line to our partner's product line.
3. Our partner's typical strategies for introducing new products is similar to ours.
4. Our partner's technological expertise is similar to ours.
5. In spite of differences in national culture, we have a similar organizational culture to our partner's.
6. Our firms do approximately the same volume of business.
7. Our long-term strategies are similar to our partner's long-term strategies.
8. Our company's philosophy is more risk-taking than that of our partner.
9. The organizational structure of our two companies is similar.
10. Our partner is more concerned with immediate growth than we are.
11. Our partner is more concerned with immediate profit than we are.
12. We are more technologically innovative than our partner.
13. Our partner firm and our firm contribute different technological skills to our alliance.
14. Although our short-term strategic goals for the alliance differ from our partner's, the differences are not in conflict.

Complementarity

Scale anchors: 1 = mostly Japanese partner, 7 = mostly foreign partner.

1. Technical skills
2. Knowledge of the market
3. Proximity of the market
4. Low-cost raw materials

5. High-quality labor
6. Management skill
7. Plant capacity

BIBLIOGRAPHY

Alpert, F., M. Kamins, T. Sakano, N. Onzo, and J. Graham. 1995. Retail buyer decision-making in Japan: What U.S. sellers need to know. Marketing Science Institute Working Paper, Report no. 95–108.

Axelrod, R. 1984. *The Evolution of Cooperation.* New York: Basic Books.

Beamish, P. 1984. Joint venture performance in developing countries. Unpublished doctoral dissertation, University of Western Ontario, London.

Blau, P. M. 1964. *Exchange and Power in Social Life.* New York: Wiley.

Bollen, K. A., and R. Lennox. 1991. Conventional wisdom on measurements: A structural equation perspective. *Psychological Bulletin,* 110: 305–314.

Borys, B., and D. B. Jamison. 1989. Hybrid arrangements as strategic alliances: Theoretical issues in organizational combinations. *Academy of Management Journal,* 14(2): 234–249.

Bradach, J. L., and R. G. Eccles. 1989. Price, authority, and trust: From ideal types to plural forms. *Annual Review of Sociology,* 15: 97–118.

Brown, L. T., A. M. Rugman, and A. Verbeke. 1989. Japanese joint ventures with Western multinationals: Synthesizing the economic and cultural explanations of failure. *Asia Pacific Journal of Management,* 6: 225–242.

Buchanan, L. 1992. Vertical trade relationships: The role of dependence and symmetry in attaining organizational goals. *Journal of Marketing Research,* 29 (February): 65–76.

Buckley, P. J., and M. Casson. 1988. The concept of cooperation. *Management International Review,* 28: 19–38.

Bucklin, L. P., and S. Sengupta. 1993. Organizing successful co-marketing alliances. *Journal of Marketing,* 57: 32–46.

Cohen, J., and P. Cohen. 1983 (second edition). *Applied Multiple Regression/Correlation Analysis for the Behavioral Sciences.* Hillsdale, N.J.: Lawrence Erlbaum.

Contractor, F., and P. Lorange. 1988. Why should firms cooperate? The strategy and economics basis for cooperative ventures. In F. Contractor and P. Lorange, editors, *Cooperative Strategies in International Business,* 3–30. San Francisco: New Lexington Press.

Cullen, J. B., J. L. Johnson, and T. Sakano. 1995. Japanese and local partner commitment to IJVs: Psychological consequences of outcomes and investments in the IJV relationship. *Journal of International Business Studies,* 26(1): 91–116.

Cullen, J. B., B. Victor, and C. Stephens. 1989. An ethical weather report: Assessing the organization's ethical climate. *Organizational Dynamics,* 18: 50–62.

Datta, D. K., and A.M.A. Rasheed. 1993. Planning international joint ventures: The role of human resource management. In R. Culpan, editor, *Multinational Strategic Alliances,* 251–272. New York: International Business Press.

Douglas, S. P., and C. S. Craig. 1983. *International Marketing Research.* Englewood Cliffs, N.J.: Prentice Hall.

Dowling, P. J., and R. S. Schuler. 1990. *International Dimensions of Human Resource Management.* Boston: PWS-Kent.

Doz, Y. L. 1988. Technology partnerships between larger and smaller firms: Some critical issues. In F. Contractor and P. Lorange, editors, *Cooperative Strategies in International Business,* 317–338. San Francisco: New Lexington Press.

Dymsza, W. A. 1988. Success and failures of joint ventures in developing countries: Lessons from experience. In F. Contractor and P. Lorange, editors, *Cooperative Strategies in International Business,* 403–424. San Francisco: New Lexington Press.

Ganesan, S. 1994. Determinants of long-term orientation in buyer-seller relationships. *Journal of Marketing,* 22 (April): 1–19.

Geringer, J. M. 1988. Partner selection criteria for developed country joint ventures. *Business Quarterly,* 53(1): 67–84.

Gouldner, A. 1960. The norm of reciprocity: A preliminary statement. *American Sociological Review,* 25: 161–178.

Gray, B., and A. Yan. 1992. A negotiations model of joint venture formation, structure and performance: Implications for global management. *Advances in International Comparative Management,* 7: 41–75.

Hagedoorn, J. 1993. Understanding the rationale of strategic technology partnering: Interorganizational modes of cooperation and sectoral differences. *Strategic Management Journal,* 14: 371–385.

Harrigan, K. R. 1985. *Strategies for Joint Ventures.* San Francisco: New Lexington Press.

Hébert, L. 1994. Division of control, relationship dynamics and joint venture performance. Unpublished doctoral dissertation, University of Western Ontario, London.

Inkpen, A. C. 1992. Learning and collaboration: An examination of North American–Japanese joint ventures. Unpublished doctoral dissertation, University of Western Ontario, London.

Johanson, J., and L.-G. Mattson. 1987. Interorganizational relations in industrial systems: A network approach compared with the transaction cost approach. *International Studies of Management and Organization,* 17(1): 34–48.

Johnson, J. L., T. Sakano, J. Cote, and N. Onzo. 1993. The exercise of interfirm power and its repercussions in U.S.-Japanese channel relationships. *Journal of Marketing,* 30 (April): 1–10.

Killing, P. 1983. *Strategies for Joint Venture Success.* London: Croom Helm.

Kogut, B. 1988. Joint ventures: Theoretical and empirical perspectives. *Strategic Management Journal,* 9: 319–332.

Kraft, F. B., and K. H. Chung. 1992. Korean importer perceptions of U.S. and Japanese industrial goods. *International Marketing Review,* 9(2): 59–73.

Larson, A. 1992. Network dyads in entrepreneurial settings: A study of the governance of exchange relationships. *Administrative Science Quarterly,* 37: 76–104.

Lolla, C., and H. J. Davis. 1991. Cultural synergy and the multicultural workforce: Bridging occidental and oriental cultures. *Advances in International and Comparative Management,* 6: 103–125.

Lorange, P., and J. Roos. 1993. *Strategic Alliances: Formation, Implementation and Evolution.* Cambridge, Mass.: Blackwell.

Madhok, A. 1995. Revisiting multinational firms' tolerance for joint ventures: A trust-based approach. *Journal of International Business Studies,* 26(1): 117–137.

Making global alliances work. 1990. *Fortune,* December 17: 121–126.

McLellan, K. 1993. Outsourcing core skills into non-equity alliance networks. Unpublished doctoral dissertation, University of Western Ontario, London.

Mendenhall, M., and G. Oddou. 1988. Acculturation profiles of expatriate managers: Implications for cross-cultural training programs. *Columbia Journal of World Business,* 21: 73–79.

Moorman, C., R. Deshpande, and G. Zaltman. 1993. Factors affecting trust in market research relationships. *Journal of Marketing,* 57 (January): 81–101.

Morgan, R. M., and S. D. Hunt. 1994. The commitment-trust theory of relationship marketing. *Journal of Marketing,* 58 (July): 20–38.

Neupert, K. 1994. Implementing strategic buyer-seller alliances for product development. Unpublished doctoral dissertation, University of Western Ontario, London.

Nunnally, J. 1978. *Psychometric Theory.* New York: Free Press.

Porter, M. E. 1986. *The Competitive Advantage of Nations.* New York: Free Press.

Pruitt, D. G. 1981. *Negotiation Behavior.* New York: Academic Press.

Pucik, V. 1988. Strategic alliances with the Japanese: Implications for human resource management. In F. Contractor and P. Lorange, editors, *Cooperative Strategies in International Business,* 487–498. San Francisco: New Lexington Press.

Ring, P. S., and A. H. Van de Ven. 1992. Structuring cooperative relationships between organizations. *Strategic Management Journal,* 13: 483–498.

Rotter, J. B. 1967. A new scale for the measurement of interpersonal trust. *Journal of Personality,* 35 (December): 651–665.

Thorelli, H. B. 1986. Networks: Between markets and hierarchies. *Strategic Management Journal,* 7: 37–51.

Tung, R. L. 1981. Selection and training of personnel for overseas assignments. *Columbia Journal of World Business,* 16(1): 68–78.

Wallets, B. A., S. Peters, and G. G. Dess. 1994. Strategic alliances and joint ventures: Making them work. *Business Horizons,* July-August: 5–10.

Wiersema, M. F., and A. Bird. 1993. Organizational demography in Japanese firms: Group heterogeneity, individual dissimilarity, and top management team turnover. *Academy of Management Journal,* 36(5): 996–1025.

Williamson, O. E. 1985. *The Economic Institutions of Capitalism.* New York: Free Press.

Zand, D. E. 1981. *Information, Organization and Power: Effective Management in the Knowledge Society.* New York: McGraw-Hill.

10

A COMMITMENT-TRUST MEDIATED FRAMEWORK OF INTERNATIONAL COLLABORATIVE VENTURE PERFORMANCE

Mitrabarun Sarkar, S. Tamer Cavusgil, and Cuneyt Evirgen

SPEARHEADED BY GLOBAL AMBITIONS and the enabling aspects of information technology, organizations and markets are undergoing rapid transformation. Along with the rise of the globally networked virtual corporation, there is growing skepticism of the long-standing neoclassical economic premise that the market operates through discrete and anonymous transactions. Growing evidence indicates that interfirm exchanges are relationship-based, and that competitive advantage lies in a firm's network of associations and the exchange ties it shares with its business partners. Based on this emerging paradigm of relationship marketing and drawing on social exchange, network, and strategic alliance literature, this chapter adapts and extends Morgan and Hunt's commitment-trust mediated framework of relationship marketing (1994) and empirically tests it in the international construction contracting industry. Modeling commitment and trust as key mediating variables that lead to successful ICV performance,

We would like to thank Thomas Page, Ajay Das, Roger Calantone, James Eckert, John Sherry, and three anonymous reviewers for their help along the way.

the authors suggest that partners need to implement policies
aimed at fostering mutual trust and commitment in order to max-
imize their chances of success in a collaborative venture.

THIS CHAPTER ADAPTS Morgan and Hunt's commitment-trust framework of relationship marketing (1994) and empirically tests its validity in international collaborative ventures (ICVs). Our contribution to the emerging literature on cooperative exchanges is in three specific directions. First, we explore the generalizability of the commitment-trust theory in the domain of international collaborative ventures. Second, we research a specific and relatively understudied industry, namely the international construction contracting industry, which has the characteristics of being global in nature and where the cooperative form of exchange is a critical success element. Third, as against Morgan and Hunt's five "qualitative outcomes" (1994: 25) that relate to the relationship, we consider specific performance variables as they relate to ICVs in the international construction contracting industry.

In this context, the theoretical contribution of this chapter should be viewed in terms of both replication and extension. Notwithstanding the difference in constructs and measures used, our study provides further evidence of the fact that Morgan and Hunt's initial theorizing has demonstrable value in other contexts. Our contribution insofar as a theoretical extension is concerned relates to the incorporation of performance variables and the international setting. More specifically, we examine the relationship between a set of antecedent variables (shared norms, partner fit, two-way communication, and relationship benefits), mediating variables (trust and commitment), and a set of outcome variables relating to ICV performance (performance efficiency, positive outcome, and strategic gains) in the international construction contracting industry.

In the discussion that follows, we integrate business networks and relationship marketing literature, and develop a commitment-trust mediated framework of ICV performance within the fabric of social exchange theories, which we subsequently test in the international construction contracting industry. Given the paucity of industry-specific studies that have actually validated the links between emerging relational theories of cooperation and performance aspects of ICVs, we believe that this study contributes to theory development, enhances our understanding of the attitudinal and behavioral relational constructs that have an impact on performance in the global marketplace while identifying their interlinkages, and sheds light on a professional service sector that has been relatively neglected by scholars.

Global Collaborations and Cooperative Theories of Exchange

Interfirm collaborations have been referred to as coalitions (Porter and Fuller 1986), cooperative arrangements (Contractor and Lorange 1988), competitive alliances (Revesz and Cauley 1986), international corporate linkages (Auster 1987), collaborative agreements, cooperative ventures (Roehl and Truitt 1987), and partnerships (Root 1988). In this study, we define an international collaborative venture as when multiple firms collaborate "in product development, manufacture, or marketing that spans national boundaries, is not based on arm's-length market transactions, and includes substantial contribution by partners of capital, technology, or other assets" (Mowery 1988: 2–3).

The compelling logic behind the value of interfirm collaborations as modes through which firms gain access to technology, products, services, knowledge, and markets (Beamish and Banks 1987; Contractor and Lorange 1988; Harrigan 1987; Hennart 1988; Kogut 1988; Porter and Fuller 1986) has been confounded by empirical findings that highlight their inherently risky nature (Beamish 1985). Studies have subsequently concluded that the dynamics of interaction between partners is of paramount importance, and that the relational constructs of trust and commitment are key to collaborative venture success (Beamish and Banks 1987; Buckley and Casson 1988). In essence, efforts to develop hitherto neglected theories of cooperation (Alderson 1965) have prompted researchers to propose that marketing should be viewed as an ongoing process of exchange that is "long-term in nature, lasting over long periods" (Sharma 1993: 2), rather than the neoclassical economic assumption of one-shot, discrete transactions with a "distinct beginning, short duration, and sharp ending by performance" (Dwyer, Schurr, and Oh 1987: 13). Snehota (1993), citing a number of studies, concluded that there is substantial empirical evidence of selective and substantial firm ties where the bulk of market exchange takes place within broad and continuous relationships and where single, discrete transactions occur only rarely. Håkansson's argument (1982) that markets display networked structures, and therefore are a different form of organization from what was assumed in microeconomic and traditional organization theory, implied that both market processes and firm behavior need to be examined from a radically different perspective (Snehota 1993: 31), where the organizing principle of interfirm exchange is the notion of continuity and the unit of analysis is the dynamics of the relational exchange between firms instead of a single transaction.

The network approach contends that the process of interfirm exchange is characterized by high levels of information flow, knowledge sharing, and relationship commitment (Sharma 1993), as the network actors carry out economic activities through the process of combining complementary resources that they own and control (Håkansson 1989). In the process of combining complementary and heterogeneous resources, actors become interdependent, thus leading to the emergence of relationship networks (Pfeffer and Salancik 1978). This in turn creates a culture of cooperation and coordination, which ultimately determines the structure of relationships within the network. The key point is that while a firm's position within the network depends on its degree of dependency on other firms within the network and their monopoly power over these resources, its overall competitive strength in the market is dependent on the overall strength of the network and the nature of its links with its suppliers, customers, collaborators, and other actors.

The management of these relationship-links that form the firm's interface with other network actors is therefore an important part of its strategy. The interdependence and cooperation inherent in this model implies that trust and commitment are critical factors because they form a check on opportunistic behavior, lead to network stability, and serve as sources of network coordination (Ford 1984).

A growing body of relationship marketing literature has reached similar conclusions. Researchers have questioned the dominant paradigm of the discrete transaction and have posited that interfirm exchanges take place in a context of continuity where relational constructs such as trust and commitment are key (Anderson and Narus 1990; Bucklin and Sengupta 1993; Cullen, Johnson, and Sakano 1995; Dwyer, Schurr, and Oh 1987; Gundlach, Achrol, and Mentzer 1995; Heide and John 1988; Madhok 1995; Moorman, Deshpande, and Zaltman 1993; Morgan and Hunt 1994).

As the nature of interfirm relationships changes from adversarial to collaborative and the domain of competition expands from individual firms to competing networks, the emerging consensus seems to be that competitive advantage lies in successful collaborations. The success of a collaboration, however, depends on relationship-based exchange processes that are coordinated by trust and commitment.

Theoretical Foundations of an Integrated Conceptual Framework

In Figure 10.1, we offer our trust-commitment mediated framework of ICV performance. The proposed framework hinges on two main issues

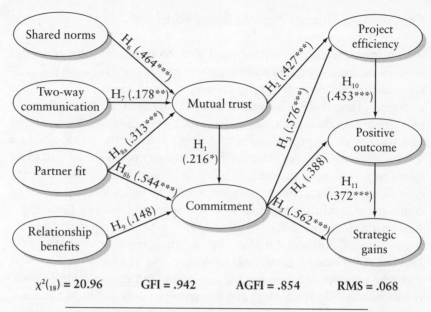

Figure 10.1. The Commitment-Trust Framework of ICV Performance.
Note: N = 68.   *p < .10   **p < .05   ***p < .01

that are elaborated in the next section: first, that interfirm collaborations represent a form of social exchange, and second, that commitment and trust are the two key variables that mediate the effects of a set of antecedent variables on ICV performance.[1]

Interfirm Collaborations as Social Exchange

As argued earlier, firms carry out various economic activities through a process that involves a matrix of exchange relationships with other firms. Explicit collaborative arrangements, through which "access to people, facilities, documents, and other forms of knowledge is traded between partners" (Hamel 1991: 100), formalize this matrix of relational exchange. As argued by the network school, interfirm interaction is a process whereby "relationships are built gradually in a social exchange process through which the parties may come to trust each other" (Håkansson and Johanson 1988: 373). Based on this line of reasoning, collaborative ventures inherently involve social exchange. The exchange of resources that have value to partners is a key characteristic of collaborative ventures. Accordingly, collaborative ventures can be said to represent a form of interorganizational interaction involving an exchange relationship (Evirgen and Yaprak 1992).

Commitment-Trust as Key Mediating Variables

A shift from the discrete transactional view of exchange to the relational network perspective implies that we need to rethink the traditional political-economic notion of power being the central coordinating mechanism for exchange (Thorelli 1986). In the relational paradigm, power needs to be participative, as these exchange networks are more purposefully organized and socially developed (Gundlach, Achrol, and Mentzer 1995; Achrol 1991). While the exercise of power by the stronger partner may lead to reduced commitment of the other (Cook and Emerson 1978), shared power reduces opportunism and exploitation, results in higher levels of trust and commitment, and thus becomes key to a successful alliance (Jain 1987; Bucklin and Sengupta 1993). Madhok (1995) notes that interfirm trust has both structural and social dimensions and these together affect the well-being of collaborative partnerships. Morgan and Hunt (1994: 22) assert that "the presence of relationship commitment and trust is central to successful relationship marketing, and not power and its ability to condition others . . . commitment and trust lead directly to behaviors that are conducive to relationship marketing success."

We therefore model commitment and trust as the key mediating variables between four antecedents (shared norms, partner fit, two-way communication, and relationship benefits) and three performance outcomes (project efficiency, positive outcome, and strategic gains). However, we go beyond the "qualitative outcomes" that Morgan and Hunt (1994: 25) examine in their model to examine performance issues that are directly related to the effectiveness and success of the collaborative relationship.

Trust

The notion of trust is assuming center stage in the new relationship-based marketing paradigm as a key construct to examine interfirm collaborations (for a review see Madhok 1995; Morgan and Hunt 1994), thus addressing Alderson's concern (1965) over the lack of cooperative theories and giving credence to MacKean's assertion (1972: 30) that a "private enterprise, market-exchange system is almost absurd unless there is a good deal of mutual trust."

While trust has been conceptualized along twin dimensions of being a cognitive expectation and a risk-taking behavior (Dwyer and LaGace 1986), Morgan and Hunt (1994: 23) operationalize trust only along cognitive lines as "when one party has confidence in an exchange partner's reliability and integrity." We prefer to treat trust along both cognitive *and* behavioral dimensions, and draw on Moorman, Deshpande, and Zaltman's definition (1993: 82) of trust being "a willingness to rely on an exchange partner in whom one has confidence." It is our contention that the presence of trust requires more than just cognitive aspects. It needs to be accompanied by a behavioral dimension, be it an intention or a report of actual behavior. Trust is thus limited if it is not accompanied by behavioral intentions. Accordingly, in measuring trust, although we have incorporated both cognitive and behavioral dimensions, we have stressed the latter. First, we expect behavioral questions to result in more valid answers than ones aimed purely at the cognitive aspects, and second, a report of behavioral intention would anyway indicate the presence of the cognitive dimension of trust. In addition, we attempt to tap into both integrity and reliability dimensions of trust.

Early work in social psychology notes that the tendency to trust is affected by an individual's perception of the other person, as well as by the individual's own intentions toward the other person (Deutsch 1960). On the premise that exchange theory supports linkages between individual-level and organizational-level variables (Smith and Barclay 1995), and that relational constructs have relevance not only at the individual level but also at the organizational level of analysis (Cullen, Johnson, and Sakano 1995), we hypothesize trust in ICVs to be an outcome of mutually perceived trustworthiness. Mutual and bilateral trust needs to be developed and maintained through the relationship, without which the collaborative venture may fail (Buckley and Casson 1988; Lorange 1989; Moorman, Deshpande, and Zaltman 1993).

Previous works have established that a positive relationship exists between trust and commitment (Doz 1988). Given that trusting relationships are highly valued, firms will desire to invest and commit to such relationships to ensure the long-term survival of these relationships (Hrebiniak 1974). Morgan and Hunt (1994) posit that since commitment entails vulnerability, firms will only seek trustworthy partners and long-term relationships. Similarly, Achrol (1991) notes that trust was an important determinant of relationship commitment.

Several studies recognize trust to be a critical factor for a successful collaboration. Madhok (1995: 126) concluded that "trust has efficiency implications, and its potential cost reduction and value enhancing properties need to be recognized." The relationship between trust and collaborative performance has been recognized (Spekman and Sawhney 1990; Ring and Van de Ven 1992). Wallace's study (1993) of U.S. and Japanese joint ventures found support for Badaracco's view (1991) that trust is a necessary success factor in knowledge-driven alliances, and as trust develops, partners start to rely more on each other. Trust has been noted to be one of the main constructs in alliance formation (Sheth and Parvatiyar 1992), and as the biggest stumbling block to a successful alliance (Sherman 1992).

Given the dynamic nature of trust (Madhok 1995), we posit in our cross-sectional study that trust has a direct influence on project efficiency.[2] If trust exists between collaborating partners, there is likely to be greater commitment to the project, more efficient use of resources, and reduced costs. This would in turn lead to higher profitability, greater client satisfaction, and long-term strategic gains. Accordingly, we hypothesize:

HYPOTHESIS 1: The greater the mutual trust among partners, the greater the level of commitment in the collaborative venture.

HYPOTHESIS 2: The greater the mutual trust among partners, the greater the level of project efficiency achieved.

Commitment

Along with trust, the concept of commitment is becoming increasingly central to the relationship-based paradigm of marketing (for reviews, see Cullen, Johnson, and Sakano 1995; Gundlach, Achrol, and Mentzer 1995).

Commitment has been defined as "an exchange partner believing that an ongoing relationship with another is so important as to warrant maximum efforts at maintaining it; that is, the committed party believes the relationship is worth working on to ensure that it endures indefinitely" (Morgan and Hunt 1994: 23), and as "an enduring desire to maintain a relationship" (Moorman, Zaltman, and Deshpande 1992: 316). Commitment involves a willingness to make short-term sacrifices to strengthen a relationship (Dwyer, Schurr, and Oh 1987), which may be made through restricting the search for alternatives and foregoing better short-term options in favor of investing in an ongoing relationship (Cook and Emerson 1978). Partners also invest in relationship-specific assets to demonstrate their reliability and commitment to their exchange partners (Anderson and Weitz 1992).

Gundlach, Achrol, and Mentzer (1995) posited that commitment is "an essential ingredient for successful long-term relationships" (p. 78), and argued that although commitment is conceptualized in diverse ways, it has three basic dimensions: behavioral, attitudinal, and temporal. Our approach partly concurs with this notion. For commitment to be present in an exchange relationship, collaborating partners need to be not only willing to express their long-term interest in the relationship but also to take affirmative action that demonstrates willingness to act on their promise. We do not consider the temporal aspect explicitly in our cross-sectional study. However, as our performance variables address venture performance, positive outcome, and strategic gains, we implicitly incorporate the view that commitment necessitates consistent behavior over a length of time.

The positive effect of commitment on collaborative venture performance has been widely reported in both conceptual and empirical studies (Beamish and Banks 1987; Jain 1987; Ohmae 1989; Badaracco 1991; Sheth and Parvatiyar 1992). Commitment, by reducing the threat of opportunistic behavior (Williamson 1975), reduces transaction costs and therefore the costs associated with partnership (Lewis 1990). Commitment therefore has a positive effect on ICV performance. Also, commitment reflects a positive valuation of a collaborative relationship (Moorman, Zaltman, and Deshpande 1992), which logically implies that it has positive and direct effects on all aspects of venture performance. Accordingly, we hypothesize:

HYPOTHESES 3–5: The greater the level of commitment, the greater will be the efficiency, positive outcome, and strategic gains achieved in the venture.

Precursors of Relationship Commitment and Trust

Compatibility in operational, financial, and technical capabilities and procedures, along with similarity in business philosophies and organizational norms facilitate a healthy and trusting collaborative environment.

Shared Norms

Harrigan (1988) reported a positive relationship between cultural homogeneity, as reflected in the values and social norms prevalent in the partnering organizations, and the success of a collaborative venture. Badaracco (1991) found that a match in values and capabilities between partners is important for a good "fit" to exist. Also, compatible philosophies between partners facilitated reduced conflict and the positive resolution of any remaining conflict. Bucklin and Sengupta (1993) noted in their study on co-marketing alliances that partner match depends on the similarity in marketing styles and corporate cultures of the partnering firms. Given that the construction industry is technology and design driven, we believe that compatibility in technological capabilities of the partners is likely to lead to a shared vision of business, which in turn should lead to a similarity in organizational cultures.

Research reports, therefore, that partner match has a direct effect on the perceived effectiveness of the alliance, while organizational compatibility is a strong predictor of alliance effectiveness. Accordingly, we posit that shared norms among collaborating partners is key to a successful ICV. We consider shared norms to comprise congruency in organizational values and social norms, and compatibility in technological capability, organizational procedures, and approaches to business dealings. If congruency and compatibility both exist, it is likely that there will be greater confidence in an exchange partner's reliability and integrity, which, in essence, is the notion of trust (Morgan and Hunt 1994). Accordingly:

HYPOTHESIS 6: The greater the degree of shared norms between partners, the greater will be the level of mutual trust in the collaborative venture.

Two-Way Communication

Open two-way communication, which is the formal and informal sharing of meaningful and timely information (Anderson and Narus 1991), helps to develop a trusting relationship between firms. Trust is facilitated by the timely exchange of information (Moorman, Deshpande, and Zaltman 1993), and this helps firms to realize mutual benefits by reducing dysfunctional misunderstandings (Dwyer, Schurr, and Oh 1987; Anderson and Narus 1991). While the norms of information exchange significantly affect partner relationships (Heide and John 1988), two-way communication, through its ability to enhance mutual disclosure, enhances relationship quality (Crosby, Evans, and Cowles 1990) and therefore leads to successful ventures (Badaracco 1991; Lewis 1990). Two-way communication helps minimize errors that arise through poor judgment, and reduces misjudged expectations of partners and aligns their expectations (Etgar 1979; Lyles 1987). Unlike Smith and Barclay (1995), who treat open communication as a function of trust, we believe that it is only through two-way communication that trust can develop among partners. Accordingly, similar to Morgan and Hunt (1994), we posit that two-way communication results in greater trust and thus in successful collaborative ventures.

HYPOTHESIS 7: The greater the level of two-way communication among the partners, the greater will be mutual trust in the collaborative venture.

Partner Fit: Complementarity and Compatibility

Collaborative ventures have been characterized as marriages (Levitt 1983; Stoltman, Gentry, and Morgan 1993), as choosing the proper partner is critical to the collaboration's success (Devlin and Bleackley 1988; Geringer 1991). We conceptualize this decision to consist of three key components: compatibility of goals and objectives, complementarity of resources, and domain congruence. Hamel, Doz, and Prahalad (1989) noted that convergence of strategic goals did not imply that individual competitive or strategic goals need to be exactly similar, as long as collaborators ensure that their attempt to achieve individual objectives does not endanger each other.

Although there is little consensus on what constitutes effective complementarity, or how contextual variables shape their relative importance (Geringer 1991), research has asserted that partner complementarity is an important determinant of collaborative venture success (Bleeke and Ernst 1991; Franko 1971; Harrigan 1988; Jain 1987; Killing 1983) and stability (Porter and Fuller 1988), as it influences the mix of skills and resources that an ICV needs to achieve its strategic objectives (Geringer 1991; Tomlinson 1970). In essence, partner fit increases when there exist complementary strengths and weaknesses (Sengupta 1993; Contractor and Lorange 1988).

Domain consensus, which is a collection of specific goals to be pursued and the functions required to complement them, enhances the quality of interorganizational relationships (Van de Ven and Ferry 1980). This also shapes and tempers partners' expectations, and is thus important for the success of the exchange relationship. We operationalize domain consensus as a mutual recognition among partners of their overall suitability in the context of the ICV.

We argue that partner fit, as measured by their complementarity and compatibility, affects both trust and commitment and enhances ICV effectiveness. A perception of good partner fit would lead, first, to demonstration of greater mutual trust, because the partners would be more willing to rely on each other's words (Rotter 1967), and second, to greater effort directed at maintaining the relationship. This would create a mutual belief that the "relationship is worth working on to ensure that it endures indefinitely" (Morgan and Hunt 1994: 23), and therefore result in increased commitment. Accordingly, we hypothesize:

HYPOTHESES 8A AND 8B: The greater the partner fit as evidenced by the degree of complementarity and compatibility of the partners, the greater will be the level of mutual trust and commitment in the collaborative venture.

Relationship Benefits

In a recent study, Cullen, Johnson, and Sakano (1995) noted that commitment develops largely as a function of perceived benefits of the relationship. Firms seek collaborations to get access to resources that they otherwise could not secure (Hamel 1991). For a collaboration to be successful, partners need to value each other's resources (Beamish and Banks 1987), as success depends on the unique contributions of the partners (Hamel, Doz, and Prahalad 1989). Given that the value of a resource to a firm depends on its need for that particular resource, and the relative scarcity of that resource (Emerson 1981), a greater need for the resource should lead to higher venture commitment; partners will be highly committed if their mutual need for each other's resources is high. Therefore, we hypothesize a direct relationship between a firm's perception of the relationship benefits that it can derive from the collaboration and the level of its commitment to the ICV. Accordingly:

HYPOTHESIS 9: The greater the perceived value of the benefits derived from the collaboration, the greater will be the mutual commitment to the venture.

Outcomes of Relationship Commitment and Trust

This study aims to examine the mediated effects of trust and commitment on the *performance* of an ICV, which we feel is an important research issue that has not yet been fully explored. Accordingly, we model performance variables as dependent outcomes. Researchers have used various indicators to assess performance of ICVs; some are financial (Tomlinson 1970), survival (Killing 1983), duration (Kogut 1988), and ownership instability (Gomes-Casseres 1987). While this multidimensionality of collaborative venture performance has been noted by Salk (1993), Geringer (1991) suggested the use of multidimensional performance measures to study international ventures. However, our position on the issue is similar to Geringer and Hébert's assertion (1989) that there exists no consensus on the appropriate definition of international joint venture performance, and that objective measures of performance often do not reflect firms' strategic motives.

There is evidence of perceptual performance measures being used to assess ICV performance (Bucklin and Sengupta 1993). Van de Ven (1976) viewed performance as the extent to which the partners *perceive* each other to have kept commitments, and how worthwhile, equitable, productive, and satisfying the relationship has been. Given our view of an ICV as an exchange relationship, its success would be reflected by partners' perceptions of having obtained benefits from the relationship (Emerson 1981). Using perceptual measures of performance was also suggested by Lorange (1989), who argued that performance needs to be measured from partner perspectives.

We view ICV performance in the global construction industry along three dimensions: the perceived efficiency with which the particular collaborative project was executed, resultant outcome in terms of project profitability and client satisfaction, and the longer-term strategic gains from the collaboration. Collectively, these three dimensions provide a comprehensive conceptualization of ICV performance.

In addition, we hypothesize that an efficiently executed project will result in positive outcomes for the collaborators, which over time will lead to a feeling that the relationship has led to strategic gains. Therefore we hypothesize:

HYPOTHESIS 10: The greater the project efficiency, the greater will be the perceived positive outcome of the collaboration.

HYPOTHESIS 11: The greater the perceived positive outcome, the greater will be the feeling of strategic gains from the collaboration.

The International Construction Contracting Industry: Rationale Behind Industry Choice

The international construction contracting market is estimated at around $3 trillion a year with global exports around $156 billion in 1993, according to the *Engineering News Record*. In spite of this, it remains a relatively underresearched industry. Strassman and Wells (1988) pointed out that this neglect may be due to the large number of different project types, numerous client types, the highly diversified market, and the various nationalities of the contractors. An additional reason, as revealed in our interviews with construction industry executives, is its traditionally closed and extremely competitive nature, which has resulted in limited sharing of interfirm information. The internationalized nature of this industry, the proliferation of international collaborations, and its understudied nature are the key reasons that motivated us to concentrate on this industry.

Method

Following analysis of secondary information, we conducted personal in-depth semistructured interviews, lasting about an hour each, with twelve construction experts from industry associations and firms to get insights into the industry, and also to get their inputs on the constructs used in the model. The draft questionnaire was subsequently modified and finalized. A mail survey was then conducted of key executives in the selected sample of contractors. We followed the key informant technique (Seidler 1974) to collect data. Campbell's criteria (1955) of being knowledgeable about the phenomenon under study and being able and willing to communicate with the researcher constituted the major criteria for informant selection.

Data Collection

The sampling frame included 561 firms in the international construction contracting industry. *Engineering News Record* (ENR), a weekly trade journal published by McGraw-Hill for the construction contracting industry, periodically collects and publishes data on the international construction contracting industry. We derived our sampling frame from its 1993 list of the top 225 international contractors and the top 400 U.S. contractors. As some of the U.S. contractors were included in both lists, the total number of discrete firms that emerged was 561. In the construction contracting industry, firms tend to specialize[3] in certain areas of competence even though they compete globally. Therefore, our definition of construction contracting was generic. Inclusion in ENR's list made them eligible for inclusion in the survey.

Data were collected using a self-administered questionnaire prepared in English. The mailing package, consisting of a cover letter, the questionnaire, and a self-addressed return envelope, was sent to a senior executive in each firm. The letters requested the addresses, if it was necessary to forward the questionnaire to an executive who had been in charge of a construction project involving a collaborative venture with a foreign partner firm over the past ten years (Van de Ven 1976). There were three reasons for including a ten-year time frame. First, we expected a fairly low response rate based on the closed and confidential nature of the industry and so a longer time to facilitate the responses. Second, construction projects generally tend to extend for a number of years. Third, we did not want to restrict responses to the post-1987 boom period in the construction industry and wished to cover the period before that too. However, we understand the possible trade-off that might have occurred due to the possible erosion of respondent memories.

The cover letter also explained the purpose of the research, and promised a summary of the findings to those who returned their business cards along with the completed questionnaires. Five weeks after the initial mailing, a second wave was mailed to those who had not responded. Only the cover letter differed from the earlier package.

There was a total of 120 returned questionnaires, for a response rate of 21.4 percent. However, not all the returned surveys were usable, either due to noncompletion or to the venture not being international. There were sixty-eight usable questionnaires, making the effective response rate 12.3 percent. As Table 10.1 indicates, we targeted and received responses from eighteen countries other than the U.S. Resource constraints limited our ability to translate the questionnaire into so many different languages, but the breakdown of the responses suggests that questionnaires in English did not cause many problems. Of the 408 surveys sent out to U.S. contractors, 76 (18.6 percent) were returned. Half the responding firms indicated that they had never had any collaborative ventures with foreign firms, thus resulting in thirty-four usable surveys. But of the 153 surveys sent to non-U.S. contractors, forty-four (28.8 percent) were returned; though the overall response rate was higher compared to U.S. contractors, only four out of the forty-four respondents reported that they never were involved in any ICV. The thirty-four usable surveys meant a usable-to-returned ratio of 79.5 percent. This ratio being almost twice that of U.S. responses, it seems that the language problem might not have been very significant. Accordingly, we feel that having the questionnaire in English did not result in the magnitude of problems that could potentially have arisen.

Measures

Table 10.2 presents the list of the constructs and measures used in the study. Following Churchill (1979), we purified the proposed measures by assessing their reliability and unidimensionality. Every variable that was measured by multiple items was subjected to a scale development and purification process. First, we examined the item-to-total correlations for the items in each of the proposed scales, and eliminated items with low correlations if they tapped no additional domain of interest. Thereafter, through confirmatory factor analysis on subsets of theoretically related measures (Moorman, Deshpande, and Zaltman 1993), we assessed the extent to which the items reflected a single dimension. We deleted items that had high correlations with items in other measures.

Results

The coefficient alphas, factor loadings, and descriptive statistics for each scale are reported in Table 10.2. Alphas range from .627 to .838, with seven of the nine values being substantially over .7, which suggests a satisfactory level of reliability (Nunnally 1978). The factor loadings are high, thus providing evidence of the unidimensional nature of the scale items.

Country	*Respondent* Origin	*Partner* Origin
Australia	0	3
Bahrain	1	0
Belgium	0	1
Brazil	2	0
Canada	1	1
Denmark	1	0
France	0	2
Germany	1	6
Holland	0	3
Hungary	1	0
Indonesia	0	2
Italy	5	4
Japan	7	4
Korea	1	1
Mexico	0	3
Philippines	1	1
Portugal	1	1
Russia	0	1
Saudia Arabia	0	2
Singapore	1	2
Slovenia	1	0
Spain	1	1
Taiwan	2	0
Turkey	2	3
United Kingdom	4	2
U.S.A.	35	24
Yugoslovia	1	0
Zambia	0	1

Table 10.1. Sample Composition and Responses by Country.

Construct	Items	Mean	SD	α	Factor Loadings
Project efficiency (EFFICIENCY)	A quality job was done on the project	3.93	0.896	.795	.734
	In general, resources were used very efficiently in this relationship.	4.10	0.866		.777
	Overall, the project was efficiently carried out.				.837
	At the completion of the project, the credibility of the project partners was confirmed or enhanced in the eyes of the owner.	4.29	0.776		.642
Positive outcome (OUTCOME)	The owner was not satisfied with the outcome of the project. (R)	4.57	0.531	.671	.771
	The owner was proud of the project at its completion.	4.63	0.554		.822
	The venture was profitable for our firm.	4.23	1.107		.646
Strategic gains (STRATEGIC GAIN)	The collaboration provided a very effective medium of learning for both firms.	4.20	0.867	.757	.837
	The collaboration met its objectives for both firms.	4.19	0.902		.572
	Collaborating with this partner in this project was a wise business decision.	4.35	0.877		.817

Table 10.2. Properties of Measures.

Note: Mean is on a scale of 1 to 5, where 1 = strongly disagree, 5 = strongly agree. (R) indicates an item is reverse scored.

Construct	Items	Mean	SD	α	*Factor Loadings*
Shared norms (SHARED NORMS)	The organizational values and social norms prevalent in the two firms were congruent.	3.26	1.080	.794	.829
	The organizational procedures of the two firms were compatible.	3.33	0.995		.856
	Executives from both firms involved in this project had compatible philosophies and approaches to business dealings.	3.67	1.010		.578
	Technical capabilities of the two firms were compatible with each other.	3.75	1.049		.663
Partner fit (PARTNER FIT)	The goals and objectives of both firms were compatible with each other.	4.09	0.781	.739	.716
	The resources brought into the venture by both partners were complementary.	4.15	0.809		.867
	Both partners were very suitable for each other.	4.12	0.832		.725
Communication (COMMUNICATION)	There was frequent communication between the two firms (such as visits to each other's firms, meetings, written and telephone communications).	4.36	0.822	.865	.93
	Exchange of information in this relationship took place frequently and informally.	4.25	0.775		.934

Table 10.2. Properties of Measures. (continued)

	Mean			
Relationship Benefits (BENEFIT)				
Both firms needed each other's resources to accomplish their goals and responsibilities.	4.07	0.967	.779	.829
The resources contributed by both firms were significant in getting the bid.	4.12	1.015		.799
Resources brought into the venture by each firm were very valuable for the other.	4.07	0.935		.818
Trust (TRUST)				
Both firms were perfectly honest and truthful with each other.	3.87	0.969	.801	.863
Both firms treated each other fairly and justly.	4.12	0.850		.751
Relying on each other was risky for both firms. (R)	4.06	1.110		.713
Both firms found it necessary to be cautious in dealing with each other. (R)	3.78	1.083		.717
Commitment (COMMITMENT)				
Both firms were willing to dedicate whatever people and resources it took to make this project a success.	4.15	0.809	.838	.761
Both firms provided experienced and capable people to the project.	4.16	0.868		.858
Both firms were committed to making this project a success.	4.54	0.698		.892

Note: Mean is on a scale of 1 to 5, where 1 = strongly disagree, 5 = strongly agree. (R) indicates an item is reverse scored.

Table 10.3 presents the means, standard deviations, intercorrelations, variances, and covariances for the summates of the research variables. The standard deviations for all nine constructs range from .65 to .803, indicating a fair amount of variance in the responses. All means are more than three, which is the center of the scale. In fact, all but one are more than four on a five-point scale. This seems to indicate that our response set is a bit skewed toward successful collaborations. However, as we are interested in examining the factors that contribute toward successful collaborative relationships, the response set is appropriate for our purpose.

The correlations in Table 10.3 provide an initial test of our hypotheses. All twelve hypotheses are supported at the $p < .01$ level. The absolute values of the correlations range from .357 to .736. For a more robust test of the framework, we employed a structural equations approach. Given the limited sample size, we use the sum scaled scores of the purified items and then use them as single-indicator items in the path analysis.

The model was tested using LISREL VII. Overall, the model performs well. The chi square is nonsignificant ($p = .281$) which indicates that the theorized model holds. The covariance matrix is shown in Table 10.3, and the results of the analysis are illustrated in Figure 10.1. Eight of the proposed twelve paths are significant at $p < .01$, one is significant at $p < .05$, another at $p < .10$, and only two turn out to be nonsignificant. The model's goodness of fit index (GFI) of .942 indicates an acceptable fit.

With the exception of H9, all hypothesized paths from the antecedents to relationship commitment and trust are supported. The squared multiple correlations (SMCs) for the structural equations for commitment and trust are high. Over half the variance (SMC = .567) in trust is explained by the direct effects of shared norms, two-way communication, and partner fit. Almost half the variance (SMC = .479) in commitment is explained by direct effects of partner fit and relationship benefit, even though the path from trust to commitment is significant only at the $p < .10$ level.

Except for the path from commitment to positive outcome (H4), all other paths are supported at $p < .001$. The model explains a substantial amount of the variance of the outcomes, as revealed by the SMCs: .393 for efficiency, .307 for positive outcome, and .455 for strategic gain. The total coefficient of determination is .687 for the whole set of structural equations.

Conclusion

The rising relevance of relationships in the context of interfirm exchanges has developed out of a recognition that the notion of competition as has

Table 10.3. Correlation-Covariance Matrix.

Constructs	Mean	SD	Shared Norm	Communication	Partner Fit	Benefit	Trust	Commitment	Efficiency	Outcome	Strategic Gain
Shared norms	3.452	.702	**.7**	.277	.502	.161	.67*	.408	.437	.25	.263
Communication	4.32	.75	.277	**.56**	.282	.114	.395*	.237	.256	.146	.153
Partner fit	4.123	.656	.282	.502	**.43**	.338	.595*	.655*	.557	.336	.398
Relationship benefits	4.095	.814	.114	.161	.338	**.66**	.201	.353*	.264	.165	.208
Trust	3.96	.803	.67	.395	.595	.209	**.64**	.53*	.607*	.343	.348
Commitment	4.294	.683	.516	.347	.655	.355	.531	**.47**	.736*	.461*	.589*
Efficiency	4.241	.652	.489	.35	.618	.392	.608	.736	**.43**	.547*	.488*
Positive outcome	4.462	.632	.231	.251	.369	.307	.291	.461	.547	**.4**	.564*
Strategic gain	4.091	.77	.479	.354	.517	.313	.384	.589	.488	.564	**.59**

Note: Correlations are above the diagonal, covariances below the diagonal, and variances on the diagonal.

*Significant at the $p < .01$ level.

been traditionally developed by neoclassical economists is less applicable today than it may have been in the past. Through an evolutionary process, spearheaded by global ambitions of the firm and the enabling aspect of information technology, the very concepts of organizations and markets have transformed quite radically. The traditional boundaries of a firm are in question, as is the process by which markets operate. The rise of the globally networked virtual organization has been accompanied by a growing skepticism that the market operates through discrete, only price-based, anonymous market transactions. Also, as research grappled with the issues that led to the competitive advantage of Asian firms, it became clear that the differentiating factors were closely related to the kind of exchange ties shared by business partners. In other words, the long-term, relationship-based structure prevalent in Asian society spilled over into the domain of firms and influenced the set of business practices that determine the exchange behavior between them. Concurrent with the shift in research focus from theories of competition to those of cooperation, the notions of continuity, long-term relations, trust, commitment, and overall cooperative behavior have come to be regarded as some of the key factors that serve as the foundations of the emerging business paradigm.

Within this context, and based on emerging commitment-trust theory of relational marketing, this study develops an integrated commitment-trust mediated theoretical framework for international collaborative venture performance, and empirically tests it in the international construction contracting industry. The theoretical framework integrates relationship marketing, network theory, and strategic alliance literature, within the basic proposition derived from social exchange theories that collaborative ventures represent a form of interorganizational relationship that involves an exchange relationship. We empirically examine the relationship between a set of antecedent variables (shared norms, partner fit, two-way communication, and relationship benefits) on the key mediating variables of trust and commitment, the impact of trust on relationship commitment, and the effects of these mediating variables on different dimensions of collaborative venture performance (performance efficiency, positive outcome, and strategic gain). The empirical validation of the framework leads us to believe that this study contributes toward furthering our understanding of how emerging relational constructs actually impact global performance, and thus helps toward the larger objective of developing a workable theory of cooperative behavior among firms.

Twelve hypotheses reflecting the relationships proposed in the theoretical model were generated and tested. The correlations for all twelve proved to be significant at $p < .01$, thus providing initial support for our model. The stronger path analysis tests conducted through LISREL, however, did not support two of the hypotheses. Two of the three hypothesized antecedents of trust (shared norms and partner fit) had very high estimates of .464 and .313 respectively, which were significant at $p < .01$ levels, while two-way communication was significant at $p < .05$. It appears that when two partnering organizations are compatible in operational, financial, technical capabilities, and procedures, they share a commonality in culture that works toward enhancing their mutual trust. This potential trust may be enhanced through practices that aim to cultivate open two-way communication between partners. Also, basic congruence in goals and objectives, mutually perceived complementarity, and overall suitability of the partners work toward enhanced trust in the collaborative venture. Given that a high level of variance (56.7 percent) in trust is explained by these three antecedent variables, trust seems to be fostered by a commonality of cultures and a mutual feeling of suitability, but maintained by open two-way communication between partners.

Almost half the variance in commitment (47.9 percent) is explained by its antecedents: partner fit, relationship benefits, and trust. However, only partner fit is significant at $p < .01$ level, while trust is significant at $p < .10$. Interestingly, similar to Morgan and Hunt's study (1994), the hypothesized relationship between relationship benefits and commitment remains unsupported, even though the correlation is positive and significant ($r = .353$), as it was in the earlier study. While this surprising consistency across studies is something that needs to be studied more carefully in the future, one of the reasons for it could be because we measured relationship benefits as a subjective perception of whether the partner's resources were valuable, whether they helped in getting a contract, and whether there was mutual need for these complementary resources to execute individual responsibilities. These measures are therefore conceptually different from Morgan and Hunt's comparative evaluations (1994), which refer to relative benefits compared to those of a potential alternative supplier. In spite of this measurement difference, the similarity in results seems to indicate that either the perceived value of resources does not affect commitment, or that individual managers believe that the relationship would not have been formalized in the first place if there were no benefits to be derived from the other partner. While perceived relationship benefit affects the formation of the collaboration, it may not affect the way the relationship develops.

More than 60.7 percent of the variance in project efficiency is explained by trust and commitment. Efficiency's significant and high positive correlations with trust ($r = .607$) and commitment ($r = .736$) further support our hypothesis, and leads to the important managerial implication that in a project-based collaboration, it is important to develop and institutionalize a set of management practices that help to nurture a trusting and committed relationship between partners.

The hypothesized paths between the execution, outcome, and longer-term strategic dimensions of performance are significant at $p < .01$ level, and their correlations are both positive and significant at a similar level. This indicates that the level of efficiency affects client perception and the profitability of the venture, which in turn leads to a feeling that there have been longer-term strategic gains from the relationship.

The hypothesized path between commitment and positive outcome (H4) was not supported. This seems *prima facie* surprising. However, one reason could be that relationship commitment to a collaboration does not directly affect a client's satisfaction level or the profitability of the collaboration. Intuitively the latter makes sense; a committed firm would engage in behavior that involves short-term sacrifices in profitability and a simultaneous increase in relationship-specific investments. Future research needs to identify the nature and type of trade-offs that occur between actions that increase a firm's demonstration of commitment versus sacrifice of short-term profitability.

On the whole, the results suggest that the commitment-trust mediated framework is indeed robust, and does influence performance of ICVs. From a theoretical point of view, this research indicates that the performance of project ventures can be measured via three constructs, which intuitively also make sense in a managerial perspective. First, the project needs to be executed efficiently, and resources need to be utilized well. This leads in turn to positive outcomes from the project, where the firm feels that profitability has been high and the client feels happy about the services offered. This in turn leads to a perception that the collaboration has worked well, the firms have learned from each other, and that overall there have been strategic gains from the partnership.

The small sample size ($N = 68$) is a limitation of this study. However, given the difficulty in getting cross-national responses in an understudied and traditionally closed industry, we feel that this study makes an important contribution. Also, none of the top ten contractors in the top 400 U.S. contractors list, and only one of the top ten contractors in the top 225 international contractors list, provided data for the study. Future research should aim to verify these results with larger sample sizes in different industries. Other global industries, such as telecommunications, may be targeted. Through validation in other industries, the findings reported here will become more useful in developing managerial implications and conceptual advances.

Also, the research addresses issues of mutual trust and commitment, but the responses viewed the relational aspect from only one partner's perspective. Thus, the likelihood of response bias exists in our study. Future research should attempt to take a dyadic perspective and collect data from both partners in the collaboration. This will enable us to check the consistency of mutuality, and correlate the responses across the antecedents and outcomes. It is only then that we can confidently assert that the relational dimensions of mutual trust and commitment play a key mediating role in ICVs.

In addition, it has been noted that contingency relationships exist between relational dimensions such as trust and performance. Studies have suggested that trust may only influence performance under uncertainty and possibility of opportunism (Heide and John 1988; Madhok 1995). Thus future research needs to incorporate the moderating effects of such issues while examining how relational variables affect performance.

With the growing importance of collaborative ventures in international business and the almost paradigmatic shift toward relationship-based business, a better theoretical understanding of the formation, operation, and maintenance of collaborative ventures is definitely required. It is hoped that the research reported here provides a building block toward such an endeavor.

NOTES

1. It is to be noted that these contingencies have been discussed in the literature for some time now (see Heide and John 1988; Bucklin and Sengupta 1993; Moorman, Deshpande, and Zaltman 1993; Madhok 1995; Gundlach, Achrol, and Mentzer 1995). This forms our point of departure into the domain of Hunt and Morgan's 1994 theoretical framework. Our theoretical contribution, as elaborated later, is in the incorporation of performance issues.

2. We expect trust to be directly related to project efficiency—one of the three performance variables. On the other hand, "Positive Outcome" is intended to measures the *results* of the manner in which the project has been executed. Thus, it measures the level of satisfaction from the perspective of the owner of the project and the construction firm. This we posit to be directly influenced by the efficiency of the project *and* the level of commitment displayed by the collaborating firms. Thus we have made a distinction here between efficiency and perceived satisfaction. Accordingly, we have hypothesized trust to directly influence only project efficiency, which along with commitment influences the perceived outcome of the project.

3. Some of the U.S. firms that were part of our sampling frame were Fluor, Ebasco, T. Y. Lin, Guy F. Atkinson, Brown and Root, and Louis Berger International. These companies carry out construction projects globally, although their areas of expertise are specialized (Fluor—energy-related work and petrochemicals, Ebasco—power generation, T. Y. Lin—structural engineering, Guy F. Atkinson—heavy construction, Louis Berger—planning, design, and construction).

BIBLIOGRAPHY

Achrol, R. 1991. Evolution of the marketing organization: New forms for turbulent environments. *Journal of Marketing,* 55(4): 77–93.

Alderson, W. 1965. *Dynamic Marketing Behavior.* Burr Ridge, Ill.: Irwin.

Anderson, E., and B. Weitz. 1992. The use of pledges to build and sustain commitment in distribution channels. *Journal of Marketing Research,* 29(1): 18–34.

Anderson, J. C., and J. A. Narus. 1991. Partnering as a focused marketing strategy. *California Management Review,* 33(3): 95–113.

Auster, E. R. 1987. International corporate linkages: Dynamic forms in changing environments. *Columbia Journal of World Business,* Summer: 3–6.

Badaracco, J. L. Jr. 1991. *The Knowledge Link: How Firms Compete Through Strategic Alliances.* Boston: Harvard Business School Press.

Beamish, P. W. 1985. Characteristics of joint ventures in developed and developing countries. *Columbia Journal of World Business,* 22: 3–6.

Beamish, P. W., and J. C. Banks. 1987. Equity joint ventures and the theory of the multinational enterprise. *Journal of International Business Studies,* 18(2): 1–16.

Bleeke, J., and D. Ernst. 1991. The way to win cross-border alliances. *Harvard Business Review,* 69(6): 127–135.

Buckley, P. J., and M. Casson. 1988. A theory of co-operation in international business. *Management International Review,* 28: 19–38.

Bucklin, L. P., and S. Sengupta. 1993. Organizing successful co-marketing alliances. *Journal of Marketing,* 57 (April): 32–46.

Campbell, D. T. 1955. The informant in quantitative research. *American Journal of Sociology,* 60 (January): 339–342.

Churchill, G. A. Jr. 1979. A paradigm for developing better measures of marketing constructs. *Journal of Marketing Research,* 16 (February): 64–73.

Contractor, F. J., and P. Lorange. 1988. Why should firms cooperate? The strategy and economics basis for cooperative ventures. In F. J. Contractor and P. Lorange, editors, *Cooperative Strategies in International Business,* 3–30. San Francisco: New Lexington Press.

Cook, K. S., and R. M. Emerson. 1978. Power, equity, and commitment in exchange networks. *American Sociological Review,* 43: 721–739.

Crosby, L. A., K. R. Evans, and D. Cowles. 1990. Relationship quality in services selling: An interpersonal influence perspective. *Journal of Marketing, 54* (July): 68–81.

Cullen, J. B., J. L. Johnson, and T. Sakano. 1995. Japanese and local partner commitment to IJVs: Psychological consequences of outcomes and investments in the IJV relationship. *Journal of International Business Studies,* 26(1): 91–116.

Deutsch, M. 1960. The effect of motivational orientation on trust and suspicion. *Human Relations,* 13: 123–39.

Devlin, G., and M. Bleackley. 1988. Strategic alliances: Guidelines for success. *Long Range Planning,* 21(5): 18–23.

Doz, Y. L. 1988. Technology partnerships between larger and smaller firms: Some critical issues. *International Studies of Management and Organization,* 27(4): 31–57.

Dwyer, F. R., and R. R. LaGace. 1986. On the nature and role of buyer-seller trust. In T. Shimp and others, editors, *AMA Summer Educators Conference Proceedings,* 40–45. Chicago, Ill.: American Marketing Association.

Dwyer, F. R., P. H. Schurr, and S. Oh. 1987. Developing buyer-seller relationships. *Journal of Marketing,* 51(2): 11–27.

Emerson, R. M. 1981. Social exchange theory. In M. Rosenberg and R. H. Turner, editors, *Social Psychology, Sociological Perspectives,* 30–65. New York: Basic Books.

Etgar, M. 1979. Sources and types of interchannel conflict. *Journal of Retailing,* 55: 77–78.

Evirgen, C., and A. Yaprak. 1992. Social exchange theory as a framework for cooperative ventures in international business. Paper presented at the Annual Meeting of the Academy of International Business, Brussels.

Ford, D. 1984. Buyer/seller relationships in international industrial markets. *Industrial Marketing Management,* 13: 101–113.

Franko, L. G. 1971. *Joint Venture Survival in Multinational Corporations.* New York: Praeger.

Geringer, J. M. 1991. Strategic determinants of partner selection criteria in international joint ventures. *Journal of International Business Studies,* First Quarter: 41–62.

Geringer, J. M., and L. Hébert. 1989. Control and performance of international joint ventures. *Journal of International Business Studies,* 20(2): 235–254.

Gomes-Casseres, B. 1987. Joint venture instability: Is it a problem? *Columbia Journal of World Business,* 22(2): 97–102.

Gundlach, G. T., R. S. Achrol, and J. T. Mentzer. 1995. The structure of commitment in exchange. *Journal of Marketing,* 59 (January): 78–92.

Håkansson, H. 1982. *International Marketing and Purchasing of Industrial Goods: An Interaction Approach.* New York: Wiley.

Håkansson, H. 1989. *Corporate Technological Behavior.* London: Routledge.

Håkansson, H., and J. Johanson. 1988. Formal and informal cooperation strategies in international industrial networks. In F. J. Contractor and P. Lorange, editors, *Cooperative Strategies in International Business,* 369–379. San Francisco: New Lexington Press.

Hamel, G. 1991. Competition for competence and inter-partner learning within international strategic alliances, *Strategic Management Journal,* 12: 83–103.

Hamel, G., Y. L. Doz, and C. K. Prahalad. 1989. Collaborate with your competitors and win. *Harvard Business Review,* 67(1): 133–139.

Harrigan, K. R. 1987. Strategic alliances: Their new role in global competition. *Columbia Journal of World Business,* 22(2): 67–69.

Harrigan, K. R. 1988. Strategic alliances and partner asymmetries. In F. J. Contractor and P. Lorange, editors, *Cooperative Strategies in International Business,* 205–226. San Francisco: New Lexington Press.

Heide, J. B., and G. John. 1988. The role of dependence balancing in safeguarding transaction-specific assets in conventional channels. *Journal of Marketing,* 52(1): 20–35.

Hennart, J.-F. 1988. A transaction costs theory of equity joint ventures. *Strategic Management Journal,* 9(4): 361–374.

Hrebiniak, L. G. 1974. Effects of job level and participation on employee attitudes and perceptions of influence. *Academy of Management Journal,* 17: 649–662.

Jain, S. C. 1987. Perspectives on international strategic alliances. In S. T. Cavusgil, editor, *Advances in International Marketing,* Vol. 2, 103–120. Greenwich, Conn.: JAI Press.

Killing, J. P. 1983. *Strategies for Joint Venture Success.* London: Croom Helm.

Kogut, B. 1988. Joint ventures: Theoretical and empirical perspectives. *Strategic Management Journal,* 9(2): 319–332.

Levitt, T. 1983. The globalization of markets. *Harvard Business Review,* May-June: 92–102.

Lewis, J. D. 1990. *Partnerships for Profit: Structuring and Managing Strategic Alliances.* New York: Free Press.

Lorange, P. 1989. Cooperative ventures in multinational settings. In S. T. Cavusgil, L. Hallen, and J. Johanson, editors, *Advances in International Marketing,* Vol. 3, 211–233. Greenwich, Conn.: JAI Press.

Lyles, M. A. 1987. Common mistakes of joint venture experience firms. *Columbia Journal of World Business,* 22(2): 79–85.

MacKean, R. N. 1972. Economics of trust, altruism and corporate responsibility. In E. S. Philips, editor, *Altruism, Morality and Economic Theory.* New York: Russel Sage Foundation.

Madhok, A. 1995. Revisiting multinational firms' tolerance for joint ventures: A trust-based approach. *Journal of International Business Studies,* 26(1): 117–138.

Moorman, C., G. Zaltman, and R. Deshpande. 1992. Relationships between providers and users of market research: The dynamics of trust within and between organizations. *Journal of Marketing Research,* 29(3): 314–328.

Moorman, C., R. Deshpande, and G. Zaltman. 1993. Factors affecting trust in market research relationships. *Journal of Marketing,* 57 (January): 81–101.

Morgan, R. M., and S. D. Hunt. 1994. The commitment-trust theory of relationship marketing. *Journal of Marketing,* 58(3): 20–38.

Mowery, D. C. 1988. *International Collaborative Ventures in U.S. Manufacturing.* New York: Ballinger.

Nunnally, J. C. 1978. *Psychometric Theory,* 2nd ed. New York: McGraw-Hill.

Ohmae, K. 1989. The global logic of strategic alliances. *Harvard Business Review,* March-April: 143–154.

Pfeffer, J., and G. R. Salancik. 1978. *The External Control of Organizations: A Resource Dependence Perspective.* New York: HarperCollins.

Porter, M. E., and M. B. Fuller. 1986. Coalitions and global strategy. In M. E. Porter, editor, *Competition and Global Industries,* 315–343. Boston: Harvard Business School Press.

Revesz, R. T., and M. L. Cauley. 1986. Competitive alliances: Strategy for global markets. *Business International,* July: 1–3.

Ring, P. S., and A. H. Van de Ven. 1992. Structuring cooperative relationships between organizations. *Strategic Management Journal,* 13(7): 483–498.

Roehl, T. W., and J. F. Truitt. 1987. Stormy open marriages are better: Evidence from U.S., Japanese and French cooperative ventures in commercial aircraft. *Columbia Journal of World Business,* 22(2): 87–95.

Root, F. R. 1988. Some taxonomies of international cooperative arrangements. In F. J. Contractor and P. Lorange, editors, *Cooperative Strategies in International Business,* 69–80. San Francisco: New Lexington Press.

Rotter, J. B. 1967. A new scale for the measurement of interpersonal trust. *Journal of Personality,* 35 (December): 651–665.

Salk, J. E. 1993. Behind the state of the union: The impact of design and social processes on relationships in shared management joint venture teams. Marketing Science Institute Technical Working Paper, Report No. 93–110.

Seidler, J. 1974. On using informants: A technique for collecting quantitative data and controlling measurement error in organizational analysis. *American Sociological Review,* 39 (December): 816–831.

Sengupta, S. 1993. Effects of industry and national origin on the complexity of alliance agreements. In M. J. Sirgy, K. D. Bahn, and T. Erem, editors, *Proceedings of the Sixth Bi-Annual International Conference of the Academy of Marketing Science,* 254–258.

Sharma, D. D. 1993. Industrial networks in marketing. In S. T. Cavusgil and D. D. Sharma, editors, *Advances in International Marketing,* Vol. 5, 1–9. Greenwich, Conn.: JAI Press.

Sherman, S. 1992. Are strategic alliances working? *Fortune,* September: 77–78.

Sheth, J. N., and A. Parvatiyar. 1992. Towards a theory of business alliance formation. *Scandinavian International Business Review,* 1(3): 71–87.

Smith, J. B., and D. W. Barclay. 1995. Promoting effective selling alliances: The roles of trust and organizational differences. Marketing Science Institute Technical Working Paper, Report No. 95–100.

Snehota, I. 1993. Market as network and the nature of market process. In S. T. Cavusgil and D. D. Sharma, editors, *Advances in International Marketing,* Vol. 5. Greenwich, Conn.: JAI Press.

Spekman, R. E., and K. Sawhney. 1990. Toward a conceptual understanding of the antecedents of strategic alliances. Marketing Science Institute Technical Working Paper, Report No. 90–114.

Stoltman, R. E., J. Gentry, and F. Morgan. 1993. Marketing relationships: Further consideration of the marriage metaphor with implications for maintenance and recovery. Working paper, Wayne State University, Detroit, Michigan.

Strassman, W. P., and J. Wells. 1988. *The Global Construction Industry: Strategies for Entry, Growth and Survival*. London: Unwin Hyman.

Thorelli, H. B. 1986. Networks: Between markets and hierarchies. *Strategic Management Journal,* 7(1): 37–51.

Tomlinson, J. W. 1970. *The Joint Venture Process in International Business: India and Pakistan*. Cambridge, Mass.: MIT Press.

The top international contractors: International contracts rise on the crest of an Asian wave. 1994. *Engineering News Record,* August 29: 26–42.

Van de Ven, A. H. 1976. On the nature, formation, and maintenance of relations among organizations. *Academy of Management Review*, 1(4): 24–36.

Van de Ven, A. H., and D. L. Ferry. 1980. *Measuring and Assessing Organizations*. New York: Wiley.

Wallace, A. 1993. American and Japanese perspectives on the determinants of successful joint ventures. Paper presented at the Annual Meeting of the Academy of International Business, Maui, Hawaii.

Williamson, O. E. 1975. *Markets and Hierarchies: Analysis of Antitrust Implications*. New York: Free Press.

11

PATTERNS OF PROCESS IN COOPERATIVE INTERORGANIZATIONAL RELATIONSHIPS

Peter Smith Ring

IN THIS CHAPTER, *an approach to assessing processes and outcomes of cooperative interorganizational relationships (CIORs) is presented. Based on data gathered during six multi-method, longitudinal case studies, five patterns of these processes are identified and outcomes associated with each are described. The chapter concludes with a brief discussion of issues raised related to the processes associated with CIORs and their study.*

IN THIS CHAPTER, I continue to explore how cooperative interorganizational relationships (CIORs)[1] "emerge, grow, and dissolve over time" (Ring and Van de Ven 1994: 90). As Doz (1996: 3) points out, "the growing literature on the strategic alliance phenomenon suffers from imbalance." He asserts that "studies of strategic alliances as evolutionary processes are

This chapter is a revised version of a paper prepared for the conference Global Perspectives on Cooperative Strategies, in London, Ontario, on March 1–3, 1996. The author is indebted to two reviewers for the conference for their extremely helpful comments. A very early version was presented at the EMOT Conference on International Networks sponsored by the European Science Foundation in Jouy-en-Josas, France, in February 1995. The assistance of the ESF and the EMOT program is gratefully acknowledged.

scarce." Parkhe (1993) observes that this is an aspect of our understanding of cooperative strategies in need of grounded empirical research.

The literature related to CIORs in general has tended to focus on antecedent conditions, on the relationships between antecedent conditions and the structure of CIORs, on relationships between antecedent conditions and outcomes with structure as a mediating variable, or on comparative studies of governance forms. These kinds of factors (inputs, structures, outcomes) are essential in providing a context for the study of collaborative processes, but their study offers little insight into the nature of the processes themselves, or how these processes contribute to the ways in which cooperative strategies unfold over time.

Despite the relative lack of interest in research on issues related to process, they remain central to any understanding of cooperative strategies. Cooperative strategies are implemented only when agents (managers, lawyers, brokers, investment bankers, and the like) acting for their principals (the boards of directors and top management teams of firms) seek each other out, engage in negotiations, and make deals. If they are successful in these efforts, they (and others) engage in the execution of cooperative strategies. These agents, and their principals, "need to know more than the input conditions, investments, and types of governance structures required for a relationship" (Ring and Van de Ven 1994: 91). Their ability to successfully develop, create, and manage cooperative strategies also depends on their understanding of the processes they employ in the course of cooperative strategies.

The central proposition offered here is that collaborative processes will vary in kind, and in intensity, contingent upon the objectives that are the focus of parties employing cooperative strategies. This conclusion is drawn from data gathered in the course of conducting six longitudinal studies of CIORs relying on ethnographic methods.

I begin with a necessarily brief discussion of cooperative strategies.[2] This is followed by a description of the six case studies from which the data on collaborative processes were gathered, after which is presented a conceptual discussion of formal and informal processes grounded in these data. Next is the presentation of five illustrative patterns of cooperative processes and their interactions. In the concluding section of the chapter, I address implications for further research on the processes that are manifest in cooperative strategies.

Cooperative Strategies

Jack Welch, General Electric's CEO, is reported as claiming that "alliances are a big part of this game [of global competition]. . . . They are critical to win on a global basis" (Yoshino and Rangan 1995: 3). Regarding CIORs in general, Olivetti's de Benedetti has observed that "the traditional multinational approach is *dépassé*. Corporations with international ambitions must turn to a new strategy of agreements, alliances, and mergers with other companies" (Symonds, Peterson, Keller, and Frons 1987).

The general interest in CIORs as strategies among practitioners is paralleled within the academic community.[3] CIORs are explored as strategies (Yoshino and Rangan 1995), governance mechanisms, organizational forms, or mechanisms for exchanges of property rights. Wide-ranging and rapid changes in technology, changes in competitive environments and in the strategies of firms, and other pressures are among the perceived reasons prompting managers to cooperate with other firms. The research I just cited reveals that the resource acquisition motivations of the managers of firms that are relying on CIORs include gaining access to new technologies, new factor markets, and new product markets. Creation of CIORs may also be motivated by a desire for the resources needed to produce economies of scale in research, production, or marketing. CIORs can also be used to build skills complementary to those of the focal firm by tapping into know-how resources located outside its boundaries.

Increasingly, CIORs are taking on many characteristics of networked organizations (Ring 1996b). A growing number involve multiorganizational collaborations. They are infused with multiplex social (see, for example, Coleman 1988) and economic exchange, and trust among the collaborators provides for more flexible governance (Ring 1996a). Interpersonal relationships are of paramount importance. Complete autonomy is easily forgone. Contributions need not be fully specified in advance, nor ongoing. Collective gains seem to be a primary objective of collaborators employing network-like CIORs (Håkansson and Snehota 1995), and economic actors in network-like settings are likely to sacrifice some of their own preferences in pursuit of collective goals.

One conclusion that may be safely drawn from the emerging body of work on cooperative strategies is that they are likely to remain as a permanent landmark on the landscape of business. Increasingly, firms will be managing numerous cooperative strategies at the same time, and the relationships developed in the course of cooperating will become longer lasting and more complex. For these kinds of reasons, understanding the processes that are employed in the emergence, evolution, maintenance, and devolution of cooperative strategies is likely to take on increasing relevance for managers and for scholars.

Case Studies

The study of process requires an approach to data collection that differs from the conventional survey methods, or from a reliance on secondary data sources, that typifies much of the CIOR research cited above. This is not to say that surveys or secondary sources are not helpful in understanding process; they can be. Exclusive reliance on these methods, however, is not likely to capture the dynamic elements of process.

Research Sites

The grounded theory about collaborative process interactions offered here, and its implications for cooperative strategies, was initially derived from a longitudinal case study of the processes of innovation. In Table 11.1, this is the 3M-NASA study. It provided the initial insights into the processes of collaboration that were reported in Ring and Rands (1989). As frequently happens with case studies, a systematic sample of representative contexts, controlling for important variables, was not a primary objective when the research was initially undertaken over a decade ago. Nonetheless, during the past eleven years, I have been able to gain access to five additional CIORs at various stages in their development. In selecting these cases I endeavored to broaden the contexts under study with the objective of increasing the possibility of generalizing the conclusions drawn from the data.[4]

Relevant characteristics of the six cases are summarized in Table 11.1. Four of the cases are disguised, either because they are ongoing or because of conditions imposed on me by the host organizations. In three of the cases, data collection efforts continue at various levels of intensity. Table 11.1 also reveals that the data collection efforts in all these cases have been extensive, spanning nearly a decade, for example, in the Alpha Mining study.

In the course of conducting this research, I intentionally sought cases in which the participants came from different sectors of the economy and from different industries. I also attempted to differentiate by ownership characteristics (for example, publicly versus privately owned). Thus, my sample includes both of these types of firms, as well as government agencies and state-owned enterprises (SOEs). There are firms from ten different countries, reflecting all regions of the Triad (Ohmae 1985). Services, manufacturing, and professional services segments of the private sector, and a governmental agency make up the sample; a number of important industries are represented. In addition to seeking such variety, three other dimensions were important criteria in my search for research sites. I sought

Dimensions used to select cases	3M-NASA	Alpha Mines	Beta Trading Co.	The Genesis Group	Delta	Bull HN
Organization type	Govt. agency, firms	Firms	Firms	Partnerships	Partnerships	Firms, state-owned enterprises
Nationalities	U.S.	U.S., Canadian, Japanese	U.S., Japanese, Australian	U.S., European, Asian	U.S., European	U.S., French, Japanese
Ownership status	Public	Public and private	Public and private	Private	Private	Public and state
Industry	Diversified mfg., auto, defense	Minerals extraction and processing	Services	Professional services	Services	Computers
Value chain focus	S, L	P	P	P, S, L	P, S, L	P, S, L
Resource types	ST, CKH, TKN, FBL	CT	CKH, TKH, FBL	GT, CT, CKH, TKH, FBL	All types	CT, CKH, TKH, CBL, FBL
Governance	MOU, STC, LTC	JV, LTC	Lic, JV, LTC	None	JV	JV

Dates of study	1985–1990	1987–present	1988–1990	1994–present	1987–1992	1986–present
Sources of data	Interviews	Interviews	Interviews	Interviews	Interviews	Interviews
	Private archival	Participant observation	Private archival	Participant observation	Participant observation	Private archival
	Public archival	Private archival		Private archival	Private archival	Public archival
	Surveys	Public archival				
		Surveys				

Key: *Governance mechanisms:* MOU = memo of understanding, STC = short-term contract, LTC = long-term contract, JV = joint venture, Lic = licensing

Value chain focus: P = production activities, S = support activities, L = legitimacy activities

Resource types: GT = generic tangible, ST = specialized tangible, CT = co-specialized tangible, CKH = codified know-how, TKH = tacit know-how, CBL = charter-based legitimacy, FBL = firm-based legitimacy

Table 11.1. Case Study Summary.

to study CIORs governed by a variety of formal governance mechanisms. I also sought CIORs that involved different kinds of resources (that is, assets). In addition, I have previously suggested that where resources are employed in a firm's value chain may also matter (Ring 1990, 1996b). Thus, I sought variety along this dimension. In the interest of space, a complete discussion of all these dimensions is forgone here; see, generally, Ring 1996b.

Sources of Data

As reflected in Table 11.1, I have gathered data on processes from a variety of sources. My primary vehicle was interviews with the principals involved in the CIORs. Most were real-time; that is, contemporaneous with important events in the evolution of the CIORs. For example, in the 3M-NASA case, data were obtained from sixty-one interviews of forty-four individuals that amounted to over ninety hours of audiotaped material. The interviewees ranged from the CEO to bench-level scientists and secretaries at 3M, and from administrators to scientists at NASA.

In some cases, the data were gathered in the course of serving as an observer to important meetings of all the parties. Much of the data for the Genesis Group have been collected in this way. In all cases, interview and participant observer data were supplemented by extensive archival research. The archival data came from public sources in some cases and from the parties' own files in all cases. Archival data included copies of memos, drafts of contracts, and other relevant documents. In the 3M-NASA cases, for example, the archival data collected over the five years of the study fill an entire file cabinet.

Collaborative Processes

Van de Ven (1992) observes that the concept of process is typically employed in one of three ways in the management literature: as an explanation for variance theory, as a category of concepts, or as a developmental sequence. The last of these is employed in this chapter. Van de Ven (1992: 170) defines this approach to process as "a sequence of events or activities that describes how things change over time, or that represents an underlying pattern of cognitive transitions by an entity in dealing with an issue." In the approach I have employed in the research described below, both aspects of Van de Ven's definition are considered.

In addressing the larger questions of process theory, Van de Ven also classifies differing approaches into four basic families of theories: life cycle, teleological, dialectic, and evolutionary. The approach taken here is consistent with teleology; the research is based on an assumption that firms seeking to implement cooperative strategies are "purposeful and adaptive." Moreover, teleology "does not presume a necessary sequence of events," nor does it imply path-dependence. This family of process theories posits "a set of functions or goals desired by an organizational unit, which it has to acquire in order to 'realize' its aspirations. Development is movement toward attaining a purpose, goal, function, or desired state" (Van de Ven 1992: 178). In our case, the purpose, goal, or desired state is the realization of cooperative strategies.

Formal Processes

The formal processes identified during our initial study of the 3M-NASA collaboration were consistent with those described by Commons (1950),[5] who argued that economic exchanges involve dynamic processes that he describes as negotiational, transactional, and administrative.

In the negotiational phase,[6] the strategies, or strategic intent (Hamel and Prahalad 1989), of the various actors begins to evolve and take shape. This phase can vary in length and intensity to a very considerable degree. In the 3M-NASA case, for example, the initial negotiational phase lasted nearly eleven months, but was largely devoted to efforts by both sides to learn more about each other. In contrast, during a second round of negotiation processes, nearly three years elapsed. A substantial part of that period was the result of delays caused by a totally uncontrollable event: the Challenger disaster.

During negotiational processes, the selection of potential participants in the CIOR will be one major outcome. At the Genesis Group, for example, this process has been ongoing for over fifteen months and the question of membership still remains an open issue for some of the parties. Delta spent over four years looking for a partner. In the case of Bull HN, on the other hand, the choice of partners for Honeywell was much more obvious, and negotiational processes lasted less than two months.

As the amount of such information as goals and core competencies that is shared between economic actors increases during negotiational processes, the likelihood that they will advance to transactional phases improves. This presents managers contemplating strategic alliances (or other contract-based CIORs) involving new partners with an obvious dilemma: Do we reflect a lack of trust from the start by conditioning information sharing, requiring confidentiality agreements and the like, or do we make (significant) unilateral investments in behavior of a trusting nature, hoping that potential collaborators will reciprocate? The latter was certainly the case with managers at both 3M and NASA and among those currently engaged in the formation of the Genesis Group. Resolution of issues surrounding the kinds of information that members of a CIOR will be expected to share with each other on an ongoing basis, and the conditions surrounding the sharing of information, are likely to be other major outcomes of a negotiational process.

During transactional processes, the wills of the parties meet as they finalize the terms by which a CIOR will be governed. In contract-based CIORs, these processes are likely to be viewed as most critical, and they frequently lead to failure as the parties confront deal-breaking conditions sought by one or more of the collaborators. This was very much the case in the Bull HN deal. Demands by one or more of the parties on a number of key issues nearly led to termination of the effort to form the joint venture.

Another outcome of transactional processes will be the rules for making rules (Hart 1961), in the form of generalized agreements on obligations, expectations, norms, and sanctions. In contract- and equity-based CIORs, these will be reduced to writing only after intense negotiational and transactional processes. At Bull HN, for instance, the rules included over a dozen "blocking rights" giving any one of the three parties absolute veto power on important strategic decisions (see for example Ring, Lenway, and Nichols 1994).

Finally, the more formal administrative processes that are associated with the management of a CIOR primarily involve the transformation of inputs into outputs whose value is (it is hoped) greater than their combined production and transaction costs. In this respect, administrative processes lead to outcomes that we would expect to find flowing from all organizational activity. The administrative process will also include the "care and feeding" of the CIOR itself, governed by the rules for making rules previously described. To the extent that these reflect the more legalistic nature of contract- or equity-based CIORs, they increase the likelihood that collaborators will face problems down the road in dealing with unforeseen consequences. Emergent strategic responses (Mintzberg and Waters 1985) in such cases will require a new round of negotiational processes. In the Alpha Mines case, the need to take into account significant changes in the industry and in the fortunes of the collaborators has produced protracted, highly legalistic negotiations that increasingly place the ongoing venture in jeopardy. Thus, an inevitable set of outcomes of administrative processes are conflict, misunderstanding, and changing expectations. These may result in new rounds of negotiational and transactional processes regarding norms, sanctions, expectations, obligations, or other outcomes. Or, these outcomes can lead to termination of the CIOR.

Informal Processes

In our studies of transactions, we have found that each of the formal processes just described is accompanied by a series of informal processes. To sustain collaborative effort between firms, reliance on interpersonal processes is essential. Turner (1987) identifies three fundamental forces motivating human thought and action that can be considered as outcomes of collaborative processes: satisfaction of the needs for identity, facticity, and inclusion. These outcomes are products of three social-psychological processes: sensemaking, understanding, and committing (Ring and Rands 1989).

Sensemaking is an enactment process (Weick 1995). This permits individuals to act more clearly in relation to the environment in which they are embedded (Morgan 1986: 243). In psychological terms, sensemaking derives from a human need to have a sense of one's own identity in relation to others (Kumon 1992; Turner 1987). In the case of the Genesis Group, much of its activity to date has been focused on this issue. Sensemaking processes help individual economic actors in a CIOR to view their own preferences in relation to those of all other economic actors in the CIOR. This was a primary outcome of the very intense sensemaking processes that accompanied transactional phases of the Bull HN joint venture. In cases in which individual and collective goals may conflict, the ability to see these differences will be essential to maintenance of the collaboration.

Understanding is an informal process that produces a social construction of a relationship. The parties seek "facticity" in their relationship (Turner 1987). Interaction is facilitated by the need among the economic actors who make up a CIOR to feel that they share a common understanding of an obdurate world. In Zucker's terms (1977), the process of understanding makes the acts of economic persons exterior—their subjective understandings are reconstructed as intersubjective understandings, permitting the acts to be seen as a part of the external world.

In those cases where understanding processes involve numerous economic actors, each relying on contrasting ways of knowing, facticity or other products of understanding processes (for example, overlapping cognitive maps, organizational learning) may not be achieved. If they are, however, they will be time-consuming and costly. This outcome is more likely to occur when the membership of a CIOR crosses boundaries of geography, politics, ideology, religion, or culture.

Committing is an informal process that produces psychological contracts (Argyris 1960; Levinson and others 1962) between economic actors. In contrast to legal contracts, psychological contracts consist of unwritten and largely unverbalized sets of expectations and assumptions held by economic actors about each other's prerogatives and obligations.

The formal and informal processes just described are employed by the parties to varying degrees of intensity. Some parties may be inclined to want to move rapidly, to cut to the chase, as it were. They may seek to truncate informal processes in the negotiational process and get on to transactional processes related to deal making. Some parties may have to do more sensemaking than others. In Figure 11.1, a model of the interactions of formal and informal processes just described is set forth. (A discussion of assessments is beyond our scope here; Ring and Van de Ven 1994 provides our views on the topic.)

Process Patterns

The foregoing discussion leads me to offer the following suppositions about the nature of collaborative processes. In cases where cooperative strategies are based on kinship ties, or on "dense transactions and a stable framework for exchange" (Gerlach 1992)—that is, networked organization—it seems probable that economic actors will not need to rely heavily on sensemaking or understanding processes. In larger, more complex CIORs (such as research consortia, or contract- or equity-based strategic alliances that cross national boundaries), sensemaking, understanding, and committing processes generally will be much more intensive for all the parties, and are likely to take much more time to conclude.

The starting points of economic exchange can vary a great deal. Conditions that affect how and with what formal processes collaboration may begin include the degree to which the parties have been previously acquainted or have had prior social or economic interactions. These kinds of conditions affect the opportunities the parties have had to come to know and understand the "self" in relation to the "other." If during these prior interactions sensemaking and understanding processes led to high levels of trust, the parties may be able to make commitments without relying on formalized, more costly governance mechanisms such as contracts. Thus, CIORs among parties who have experienced prior economic relationships, or who benefit from friendship or social ties, can be expected to evolve more rapidly than when reciprocal sensemaking, understanding, or committing processes have not been employed repeatedly between them in the past.

The studies of cooperative strategies I have conducted indicate that sensemaking, understanding, and committing processes will occur at varying levels of intensity within differing types of CIORs. I conclude this section by describing five potential patterns. Needless to say, this discussion should be

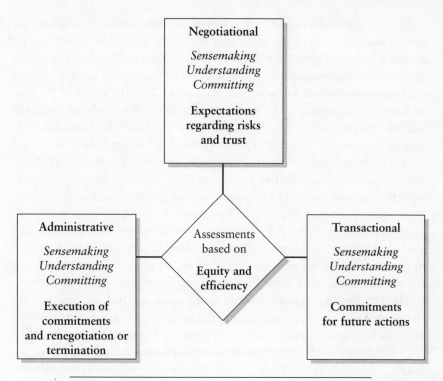

Figure 11.1. Process Framework for the Development of CIORs.

considered as extremely tentative, based as it is on a limited number of observations of CIOR processes.

New Collaboration in an Existing CIOR

The first pattern of processes occurs in an existing CIOR in which the members are engaged in a new collaboration. This pattern has been present in the 3M-NASA, Beta Trading, Alpha Mining, and Honeywell-Bull cases. In each, the most intense interpersonal processes occurred during transactional phases. In most important respects, the members of the CIOR relied on established routines that minimized the need for extensive informal processes in negotiational phases. Cognitive maps of the relationship were established and generally understood. The parties were committed to continuing their relationship. Some external pressure had produced a need to change the nature of the existing CIOR, and the members of the CIOR were responding to time pressures such as market demands, regulatory changes, and the like.

In these four cases, defining the terms of the new relationships among the parties was the cause of the most intense activity. Sensemaking and understanding processes were centered around reaching agreement on consideration and the duration of the relationship. The conduct of these processes tends to be intensified by these time pressures. Once the terms of the new exchange were agreed to, however, the administrative phase played itself out via processes with which the members of the CIOR had become quite familiar. In the 3M-NASA and the Beta Trading collaborations, trust had been established, information flowed freely, the same language was (now) spoken, and mechanisms for private ordering were in place. Hence, the need for extensive sensemaking, understanding, and committing processes during administrative phases was also reduced. At Alpha Mining, the absence of trust was replaced by extensive monitoring mechanisms that were well established. At Honeywell-Bull, the creation of the joint venture had its greatest impact, initially, on headquarters personnel; operations tended to continue as they had in the past (see Ring, Lenway, and Nichols 1994).

The benefits that should flow to members of a CIOR in this case include an ability to capitalize more quickly on new technologies, to enter new markets more rapidly, or to gain greater advantage from cost reduction initiatives. In short, whenever time-based imperatives confront economic actors, those who are already functioning within an established CIOR (or have collaborated with each other in the past) ought to act more quickly than economic actors who must act independently or develop cooperative strategies from square one. Their existing relationship should permit them to focus their attention on much less intense informal processes in the course of conducting transaction processes. Parties who face the same time pressures without the benefit of prior interaction will experience more intensive informal processes in the course of conducting formal processes.

Creation of a New CIOR: The U.S. "Legalistic" Approach

As I will discuss further in this section, the limited data I have gathered suggest that new CIORs produce widely varying patterns of process interactions. For example, the managers of U.S. firms reveal a tendency to rush through informal processes of sensemaking, understanding, and committing in negotiational processes. In transactional processes, however, they engage in intensive sensemaking and understanding processes. Committing processes are present in the course of transactional processes, but they appear to be less important (and conducted less intensively) than is understanding the nature of the deal. It is my impression that this more intensive focus on sensemaking and understanding processes in the transactional phase of CIOR creation is a function of the legalistic approach to deal making that is characteristic of U.S. firms. The sensemaking and understanding processes will be needed if the parties are to reach agreement on the objectives for the CIOR, or on their impacts on the organizations that make up the CIOR. This was so, initially, in all of the cases outlined in Table 11.1 (with the exception of the Bull HN collaboration).

A new CIOR may also alter preexisting relationships between some of the parties to such an extent that new committing processes will be required, as was the case for Honeywell, NEC, and Companie de Machines Bull. The nature of the new relationships was resolved in transactional phases, not during administrative phases. Aware of the value of a CIOR as a means of reducing cost or enhancing information sharing, the parties look to identify problems related to the ways in which production activities will be conducted in advance, and seek to resolve them as they work out the design of the CIOR in negotiational and, most intensely, in transactional phases. Once the details of the CIOR are established in the transactional phases, sensemaking and understanding processes, although ongoing, will be less intense than those that occur during transactional phases, at least until problems arise. Committing processes, to the extent that the new CIOR changes established relationships, however, are likely to intensify during administrative phases, as new or renewed levels of trust are sought. However, the need for more intensive sensemaking, understanding, and committing processes during negotiational and transactional phases means that the benefits that flow from collaborative relationships will take longer to emerge than is the case in the existing CIOR described in the first pattern. In cases in which a CIOR is being formed to take advantage of scale or scope economies, this may not be a liability, but it will be if time-based imperatives are at work in the competitive environment.

Creation of a New CIOR: Two-Culture CIORs

In our third pattern, negotiational and administrative phases leading to the emergence of the CIOR are more intense than in transactional phases. I believe this pattern of processes will be associated with CIORs in which parties from very different cultures are engaged, or in cases in which sovereignty or institutional guarantors are absent. This was the case in the 3M-NASA collaboration and in Beta Trading's initial forays into Japan. On the other hand, as Beta moved into Australia, it truncated sensemaking and understanding processes in negotiational processes by the relatively simple expedient of gaining the products of those processes by acquiring the individual owner of a firm with the reputation for best understanding the Australian market. That person then conducted sensemaking and understanding processes in subsequent efforts by Beta to develop collaborative relationships with other firms in the Australian market.

Creation of a New CIOR: Japanese Style

There are also collaborative dynamics that can produce lower levels of uncertainty. The ability to share information during intense sensemaking and understanding processes can lower uncertainty of the state-contingent variety (Thompson 1967). Information sharing during sensemaking and understanding processes may also help the members of a CIOR to reduce the effects of behavioral uncertainty (that is, opportunism).

I refer to this pattern of processes as Japanese-style collaborations because in many important respects it appears to reflect an approach to decision making and exchange thought to be favored by the Japanese. In this pattern the most intense processes occur during negotiational phases, whereas in the transactional and administrative phases of the collaboration the intensity of informal processes is predicted to fall off dramatically.

Although I refer to this pattern as a Japanese style, this does not imply that the approach is always reflected in collaborations involving Japanese firms. The two-culture pattern (our third pattern) also reflects data gathered in observing collaborations involving Japanese firms. In fact, I have a colleague in the legal profession who counsels clients dealing with Japanese firms to rely on a two-culture approach in first-time deals. The formal contracts that the parties rely on in these cases are simply well-crafted legal agreements to conduct formal strategic planning processes and to manage their relationship by the terms of the strategic plan and its annual operationalization in a budget. Where time is not a fundamental factor in governing the pace of collaborative processes, however, the Japanese-style approach offers significant potential gains in eliminating conflicts during administrative phases that could require new rounds of negotiational and transactional processes, or worse still lead to exit (Hirschman 1970) by one of the parties.

CIORs in an Embedded Context

I believe that in simple CIORs—those deeply embedded in family ties, in a single culture, or within well-established legal systems (such as the Uniform Commercial Code)—informal processes will not vary much between formal phases. If a CIOR is deeply and culturally embedded, little additional sensemaking, understanding, or committing will be required in the first instance. These are well-acquainted parties, performing well-established routines (March and Simon 1958). Consequently, I expect that processes will not vary across formal phases and will evidence relatively low levels of intensity throughout. At Beta Trading, for example, the nature of the relationship between the U.S. and Japanese firms that has emerged over twenty years has made new deals between them very routine. Lorenzoni and Lipparini (1995) report similar outcomes among the firms that they studied.

This fifth pattern of processes implies that in a particular CIOR the transaction costs incurred by the parties may be significantly reduced. This is one of the benefits of social embeddedness. This pattern also reflects the benefits that can be obtained by private parties from more formalized institutional efforts to reduce the costs of economic exchange, such as the U.C.C.

Conclusion

As previously stated, the five patterns described above must be treated with caution. They are based on observations derived from longitudinal study of a small number of CIORs. They are consistent, however, with observations derived from other studies (see for example Browning, Beyer, and Shelter 1995; Larson 1992; Lazerson 1988; Lorenzoni and Lipparini 1995). And they are grounded in well-established concepts derived from studies of organizational behavior, in theories of social psychology, cognition, and the epistemology of knowledge. Finally, there are well-established ethnographic methods for studying these processes.

Scholarly interest in the structure and processes of CIORs is clearly on the upswing, and it seems to be the case that collaborations, especially of the network variety, are appearing more today than in the past. Whether there are more networks today is, of course, an empirical question that is not very tractable. Whether the factors that apparently motivate managers to use cooperative strategies as a means of conducting economic exchange are permanent or transient remains to be seen. Whether they necessarily lead to reliance on CIORs is another empirical question worthy of investigation. We may be witnessing something very much like the paradox of Say's Law: supply (of CIORs) can create its own demand (for more CIORs).

Extant research on CIORs reveals that they currently are manifest in a wide variety of forms, and are governed by a number of mechanisms. Less is known about the extent to which the processes by which networks emerge, evolve, are sustained, or terminated are common across cooperative strategies or governance mechanisms. These are also questions that will require further rigorous empirical investigations if we are to help managers enjoy the benefits that seem to flow from reliance on CIORs as a means of governing economic exchanges.

A focus on the outcomes of CIORs also raises another question. Much of the research on CIORs explores the CIOR. Less attention is given to those whose economic lives also are affected by the CIORs: their stakeholders (Freeman 1984). Perhaps it is time to broaden the scope of our investigations to include a better assessment of boundary questions. As we explore CIORs, do we include all those within the CIOR who are really a part of it? The techniques of network analysis certainly permit us to explore these kinds of questions. These same techniques also permit us to compare perceptions of the efficiency and effectiveness of cooperative strategies held by those who are the primary stakeholders of a CIOR with those held by members of the CIOR.

Finally, because cooperative business arrangements are becoming more pronounced, researchers are looking for concepts by which issues related to collaboration can be explored. The variety in forms of governance described earlier as falling under the umbrella of a CIOR may indicate that we need greater conceptual clarification of the term *strategic alliance*. The concepts of network and alliance (for example) are used interchangeably in many instances. If, as I have suggested, these are distinct forms of governance of economic exchanges, then the conceptual confusion must be resolved.

NOTES

1. Whether cooperative interorganizational relationships (CIORs) are strategies or the outcomes (or instruments) of strategies is a question beyond the scope of this chapter. There appears to be an assumption, implicit in much of the research on cooperative strategies, that CIORs are vehicles used to achieve strategic objectives.

2. Presenting data derived from ethnographic studies within the usual page limits of this kind of chapter is a daunting task. Typically something must be sacrificed. I have chosen to forgo the usual approach to a literature review for two reasons. First, more relevant literatures will be addressed in the discussion of the processes observed in the course of the studies that provide the data. Second, extensive reviews of the literature on cooperative strategies are readily available to the interested reader.

3. See generally: institutional economics (for example, Barney and Ouchi 1986; North 1990; Williamson 1991); interorganizational relations (for example, Oliver 1990), a cultural-structural approach first taken by socio-

logists, and more recently relied upon by management and marketing scholars, focusing on networks (for example, Aldrich and Whetten 1981; Axelsson and Easton 1992; Häkansson 1989; Jarillo 1988; Nohria and Eccles 1993; Powell 1990). In reviewing these literatures, one shortcoming common to each emerged: none provides a complete picture of the processes by which CIORs emerged (or were formally planned). The cross-sectional nature of survey research characterizing much of the empirical work precludes developing such insights (see for example Gulati 1995; Parkhe 1993). Nor do they appear in case studies of collaborative efforts of single firms, industrial districts, consortia, or networks (see for example Barley, Freeman, and Hybels 1993; Casson and Cox 1993). Exceptions to my general statement about studies of process can be found in Doz (1996), Larson (1992), and Ring and Van de Ven (1994, 1992).

4. I use the term *select* advisably because some of the cases came to me quite fortuitously. In other instances, I passed up opportunities while looking for cases that added new dimensions to the research. The time-intensive aspects of longitudinal field work grounded in ethnographic methods mandate this kind of selectivity. They also prolong the time within which grounded theory is developed. And they raise the ante in passing up opportunities.

5. Space limitations prevent a more complete description of the formal and informal collaborative processes observed in the CIORs under study here. More complete discussions of these processes, their theoretical grounding, and some of their implications for managers pursing cooperative strategies, or researchers studying cooperative strategies, will be found in Ring and Rands (1989) and Ring and Van de Ven (1989, 1992, 1994).

6. Negotiational processes may occur when economic actors seek to create a new CIOR, when they attempt to join an existing CIOR to which they do not belong, or when they redefine their relationships within an existing CIOR (including an exit from the CIOR).

Bibliography

Aldrich, H., and D. A. Whetten. 1981. Organizational sets, action sets, and networks: Making the most of simplicity. In C. P. Nystrom and W. H. Starbuck, editors, *Handbook of Organizational Design,* 385–408. New York: Oxford University Press.

Argyris, C. 1960. *Understanding Organizational Behavior.* Homewood, Ill.: Dorsey.

Axelsson, B., and G. Easton, editors. 1992. *Industrial Networks: A New View of Reality.* New York: Routledge.

Barley, S. R., J. Freeman, and R. C. Hybels. 1993. Strategic alliances in commercial biotechnology. In N. Nohria and R. Eccles, editors, *Networks and Organizations.* Boston: Harvard Business School Press.

Barney, J., and W. G. Ouchi, editors. 1986. *Organizational Economics: Toward a New Paradigm for Understanding and Studying Organizations.* San Francisco: Jossey-Bass.

Beamish, P. W. 1988. *Multinational Joint Ventures in Developing Countries.* London: Routledge.

Berg, S. V., J. Duncan, and P. Friedman. 1982. *Joint Venture Strategies and Corporate Innovation.* Cambridge, Mass.: Oelgschlager, Gunn and Hain.

Bromiley, P., and L. L. Cummings. 1995. Transactions costs in organizations with trust. In R. J. Bies, R. J. Lewicki, and B. L. Sheppard, editors, *Research on Negotiations in Organizations,* Vol. 5, 219–247. Greenwich, Conn.: JAI Press.

Browning, L. D., J. M. Beyer, and J. C. Shelter. 1995. Building cooperation in a competitive industry: SEMATECH and the semiconductor industry. *The Academy of Management Journal,* 38: 113–151.

Casson, M., and H. Cox. 1993. Modelling inter-firm networks. In M. Ebers and A. Grandori, editors, *Proceedings of the European Science Foundation Conference, Forms of Inter-Organizational Networks: Structures and Processes,* 269–310. Berlin: European Science Foundation.

Coleman, J. S. 1988. Social capital in the creation of human capital. *American Journal of Sociology,* 94 (Special Supplement): S95–S120.

Commons, J. R. 1950. *The Economics of Collective Actions.* Madison: University of Wisconsin Press.

Doz, Y. L. 1996. The evolution of cooperation in strategic alliances: Initial conditions or learning processes? *Strategic Management Journal,* 17: 55–83.

Freeman, R. E. 1984. *Strategic Management: A Stakeholder Perspective.* Boston: Pitman.

Gerlach, M. L. 1992. *Alliance Capitalism: The Social Organization of Japanese Business.* Berkeley: University of California Press.

Gulati, R. 1995. Does familiarity breed trust? The implications of repeated ties for contractual choices in alliances. *Academy of Management Journal,* 38: 85–112.

Håkansson, H. 1989. *Corporate Technological Behavior: Cooperation and Networks.* London: Routledge.

Håkansson, H., and I. Snehota, editors. 1995. *Developing Relationships in Networks.* London: Routledge.

Hamel, G., and C. K. Prahalad. 1989. Strategic intent. *Harvard Business Review,* 67: 63–76.

Hart, H.L.A. 1961. *The Concept of Law.* Oxford: Clarendon Press.

Hirschman, A. O. 1970. *Exit, Voice, and Loyalty: Responses to Decline in Firms, Organizations, and States.* Cambridge, Mass.: Harvard University Press.

Jarillo, J. C. 1988. On strategic networks. *Strategic Management Journal,* 9: 31–41.

Kumon, S. 1992. Japan as a network society. In S. Kumon and H. Rosovsky, editors, *The Political Economy of Japan.* Vol. 3, 109–142. Stanford, Calif.: Stanford University Press.

Larson, A. 1992. Network dyads in entrepreneurial settings: A study of the governance of exchange relationships. *Administrative Science Quarterly,* 37: 76–104.

Lazerson, M. H. 1988. Organizational growth of small firms: An outcome of markets and hierarchies. *American Sociological Review,* 53: 330–342.

Levinson, H., C. R. Price, K. Munden, H. J. Mandl, and C. M. Solley. 1962. *Men, Management, and Mental Health.* Cambridge, Mass.: Harvard University Press.

Lorenzoni, G., and A. Lipparini. 1995. Relational capability as a source of competitive advantage. *Mimeo.* Bologna, Italy: University of Bologna.

March, J. G., and H. A. Simon. 1958. *Organizations.* New York: Wiley.

Mintzberg, H., and J. A. Waters. 1985. Of strategies, deliberate and emergent. *Strategic Management Journal,* 6: 257–272.

Morgan, G. 1986. *Images of Organization.* Thousand Oaks, Calif.: Sage.

Murakami, Y., and T. P. Rohlen. 1992. Social-exchange aspects of the Japanese political economy: Culture, efficiency, and change. In S. Kumon and H. Rosovsky, editors, *The Political Economy of Japan.* Vol. 3, 63–105. Stanford, Calif.: Stanford University Press.

Nohria, N., and R. Eccles, editors. 1993. *Networks and Organizations.* Boston: Harvard Business School Press.

North, D. 1990. *Institutions, Institutional Change, and Economic Performance.* Cambridge, England: Cambridge University Press.

Ohmae, K. 1985. *Triad Power: The Coming Shape of Global Competition.* New York: Free Press.

Oliver, C. 1990. The determinants of interorganizational relationships: Integration and future directions. *Academy of Management Review,* 16: 241–265.

Osborn, R., J. G. Denekamp, M. F. Zhang, and C. C. Baughn. 1993. Networks of interfirm alliances in the high-tech: Implications of international trade. In M. Ebers and A. Grandori, editors, *Proceedings of the European Science*

Foundation Conference, Forms of Inter-Organizational Networks: Structures and Processes, 153–188. Berlin: European Science Foundation.

Parkhe, A. 1993. "Messy" research, methodological predispositions and theory development in international joint ventures. *Academy of Management Review,* 18: 227–268.

Powell, W. W. 1990. Neither market nor hierarchy: Network forms of organization. In L. L. Cummings and B. M. Staw, editors, *Research in Organizational Behavior,* Vol. 12, 295–336. Greenwich, Conn.: JAI Press.

Ring, P. S. 1990. Strategic alliances: A conceptual framework. Paper presented at the Academy of International Business, Toronto, October 11–14, 1990.

Ring, P. S. 1996a. Processes facilitating reliance on trust in the development of inter-organizational networks. In M. Ebers, editor, *The Formation of Inter-Organisational Networks.* London: Oxford University Press.

Ring, P. S. 1996b. *Networked Organization: A Resource-Based Perspective.* Uppsala: Uppsala University Press.

Ring, P. S., S. Lenway, and M. L. Nichols. 1994. Industry exit via strategic collaboration: The Honeywell approach. In J. Roos, editor, *European Casebook on Cooperative Strategies.* Hemel Hempstead, England: Prentice Hall International.

Ring, P. S., and G. Rands. 1989. Sensemaking, understanding, and committing: Emergent transaction processes in the evolution of 3M's microgravity research program. In A. H. Van de Ven, H. Angle, and M. S. Poole, editors, *Research on the Management of Innovation: The Minnesota Studies,* 337–366. New York: Ballinger.

Ring, P. S., and A. H. Van de Ven. 1989. Formal and informal dimensions of transactions. In A. Van de Ven, H. Angle, and M. S. Poole, editors, *Research on the Management of Innovation: The Minnesota Studies,* 171–192. New York: Ballinger.

Ring, P. S., and A. H. Van de Ven. 1992. Structuring cooperative relationships between organizations. *Strategic Management Journal,* 13: 483–498.

Ring, P. S., and A. H. Van de Ven. 1994. Developmental processes of inter-organizational relationships. *Academy of Management Review,* 19: 90–118.

Symonds, W. C., T. Peterson, J. J. Keller, and M. Frons. 1987. Dealmaker de Benedetti: Olivetti's CEO doubles as an entrepreneur. *Business Week,* August 24, 42–47.

Thompson, J. D. 1967. *Organizations in Action.* New York: McGraw-Hill.

Turner, J. H. 1987. Toward a sociological theory of motivation. *American Sociological Review,* 52: 15–27.

Van de Ven, A. H. 1992. Suggestions for studying strategy process: A research note. *Strategic Management Journal,* 13 (Summer): 169–188.

Weick, K. E. 1995. *Sensemaking in Organizations.* Thousand Oaks, Calif.: Sage.

Williamson, O. E. 1991. Comparative economic organization. *Administrative Science Quarterly,* 36: 269–296.

Yoshino, M., and U. S. Rangan. 1995. *Strategic Alliances: An Entrepreneurial Approach to Globalization.* Boston: Harvard Business School Press.

Zucker, L. G. 1977. The role of institutionalization in cultural persistence. *American Sociological Review,* 42: 726–743.

12

INTERNATIONAL JOINT VENTURE TRUST

An Empirical Examination

Andrew C. Inkpen and Steven C. Currall

ALTHOUGH TRUST HAS BECOME *a central concept in the international joint venture (IJV) literature, little empirical research has been conducted on trust's contribution to the workings of IJV relationships and its impact on IJV performance. In this chapter we examine trust and its role in the process of IJV management. We focus on IJV manager trust, which was operationalized in two ways: trust in a counterpart IJV manager and trust in the IJV partner firm as a whole. The antecedents of IJV manager trust (length of the prior joint venture relationship, joint venture risk, forbearance, and joint venture partner control), as well as the impact of trust on JV performance, were analyzed using a sample of managers from North American–Japanese JVs.*

AS SUGGESTED BY TRANSACTION cost theory, opportunism is a potential risk in any interfirm relationship. To mitigate the dangers of opportunism,

Research assistance from Stephanie Hughes is gratefully acknowledged. An earlier version of this chapter was presented at the 1995 Academy of Management Meeting.

researchers have argued that IJVs (Beamish and Banks 1987; Buckley and Casson 1988; Madhok 1995) and, more generally, interorganizational collaboration (Alter and Hage 1993; Fichman and Levinthal 1991; Granovetter 1992; Jarillo 1988) should be established in a spirit of mutual trust and commitment. It has been posited, for example, that trust is advantageous because it strengthens interorganizational ties (Fichman and Levinthal 1991), speeds contract negotiations (Reve 1990), and reduces transaction costs (Bromiley and Cummings 1993).

Breakdowns in the value creation process in collaborative relationships often stem from problems in managing interdependencies; a lack of trust between partners is one such problem (Borys and Jemison 1989). As Harrigan (1986: 148) asserted, "managers can be as crafty as they please in writing clauses to protect their firm's technology rights, but the JV's success depends on trust." With a foundation of trust, JV partners will be more willing to exercise the tolerance and mutual forbearance that allow the JV to overcome problems that could lead to opportunistic behavior. An atmosphere of trust may contribute to a free exchange of information between committed partners because the decision makers do not feel that they have to protect themselves from the others' opportunistic behavior (Blau 1964; Jarillo 1988). Without trust, information exchanged may be low in accuracy, comprehensiveness, and timeliness (Zand 1972), contributing to breakdowns in the JV value creation process.

Although trust has become a central concept in the IJV literature (Parkhe 1993a), little empirical research has been conducted on trust's contributions to the workings of IJV relationships and its impact on IJV performance. Gulati (1995: 107) pointed out that a "vast gap in understanding the many dimensions of trust and their operation within alliances remains." On the premise that trust is both a critical IJV concept and one that has received limited empirical examination in IJV research, the study discussed in this chapter had two main objectives. The first was to carry out a preliminary empirical examination of trust and its role in the process of IJV management, with an emphasis on both the antecedents of IJV manager trust and the impact of trust on IJV performance. Our findings on the antecedents of trust are of particular importance because of their implications concerning how IJV trust develops and the factors that determine the extent of IJV trust.

The second objective was to go beyond reliance on a single measure of IJV trust, as has been characteristic of previous studies. We used two operational measures of the IJV trust construct. Our decision to use two measures was based on Nunnally and Bernstein's recommendations (1994) concerning the desirability of triangulation and the use of multiple operational measures of a construct to better understand its properties. Both measures assessed trust from the perspective of an IJV manager, yet they differed in their referent object. One measure assessed the extent to which an IJV manager trusts the main counterpart IJV manager. The second measure assessed the extent to which an IJV manager trusts the IJV partner firm as a whole. By using two operational measures, our aim was to ensure that our findings were not a function of a single method of measuring trust.

Conceptual Background and Hypotheses

Trust is a fundamental dimension of interpersonal relations and organizational life (Gibb 1964) and an essential element in the effective functioning of both large and small social systems (Barber 1983). Arrow (1973: 21) linked trust and organizational efficiency by suggesting that "ethical elements enter in some measure into every contract; without them no market could ever function." Williamson (1975) assumed the opportunism of some human agents; accordingly, this assumption contributes to increased monitoring and control costs associated with every transaction. If an individual's trustworthiness could be ascertained beforehand, transaction costs would diminish and the use of the market to facilitate transactions would increase.

Despite the lack of both a unifying definition of trust and a generalized means of operationalization, there are some common themes in the conceptual treatments of trust. For example, trust is often conceptualized as occurring in situations of social exchange where expectations can either be met or violated. This conception of trust is supported by Schelling's characterization of trust in terms of the potential for reciprocity (1960). According to Schelling, trust can be achieved through relationship continuity and the recognition by parties that what might be gained by cheating in the short run is outweighed by the value of the tradition of trust that makes possible a stable long-term relationship.

Interorganizational relationships introduce added complexity to the investigation of trust within an organizational setting. Strategic alliances, as a form of interorganizational relationships, represent a coalition of two or more firms collaborating to achieve strategically significant goals that are mutually beneficial (Parkhe 1993a). Included in this definition are a broad range of organizational forms such as JVs, licensing, contracting, and consortia. The focus of this chapter is on equity IJVs, which are formed when two or more distinct firms (the parents) pool a portion of their resources within a separate jointly owned organization.

Trust in IJVs

Although there is widespread agreement that trust in IJVs is central to their success, there is limited understanding of the nature and mechanisms that firms use to build and maintain a relationship characterized by trust. Since trust evolves over time through repeated interactions between the partner firms (Madhok 1995), the relationships between the managers involved in the collaborative relationship are critical to the establishment of interorganizational trust (Yoshino and Rangan 1995). These managers, termed alliance managers by Yoshino and Rangan, are responsible for the day-to-day operations of the IJV and the relationships between the IJV partners. Alliance managers can foster trust by building one-to-one relationships with partner managers and by developing a familiarity with the partner's strategy, organization, and culture. In larger IJVs, a separate alliance interface office may be established to oversee the IJV operation, provide linkages with the parents, and manage the collaborative relationship. In smaller IJVs of the type studied in this research, the senior IJV managers in the IJV, such as the general manager or president, perform the role of alliance managers.

There is substantial support for the importance of interpersonal trust in the development of interfirm trust. Macaulay described how close personal ties between individuals in firms contracting with each other could "exert pressure for conformity to expectations" (1963: 63). Ring and Van de Ven (1989) suggested that informal connections across organizations play an important role in the governance structure of interfirm transactions. At its core, interfirm trust is based on strong cognitive and emotional bases (Gulati 1995), which can only result through close interpersonal relationships.

In this research, we examined IJV trust from two perspectives. The first was an IJV manager's trust in the counterpart IJV manager. Consistent with Yoshino and Rangan's findings, we view trust in collaborative relationships as largely dependent on the managers who have responsibility for the management of the relationship. Because they provide the linking mechanism across organizational boundaries, IJV managers are "organizational boundary role persons" (BRPs) (Adams 1976). The focus on IJV managers as BRPs is consistent with recent interaction models studying interorganizational collaboration in the context of a specific relationship between BRPs (Heide and Miner 1992; Kumar, Stern, and Anderson 1993; Ring and Van de Ven 1994).

Based upon the idea that BRP behaviors shape and modify the interorganizational relationship (Jarillo 1988; Ring and Van de Ven 1994), of key interest is the BRP's willingness to engage in trusting behavior (for example, entering into an informal agreement) toward a counterpart BRP. Our conceptual definition of trusting behavior is based on two principal concepts: reliance (Giffin 1967; Rotter 1980) and risk (Deutsch 1962; Gambetta 1988; Kee and Knox 1970; Lorenz 1993). Drawing from this research, trust was defined as an individual's behavioral reliance on another person under a condition of risk (Currall and Judge 1995). Risk is defined in terms of magnitude of potential negative outcomes—that is, injury or loss (Isen, Nygren, and Ashby 1988). Empirical evidence has shown that this definition of risk is the one that best describes how individuals in organizations use the concept of risk (March and Shapira 1987). Applying our definition of trust to BRP A and BRP B, the extent of A's risk concerns the magnitude of potential negative outcomes that occur from the untrustworthiness of B. Reliance is volitional behavior by A that allows A's fate to be determined by B (Zand 1972). Thus, under a condition of risk, A's trusting behavior is signified by behavior (that is, reliance) that puts his or her fate in the hands of B.

The second perspective of IJV trust, and the one often adopted in empirical studies involving interorganizational trust (for example, Anderson and Narus 1990; Zaheer and Venkatraman 1995), views trustworthiness as a characteristic of the IJV partner firm. In the strictest sense, firms cannot trust one another. However, firm-level treatments of trust are widely used in the IJV literature when trust is discussed from a conceptual perspective (for example, Buckley and Casson 1988; Madhok 1995). Although expectations of trust reside in individuals, economic transactions between firms are often shaped by trading relationships based on interfirm trust. From this perspective, a firm-level view of trust is a reflection of closely interwoven personal relationships (Zaheer and Venkatraman 1995) that develop incrementally over time (Gulati 1995). For this reason, we define trust in the partner firm in terms of an IJV manager's perception of the perceived trustworthiness of the partner firm. Note that we view trustworthiness as relationship specific. Although Firm A may view Firm B as trustworthy, Firm C may view Firm B as untrustworthy.

The Antecedents of IJV Trust

There are at least four of these.

LENGTH OF PRIOR RELATIONSHIP. Several theories suggest that cooperative behavior between firms increases with the length of the prior relationship. Interaction over time may lead to commitment (Deutsch 1962) and to the development of relationship-specific assets such as a partner's knowledge of the other's procedures and values (Levinthal and Fichman 1988). This suggests that when firms repeat transactions with partners over time, an opportunity is created for the development of interpartner trust. Ring and Van de Ven (1992: 489) argued that reliance on trust by organizations can be expected to emerge between business partners when they have successfully completed transactions in the past and they perceive one another as complying with norms of equity. The authors suggest that this shift in trust between partners leads to a greater reliance on alternative governance structures emphasizing relational contracts over market or hierarchical contracts.

A history of relations between firms can shape the context for new exchange by reducing uncertainty. A social context provides the environment within which economic exchange can be initiated (Larson 1992). If firms have worked together in the past, they will have basic understandings about each other's skills, capabilities (Heide and Miner 1992), and idiosyncrasies (Parkhe 1993c). Building on Zucker's conceptualization of process-based trust (1986), Parkhe (1993b) argued that a partner's cooperative history allows each partner the opportunity to assess the ability and willingness of each to follow through on its promises. The passage of time lays the foundation for future expectations based on shared norms and values, and hence greater trust (Fichman and Levinthal 1991; Granovetter 1992).

As well, a multinational firm's knowledge about its local partner, generated through previous interactions, can play an important role in determining its equity position in the host country (Sohn 1994). This prior interaction at the organization level may lead to IJVs that begin with an existing stock of "relationship assets" (Fichman and Levinthal 1991) and a high degree of interpartner trust (Gulati 1995). Therefore, when IJV partners are familiar with each other through a history of interaction and collaboration, there should be greater trust between the partners.

HYPOTHESIS I: The greater the length of the prior relationship between the partners, the higher the trust.

RISK. A recurring source of risk in all transactions is the need to make decisions in the face of uncertainty in accomplishing tasks that require sustained cooperation with others (Ring and Van de Ven 1989). When the tasks represent difficult or novel ventures, the risk and uncertainty will usually be higher. In high risk ventures, partner firms are in a potential position of vulnerability because of the ambiguity about the venture's future direction. Ring and Van de Ven suggested that when there is high risk in cooperative relationships, high levels of trust can reduce the need for designing complex safeguards. Moorman, Zaltman, and Deshpande (1992) suggested that because trust increases the extent to which partners engage in risky exchanges, trust is expected to increase the likelihood that partners will become committed to the relationships.

Although trust can be an effective substitute for formal safeguards in high-risk cooperative relationships, when the partners are transacting in new international markets and are still learning about each other there may be a reluctance to rely on trust (Ring and Van de Ven 1992). This scenario is applicable to IJVs. As evidenced by failure rates of as high as 50 percent (Kogut 1988), many new IJVs begin (and often continue) under high-risk conditions.[1] In these high-risk conditions, governance and control structures may be employed to lessen the need for reliance on trust. Thus, we expect that in an IJV characterized by high risk, trust will be lower relative to a low-risk relationship because of greater ambiguity and uncertainty about the future outcomes of the relationship. Therefore:

HYPOTHESIS 2: The higher the IJV risk, the lower the trust.

FORBEARANCE. In a truly cooperative IJV, mutual forbearance is an essential feature of the relationship. When parties in a cooperative relationship refrain from acting opportunistically, they are said to forbear. Forbearance, in turn, can generate trust between the partners (Buckley and Casson 1988). If a partner is unwilling to refrain from exploiting another partner, it is unlikely that trust between the partners will develop. Buckley and Casson (1988) also argued that IJVs with a reputation for mutual forbearance enhance their chances of future success. They reasoned that a party with a reputation for forbearance gives partners a greater incentive to forbear themselves, because it increases the likelihood that if they forbear, then the venture as a whole will be a success.

Forbearance, like trust, evolves through interactions between alliance managers. It is the alliance managers that must make the decision, on behalf of the partners, to refrain from acting opportunistically. Alliance managers who have observed in their counterpart managers a willingness to refrain from oportunistic behavior are more likely to engage in trusting behavior. Thus:

HYPOTHESIS 3: The greater the partner forbearance, the greater the trust.

PARTNER CONTROL. Every organization requires a method of monitoring or controlling the processes that lead to task or goal attainment. Organizational control has been defined as any action that aligns the interests of the individual with the interests of the organization (Tannenbaum 1966). In an IJV, control issues are usually an important consideration for the partners (Geringer and Hébert 1989; Killing 1983; Yan and Gray 1994). In comparison with wholly owned subsidiaries, exercising effective control over IJVs is often difficult for the parent firms, especially if they are unable to rely solely on their ownership position (Geringer and Hébert 1989).

When one firm controls an "irreplaceable" IJV resource or input, or has control over an important IJV decision area, a dependency situation is created (Yan and Gray 1994). In a cooperative relationship, dependence can be a source of power for the firm controlling the key resources because, to some degree, each firm can increase or withhold resources that are attractive to its partner (Bacharach and Lawler 1980). For the firm in the dependent position, a lack of bargaining power is potentially a key factor in the determination of IJV trust. If a firm lacks bargaining power over a strategic IJV area, the firm may perceive that it cannot influence the IJV's output and performance. The firm may also perceive that its partner is in a position to act opportunistically. Thus, we expect that as a partner increases its relative control, trust from the other partner's perspective will decrease.

HYPOTHESIS 4: There is a negative relationship between the extent of one partner's IJV control and the other partner's trust.

IJV Performance and Trust

A controversial issue in IJV and strategic alliance research is the relationship between trust and venture performance. In interviews with IJV managers we have often heard opinions such as: "the most important factor in the success of our venture is trust between the partners." The direction of the relationship has generally been argued as trust leading to performance (for example, Harrigan 1986), although Yan and Gray (1994) suggested that performance may also have a feedback effect on trust. Poor performance may cause distrust between the partners, which in turn leads to poor long-term IJV performance (Killing 1983).

The rationale for the trust-to-performance relationship is that trust ensures a sound and cooperative working relationship between the partners. The higher the trust, the more efficient the IJV will be in transforming an input of cooperation into a collaborative output (Buckley and Casson 1988). A foundation of trust, although time-consuming and expensive to create, can contribute to the sustained continuation of cooperative relationships (Madhok 1995). Thus, IJV performance should be viewed as a consequence of IJV trust, with more successful partnerships characterized by higher levels of trust. This relationship was supported by Mohr and Spekman's study (1994) of marketing channel relationships. They found a significant relationship between trust and satisfaction with profit.

HYPOTHESIS 5: The greater the trust, the better the IJV performance.

Methods

North American–Japanese IJVs located in North America provided the empirical base for our study.

Sample

Although there were several Canadian firms in our sample, we will refer to the sample of firms as American rather than North American for brevity. All the IJVs competed in the automotive supply industry. Using a single industry with a homogeneous set of organizations imposes certain constraints. In particular, theory development is restricted to limited domain or middle-range theories (Pinder and Moore 1980), and generalizability is limited to other industries sharing similar structural characteristics. A single industry does, however, provide a greater degree of control over market and environmental peculiarities (Conant, Mokwa, and Varadarajan 1990) and increases the internal validity of the study. This was considered critical given the preliminary nature of the study.

To develop the sample, a Toronto-based organization called Pacific Automotive Cooperation (PAC) was contacted. PAC provided a list of 125 two-partner Japanese–North American IJVs involved in the manufacture of automotive parts (such as brakes, mufflers, seats), and automotive materials (such as glass and paint). Each of these IJVs was contacted to determine the identity of the senior American manager in the venture. A questionnaire was sent to each manager. We used two questionnaire mailings plus a follow-up reminder letter. We received thirty-five usable responses, for a response rate of 28 percent. The mean score for the number of years the managers had been with their IJVs was 4.33 (s.d. = 2.24) and was greater than one for all but three managers (there were no significant relationships between the number of years IJV managers had worked in the IJVs and the trust scores). The mean score for the number of years the managers had worked for the American parent prior to joining the IJV was 10.0 years. The IJVs ranged in age from fifteen years to one year, with twenty-six ventures being five to eight years old.

Trust Measures

The present study used two measures of IJV trust: the level of IJV manager trust in the counterpart IJV manager, and the level of trust in the partner firm as a whole. These measures are discussed below, with greater attention devoted to the measure of trust in the counterpart IJV manager because this measure represents a new approach to operationalizing IJV trust.

TRUST IN THE COUNTERPART IJV MANAGER. Our measure of trust in the counterpart IJV manager adapted a measure of BRP trust previously developed by Currall and Judge (1995). The theoretical basis for their measure was Fishbein-Ajzen's theory of reasoned action (Ajzen and Fishbein 1980). Experimental and field research has supported the theory of reasoned action's underlying causal sequence: from attitudes and social norms come behavioral intentions and from intentions come behaviors. As we argued earlier, BRP behaviors shape and modify the interorganizational relationship (Jarillo 1988; Ring and Van de Ven 1994). Thus, our trust measure focused on the behavioral intention construct in the theory of reasoned action; it tapped a BRP's willingness to engage in trusting behavior toward a counterpart BRP. In this way, our survey instrument measured the most proximal antecedent of trusting behavior. Furthermore, our measure's focus upon willingness to engage in trusting behavior differs from previous trust measures (for example, Cook and Wall 1980; Swan, Trawick, Rink, and Roberts 1988) that assessed the social judgment determinants of trusting behavior (for example, the target person's integrity). Social judgment determinants are more distal (Fishbein 1980) antecedents of BRP trusting behavior compared to our measure of behavioral intentions to trust.

In developing the measure of BRP trust, Currall and Judge (1995) followed the construct validity process (Ghiselli, Campbell, and Zedeck 1981) by first formulating the general conceptual definition of trusting behavior that was presented earlier in this chapter. Psychometric properties of the measure were investigated on the basis of BRPs who operate at critical interorganizational boundaries in public education institutions. To create trusting behavior items, sixty-two interviews were carried out, as was a process analysis of item content validity (Ghiselli, Campbell, and Zedeck 1981: 287). A total of twenty items were developed, five for each of four dimensions (manifestations) of trusting behavior: open and honest communication with the counterpart BRP, entering into an informal agreement with the counterpart BRP, task coordination with the counterpart BRP, and maintaining surveillance over the counterpart BRP (reversed). This focus on four dimensions of trust is consistent with recent literature that has emphasized trust's multidimensionality (for example, McAllister 1995).

Analyses of survey data on a total of 598 BRPs supported the construct validity of the measure. Confirmatory factor analysis results (using LISREL 8) supported the hypothesized four-dimensional model of trust, and further tests showed that, although the trust dimensions were correlated, they were distinguishable. The overall trust scale was formed by summing unit-weighted means of the four trust dimensions. A nomological network of correlates of BRP trust also was developed and tested. Both survey and archival data showed a pattern of results providing support for the hypothesized associations outlined in the network, thereby supporting the measure's construct validity.

We adapted Currall and Judge's measure to create an index of an IJV manager's willingness to engage in trusting behavior toward the counterpart IJV manager. In-depth field interviews with IJV managers (Inkpen 1995) provided the contextual knowledge necessary to adapt the Currall and Judge trust items to the IJV setting. To apply the measure to IJVs, the critical BRPs in IJVs were identified. Again, based upon prior research (Inkpen 1995), we chose senior IJV managers such as managers or JV presidents. These managers operate at the boundary between the IJV partner firms and deal with boundary-spanning issues on a daily basis. As managers of the interface between IJV firms, these individuals are knowledgeable about interpartner relationships and are a reliable source of data (Geringer and Hébert 1991).

Because Currall and Judge's survey items measuring the communication, informal agreement, and surveillance dimensions of trust were common to all BRPs, we applied them to IJV managers. Of these items, however, five were dropped because they were inconsistent with the IJV context. Because the task coordination dimension of trust varies on the basis of organizational context, we developed task coordination items to fit the IJV context. Our final measure of IJV manager trust contained fifteen items and had a coefficient alpha of .80.

TRUST IN THE PARTNER FIRM. We measured trust in the partner firm using a three-item measure. This measure drew on Anderson and Narus's study (1990) of marketing channel partnerships and Beamish's IJV trust measure (1984) and was used to assess an IJV manager's trust in the partner firm as a whole. The coefficient alpha for this scale was .86. As evidence of convergent validity, the correlation between the measure of trust in the partner firm and the measure of trust in the counterpart IJV manager was .57 ($p < .01$). The Appendix contains all survey items.

Other Measures

We used five of these.

PRIOR LENGTH OF RELATIONSHIP. Respondents were asked to indicate the number of years cooperative relationships between the partners had been in existence prior to the formation of the current IJV. We then transformed the results to logarithms for use in the analysis. The transformation to logarithms was done because we assumed the effect of prior relationship is not linear and that duration has diminishing effects on interfirm trust at higher levels (Currall and Judge 1995; Heide and Miner 1992).

RISK. The measure of IJV risk was based on the predictability of IJV operations. Respondents indicated the predictability of IJV operations in five areas: profitability, raw materials costs, sales, labor costs, and market share. A five-item scale was used for each area, ranging from completely unpredictable to completely predictable. The five items were summed to yield a measure of IJV risk. On the basis that a high degree of uncertainty increases the IJV's riskiness, the lower the score, the higher the risk.

FORBEARANCE. To measure forbearance, we adapted the measure of restraint in the use of power developed by Heide and Miner (1992). This is a three-item scale measuring the degree to which the partners refrain from exploiting each other, given the opportunity to do so. We expected forbearance to manifest itself in a partner's willingness to forgo short-term benefits at the expense of the other party (alpha = .68).

JAPANESE PARTNER CONTROL. The extent of partner control was measured by examining decision-making responsibility over twelve IJV decision areas. The decision areas selected were based on research by Beamish (1984) and Killing (1983). Respondents were asked to allocate 100 points between the Japanese partner, the North American partner, and the IJV itself. For example, if both partners and the IJV had equal responsibility for a decision making area, thirty-three points would be allocated to each partner and to the IJV. If the North American partner had complete control over an area, 100 points would be allocated to the North American partner, zero points to the Japanese partner, and zero points to the IJV. Because the decision areas could be more or less important across the IJVs, respondents were asked to indicate the importance of each decision area to the success of the IJV. A five-point scale ranging from "not important" to "very important" was used as the basis for weighting the point allocations. The weighted responses for the Japanese partner were summed to give a measure of Japanese partner control.

PERFORMANCE. IJV performance was measured by asking respondents to evaluate how satisfied the North American partner was relative to initial expectations in ten areas, including return on investment, sales growth, and market share (see the chapter appendix for the complete list). Because some areas may be more important than others in evaluating performance, respondents were also asked how important each of the areas was in the overall evaluation of performance. A five-point scale ranging from "not important" to "very important" was used as the basis for weighting the performance measure.

Results

Table 12.1 shows the means, standard deviations, and correlations between the dependent and independent variables. To test the hypotheses, measures of both trust in the counterpart IJV manager and trust in the partner firm were used.

Table 12.2 summarizes the results of OLS regression analyses of the four independent variables and trust. Both equations were statistically significant at the .05 level, with the adjusted R^2 ranging from .201 to .474. The higher R^2 for the measure of trust in the partner firm (.474) versus the measure of trust in the IJV counterpart manager (.201) was likely attributable to the strong measurement correspondence (Ajzen and Fishbein 1977) between trust in the partner firm as a whole and the measures of the antecedents of trust, which were also assessed as characteristics of the partner firm as a whole.

The negative relationship between risk and trust for both models supports Hypothesis 2. In both equations, forbearance is significant and in the predicted direction, supporting Hypothesis 3. The coefficients for Japanese partner control and length of the prior relationship are not significant. Thus, we found that two of the predicted antecedents are significantly associated with the measures of trust in the counterpart manager and trust in the partner firm. No support was found for Hypotheses 1 and 4.

The results for both models are similar, which provides additional support for the convergent validity of the measure of trust in the counterpart IJV manager that was adapted from Currall and Judge (1995). A primary objective in this study was to empirically test a trust measure that goes beyond a "global" type of firm-level measure. The results of the two models provide evidence that this objective was accomplished.

Conclusion

The primary objective of our study was to address the concerns of Parkhe (1993a), Gulati (1995), and others that insufficient empirical attention has been paid to the core concepts in IJV theory. As an initial empirical

Table 12.1. Descriptive Statistics and Correlations.

Variables	Means	SD	1	2	3	4	5	6
Length of the prior relationship	0.34	0.49						
Risk	2.58	0.52	.015					
Forbearance	4.92	1.41	.007	-.127				
Japanese partner control	7.49	5.14	.052	.324	.177			
Trust in counterpart IJV Manager	4.46	0.82	.073	-.289	.453***	.115		
Trust in partner firms	5.41	1.50	.058	-.336**	.548***	-.130	.487***	
Performance	143.17	65.97	.174	-.231	.579***	-.134	.334	.518***

$**p < .05$ $***p < .01$

Table 12.2. Regression Analysis: Trust as Dependent Variable.

Independent Variables	TRUST IN COUNTERPART IJV MANAGER			TRUST IN PARTNER FIRM		
	b	Std. Error	t	b	Std. Error	t
Length of the prior relationship	-.025	.280	-0.09	.591	.419	1.41*
Risk	-.494	.277	-1.78**	-1.32	.426	-3.10***
Forbearance	.237	.100	2.36**	.572	.154	3.71***
Japanese partner control	.023	.028	0.82	-.025	.043	-.585
R^2	.311			.546		
Adjusted R^2	.201**			.474***		

$*p < .10$ $**p < .05$ $***p < .01$

effort, we triangulated (Nunnally and Bernstein 1994) our measures of trust by using one that focused upon the IJV manager's trust in the counterpart IJV manager and a second measure that focused upon the IJV manager's trust in the partner firm as a whole. Both measures showed parallel results when used in hypothesis tests on the antecedents of trust and in further tests on factors associated with IJV performance. We urge future researchers to triangulate their measures of trust when conducting hypothesis tests concerning trust and IJV relationships.

Hypothesis testing yielded support for three of the five hypotheses. Hypothesis 1, predicting a relationship between trust and the length of the prior relationship between the partner firms, was not supported. The explanation for the lack of support may involve the nature of the American firms' experiences with their IJVs. Prior research has shown that these experiences are often very different than anticipated and, therefore, may have been inadequate in preparing the American partners for their Japanese IJVs (Inkpen and Crossan 1995). Managers in the American partners may have been unprepared to deal with their Japanese partners and particularly unprepared for the rigors of Japanese just-in-time systems and customer demands for flexible production. Shortell and Zajac (1988) found a similar result in their study of internal corporate IJVs. They expected a positive relationship between prior experience in related programs and profitability of IJVs, but instead found a negative relationship. Because the prior experience involved different types of activities than the IJV, the learning that occurred from the prior experiences had little transferability to the new IJV situation. Similarly, although a firm may have worked with its partner for many years, the formation of an IJV creates a new type of relationship between the partners. A prior partner relationship may influence the structure of the relationship (for example, the equity split) and smooth the start-up period. However, because the IJV establishes a new organization, new roles have to be learned by the two partners. These can be sufficiently different from those of prior relationships that the carryover of prior knowledge and its impact on the IJV learning experience is limited. For future research it would be instructive to identify the specific forms of prior relationships and determine if and how trust varied across these forms.

The lack of support for the Japanese partner control hypothesis is more difficult to interpret. We expected that the more control held by the Japanese partner, the lower the interpartner trust. The rationale was based on the premise that control provides an opportunity for a partner to act opportunistically. The nonsignificant findings suggest that IJV partners may not associate control and opportunism. Control, as it was operationalized for this study, was based on control over specific areas and activities. Perhaps a different operationalization of control would yield different results. As well, there may be some interaction between control and IJV performance. When partners with limited control profit financially, these rewards may appease their fear of opportunistic behavior by their counterparts, and as a result trust may be higher. As Yan and Gray (1994) found, the control-performance relationship is very complex, with informal and formal control mechanisms interacting and jointly affecting performance. In contrast to our prediction, Yan and Gray suggest that high levels of trust can offset the potential partner conflict associated with dominant control. The control-trust relationship is most likely a dynamic one. From a temporal perspective, trust may influence the original configuration of IJV control. As the relationship matures and management control shifts with changes in partner bargaining power, the trust between the partners will also shift.

For IJV managers this research has several implications. Drawing on the findings of this and other research in a similar setting (Inkpen 1995), the relationships between IJV managers can be viewed as a strong predictor of interfirm trust. Given the strong relationship between the two trust measures, the research lends support to Yoshino and Rangan's argument (1995) that alliance managers are critical in fostering interorganizational trust and that one-on-one relationships between partner managers can have a direct influence on alliance performance. Although the situation could arise where an IJV manager in Firm A trusts a manager in partner Firm B but not the whole Firm B, we view this scenario as unlikely. Similarly, we view as unlikely the scenario of an IJV manager in Firm A not trusting a senior IJV manager in Firm B but still trusting Firm B. Note that we offer these conclusions with two caveats associated with the research setting. First, they may not apply to large IJVs with a high degree of turnover in the IJV managerial team. Second, all of the IJVs in this study involved Japanese firms, and the importance of personal relationships in Japanese firms is well documented.

Trust, Forbearance, and Performance

Hypothesis 5 predicted a positive relationship between trust and IJV performance. In the models tested in Table 12.3, we used the four trust antecedents and trust itself as predictors of IJV performance. Although both models were significant, the trust measures were not significant. Hypothesis 5 therefore was not supported on the basis of these models. Because forbearance was found to be a significant predictor of IJV performance, we investigated the possibility that trust affects forbearance, which, in turn, affects performance. This amounts to an indirect effect of trust on performance, mediated by forbearance. Following Darlington's discussion (1990) of mediator effects, this indirect effect was tested by conducting two types of regressions: predicting forbearance from trust and predicting IJV performance from both forbearance and trust. If forbearance acts as a mediator, trust will significantly predict forbearance, and only forbearance, not trust, will predict IJV performance. Both types of regressions were tested twice: first using the measure of trust in the counterpart IJV manager, and second using the measure of trust in the partner firm.

Consistent with the idea of forbearance as a mediator, trust in the counterpart IJV manager predicted forbearance ($b = .77$, $t = 2.84$, $p < .01$). In the subsequent test, trust in the partner firm predicted forbearance ($b = .52$, $t = 3.71$, $p < .01$). The second type of regression showed a pattern consistent with forbearance as a mediator as well. That is, forbearance significantly predicted performance ($b = 27.44$, $t = 3.46$, $p < .01$), yet trust in the counterpart IJV manager was nonsignificant ($b = 5.55$, $t = .42$, ns.). Subsequently, forbearance significantly predicted performance ($b = 19.89$, $t = 2.47$, $p < .05$), yet trust in the partner firm was nonsignificant ($b = 12.32$, $t = 1.64$, ns.). Therefore, it appears that trust affects forbearance, which in turn affects performance. These findings, combined with Table 12.2's results showing that forbearance predicts trust, suggest that there is a two-directional relationship between trust and forbearance. Future research should conduct additional tests of this relationship.

In summary, our results found support for the argument that trust has an indirect effect on performance mediated by forbearance. However, the alternative hypothesis of performance leading to trust also has merit. A firm's review of past IJV results in comparison with expectations can lead to a firm's prediction of the extent to which the partner firm will follow through on its current promises. If IJV performance is worse than expected, IJV partners are likely to question the competence and capabilities of their partners. The level of trust in the relationship will suffer accordingly. Thus, when IJV managers say "our relationship is built on trust," they may mean that, because performance outcomes exceed expectations, neither partner has questioned the actions and motives of the other.

Limitations and Avenues for Future Research

In this research, ownership and other structural dimensions were deemphasized because of the focus on IJV manager interactions and because in our view trust is primarily a product of those interactions. Therefore, although this research focused on IJVs as a specific form of collaborative relationship, the basic arguments can be extended to other alliances in which there are

Independent Variables	MODEL 1			MODEL 2		
	b	Std. Error	t	b	Std. Error	t
Length of the prior relationship	30.77	20.67	1.49**	30.96	21.40	1.45**
JV risk	−30.30	22.27	−1.36**	−30.67	24.58	−1.25
Forbearance	28.09	8.52	3.30***	28.26	9.65	2.93***
Japanese partner control	−.024	.022	−1.08	−.024	.022	−1.09
Trust in counterpart IJV manager	−.114	15.05	−.008			
Trust in partner firm				9.84	−.034	−.332
R^2	.468			.468		
Adjusted R^2	.352***			.353***		

Table 12.3 Regression Analysis: Performance as Dependent Variable.

$**p < .10$ $***p < .01$

managers at the interface between the partners. Researchers wishing to use the measure of trust in the counterpart BRP in other alliance settings have two options. One is to use the Informal Agreement, Communication, and Surveillance dimensions only. These items are generic to alliances and can be used to measure trust in a variety of alliances. A second option involves the use of all four dimensions, including Task Coordination. To develop Task Coordination items requires an in-depth understanding of the specific alliance context based on managerial interviews, a procedure that was followed in developing the Task Coordination items for the current research.

One of the limitations of the study is that a key informant approach was used (Kumar, Stern, and Anderson 1993). Ideally, multiple managers from both IJV partner firms would be surveyed and the responses combined to generate a comprehensive trust measure. Although this was not done, the trust measures used in the study should lend themselves to this type of research in the future. Additionally, the size and nature of the sample limit the generalizability of the results. However, this research was intended as a first step toward systematic study of IJV trust. Therefore, given our primary objective of measurement adaptation and development, and given the paucity of empirical research in this area, we hope our research will mark a beginning point for future research.

The present research is an initial attempt to empirically assess trust as one of the core concepts in the IJV process. However, much more research on both the antecedents and the consequences of trust is required. This chapter has taken a first step in testing a new measure of IJV manager trust and applying it to a sample of Japanese-American IJVs. Future research should focus on developing a more fully specified model, extending the trust measure across both IJV partners, and using non-self-reporting data.

Appendix: Measures

Trust in Counterpart IJV Manager

What actions are you willing to take when dealing with the partner manager? The response scale indicated the likelihood of action, ranging from 1, "unlikely," to 7, "likely."

INFORMAL AGREEMENT

1. Enter into an agreement with the partner manager even if his obligations concerning the agreement are not explicitly stated.

2. Enter into an agreement with the partner manager even if it is unclear whether he would suffer any negative consequences for breaking it.

3. Decline an offer by a partner manager to engage in activities that were not dealt with in the JV agreement.

4. Engage in important activities with the partner manager even if the activities are not explicitly documented in the JV agreement.

COMMUNICATION

5. Think carefully before telling the partner manager my opinions (reverse coded).

6. Minimize the information I give to the partner manager (reverse coded).

7. Deliberately withhold some information when communicating with the partner manager (reverse coded).

TASK COORDINATION

8. Feel confident when the partner manager tells me he will do something.

9. Rely on the partner manager to develop human resource policies for the JV.

10. Rely on the partner manager to make managerial hiring decisions for the JV.

11. In a tough spot with the North American parent, rely on the partner manager to help me.

SURVEILLANCE

12. Watch the partner manager attentively in order to make sure he doesn't do something detrimental to the North American parent company (reverse coded).

13. Keep surveillance over the partner manager (that is, "look over his shoulder") after asking him to do something (reverse coded).

14. Check with other people about the activities of the partner manager to make sure he is not trying to "get away" with something (reverse coded).

15. Check records to verify facts stated by the partner manager (reverse coded).

Trust in Partner Firm

On a scale of 1 to 7, 1 = strongly disagree, 7 = strongly agree.

1. The Japanese partner can be trusted to make sensible JV decisions.

2. The Japanese partner would be quite prepared to gain advantage by deceiving the North American partner (reverse coded).

3. The North American partner can rely on the Japanese partner to abide by the JV management agreement.

Length of the Prior Relationship

Indicate how many years the relationship existed prior to the formation of the current JV. The results were transformed to logarithms for use in the models.

Risk

On a scale of 1 to 5, 1 = completely unpredictable, 5 = completely predictable

1. Future profitability
2. Future sales
3. Future market share
4. Future raw materials costs
5. Future labor costs

Forbearance

On a scale of 1 to 7, 1 = strongly disagree, 7 = strongly agree

1. The partners feel it is important not to use any proprietary information to the other partner's disadvantage.
2. Neither partner makes demands that might be damaging to the other partner.
3. The more powerful partner uses its power to get its way (reverse coded).

Japanese Partner Control

Decision areas:

1. JV pricing
2. JV product design
3. JV manufacturing processes
4. JV marketing and distribution

5. JV human resources
6. Hiring of managers in the JV
7. JV production scheduling
8. Quality control in the JV
9. JV accounting
10. JV sales budgeting
11. JV financial management
12. JV capital expenditures

JV Performance

On a scale of 1 to 7, 1 = definitely did not meet expectations, 7 = definitely met initial expectations

1. Return on investment
2. Market share
3. Return on equity
4. Customer satisfaction
5. Sales growth
6. Industry reputation
7. Reduction of operating costs
8. Cost position in the industry
9. Productivity gains
10. Access to Japanese technology

NOTE

1. Note that we do not equate JV longevity with JV success. Many firms view JVs as intentionally temporary and recognize that their ventures will not last indefinitely. If a JV termination is an orderly and mutually planned event, the JV may well be evaluated as extremely successful. In fact, a JV that is prematurely terminated may also be evaluated as successful, depending on the criteria used to evaluate performance.

BIBLIOGRAPHY

Adams, J. S. 1976. The structure and dynamics of behavior in organizational boundary roles. In M. Dunnette, editor, *The Handbook of Industrial and Organizational Psychology*, 1175–1199. Skokie, Ill.: Rand McNally.

Ajzen, I., and M. Fishbein. 1977. Attitude-behavior relations: A theoretical analysis and review of empirical research. *Psychological Bulletin,* 84: 888–918.

Ajzen, I., and M. Fishbein. 1980. *Understanding Attitudes and Predicting Social Behavior.* Englewood Cliffs, N.J.: Prentice Hall.

Alter, C., and J. Hage. 1993. *Organizations Working Together.* Thousand Oaks, Calif.: Sage.

Anderson, J. C., and J. A. Narus. 1990. A model of distributor firm and manufacturer firm working partnerships. *Journal of Marketing,* 54 (January): 42–58.

Arrow, K. 1973. *Information and Economic Behavior.* Stockholm: Federation of Swedish Industries.

Bacharach, S., and E. Lawler. 1980. *Power and Politics in Organizations.* San Francisco: Jossey-Bass.

Barber, B. 1983. *The Logic and Limits of Trust.* New Brunswick, N.J.: Rutgers University Press.

Beamish, P. W. 1984. *Joint Venture Performance in Developing Countries.* Unpublished doctoral dissertation, University of Western Ontario, London.

Beamish, P. W., and J. C. Banks. 1987. Equity joint ventures and the theory of the multinational enterprise. *Journal of International Business Studies,* 18 (Summer): 1–16.

Blau, P. M. 1964. *Exchange and Power in Social Life.* New York: Wiley.

Borys, B., and D. B. Jemison. 1989. Hybrid arrangements as strategic alliances: Theoretical issues in organizational combinations. *Academy of Management Review,* 14: 234–249.

Bromiley, P., and L. L. Cummings. 1993. Organizations with trust: Theory and measurement. Paper presented at the Academy of Management Meeting, Atlanta.

Buckley, P. J., and M. Casson. 1988. A theory of cooperation in international business. In F. Contractor and P. Lorange, editors, *Cooperative Strategies in International Business,* 31–54. San Francisco: New Lexington Press.

Conant, J. S., M. P. Mokwa, and P. R. Varadarajan. 1990. Strategic types, distinctive marketing competencies, and organizational performance: A multiple measures-based study. *Strategic Management Journal,* 11: 365–383.

Cook, J., and T. Wall. 1980. New work attitude measures of trust, organizational commitment, and personal need non-fulfillment. *Journal of Occupational Psychology,* 53: 39–52.

Currall, S. C., and T. A. Judge. 1995. Measuring trust between organizational boundary role persons. *Organizational Behavior and Human Decision Processes,* 64: 151–170.

Darlington, R. B. 1990. *Regression and Linear Models*. New York: McGraw-Hill.

Deutsch, M. 1962. Cooperation and trust: Some theoretical notes. In M. R. Jones, editor, *Nebraska Symposium on Motivation*, 275–320. Lincoln: University of Nebraska Press.

Fichman, M., and D. A. Levinthal. 1991. Honeymoons and the liability of adolescence: A new perspective on duration dependence in social and organizational relationships. *Academy of Management Review*, 16: 442–468.

Fishbein, M. 1980. A theory of reasoned action: Some applications and implications. In H. Howe, editor, *Nebraska Symposium on Motivation*, 65–116. Lincoln: University of Nebraska Press.

Gambetta, D. 1988. Can we trust trust? In D. Gambetta, editor, *Trust: Making and Breaking Cooperative Relations*, 213–237. Oxford: Blackwell.

Geringer, J. M., and L. Hébert. 1989. Control and performance of international joint ventures. *Journal of International Business Studies*, 20: 235–254.

Geringer, J. M., and L. Hébert. 1991. Measuring performance of international joint ventures. *Journal of International Business Studies*, 22: 249–263.

Ghiselli, E. E., J. P. Campbell, and S. Zedeck. 1981. *Measurement Theory for the Behavioral Sciences*. New York: W. H. Freeman.

Gibb, J. 1964. Climate for trust formation. In L. Bradford, J. Gibb, and K. Benne, editors, *T-Group Theory and Laboratory Method*, 279–301. New York: Wiley.

Giffin, K. 1967. The contribution of studies of source credibility to a theory of interpersonal trust in the communication process. *Psychological Bulletin*, 68: 104–120.

Granovetter, M. 1992. Problems of explanation in economic sociology. In N. Nohria and R. Eccles, editors, *Networks and Organizations: Structure, Form, and Action*, 25–56. Boston: Harvard Business School Press.

Gulati, R. 1995. Does familiarity breed trust? The implications of repeated ties for contractual choice in alliances. *Academy of Management Journal*, 38: 85–112.

Harrigan, K. R. 1986. *Managing for Joint Venture Success*. San Francisco: New Lexington Press.

Heide, J. B., and A. S. Miner. 1992. The shadow of the future: Effects of anticipated interaction and frequency of contact on buyer-seller cooperation. *Academy of Management Journal*, 35: 265–291.

Inkpen, A. 1995. *The Management of International Joint Ventures: An Organizational Learning Perspective*. London: Routledge.

Inkpen, A., and M. M. Crossan. 1995. Believing is seeing: Joint ventures and organizational learning. *Journal of Management Studies,* 32: 595–618.

Isen, A., T. Nygren, and G. Ashby. 1988. Influence of positive affect on the subjective utility of gains and losses: It is just not worth the risk. *Journal of Personality and Social Psychology,* 55: 710–717.

Jarillo, J. C. 1988. On strategic networks. *Strategic Management Journal,* 9: 31–41.

Kee, H., and R. Knox. 1970. Conceptual and methodological considerations in the study of trust. *Journal of Conflict Resolution,* 14: 357–366.

Killing, J. P. 1983. *Strategies for Joint Venture Success.* New York: Praeger.

Kogut, B. 1988. Joint ventures: Theoretical and empirical perspectives. *Strategic Management Journal,* 9: 319–322.

Kumar, N., L. W. Stern, and J. C. Anderson. 1993. Conducting interorganizational research using key informants. *Academy of Management Journal,* 36: 1633–1651.

Larson, A. 1992. Network dyads in entrepreneurial settings: A study of governance exchange relationships. *Administrative Science Quarterly,* 37: 76–104.

Levinthal, D. A., and M. Fichman. 1988. Dynamics of interorganizational attachments: Auditor client relationships. *Administrative Science Quarterly,* 33: 345–369.

Lorenz, E. H. 1993. Flexible production systems and the social construction of trust. *Politics and Society,* 21: 307–324.

Macaulay, S. 1963. Non-contractual relations in business: A preliminary study. *American Sociological Review,* 28: 55–67.

Madhok, A. 1995. Revisiting multinational firms' tolerance for joint ventures: A trust-based approach. *Journal of International Business Studies,* 26: 117–138.

March, J. G., and Z. Shapira. 1987. Managerial perspectives on risk and risk taking. *Management Science,* 33: 1404–1418.

McAllister, D. J. 1995. Affect- and cognition-based trust as foundations for interpersonal cooperation in organizations. *Academy of Management Journal,* 38: 24–59.

Mohr, J., and R. Spekman. 1994. Characteristics of partnership success, partnership attributes, communication behavior, and conflict resolution techniques. *Strategic Management Journal,* 15: 135–152.

Moorman, C., G. Zaltman, and R. Deshpande. 1992. Relationships between providers and users of market research: The dynamics of trust within and between organizations. *Journal of Marketing Research,* 29: 314–328.

Nunnally, J. C., and I. H. Bernstein. 1994. *Psychometric Theory,* (3rd ed.). New York: McGraw-Hill.

Parkhe, A. 1993a. "Messy" research, methodological predispositions, and theory development in international joint ventures. *Academy of Management Review,* 18: 227–268.

Parkhe, A. 1993b. Trust in international joint ventures. Paper presented at the Academy of International Business Meeting, Hawaii.

Parkhe, A. 1993c. Strategic alliance structuring: A game theoretic and transaction cost examination of interfirm cooperation. *Academy of Management Journal,* 36: 794–829.

Pinder, C. C., and L. F. Moore. 1980. The inevitability of multiple paradigms and the resultant need for middle-range analysis in organizational theory. In C. Pinder and L. Moore, editors, *Middle Range Theory and the Study of Organizations,* 87–100. Boston: Martinus Nijhof.

Reve, T. 1990. The firm as a nexus of internal and external contracts. In M. Aoki, B. Gustafson, and O. Williamson, editors, *The Firm as a Nexus of Treaties,* 133–161. Thousand Oaks, Calif.: Sage.

Ring, P. S., and A. H. Van de Ven. 1989. Legal and managerial dimensions of transactions. In A. Van de Ven, H. Angle, and M. Poole, editors, *Research on the Management of Innovation: The Minnesota Studies,* 171–192. New York: Ballinger.

Ring, P. S., and A. H. Van de Ven. 1992. Structuring cooperative relationships between organizations. *Strategic Management Journal,* 13: 483–498.

Ring, P. S., and A. H. Van de Ven. 1994. Developmental processes of cooperative interorganizational relationships. *Academy of Management Review,* 19: 90–118.

Rotter, J. 1980. Interpersonal trust, trustworthiness, and gullibility. *American Psychologist,* 35: 1–7.

Schelling, T. C. 1960. *The Strategy of Conflict.* Cambridge, Mass.: Harvard University Press.

Shortell, S. M., and E. J. Zajac. 1988. Internal corporate joint ventures: Development processes and performance outcomes. *Strategic Management Journal,* 9: 527–542.

Sohn, J.H.D. 1994. Social knowledge as a control system: A proposition and evidence from the Japanese FDI behavior. *Journal of International Business Studies,* 25: 295–324.

Swan, J. E., I. F. Trawick, D. R. Rink, and J. J. Roberts. 1988. Measuring dimensions of purchaser trust of industrial salespeople. *Journal of Personal Selling and Sales Management,* 8: 1–9.

Tannenbaum, A. S. 1966. *The Social Psychology of Work Organization.* Pacific Grove, Calif.: Brooks/Cole.

Williamson, O. E. 1975. *Markets and Hierarchies: Analysis and Antitrust Implications*. New York: Free Press.

Yan, A., and B. Gray. 1994. Bargaining power, management control, and performance in United States–Chinese joint ventures: A comparative case study. *Academy of Management Journal*, 37: 1478–1517.

Yoshino, M. Y., and U. S. Rangan. 1995. *Strategic Alliances: An Entrepreneurial Approach to Globalization*. Boston: Harvard Business School Press.

Zaheer, A., and N. Venkatraman. 1995. Relational governance as an interorganizational strategy: An empirical test of the role of trust in economic exchange. *Strategic Management Journal*, 16: 373–392.

Zand, D. 1972. Trust and managerial problem solving. *Administrative Science Quarterly*, 17: 229–239.

Zucker, L. G. 1986. Production of trust: Institutional sources of economic structure, 1840–1920. In B. Staw and L. Cummings, editors, *Research in Organizational Behavior*, Vol. 8, 53–112. Greenwich, Conn.: JAI Press.

PART FOUR

THE ROLE OF INFORMATION AND KNOWLEDGE IN COOPERATIVE ALLIANCES

13

AN EXAMINATION OF KNOWLEDGE MANAGEMENT IN INTERNATIONAL JOINT VENTURES

Andrew C. Inkpen

OVER THE PAST TWO *decades there has been a substantial increase in the formation of international strategic alliances. As an explanatory factor for the increasing number of international alliances, it has been argued that alliances provide a platform for organizational learning. This chapter addresses the process of learning through international alliances. The underlying premise is that alliances can provide firms with access to the embedded knowledge of other organizations. Two primary questions are posed: (1) What is the process used by alliance partners to transfer knowledge from an alliance context to a partner context? and (2) Why are some firms more effective at using alliances to create*

Research support from the Carnegie Bosch Institute for Applied Studies in International Management and Temple University's Center for East Asian Studies is gratefully acknowledged. Earlier versions of this chapter were presented at the Carnegie Bosch Institute's 1994 International Research Conference and the 1995 Academy of Management Meeting, Vancouver. Thanks to John Stopford and other participants in the Carnegie Bosch Institute's International Research Conference. I am also grateful to Stewart Black, Russell Coff, Anoop Madhok, and Kent Neupert for their helpful comments.

organizational knowledge than others? The data, collected from a longitudinal study of North American–based joint ventures between North American and Japanese firms, identified several organizational processes used by firms to access and exploit alliance knowledge. Factors that promote a favorable climate for effective knowledge creation are discussed and a set of propositions on the relationships between these factors and knowledge creation are developed.

OVER THE PAST TWO DECADES there has been a substantial increase in the formation of international strategic alliances. Since 1990, the number of domestic and international alliances has grown by more than 25 percent annually (Bleeke and Ernst 1995). Drucker (1995) has suggested that the greatest change in the way business is being conducted is the accelerating growth of relationships based not on ownership but on partnership. It has been argued that an important explanatory factor for this trend is that alliances provide a platform for organizational learning, giving partner firms access to the knowledge of their partners (Hamel 1991; Inkpen and Beamish 1997; Kogut 1988; Westney 1988).

In the alliance context, the kind of knowledge that is useful to a parent firm can be viewed from three perspectives. First, firms may acquire knowledge useful in the design and management of other alliances (Lyles 1988). This knowledge may be applied to future alliances. Second, firms may seek access to other firms' knowledge and skills but will not necessarily wish to internalize the knowledge in their own operations. As Hamel (1991) pointed out, knowledge that is embodied only in the specific outputs of an alliance has no value to the parents outside the narrow terms of the collaborative agreement. Third, an alliance may generate knowledge that can be used by parent companies to enhance their own strategy and operations. The current research is concerned with this type of knowledge. Knowledge useful to one parent may be knowledge transferred by another alliance partner to the alliance. The knowledge may be created independently by the alliance through its interactions with customers, competitors, and other firms. The alliance may also create a forum for interactions between the parents that is itself a source of new knowledge.

When alliance knowledge is incorporated into parent systems and structures, new organizational knowledge is being created. For example, Sony Corporation, a firm with a culture of independence in product development, has formed various alliances with computer and telecommunications firms in an effort to forge new technology linkages for its consumer electronics products (Hamilton 1995). These alliances provide Sony with access to a wealth of new knowledge, such as how to manage the product development cycles of the computer industry that are much faster than those of consumer electronics. In forming these alliances, various Sony managers will gain access to new knowledge. The challenge for Sony and other firms involved in alliances, and for all firms seeking access to knowledge beyond their boundaries, is to incorporate disparate pieces of individual knowledge into a wider organizational knowledge base.

Although still small, there is a growing body of theoretical research (Inkpen and Beamish 1997; Kogut 1988; Parkhe 1991; Pucik 1991; Westney 1988) and empirical studies (Dodgson 1993; Hamel 1991; Inkpen 1995a; Inkpen and Crossan 1995; Simonin and Helleloid 1993) that addresses the issue of alliances and learning, particularly the important questions associated with how organizations exploit alliance learning opportunities. However, prior alliance research has not addressed in any detail the nature of alliance knowledge nor how knowledge is managed in the alliance context. In organizational studies in general, knowledge management has received limited attention, perhaps because the dominant theoretical paradigms are inadequate to address these issues (Hedlund 1994).

The management of knowledge is emerging as an important role of top management (Prahalad and Hamel 1994; Quinn 1992). Drawing on recent work on knowledge creation (Hedlund 1994; Hedlund and Nonaka 1993; Nonaka 1991, 1994; Von Krogh, Roos, and Slocum 1994), this chapter explores how American firms access and exploit joint venture (JV) knowledge that originated with the Japanese partner. Using data from a longitudinal study of North American–based JVs between North American and Japanese firms, several research questions are addressed: (1) How is alliance-based knowledge transformed to knowledge that is useful to an alliance parent? (2) What is the *process* used by alliance partners to restructure, recontextualize, and amplify alliance-based knowledge? (3) Why is the knowledge creation process more effective in some alliances than in others?

Conceptual Background

The concept of organizational learning refers to the development of skills and knowledge and to associations between past actions, the effectiveness of those actions, and future actions (Fiol and Lyles 1985). The development of a firm's skills through a learning process involves the interpretation of past experiences and strategy choices as a basis for present and future actions (Cohen and Sproull 1991; Porter 1991). The knowledge generated through learning supports a firm's ability to understand the consequences of past actions and respond to environmental stimuli. Thus, effective learning results in an enhancement of an organization's skills and capabilities (Levinthal 1991).

Mintzberg (1990), in arguing that strategy making is a learning process, suggested that strategic initiatives create experiences, actions, and strategic choices that provide the foundation for learning. The focus of this study is on a particular strategic initiative—the formation of an international alliance. The alliance-forming experience can be the action that "triggers" learning because it provides new stimuli that may force changes in the mental maps of the organization (Nonaka and Johansson 1985). An underlying assumption is that managers have some understanding of the causal relationships associated with knowledge creation.

The outcome of the learning process is the capacity for organizational action. When individual knowledge is integrated into a collective knowledge base or organizational memory, the stored information from an organization's history can be retrieved and translated into action (Walsh and Ungson 1991). Action is represented by the incorporation of managerial experiences into the activities of organizations (Daft and Weick 1984; Nelson and Winter 1982). The translation of new knowledge into action is the basis for creating new skills that underpin a firm's competitive advantage. Thus, as an organization learns, it strengthens and possibly renews its core competencies. In turn, core competencies can be seen to represent the collective learning in the organization (Prahalad and Hamel 1990).

Organizational Knowledge Creation

Knowledge is an organized flow of information that is anchored in the commitment and beliefs of its holder (Nonaka 1994).[1] Organizational knowledge is shared among organizational members and is connected to the organization's history and experiences (Von Krogh, Roos, and Slocum 1994). Organizational knowledge is created when personal knowledge is transformed into organizational knowledge (Nonaka and Takeuchi 1995). This occurs in a dynamic process involving various organizational levels and actors. At each level, different learning processes are at work. At the individual level, the critical process is interpreting; at the group level, integrating; and at the organization level, integrating and institutionalizing (Inkpen and Crossan 1995). To capture the dynamic movement of knowledge across the various levels, Nonaka (1994) developed the concept of a spiral of knowledge creation. In the spiral, knowledge moves upward in an organization, starting at the individual level, moving to the group level, and then up to the firm level. As the knowledge spirals upward in the organization, it may be enriched and amplified as individuals interact with each other and with their organizations.

This multilevel perspective suggests that although individuals are integral to the process, organization knowledge creation is different than the sum of individual learning. Nelson and Winter (1982), in their work on organizational evolution, argued that reducing organizational memory to individual memories overlooked or undervalued the linking of those individual memories by shared experiences in the past. Furthermore, organizations represent patterns of interactions among individuals that endure even when individuals leave (Hedberg 1981; Weick 1979).

Although much of the learning literature addresses the product or content of learning, the *process* of learning and knowledge creation is of equal importance. A focus solely on content ignores the complex cognitive and behavioral changes that must occur before a learning "outcome" can be identified. Given that the question of whether or not organizations learn is controversial, studying knowledge creation may provide a more valid foundation for understanding how knowledge travels and changes within organizations (Hedlund and Nonaka 1993). Clearly, organizations are repositories of knowledge. The important question is how individual and group interactions contribute to organizational knowledge creation. Although organizations cannot create knowledge without individuals, unless individual knowledge is shared with other individuals and groups the knowledge will have a limited impact on organizational effectiveness. Thus, organizational knowledge creation should be viewed as a process whereby the knowledge held by individuals is amplified and internalized as part of an organization's knowledge base (Nonaka 1994). As individual knowledge becomes accepted by other organizational members and is utilized in organizational processes, the knowledge creation process is occurring because knowledge is moving beyond one individual's perspective.

Knowledge Creation in Alliances

Knowledge creation through alliances can be viewed as a multistage process, following Nonaka (1994) and analogous to the innovation diffusion process (for example, Tushman and Scanlon 1981). The first stage begins with the formation of the alliance and interactions between individuals from the two (or more) partners. The interactions and the managers' exposure to their partner's knowledge may lead to the recognition of partner skill differences embodied in the alliance operation, which in turn may lead to knowledge creation at the alliance level.

Knowledge acquired from outside the organization can be used strategically only to the extent that it is disseminated and integrated within the organization (Aguilar 1967; Jelinek 1979). Thus, a second stage involves the integration of knowledge acquired by individual managers at the alliance level into the parent's collective knowledge base. Huber (1991) referred to this process as grafting, the process by which organizations increase their store of knowledge by internalizing knowledge not previously available within the organization. For this internalization to occur, the parents must first engage in efforts to transfer their partner's skill-related knowledge from the alliance back to the parent. These efforts create the "connections" for individuals to share their observations and experiences. The intensity of the parent firm's learning efforts reflects the degree to which the parent is actively trying to internalize the skills and capabilities of its partner.

Transferred knowledge will usually involve both explicit codifiable knowledge and tacit and highly context-dependent knowledge. For example, the skills associated with how to manufacture high-precision products consist of a combination of both tacit and explicit knowledge. Because tacit and explicit knowledge are mutually complementary (Nonaka and Takeuchi 1995), there will be a strong tacit dimension associated with how to use and implement the explicit knowledge. This tacit, difficult-to-transfer dimension is the "glue" that holds together the organizational routines associated with other partners' skills.

Although the transfer of alliance knowledge is a necessary condition for knowledge creation, the parent must also ensure that the transferred knowledge is moved and shared within the parent organization. The risk, particularly with tacit knowledge, is that knowledge transferred from an alliance to a parent will dissipate as it spirals its way to the organization level. The rate of dissipation will be influenced by a variety of factors. For example, when confronted with learning opportunities, successful firms may see little need to change behavior and thus become trapped by their distinctive competence (Levinthal and March 1993). The strength of a firm's learning intent will help determine the organizational resources committed to learning (Hamel 1991). The type of knowledge creation mechanisms plays a key role in how new knowledge is "managed" by JV parent firms (Hedlund and Nonaka 1993). Finally, the nature of managerial belief systems permeates all levels of knowledge creation and correspondingly contributes to knowledge dissipation (Inkpen and Crossan 1995).

In summary, this study focuses on the learning efforts and processes used by firms to transfer and gain access to alliance-based knowledge. An important assumption is that alliance partners have knowledge that, at least in part, should be considered valuable by the other partner(s). Thus, the processes used to gain access to partner knowledge and the role played by the collaborative process between alliance partners are fundamental elements in alliance-based knowledge creation.

Methods

This study used a two-stage research design. The first stage established the industry context and basis for the selection of cases for longitudinal study. The second stage used an open-ended approach of grounded theory building (Glaser and Strauss 1967) to examine the process of alliance knowledge management. This chapter is based primarily on the second stage, although the industry, alliance, and partner contextual data from stage one were critical in interpreting the case study data.

Because research in the area of knowledge management was at an early stage of development, an inductive process was used. The study was exploratory in that key constructs were tentatively identified *a priori,* but the specific relationships among the constructs and the dimensions of the constructs were not known. For example, technology sharing as a knowledge creation process was identified in the first research stage, but the components and specific types of technology sharing processes were unknown before the study. Also, a preliminary identification of the organizational conditions supporting knowledge creation was possible prior to data collection, but the important linkages with the learning processes emerged from the case studies in stage two.

Stage One: Context Definition

The initial research stage, reported in detail in Inkpen (1995b), was designed to provide contextual understanding of the alliance learning issues and to gain a cross-sectional perspective on the basic dimensions of alliance learning. Two research questions were explored: (1) Do alliance parents recognize and seek to exploit alliance learning opportunities? and (2) What organizational and strategic factors play a role in the learning process?

A sample of North American–Japanese JVs located in North America provided the empirical base. (Although there were two Canadian firms in the sample, for brevity, future references to the sample of firms will use American rather than North American.) The primary data collection method for stage one was field interviews with fifty-eight managers associated with forty two-partner JVs. The majority of managers held positions such as JV president or JV general manager and were either employed by the

American partners or appointed by the American partners to senior management positions in the JVs. Geringer and Hébert (1991) found that these managers were a valid source of JV data. As the managers at the boundary between the JV and parent firms, these managers were expected to have an important influence on parent access to and management of alliance knowledge.

All JVs were suppliers to the automotive industry and only one had less than 50 percent of its sales to automotive customers. The motive for JV formation by the majority of the American partners was to gain access to the Japanese transplant market in the United States. Most of the JVs were direct suppliers to the automotive assemblers (that is, tier-one suppliers). With two exceptions, all JVs were start-up or greenfield organizations. In terms of ownership, seventeen ventures were fifty-fifty, in fifteen ventures the Japanese partners had majority equity, and in eight ventures the American partners had majority equity.

Stage Two: Longitudinal Case Study

Stage one of the research found evidence that the JVs created important learning opportunities for the American JV parents. The American firms were provided with an excellent "window" into their Japanese partners' capabilities. The window had two main sources of potential value. First, all but five JVs were transplant suppliers, generally making products similar to those manufactured by the Japanese partners in Japan. The JVs provided the American partners with access to skills created by the Japanese partner for the Japanese market and also access to how those skills could be adapted to North American work style and infrastructure. Second, the JVs were often the American partners' initial experience in supplying Japanese automakers. Because in most cases the Japanese partners had established relationships with Japanese automakers, the JVs provided the American partners with an opportunity to learn how to manage a long-term Japanese customer relationship, albeit adapted to the North American context.

Stage one also provided the foundation for an emerging understanding of alliance knowledge creation. The second research stage explored the knowledge management process in detail. An emphasis on process suggested the need for a longitudinal approach that provided deeper and more extensive access to the individuals involved in collaborative exchange.

A multiple case study design was used, based on theoretic replication (Yin 1989) because the choice of cases was directed by the emerging theory developed from stage one. To gain efficiencies in data collection and to capitalize on established industry contacts, the five cases selected were a subset of those from stage one. Several criteria were used to select the cases, with the objective of finding variance across several dimensions. Of particular interest was the learning potential created by the JVs. This factor, based on differences in partner skills, was important because it influenced the knowledge management processes initiated by the JV parents and the motivation of the American parents to exploit the learning potential. Because it is better to initiate historical study before the outcomes of strategic change processes become known (Van de Ven 1992), the JVs selected were all still in existence.

Table 13.1 shows the case selection criteria plus other characteristics of the five JVs studied in stage two. To evaluate JV skill differences, JV manufacturing performance relative to the American parent was considered. In each of the cases, the JV product line was functionally similar to the American parent product line. In the absence of product similarity, evaluating skill differences would have been more difficult. I looked for qualitative evidence that the JV was exceeding the parent's quality efforts because this was an indication of partner skill differences at the manufacturing process level.[2] JV performance was evaluated from the perspective of the American parent and was based on the American parent's overall satisfaction with performance. Partner history reflects the extent of previous collaborative relationships between the partners. Knowledge management processes initiated was a first-cut identification of several processes, including the rotation of personnel, regular visits and tours by parent company executives, information sharing between the JV and the American parent, and senior American parent management involvement in JV activities.

Building on the data collected in the first stage, second-stage site visits and interviews began in May 1993 and continued to September 1994. The interviews in this stage were usually one and a half to two hours in length, although a few were a half day or more. For the cases studied in stage two, a total of twenty interviews were conducted with senior American managers in the JVs and parent organizations. Including the first-stage interviews, observations were collected over three and a half years.

Data Analysis

INTERVIEW WRITE-UPS. For all interview data, data reduction began immediately following the interview and helped bring the raw data into a manageable form. Within twenty-four hours, the detailed interview write-ups were completed. The write-ups summarized the interviews in a consistent and logical manner, their objective being a "product intelligible to

	Alpha	Beta	Gamma	Kappa	Sigma
JV skill differences	High	Medium	Medium	High	Low
JV performance	Low	Medium	High	Medium	High
Partner history	None	Limited	Limited	Extensive	None
Knowledge management processes initiated	Limited	Moderate	Extensive	Extensive	Moderate
Senior JV management	President from outside, Japanese VP	Japanese president, American COO and plant managers	American general manager and plant manager, Japanese sales managers	American president or general manager, Japanese VP	American president and plant managers, Japanese sales managers
Ownership	50–50	65 percent Japanese, 35 percent American	50–50	50–50	50–50

Table 13.1. Characteristics of the Five JVs Studied.

anyone, not just the fieldworker" (Miles and Huberman 1984: 50). All write-ups were reviewed for omissions and clarity problems, and follow-up data was collected if necessary.

The write-ups were based on a classification scheme approximating the main analytic concepts, such as parent experience, JV performance, and partner interactions. The write-ups also incorporated information on company history, background of the informant, and data from several other sources such as company documents (for example, organization charts and promotional literature), business press articles, and annual reports. As the classification scheme evolved, revisions were made to earlier interview write-ups. By the end of the fieldwork, the interviews were written up using a similar format. This consistency in format greatly simplified the cross-site analysis.

MEMOING. An analysis activity that occurred throughout the research project was the development of analytic memoranda. This process, called "memoing" by Glaser (1978), involved the recording of conceptual and analytic impressions as they occurred. The impressions reflected several different themes including the preliminary identification of patterns, summaries of unique or surprising site attributes, and ideas on data analysis. As the research progressed, the categorized data, write-ups, and memos were examined for emerging patterns, themes, and processes that might account for the frequency and absence or presence of data categories. An objective of exploratory research is the discovery of new categories of data that emerge out of the data, rather than having been decided prior to data collection and analysis (Patton 1987). For example, a pattern that emerged early in the study was a relationship between JV performance and knowledge creation.

KNOWLEDGE MANAGEMENT PROCESSES. As indicated earlier, the first stage resulted in the identification of several processes considered fundamental to knowledge creation and management. These processes provided an important input to the second-stage case studies. As the research progressed, the classification of these processes evolved into the categories discussed in the results section.

ASSESSING RELATIONSHIPS. The analysis yielded data on variables such as performance, prior partner history, and top management involvement in JV management. Over the several years of data collection for both stages of the research, relationships emerged between knowledge management processes and organizational conditions that either supported or created barriers to knowledge creation. Propositions based on these relationships are introduced later.

Results

A primary objective in this research was to develop further understanding of how American firms access and exploit JV knowledge that originated with the Japanese partner. Several collaborative activities emerged as the basis for accessing and exploiting alliance knowledge. For example, here is a summary of knowledge management activities in the Kappa JV.

- The American parent (AP) has studied various aspects of the JV's operation, including its use of employee involvement programs, *kaizen* teams, and its scheduling system. The AP has also studied some of the JV's process innovations, one of which the JV considers proprietary.

- Several JV managers were promoted to positions within the AP. One manager was promoted into a staff training position at AP headquarters. Several engineers have also been promoted.

- AP senior management are committed to the JV and to an Asian connection. The JV is the strongest Asian connection. The president of the AP has a very close relationship with the former Japanese parent chairman.

- The AP has formed teams to share information on forming and fabrication. The idea is that representatives from the various AP plants (the JV included) will get together regularly and share information.

- The AP has set up what it calls "gatekeepers," units of the company responsible for certain aspects of manufacturing. A gatekeeper is expected to be available to all units of the company on the specific process or technology. The JV was asked to be the gatekeeper for just-in-time (JIT) scheduling expertise.

- The AP has several engineers temporarily working in Japan in the Japanese parent organization.

- The AP and the Japanese parent have initiated a joint engineering project. A piece of manufacturing equipment will be made by the Japanese partner in Japan, with an American engineer visiting Japan during the project period. The equipment will be installed in an AP plant and the AP will pay the Japanese parent for the developmental work.

- More than fifteen employees in the JV have visited Japan.

Similar data were collected for each of the cases. From this data, four critical processes were identified: technology sharing, JV-parent interaction, personnel movement, and strategic integration.[3] The four processes share a conceptual underpinning in that each represents what Von Krogh, Roos, and Slocum (1994) referred to as a "knowledge connection." Knowledge connections create the potential for individuals to share their observations and experiences. An organization's set of internal relationships facilitates the sharing and communicating of new knowledge. Each of the four processes identified, described in detail below, creates a connection for individual managers to communicate their JV experiences to others. Table 13.2 classifies the cases on the strength of each process.

The four knowledge management processes are not complex or difficult to understand. However, the lack of complexity should not be associated with a lack of effectiveness. The creation of organizational knowledge re-

	Alpha	Beta	Gamma	Kappa	Sigma
Technology sharing	Low	Low	High	High	Medium
Interorganizational interaction	Medium	Medium	High	High	High
Personnel movement	Low	Medium	Medium	High	Medium
Strategic integration	Low	Low	High	High	Medium

Table 13.2. Knowledge Management in the Five Cases.

quires the sharing and dissemination of individual experiences. This research suggests that each process provides an avenue for JV parent managers to gain exposure to knowledge and ideas outside their traditional organizational boundaries.

Technology Sharing

In the cases studied, the JVs were manufacturing products functionally similar to those of the American parent. In four cases, the Japanese partners were responsible for implementing the manufacturing process, installing the equipment, and supplying the product technology. Consequently, those four JVs provided the American partners with a unique opportunity to study a new, state-of-the art manufacturing organization that would not have been possible without a collaborative relationship. In the fifth case (Sigma), the American partner had responsibility for the manufacturing process.

Parent firms instituted various processes to gain access to JV manufacturing process and product technology. The most evident approach was through meetings between JV and parent managers. Gamma had monthly meetings, with the location alternating between the JV and one of the American parent plants. In attendance were plant managers, heads of quality control, R&D managers, the vice president of manufacturing at the American parent head office, and several senior JV managers. In addition, the JV and American parent had quarterly R&D meetings.

The manufacturing vice president of one of the American parents said that although he hated to admit it, the quality of the JV product was superior to that in the parent. As a result, he initiated a program with his plant managers to improve quality and customer service.

Access to partner technology skills also occurred through direct linkages between Japanese and American partners. In both Kappa and Sigma, there were regular visits by American parent personnel to Japanese parent facilities. Consistent with the argument that Western firms find it difficult to undertake activities not fitting prevailing notions of what the company is about (Hedlund and Nonaka 1993), the president of Kappa's American parent expressed frustration at the lack of tangible output from these visits and the unwillingness of the engineers to give up their existing methods. "Our engineers go to Japan and come back with some good ideas but nothing ever happens. They [the American engineers] are too protective of their technology and way of doing things."

To capitalize on the Japanese partner's fabrication knowledge and ability to operate with fewer equipment operators, several Japanese engineers were invited to the United States to train parent engineers. The Japanese engineers brought very detailed equipment designs that would allow the American firm to replicate the Japanese manufacturing process. When no visible progress was made on designing new equipment, the American president decided to contract the design and manufacturing of the equipment to the Japanese partner. An American engineer would be sent to Japan to learn about the equipment so it could be installed in the United States.

In another case, the partners signed a very broad global technology agreement. Both partners agreed to be completely open in sharing both product and manufacturing technology. For product technology, explicit terms on licensing and royalties were established. For manufacturing technology there were no terms. For example, the American parent may ask to borrow an engineer from the Japanese partner for a few weeks. When this had happened in the past there were no financial considerations involved because "it all comes out in the wash." The American partner recognized the need for reciprocal commitment (Gulati, Khanna, and Nohria 1994) and tried to make the technology sharing a two-way relationship.

Not all the American parents were interested in access to Japanese partner technology. Worried about inroads its Japanese competitor was making with the U.S. domestic automakers, Alpha's Japanese parent offered to share its proprietary manufacturing technology with its American partner at no cost. The technology was used in the JV. The offer was communicated in a written memo from a JV manager to the American partner president. The American firm never followed up on the offer. One JV manager's opinion was that "the people from the American parent do not want to learn because they see the JV as an upstart."

JV-Parent Interactions

JV-parent interactions beyond those discussed under technology sharing play a key role in knowledge management. Individual knowledge and perspectives remain personal unless they are amplified and articulated through social interaction (Nonaka 1994). Interactions between parent and JV managers can create the social context necessary to bring JV knowledge into a wider arena. In effect, these interactions provide the foundation for evolving communities of practice (Brown and Duguid 1991). Community members share knowledge and may be willing to challenge the organization's conventional wisdom. Communities emerge not when the learners absorb abstract knowledge but when the learners become insiders and acquire the particular community's subjective viewpoint and learn to speak its language. In several interviews, JV managers referred to parent managers as "transformed" because the parent and JV managers both saw the learning potential in the JVs. From Brown and Duguid's perspective, a community of practice had emerged. A JV manager explained that in another case a community began emerging because "over time the JV has become grudgingly accepted as more people have been exposed to the JV. Now, there is high regard for what is going on." As a result, the JV was incorporated into the parent's strategic planning processes and was expected to contribute new ideas and provide leadership in a particular technology area.

Visits and tours of JV facilities provide an effective and simple interactive means for parent managers to learn about their JVs. The JV managers were generally convinced that the differences embodied in the JV were visible and parent managers would appreciate the differences if they spent more time in the JV. However, visits were not always perceived as effectively utilized, as a Beta manager explained: "Plant managers have been invited and some have visited. However, the American parent organization is so lean that these people have little time to invest in learning. . . . A group of first-line supervisors spent two weeks in the JV. They spent time learning about the JV systems and took videos, notes, etcetera, back to the parent. They went back to the parent plants and nothing happened."

The previous quote suggests that the absence of highly visible changes to systems and processes was equated with low knowledge transference. This supports the view that Western organizations try to learn in large, discrete steps (Hedlund and Nonaka 1993) and often fail to recognize the value of incremental learning.[4] This research suggests that the differences in partner skills and capabilities arose from a multitude of factors, many of which were not only difficult to see but difficult to replicate. In contrast, the Japanese partners were often seen as much more proactive at learning, as the following quote from a manager suggests: "The Japanese partner, on the other hand, sends many people to the JV with a learning objective. They are not afraid to ask questions and spend a lot of time in the JV doing that. There are always Japanese people visiting, both from Japanese parent divisions and from Japanese parent world headquarters. It is not always clear what they are here for. Sometimes they just observe; other times they ask a lot of questions."

One JV visit that produced an observable change occurred when an American parent sent several managers to visit its JV to study the JV's human resource management systems. In contrast to most of the American parent plants, the JV was a nonunion operation with hybrid Japanese and American human resource practices. The American parent was establishing a new nonunion operation and decided to use the JV as a model. With the JV managers' support, the visiting managers spent several days studying the JV and then incorporated much of their knowledge in the new nonunion plant. One explanation for the success of the knowledge transfer is that the learning focus was on a discrete system that could easily be replicated.

Customer-supplier relationships between the JV and the American parent also created a basis for extensive, although not always amicable, interaction. In the Alpha case, the JV acted as both supplier and customer for the American parent. Neither relationship was considered satisfactory, although it was a rich source of knowledge for the American parent. As a customer, Alpha had so many quality problems with the American parent's products that most of the business was shifted to an outside firm. As a supplier, there were also problems. For example, the parent asked Alpha to carry out a special order because the parent was behind in its deliveries. When Alpha management refused the business because of concerns about the product quality, the reaction from the American parent was "those [JV] people are too inflexible and going too far with the quality issue." In another example, the American parent substantially increased its quality because of pressure from the JV as a customer, which in turn was under pressure from its Japanese transplant supplier. Until the JV was formed, the American parent had not had any extensive interactions with Japanese customers. In supplying the JV, and indirectly becoming a transplant supplier, the American parent was forced to evaluate some of its manufacturing operations.

Meetings, such as monthly sales meetings between parent divisions and the JV, were also a means of interacting and exchanging information. Finally, in several cases the JV relied extensively on the American parent for various services, such as purchasing, accounting, human resource management, and in one case laboratory facilities. When this occurred, American parent managers had no choice but to be involved with the JV.

Personnel Movement

Personnel rotation can be considered a process of organizational reflection (Hedlund and Nonaka 1993) and a means of mobilizing personal knowledge. Rotation helps members of an organization understand the business from a multiplicity of perspectives, which in turn makes knowledge more fluid and easier to put into practice (Nonaka 1994: 29). The rotation of managers through JV positions and back to the parent may encourage the "bleedthrough" of ideas from the venture to the parent (Harrigan 1985).

Interestingly, none of the cases studied had an explicit process of rotation between the JV and the parent. However, with Kappa (Table 13.2) there was an extensive informal system of personnel movement between the organizations. For example, the American parent promoted a Kappa manager to a staff training position at the parent headquarters. Several engineers also were promoted. In four of the cases, senior managers in the JV were transferred to the JV when the JV was formed. The careers of these managers were closely linked to the American parent, not just to the JV. In Gamma, the chief operating officer of the JV came from the American parent to act as mentor for the younger JV management. This manager will eventually return to the American parent. In Beta, two plant managers spent time in the JV and then returned to plant management positions in American parent plants.

Although I found no evidence that the Japanese partners saw knowledge transfer as a threat, the Japanese parent sometimes constrained rotation. In one case, the Japanese parent preferred that JV personnel not move to the American parent. The Japanese parent saw the JV as distinct and separate from the American parent and preferred that both organizations operate at arm's length. Despite this concern, the American parent has moved personnel from the JV to the parent. In another case, personnel were willing to move from the parent to the JV but less willing to return to the American parent because of the perception that career opportunities within the JV were better than in the parent firm. This prompted the American parent to ask its JV not to "poach" any more personnel from the parent.

Strategic Integration

Strategic integration is the linking of an alliance strategy with the strategy of the parent organization (Harrigan and Newman 1990). Cohen and Levinthal (1990) suggested that effective integration at the learning interface will augment an organization's learning capacity. Thus, a JV perceived as peripheral to the parent organization's strategy will likely yield few opportunities for the transfer of alliance knowledge to the parent. A JV considered closely related to the parent's strategy may receive more attention from the parent organization, leading to substantial parent-JV interaction and a greater commitment of resources to the management of the collaboration. This supports Hamel's argument (1991) that receptivity to learning is enhanced if the parent and its alliance are closely related.

Through strategic linkages between the JV and the parent, the partners can gain important insights into each other's businesses. For example, one of the American parents won a contract to supply a part but was unable to meet the target cost. The parent decided to use its JV to produce the parts because of the JV's superior process technology. This type of linkage indicates that the American parent had internalized the knowledge associated with differences between the parent and JV. The linkage also opened the door for more knowledge sharing and cooperation in the future.

To maximize exposure to partner knowledge, alliance partners must go beyond the narrow confines of the JV agreement. In Gamma and Kappa, the JV functioned like a related division of the American parent, with the parent focused on managing the partner relationship, not just the JV itself. According to the president of Kappa's American parent: "The JV is treated exactly the same as our other divisions. The JV participates in all our meetings and all of the JV's salaried employees have the same benefits as their counterparts at other divisions. This makes it easier to move people back and forth between the JV and parent."

In this case, the relationship between the partners was getting much tighter. The JV started off strictly as a transplant supplier relatively independent of its American parent, relying extensively on the Japanese partner for product technology and marketing support. Over the years, Kappa became less independent as ties between the two partners increased. A similar situation existed in Gamma. When the JV was formed it was initially presented as a Japanese company to the transplant customers. The JV evolved into a much less "Japanese" firm and through its American parent's contacts developed a substantial amount of business with domestic customers. The objective, remarked a Gamma manager, was for the benefit of both the JV and the parents.

Suggesting that strategic linkages are important to knowledge creation assumes that the linkages are consistent with the strategic goals of the parents and JVs. If a JV is in a business unrelated to that of the parent, linkages may not be possible or useful. For that reason, a lack of strategic linkages should not be equated with the success of the international joint venture (IJV) or its importance. If the IJV is involved in an unrelated business, it is unlikely that the primary rationale for collaboration will be knowledge creation.

Managing the Knowledge Creation Process

A firm involved in an alliance has a choice as to the resources and effort to devote to alliance-based knowledge creation. The previous section considered the question of *how* firms accessed JV knowledge. This section considers two further questions: (1) Why are some firms more willing to initiate knowledge creation efforts than others? (2) Why is the alliance knowledge creation process more effective in some cases than others? To address these questions, organizational enabling conditions that promote a favorable climate for effective knowledge creation (Nonaka 1994: 27) are introduced.[5] The absence of these conditions creates obstacles to knowledge creation. Four conditions are examined: partner intent, managerial commitment, redundancy, and trust. In addition, performance myopia is discussed as a barrier to knowledge creation.

This discussion provides the rationale for a set of testable propositions. Note that the relationships are identified as propositions, rather than hypotheses, because they deal with approximated constructs that cannot be observed directly (Bacharach 1989). Although the propositions are based on observed data, the development of concrete and parsimonious operationalizations of the constructs was not an objective of this research.

Flexible Partner Intent

The collaborative objectives of the JV partners have been identified as a key element in alliance learning. As Hamel, Doz, and Prahalad (1989: 138) asserted, "It is self-evident: to learn, one must want to learn. . . . Western companies must become more receptive [to the benefits of alliance learning]." Hamel (1991), in his inductive model of alliance learning, argued that learning intent was one of the critical learning determinants. When a firm seeks to internalize knowledge from its JV, it can be said to have a learning intent. Hamel (1991: 89–90) defined an alliance learning intent as "a firm's initial propensity to view collaboration as an opportunity to learn."

The findings in this study suggest that the relationship between initial learning intent and knowledge creation is more complex than Hamel described. If a learning intent is associated with the formation of a JV, a parent firm may enter more actively into the search for knowledge. However, if the initial learning objective is not correctly focused and management is unwilling or unable to adjust the objective, knowledge management efforts may be ineffective. For example, in the Alpha case, the American parent had a very explicit technology learning objective. However, this firm's knowledge management efforts were weak and inconsistent because the firm did not have a clear understanding of its partner's skills, probably because of causal ambiguity (Reed and DeFillippi 1990) about the source of their Japanese partner's competitive advantage. Although the Japanese firm was highly skilled in specific manufacturing technology areas, its success was also the result of skills in other areas such as customer management and scheduling. The American partner showed an unwillingness to adjust its original, narrow technology learning objective.

With Sigma, the situation was almost the reverse. The American parent was interested in forming a JV primarily to gain access to the Japanese transplant market. When negotiations to form the JV were started, American parent management made it clear that they were only willing to be involved if they managed the JV. According to Sigma's president, "We have a quality reputation which we should be able to carry over to the JV." But, after working together for several years, American parent management realized that alliance knowledge could be important to their firm and made greater effort to gain access to Sigma operations and to the Japanese parent's store of knowledge. The American parent formed its JV with a weak learning objective that grew stronger with exposure to the JV and to the partner.

In several cases in the stage one study, the American firm did not have an initial learning objective until skill discrepancies became obvious and unavoidable. For example, an American firm that had prided itself on its high-quality product status found its quality lacking when it attempted to supply a Japanese transplant automaker.

As the basis for the initiation of effective knowledge creation, a firm must have a learning intent. However, the intent can rise at any time, not just at the time of IJV initiation. Also, if the initial learning intent is based on an incorrect assessment of partner competencies, learning and knowledge creation efforts may be ineffective. As a firm builds a relationship with its partner, the learning intent should become more focused as ambiguity about the partner disappears. As a result, the learning intent and the efforts devoted to knowledge creation should evolve together. Thus the first proposition:

PROPOSITION 1: The parent firm's learning intent at the time of JV formation will be positively related to the initiation of knowledge creation efforts in the JV's initial years of existence, but over time the relationship between initial intent and knowledge creation efforts will weaken as a new learning intent takes shape.

Managerial Commitment

In a receptive learning environment, top management of the parent firms are enthusiastic about learning and are willing to be "taught" by their partners (Hamel 1991). Similarly, Hedlund (1994) saw top management's roles in managing knowledge as those of catalyst and architect. Commitment from top managers to the JV and their involvement in JV management is a critical element in exploiting alliance-based knowledge and is especially important in facilitating the strategic integration discussed earlier. When parent management adopts a passive approach, it may not be in a position to adapt to changes in collaborative roles and circumstances (Gulati, Khanna, and Nohria 1994).

Top management creates the "organizational intentions" by asking questions on behalf of the entire organization and creating the challenges for intellectual growth (Nonaka 1994). Thus the second proposition:

PROPOSITION 2: The commitment of top management to the strategic value of the jv will have a positive impact on the degree to which the parent perceives knowledge creation to be a valuable collaborative activity.

The next example from the Alpha case illustrates the consequences of weakening leadership commitment. The CEO of the American parent joined the parent shortly after Alpha was formed. In the JV's initial years, there was a moderate amount of ideas shared between the two firms, primarily because the JV was formed as an offshoot of a licensing agreement between the Japanese and American partners. After joining the American parent, the CEO found that the relationship between Alpha and the American parent was deteriorating. To improve communication, regular "differences meetings" between the two sides were organized. For example, an issue raised at one meeting was the American parent's role in performing some intermediate manufacturing for Alpha. Alpha management accused the American parent of making poor-quality products and charging high prices. After a few meetings, the parent CEO stopped attending and no more meetings were held. According to the CEO: "The two sides are too different. They are like oil and water. Alpha is in a different business. They do not have traditional customer relationships and they make a handful of parts compared to us. Everything takes so long to get done there. They are experts at nitpicking."

From the perspective of Alpha's president, the American parent was aware that there were technology differences between the two firms because in his view, the differences were highly visible. In interviewing the parent CEO and manufacturing vice president, it was clear that although they questioned the usefulness of these differences, there was a shared understanding of their existence. In that sense, knowledge was being created in the parent, although not in the manner anticipated when the JV was formed. Thus, despite the poor communication between the JV and its American parent, the partners were learning about each other. Board meetings were reasonably amicable and neither partner was actively seeking to end the relationship. As Fichman and Levinthal (1991) argued, the persistence of interfirm relationships can be viewed as the result of a sorting process in which firms are learning about each other.

Redundancy

Redundancy, in the sense of superfluity, means that there is information that goes beyond what organizational members require for immediate operational requirements. In an organization, redundancy refers to a conscious overlapping of company information, activities, and management responsibilities (Nonaka and Takeuchi 1995). Redundancy is important for knowledge creation to occur because individuals and groups must share and discuss information. If redundancy is not tolerated in an organization, individuals may be reluctant to discuss information they deem not to be immediately usable. The knowledge creation processes discussed earlier involved elements of redundancy. Much of the discussion revolved around concepts such as sharing, interaction, and integration, all of which imply the transfer of knowledge between individuals.

My observations suggest that managerial tolerance for redundancy was not consistent across the cases. In Gamma, the regular attendance of JV managers at meetings involving parent division managers could have been seen as redundant given that the JV was initially formed with a narrow mandate to supply one transplant firm. For Kappa, the American parent's president realized that the parent had to make a large commitment in managerial time when the JV was formed if the JV was going to be successful. The result was a JV that was closely integrated with the parent's strategy, and a clear overlapping of strategic and operational roles.

In a case of low tolerance for redundancy, Beta's general manager actively encouraged parent management to use the JV as a training ground for parent managers. However, Beta's American parent was generally unwilling to incur the minimal expense of sending key parent managers to the JV on a regular basis to experience the JV firsthand. This type of action may have been seen as wasteful by the American parent and not directly associated with successful management of the JV. However, as

Nonaka (1990) suggested, allowing individuals to enter each others' areas of operation promotes the sharing and articulating of individual knowledge, which may lead to problem generation and knowledge creation. This study found that the Japanese parents frequently took the opportunity to send Japan-based managers to visit the JV, probably because of a greater tolerance for redundancy and because lifelong learning is often an explicit element in the career path of Japanese managers (Hedlund and Nonaka 1993; Keys, Denton, and Miller 1994).

PROPOSITION 3: The greater the parent organization's tolerance for information redundancy, the more likely knowledge creation will be viewed as a valuable collaborative activity.

Trust

Trust between JV partners has been identified as an important element in collaborative relationships (Gulati 1995; Madhok 1995). Breakdowns in the value creation process in JVs often stem from a lack of trust between partners (Borys and Jemison 1989). Trust between the partners reflects the belief that a partner's word or promise is reliable and that a partner will fulfill its obligations in the relationship. In the knowledge creation process, an atmosphere of trust should contribute to the free exchange of information between committed exchange partners because the decision makers do not feel that they have to protect themselves from the other's opportunistic behavior (Blau 1964; Jarillo 1988). Without trust, the information exchanged between the parents directly or through the JV may not be highly accurate, comprehensive, or timely (Zand 1972) because the partners are unwilling to take the risks associated with sharing more valuable information.

Trust between the partners appeared to be a function of both top management involvement in the relationship and a history of cooperation prior to the formation of the JV. A Kappa manager suggested that the high trust relationship between the "patriarchs" in each partner was critical to the partner relationship. In another case, in response to a question as to the single most important factor in ensuring an enduring partner relationship, the American parent president indicated that a long history of cooperation was essential. This supports Gulati's finding (1995) that repeated ties between alliance partners generates trust. If there is no history of stable ties and interrelationships between partners, the initial state of trust will be precarious and will contribute to the liability of newness that characterizes JVs (Fichman and Levinthal 1991).

PROPOSITION 4A: The level of trust between the JV partners will influence the nature and extent of knowledge exchanged between the partners.

Mutual trust between the JV and the parent was also important as a basis for sharing and cooperating. This is consistent with Hedlund's argument (1994) that long-term collaboration and sharing of knowledge across channels require trust between agents. In both stages of this research, JV managers often indicated that the JVs were viewed by middle managers in parent organizations with distrust. In three of the cases studied in the second stage, the JV-parent relationship had evolved into a high-trust relationship. With Alpha, there was a high level of distrust about the nature of the relationship and the motives of the two organizations.

PROPOSITION 4B: The level of trust between the JV and its parent will influence the parent's willingness to initiate knowledge creation efforts.

Performance-Induced Myopia

Managers intent on learning and knowledge creation must cope with confusing experiences (Levinthal and March 1993). One such experience for JV parents is the assessment of JV performance by the parents. In the first stage of the research, several managers in American parent companies pointed to the poor financial performance of their JVs as evidence that learning was not occurring, and perhaps more importantly, could not occur. More generally, a preoccupation with short-term issues was a common characteristic of the American partners. Although it is too simplistic to describe Japanese management as long-term oriented and American management as short-term oriented, the Japanese partner firms in this study appeared to focus on customer satisfaction and product quality measures rather than profit-based performance. Consistent with other studies (such as Abegglen and Stalk 1985, and Doyle, Saunders, and Wong 1992), the Japanese firms seemed less constrained by issues of share price and impatient boards of directors than their American counterparts.

Because the American partners were heavily focused on financial performance issues, knowledge creation may have been a secondary and less tangible concern. Whereas North Americans focused on the bottom line, the Japanese focused on improving productivity, quality, and delivery. For American managers, it was difficult to conceive that learning could be occurring coincident with poor performance. Consequently, there was a reluctance to commit to or even try out proposals in the parent that were generated at the JV level. A quote from the report on the stage one study is indicative of this perspective: "The American parent's emphasis on the profitability of the JV clouded their judgment. Learning was never allowed to surface. Their attitude became, they (the Japanese partner) don't know anything so how can we learn from these people?"

This research supports the argument that organizational learning oversamples successes and undersamples failures (Levinthal and March 1993). As a result, learning processes tend to eliminate failures and sustained experimentation becomes difficult.

PROPOSITION 5: Poor JV performance will act as a barrier to the initiation of knowledge creation efforts.

Levinthal and March (1993) suggested that learning is a balancing act between the competing goals of developing new knowledge and exploiting current competencies. This balancing act can be seen in the paradoxical challenge faced by JV general managers. On one hand, general managers were charged with generating an adequate financial return for the American parents; on the other hand, they were expected to act as the conduit for the parent's learning initiative. A focus on one objective detracted from the other. More importantly, when either learning or performance was less than satisfactory, there were implications for the assessment of the other objective. Thus, although poor performance can act as a barrier to knowledge creation, unexploited learning opportunities may lead to perceptions of unsatisfactory JV performance. Poor performance can also provide an opportunity to delve into a situation and learn why performance is less than satisfactory.

Conclusion

Organizations must not only process information but also create new information and knowledge. This chapter explored how organizations involved in international alliances can use their alliance experience as the basis for managing and creating knowledge. The inductive framework developed in the chapter is intentionally broad in order to convey the experimental nature of knowledge creation. Several underlying assumptions are associated with the framework. First, there can be a significant payoff in interorganizational cooperating, namely knowledge creation. Although not all knowledge creation efforts will have immediate performance payoffs, over the long term successful knowledge creation should strengthen and reinforce a firm's competitive strategy. Second, knowledge creation is not confined to identifiable points of input-output sequences but is in fact far more continuous, random, and idiosyncratic. It may occur unintentionally and it may occur even if success cannot be assessed in terms of objective outcomes. Finally, knowledge creation is a dynamic process involving interactions at various organizational levels and an expanding community of individuals that enlarge, amplify, and internalize the alliance-based knowledge.

This study's findings document knowledge management processes in international alliances and propose new relationships among alliance context, collaborative process, and knowledge creation. The distinct characteristics of the alliances studied and the automotive industry setting may limit generalizations to other alliances. Using a single industry with a homogeneous set of organizations imposes certain constraints. In particular, theory development is restricted to limited domain or middle-range theories (Pinder and Moore 1980), and generalizability is confined to other industries sharing similar structural characteristics. However, a single industry offers greater control over market and environmental peculiarities, an important consideration in exploratory and theory building research.

The four key knowledge management processes discussed are important regardless of the industry context. However, the nature of the processes and the type of knowledge involved will differ. For example, in four of the five cases (all but Sigma), the Japanese partner was responsible for the manufacturing process and product technology, which obviously influenced the type of technology knowledge that could be exchanged between the partners. Also, industry conditions can influence the learning intent and managerial commitment of a parent firm. When this research began in 1990, the U.S. automotive industry was under serious attack by Japanese firms. Suppliers had to cope with new competitors, and their traditional customers were losing market share. By 1994, the situation was very different. The U.S. domestic auto industry was recapturing some of its market share, and their suppliers were reaping the benefits. The learning imperative that existed in 1990 was no longer as explicit. This highlights one of the problems with cross-sectional research, namely that firms and industries are in constant evolution. Longitudinal research captures the evolutionary patterns in the underlying research context.

The study did not attempt to explicitly link knowledge management with organizational performance. A tentative conclusion based on Tables 13.1 and 13.2 is that successful creation and management of knowledge are positively related to performance. For example, Alpha was the poorest performing JV and had the least active knowledge management processes. Gamma was classified as high performance and three of four knowledge management activities were also classified as high. In the case of Alpha, poor performance clearly acted as a barrier to the initiation of knowledge management efforts. For Gamma, the early profitability of the JV eliminated doubts about the JV's viability, which in turn helped foster greater interaction between the JV and the parent.

An alternative hypothesis for the relationship between JV performance and knowledge creation is that stages in the development of a cooperative relationship occur sequentially rather than simultaneously. In four of the cases, the initial development phase had been completed; the JV was stable and performing at a level satisfactory to the American parent. The parent could shift its attention to exploit learning opportunities. In Alpha, the initial development phase was still under way; and until the completion of this phase, knowledge creation was a minor objective. Thus, the static relationship between performance and knowledge creation may be less important than a dynamic understanding of the JV's life cycle stages.

An area for further research is the question of which knowledge management processes are most important and most successful. Table 13.2 shows four different knowledge management strategies. Does a firm need to be good at all the processes to create knowledge, or will an "unbalanced" approach to knowledge management also work? The answer depends on the type of knowledge sought (for example, tacit versus explicit) and the strategic value that parents attach to knowledge created in the JV. In their approach to organizational knowledge, Western firms tend to focus on explicit knowledge that can be created through analytical skills and concrete forms of oral and visual presentation (Nonaka and Takeuchi 1995). This study found that although the American firms formed JVs with an objective of learning from their Japanese partners, their expectations revolved around "what" the Japanese knew, rather than "how" and "why" the Japanese firms knew what they knew. There was an initial emphasis on knowledge based on visible differences that could be analyzed and incorporated readily by the parent. As it turned out, there were valuable learning experiences associated with specific techniques *and* with an overall philosophy of organizing and competing.

Because of the focus on explicit knowledge, the American firms tended to begin their collaborations with the view that the knowledge management processes based on technology sharing and interorganizational interaction were the most viable. However, in one of the cases, the focus on narrow objectives of technology learning resulted in an early abandonment of technology sharing efforts. The parent firms that were most successful in knowledge creation recognized that important knowledge could not be internalized without substantial interaction between managers in both the parent and JV. Also, these firms increasingly used strategic relationships between the two organizational units as a means of solidifying the knowledge linkages. Unlike the technology sharing process, the strategic integration process involved less visibly defined objectives and, in that sense, had a more tacit dimension.

Clearly, firms will attach different values to JV knowledge; therefore, knowledge creation strategies will differ across organizations and also evolve over time. This research found that although different strategies can be viable, some fundamental organizational enabling conditions promote a favorable climate for effective knowledge creation. Future research should address the relationships between the enabling conditions and knowledge creation processes. The integration of a typology of organizational knowledge with the management processes necessary to access and transfer the knowledge would be an important step toward developing a deeper understanding of these relationships.

NOTES

1. An example might help in differentiating knowledge and information. In explaining how the JV differed from its American parent, a JV manager said that there were simple things, such as shipping exactly 7,200 parts, not 7,201. The fact that 7,200 parts were shipped is information; the deeper meaning associated with customer satisfaction with quality delivery is knowledge.

2. It should be noted that differences in quality may be associated with different skill levels and may also be a function of different equipment, raw materials, and production conditions. The view here is that the *explanation* for the difference in quality can be the source of new knowledge for the American parent. For example, the JV may have a particular piece of equipment with which the parent is unfamiliar. If the parent learns how this equipment works and integrates this knowledge in its knowledge base, organizational knowledge is created.

3. Hamel (1991) argued that when a firm is able to successfully build new capabilities through the acquisition of alliance knowledge, the firm strengthens its bargaining power and increases its ability to exert control over the alliance. On this basis, the knowledge management processes identified in this study could be viewed as control mechanisms, because if a firm is successfully exploiting an alliance learning opportunity, the firm may be increasing its bargaining power.

4. For a detailed discussion of Western versus Japanese knowledge management processes, see Hedlund and Nonaka (1993). In Chapter 8 of Nonaka and Takeuchi (1995), the authors use several Japanese company examples to describe how organizational knowledge creation takes place on a global scale.

5. Nevis, DiBella, and Gould (1995) referred to facilitating factors that affect how easy or hard it is for learning to occur and how much effective learning takes place.

BIBLIOGRAPHY

Abegglen, J. C., and G. Stalk. 1985. *Kaisha: The Japanese Corporation.* New York: Basic Books.

Aguilar, F. J. 1967. *Scanning the Business Environment.* New York: Macmillan.

Bacharach, S. B. 1989. Organizational theories: Some criteria for evaluation. *Academy of Management Review,* 14: 496–515.

Blau, P. M. 1964. *Exchange and Power in Social Life.* New York: Wiley.

Bleeke, J., and D. Ernst. 1995. Is your strategic alliance really a sale? *Harvard Business Review,* 73(1): 97–105.

Borys, B., and D. B. Jemison. 1989. Hybrid arrangements as strategic alliances: Theoretical issues in organizational combinations. *Academy of Management Review,* 14: 234–249.

Brown, J. S., and P. Duguid. 1991. Organizational learning and communities of practice: Towards a unified view of working, learning, and organization. *Organization Science,* 2: 40–57.

Cohen, M. D., and L. S. Sproull. 1991. Editor's introduction. *Organization Science,* 2(1).

Cohen, W. M., and D. A. Levinthal. 1990. Absorptive capacity: A new perspective on learning and innovation. *Administrative Science Quarterly,* 35: 128–152.

Daft, R. L., and K. E. Weick. 1984. Towards a model of organizations as interpretation systems. *Academy of Management Review,* 9: 284–295.

Dodgson, M. 1993. Learning, trust, and technological collaboration. *Human Relations,* 46: 77–95.

Doyle, P., J. Saunders, and V. Wong. 1992. Competition in global markets: A case study of American and Japanese competition in the British market. *Journal of International Business Studies,* 23: 419–442.

Drucker, P. F. 1995. The network society. *Wall Street Journal,* March 29: 12.

Fichman, M., and D. A. Levinthal. 1991. Honeymoons and the liability of adolescence: A new perspective on duration dependence in social and organizational relationships. *Academy of Management Review,* 16: 442–468.

Fiol, C. M., and M. A. Lyles. 1985. Organizational learning. *Academy of Management Review,* 10: 803–813.

Geringer, J. M., and L. Hébert. 1991. Measuring performance of international joint ventures. *Journal of International Business Studies,* 22: 249–263.

Glaser, B. 1978. *Theoretical Sensitivity.* Mill Valley, Calif.: Sociology Press.

Glaser, B., and A. L. Strauss. 1967. *The Discovery of Grounded Theory: Strategies for Qualitative Research.* New York: Aldine.

Gulati, R. 1995. Does familiarity breed trust? The implications of repeated ties for contractual choice in alliances. *Academy of Management Journal,* 38: 85–112.

Gulati, R., T. Khanna, and N. Nohria. 1994. Unilateral commitments and the importance of process in alliances. *Sloan Management Review,* 35 (Spring): 61–69.

Hamel, G. 1991. Competition for competence and inter-partner learning within international strategic alliances. *Strategic Management Journal,* 12 (Special Issue): 83–104.

Hamel, G., Y. Doz, and C. K. Prahalad. 1989. Collaborate with your competitors—and win. *Harvard Business Review,* 67(2): 133–139.

Hamilton, D. P. 1995. Sony expands in computer-linked gear: Effort requires shift in go-it-alone tradition. *Wall Street Journal,* April 14: A8.

Harrigan, K. R. 1985. *Strategies for Joint Ventures.* San Francisco: New Lexington Press.

Harrigan, K. R., and W. H. Newman. 1990. Bases of interorganizational co-operation: Propensity, power, persistence. *Journal of Management Studies,* 27: 417–434.

Hedberg, B. 1981. How organizations learn and unlearn. In P. Nystrom and W. Starbuck, editors, *Handbook of Organizational Design,* 8–27. London: Oxford University Press.

Hedlund, G. 1994. A model of knowledge management and the N-form corporation. *Strategic Management Journal,* 15: 73–90.

Hedlund, G., and I. Nonaka. 1993. Models of knowledge management in the West and Japan. In P. Lorange, B. Chakravarthy, J. Roos, and A. Van de Ven, editors, *Implementing Strategic Processes: Change, Learning, and Co-operation,* 117–144. Oxford, England: Blackwell.

Huber, G. P. 1991. Organizational learning: The contributing processes and a review of the literatures. *Organization Science,* 2: 88–117.

Inkpen, A. 1995a. Organizational learning and international joint ventures. *Journal of International Management,* 1: 165–198.

Inkpen, A. 1995b. *The Management of International Joint Ventures: An Organizational Learning Perspective.* London: Routledge.

Inkpen, A., and P. W. Beamish. 1997. Knowledge, bargaining power, and international joint venture instability. *Academy of Management Review,* forthcoming.

Inkpen, A., and M. M. Crossan. 1995. Believing is seeing: Joint ventures and organizational learning. *Journal of Management Studies,* 32: 595–618.

Jarillo, J. C. 1988. On strategic networks. *Strategic Management Journal,* 9: 31–41.

Jelinek, M. 1979. *Institutionalizing Innovations: A Study of Organizational Learning Systems.* New York: Praeger.

Keys, J. B., L. T. Denton, and T. R. Miller. 1994. The Japanese management theory jungle—revisited. *Journal of Management,* 20: 373–402.

Kogut, B. 1988. Joint ventures: Theoretical and empirical perspectives. *Strategic Management Journal,* 9: 319–322.

Levinthal, D. A. 1991. Organizational adaptation and environmental selection: Interrelated processes of change. *Organization Science,* 2: 140–145.

Levinthal, D. A., and J. G. March. 1993. The myopia of learning. *Strategic Management Journal,* 14: 95–112.

Lyles, M. A. 1988. Learning among JV-sophisticated firms. In F. Contractor and P. Lorange, editors, *Cooperative Strategies in International Business,* 301–316. San Francisco: New Lexington Press.

Madhok, A. 1995. Revisiting multinational firms' tolerance for joint ventures: A trust-based approach. *Journal of International Business Studies,* 26: 117–138.

Miles, M. B., and A. M. Huberman. 1984. *Qualitative Data Analysis: A Sourcebook of New Methods.* Thousand Oaks, Calif.: Sage.

Mintzberg, H. 1990. Strategy formation: Schools of thought. In J. Frederickson, editor, *Perspectives of Strategic Management,* 105–235. New York: Harper Business.

Nelson, R. R., and S. G. Winter. 1982. *An Evolutionary Theory of Economic Change.* Cambridge, Mass.: Harvard University Press.

Nevis, E. C., A. J. DiBella, and J. M. Gould. 1995. Understanding organizations as learning systems. *Sloan Management Review,* 36 (Winter): 73–85.

Nonaka, I. 1990. Redundant, overlapping organizations: A Japanese approach to managing the innovation process. *California Management Review,* 32(3): 27–38.

Nonaka, I. 1991. The knowledge-creating company. *Harvard Business Review,* 69(6): 96–104.

Nonaka, I. 1994. A dynamic theory of organizational knowledge. *Organization Science,* 5: 14–37.

Nonaka, I., and J. K. Johansson. 1985. Organizational learning in Japanese companies. In R. Lamb and P. Shrivastava, editors, *Advances in Strategic Management,* Vol. 3, 277–296. Greenwich, Conn.: JAI Press.

Nonaka, I., and H. Takeuchi. 1995. *The Knowledge-Creating Company: How Japanese Companies Create the Dynamics of Innovation.* New York: Oxford University Press.

Parkhe, A. 1991. Interfirm diversity, organizational learning, and longevity in global strategic alliances. *Journal of International Business Studies,* 22: 579–602.

Patton, M. Q. 1987. *How to Use Qualitative Methods in Evaluation.* Thousand Oaks, Calif.: Sage.

Pinder, C. C., and L. F. Moore. 1980. The inevitability of multiple paradigms and the resultant need for middle-range analysis in organizational theory. In C. Pinder and L. Moore, editors, *Middle Range Theory and the Study of Organizations,* 87–100. Boston: Martinus Nijhof.

Porter, M. E. 1991. Towards a dynamic theory of strategy. *Strategic Management Journal,* 12 (Special Issue Winter): 95–117.

Prahalad, C. K., and G. Hamel. 1990. The core competence of the corporation. *Harvard Business Review,* 68(3): 79–91.

Prahalad, C. K., and G. Hamel. 1994. Strategy as a field of study: Why search for a new paradigm? *Strategic Management Journal,* 15: 5–16.

Pucik, V. 1991. Technology transfer in strategic alliances: Competitive collaboration and organizational learning. In T. Agmon and M. A. Von Glinow, editors, *Technology Transfer in International Business.* New York: Oxford University Press.

Quinn, J. B. 1992. *The Intelligent Enterprise.* New York: Free Press.

Reed, R., and R. J. DeFillippi. 1990. Causal ambiguity, barriers to imitation, and sustainable competitive advantage. *Academy of Management Review,* 15: 88–102.

Simonin, B. L., and D. Helleloid. 1993. Do organizations learn? An empirical test of organizational learning in international strategic alliances. In D. Moore, editor, *Academy of Management Proceedings 1993.*

Tushman, M., and T. J. Scanlon. 1981. Boundary-spanning individuals: Their role in information transfer and their antecedents. *Academy of Management Journal,* 24: 289–305.

Van de Ven, A. H. 1992. Suggestions for studying strategy process: A research note. *Strategic Management Journal,* 13 (Special Issue): 169–188.

Von Krogh, G., J. Roos, and K. Slocum. 1994. An essay on corporate epistemology. *Strategic Management Journal,* 15: 53–71.

Walsh, J. P., and G. R. Ungson. 1991. Organizational memory. *Academy of Management Journal,* 16: 57–91.

Weick, K. E. 1979. *The Social Psychology of Organizing,* 2nd ed. Reading, Mass.: Addison-Wesley.

Westney, D. E. 1988. Domestic and foreign learning curves in managing international cooperative strategies. In F. Contractor and P. Lorange, editors, *Cooperative Strategies in International Business,* 339–346. San Francisco: New Lexington Press.

Yin, R. K. 1989. *Case Study Research: Design and Methods,* rev. ed. Thousand Oaks, Calif.: Sage.

Zand, D. E. 1972. Trust and managerial problem solving. *Administrative Science Quarterly,* 17: 229–239.

14

KNOWLEDGE MANAGEMENT IN INTERNATIONAL JOINT VENTURES

Iris Tiemessen, Henry W. Lane,
Mary M. Crossan, and Andrew C. Inkpen

EXISTING RESEARCH ON *international joint ventures (IJVs)*
provides an understanding of joint venture (JV) structures, the
resources flowing through them, and the conditions affecting
their success. However, even though the acquisition of new
knowledge and skills is cited as an important reason for the for-
mation of JVs, the literature does not provide insight into the
processes by which these learning opportunities are seized and
institutionalized into organizational competencies. This chapter
integrates research on IJVs with the literature on organizational
learning (OL) to provide an understanding of the complexities
of the process and a framework to guide future research. The
conceptual framework describes the multilevel interactive pro-
cesses through which organizations learn and create knowledge.
The knowledge management framework maps the transfer of
knowledge in alliances, the transformation or creation of new
knowledge in the venture, and the harvesting or active and con-
scious integration of knowledge into parent company routines.

The authors gratefully acknowledge the financial support of the Social Sciences
and Humanities Research Council of Canada for the research project on which
this chapter is based.

In addition to firm-specific and market-specific knowledge, this chapter considers partnering knowledge and resource-integration knowledge to be critical resources in developing and maintaining sustainable competitive advantage on a global scale. Barriers that can prevent new knowledge and skills from developing or being absorbed by the organization are also discussed.

OVER THE LAST TWO decades there has been a substantial increase in the formation of international joint ventures (IJVs). The IJV literature identifies numerous conditions associated with JV performance, such as partner choice (Blodgett 1991; Geringer 1988a, 1988b, 1991; Parkhe 1991), motivation or intent (Beamish 1985; Hamel 1991; Killing 1983; Mariti and Smiley 1983), expectations (Beamish 1988; Buckley and Casson 1988), and control (Anderson and Gatignon 1986; Geringer and Hébert 1989; Killing 1982; Kim and Hwang 1992). However, the actual processes by which JVs are successfully managed has received limited attention and the "larger problems of interorganizational relations" (Toyne 1989: 1) have remained largely unexamined. Managing relationships is a behavioral process; mapping the dynamic interaction of two parents and the JV is the "missing link in understanding JV strategies" (Harrigan 1985: 40).

Organizational learning (OL) has been recognized as a process associated with JVs (Badaracco 1991; Hamel 1991; Kogut 1989; Parkhe 1991; Pucik 1991; Westney 1988) and with long-term competitive advantage (Hedlund 1994; Powell 1987). Ghoshal (1987) observed that while the initial pool of competencies allows a multinational corporation (MNC) to expand into new markets, the ongoing pool of competencies from which it draws leads to the MNC's sustained success. Ghoshal argues that the "one key asset of the MNC [is] the potential for learning from its many environments" (1987: 437). Therefore, one of the critical management processes in JVs is the management of learning and the continued acquisition of knowledge.

The organizational learning perspective is appearing more frequently in the international business literature, in particular with respect to strategic alliances and international joint ventures. We believe that its application holds great potential to increase our understanding of alliances. However, researchers importing this perspective into the international field to interpret interorganizational phenomena must use a common model of OL or risk perpetuating the lack of consensus that has already developed in the broader OL field.

The term *organizational learning* has existed in the literature at least since Cangelosi and Dill (1965) discussed the topic thirty years ago. However, little convergence or consensus on the meaning of the term or the basic nature of the phenomenon has emerged (Huber 1991; Kim 1993). Pfeffer (1993: 611) has suggested that the ability of a field to make progress and to attract resources requires some convergence among the scholars in the area. He states that "without some minimal level of consensus about research questions and methods, fields can scarcely expect to produce knowledge in a cumulative, developmental process." After nearly thirty years, the OL field has yet to achieve a coherent and comprehensive view and, despite the current popularity of OL, the lack of consensus threatens the continued intellectual development of the field (Crossan, Lane, White, and Djurfeldt 1995).

This lack of consensus about what OL is and how it occurs has arisen primarily along three dimensions: the emphasis placed on learning as a change in cognition or behavior; the tightness of coupling in learning-performance outcomes; and the level of analysis—individual, group, organizational. To this third dimension we would add the interorganizational level of analysis associated with alliances. No current OL framework exists that completely addresses these three dimensions to synthesize the existing OL literature and provide an integrated view while also incorporating the IJV literature. Unless progress is made on achieving consensus, researchers applying OL to alliances are in danger of finding pieces to the puzzle but never formulating a comprehensive understanding.

There have been calls to consider knowledge as a resource, to recognize the need for global organizations to develop learning competencies, and to take advantage of the learning opportunities that JVs provide; however, there has been little research on learning in international collaborations that describes or explains how learning takes place or how competency in learning develops. It is imperative to develop a framework that integrates the conditions, processes, and phases already established as being important in global alliances with a deeper understanding of organizational learning so that more accurate conceptualizations of knowledge management and the knowledge management process are possible.

By knowledge management, we mean the consciously embedded structures, systems, and interactions designed to permit the management of the firm's pool of knowledge and skills. Explicit knowledge management enhances the learning that takes place and ensures that competencies are developed, but, as Ghoshal (1987) points out, multinationals must put mechanisms into place through which learning can be fostered and managed. Although knowledge has been described as an important firm resource (Dorroh, Gulledge, and Womer 1994; Hedlund 1994; Nonaka 1994; Wernerfelt 1984), it is often underutilized and ineffectively deployed (Ernst and Young 1995).

Organizational learning is the study of changes to a knowledge base and its application in an organizational context. Hence OL provides the cognitive and behavioral understanding of how to manage knowledge resources such that partner companies can increase their knowledge and capabilities in ways that they could not do alone.

The present study integrates previous research on the structure and conditions of IJVs with OL research to provide the beginning of a common base for researchers in the area of learning in alliances. It examines the IJV literature to specify the conditions associated with successful IJVs, which become the context within which learning and knowledge transfer take place. Then it clarifies the dimensions of knowledge, before identifying the four learning processes of intuiting, interpreting, integrating, and institutionalizing and explaining their relationship to the facilitation of learning within an organization. Next, it establishes a framework for investigating interorganizational learning and the knowledge management process (KMP); the KMP is defined as the interorganizational transfer, transformation, and harvesting of knowledge. Finally, the study discusses potential barriers to knowledge enhancement and explains the implications for researchers and managers. The primary contribution of this study is an integration of current understanding and the development of a framework complete enough to begin moving the field beyond the lack of consensus and the narrow perspectives that exist.

Knowledge Management Framework

The knowledge management framework for IJVs presented here follows Parkhe's suggestion (1993: 227) for "a strong theoretical core or an encompassing framework that effectively integrates past research and serves as a springboard for launching future research." The development of this framework required us to keep an open mind to nontraditional concepts (Buckley 1991). Our framework integrates diverse literature from international and cross-cultural management, and from OL research, into the structure, conditions, and process framework proposed by Toyne (1989). We have modified Toyne's framework to follow an input-process-output model: we have included his structure and process as inputs, and we have added outcomes as the output. The type of international collaboration is the IJV. As a result, the structures relevant to the KMP are the individual entities—two parents and the IJV—and the interactions between them. The resources are the knowledge resources that both flow through and are created within this model. The conditions are the context within which the knowledge management process both operates and establishes parameters

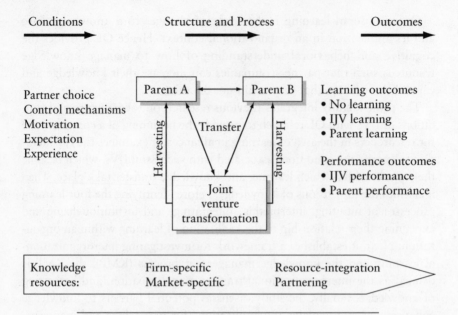

Conditions — Structure and Process — Outcomes

Partner choice
Control mechanisms
Motivation
Expectation
Experience

Parent A ←→ Parent B

Harvesting   Transfer   Harvesting

Joint
venture
transformation

Learning outcomes
• No learning
• IJV learning
• Parent learning

Performance outcomes
• IJV performance
• Parent performance

Knowledge
resources:

Firm-specific
Market-specific

Resource-integration
Partnering

Figure 14.1. Knowledge Management Framework.

that influence processes. The processes are the ways in which knowledge resources flow into, through, and out of the structure, and the ways in which existing knowledge is transformed or new knowledge is created. The outcomes are both learning and performance results realized by the parents and the IJV. The following sections provide an overview of each of the constructs of the framework presented in Figure 14.1. The intent is not to provide a full review of the constructs, but rather to attempt to synthesize our current understanding of areas that become important contextual variables of the knowledge management process in international alliances.

Structure

There are a variety of international collaborative structures that define networks of exchange and relationships, and that create different learning opportunities. Although we believe that the knowledge management framework given in this chapter has wide applicability, the structure of an IJV, with at least two parents from different countries and a new organizational form, provides an excellent opportunity to investigate knowledge management. Equity JVs (EJVs), a specific form of international alliance with distinct ownership and risk structures (Root 1988), potentially offer the highest degree of interfirm cooperation because the owners have a legal right to jointly manage the JV and they jointly assume its risk. EJVs are also the best vehicle for investigating learning because they offer greater access to new knowledge than internalization options, and they do so more cheaply than buying it through arm's-length transactions (Madhok 1995). Theoretically, within the context of an EJV, resources flow from the parent firm to the JV, where they are transformed into resources of higher value, which are then partitioned and flow back to the parent firms. EJVs in particular lead to an increase in the value of resources, as the resources are contributed for the specific purpose of producing outputs of higher value to parents (Gulati 1995). The implication here is not that EJVs are the only interorganizational form through which knowledge can be exchanged and created. Rather, the idea is that the structure of the relationship will determine the barriers and gateways to the interorganizational knowledge flow.

Conditions

Various conditions influence an IJV's success. In this section, we review the conditions that have been identified as most salient for joint venture success: partner choice, control mechanisms, motivation, expectations, previous IJV experience, nature of cooperation, and cultural context. These conditions, which create the context within which the knowledge management process operates, are both interactive and dynamic. For example, motivation can influence the choice of partner, and the choice of partner can have an impact on the control mechanisms implemented. Also, a change in the motivations of partners over time can influence expectations. As the IJV's performance stabilizes or changes, the control mechanisms may be changed; even the choice of partner may be reassessed. Although the discussion of each condition and its effect on an IJV's success may suggest a static and oversimplified view, we caution researchers to recognize the interactive and dynamic nature of these conditions. Our intent is to identify the specific conditions that have important influences on IJV success and knowledge management, but the actual interactive effects and their influence on learning and knowledge management will have to be determined through further research.

PARTNER CHOICE. Partner choice has been identified as important to IJV success (Beamish 1988; Blodgett 1991; Geringer 1988a, 1988b, 1991). The choice of IJV partner will determine what resources are available to be contributed and how well the two partners work together (Killing in foreword to Geringer 1988a). In integrating pools of resources, attention must be paid to the tacit (that is, implicit and experiential [Polanyi 1966]), knowledge held by each partner. For example, the partner contributing technology will hold proprietary knowledge that incorporates technological know-how. Similarly, the partner contributing market knowledge will have proprietary knowledge of relationships with suppliers, employees, and government, which is often ill-codified and difficult to transmit (Calvet 1981). Firms with complex, uncodified knowledge possessed by their employees will have more difficulty diffusing that knowledge than firms whose knowledge is coded in documents or objects (Boisot 1995).

The diversity between partners will have implications for what they need to learn (Parkhe 1991). Parkhe differentiates alliances formed between partners of reciprocal strength and complementary resources (Type I diversity), and partners with differing characteristics (Type II diversity). In his study, Parkhe focuses on Type II diversity, "the interorganizational interface at which inherent interfirm diversity between (Global Strategic Alliance) partners often makes effective management of pooled resource contributions problematic" (p. 582). He argues that in culturally diverse partnerships, OL is a threshold condition for alliance success, and that the interfirm differences stemming from societal culture, national culture, or corporate culture have to be identified and managed in the early phases of the relationship. If, however, diversity arises in strategic direction and management practices, OL becomes an adaptive process necessary to ensure that the alliance survives new circumstances.

The literature on partner choice has tended to focus on the partners' need for strategic complementary and compatible technical skills, such as technology and marketing. However, as Geringer (1988) pointed out, these should be considered the minimum qualifications, and more attention should be paid to selecting compatible partners, defined as those having compatible operating policies and management teams. Compatible partners will communicate effectively and have a relationship built on trust and commitment. The diversity of partner perspectives and resources provides the potential for learning if those resources are appropriately matched and deployed to the IJV activities. A diversity of perspectives, however, also can be a barrier to learning if not recognized, understood, and managed.

CONTROL MECHANISMS. Firms use control as a way to ensure that risk is minimized and return is maximized, and to efficiently coordinate activities, utilize resources, and implement strategy (Anderson and Gatignon 1986; Geringer and Hébert 1989; Killing 1982; Kim and Hwang 1992; Schaan 1983). Positive relationships have been found between the use of appropriate control measures and successful JV performance. Differences in corporate control affect the knowledge flows in multinational corporations (Gupta and Govindarajan 1991). The control literature has not considered the specific impact of control measures on learning processes in IJVs; however, it seems likely that factors such as the locus of control (relative autonomy of the IJV) and temporal orientation (long- or short-term orientation) of the control systems would effect the flow of resources into and out of the IJV, and could therefore influence the processes by which new knowledge is created within the IJV.

MOTIVATION. Although some firms may have intentions other than taking advantage of the learning opportunities in their IJVs, such as gaining access to needed assets (Beamish 1988; Killing 1983) and achieving economies of scale (Killing 1983), acquiring knowledge has been suggested as a primary motivation for forming JVs (Badaracco 1991; Hamel 1991; Kogut 1989; Mariti and Smiley 1983; Powell 1987; Pucik 1991; Westney 1988). The need for partner skills (Beamish 1988; Killing 1983) and the need for local market knowledge (Casson 1993) have been empirically examined. Knowledge and skills that should be learned by the parents and the JV include managerial know-how, process technology, and product technology (Inkpen 1992).

Learning intent is an important determinant of the efforts that a firm makes in learning from a JV partner (Hamel 1991). In discussing the potential multinationals have for learning from their diverse operations and markets, Ghoshal (1987: 432) warns that to exploit this potential, "the organization must consider learning as an explicit objective, and must create mechanisms and systems for such learning to take place." The acquisition of new knowledge is only a potential outcome of an IJV, not a given; the intent to learn must be matched by actions that encourage and support learning.

EXPECTATIONS. Expectations are different from motivations. Motivations represent the ultimate aim or purpose of the IJV; expectations are the anticipated probable outcome of the IJV. The distinction can be expanded by suggesting that motivations answer "why are we doing this?" while expectations answer "what do we expect as an outcome?" Expectations include outcomes that are usually favorable at the start of the collaboration, but which can change dramatically during the relationship depending on, for example, unexpected developments in the environment or changes in the behavior of the partner.

One expectation raised by Buckley and Casson (1988) is that the partners will not cheat on each other. They define cooperation as "coordination affected through mutual forbearance" (p. 32), where forbearance is defined as refraining from cheating on another party. If the parties in a JV are concerned about cheating, perhaps the best they can hope for is mutual forbearance, in which case protectionism will be evident and IJV failure probable. However, if the parties to a JV believe in mutual benefits, true cooperation may occur. It is interesting to note that Buckley and Casson assume that cooperation is only a product of mutual forbearance. A different perspective would be to focus on the mutually oriented behavior that might enhance the relationship's value, rather than on protectionism that might prevent value depletion (Madhok 1995).

The existence of trust and commitment in a relationship will influence the willingness of parents to share proprietary capabilities (Geringer 1988a, 1988b). This situation becomes more complicated when competitors form an alliance to develop a product or capability that neither could develop alone. A common understanding and shared set of expectations are essential for success. Without sharing, however, knowledge exchange and learning will be diminished. The degree of openness to sharing information and knowledge in the IJV will influence the amount of learning that takes place.

EXPERIENCE. Previous IJV experience has been included as a factor because learning processes and outcomes change and develop as firms gain experience in international collaborations (Hagedoorn 1995; Chang 1995). More importantly, companies that are more alliance-experienced have higher returns on investment (Harbison and Pekar 1993); however, researchers have not identified the specific knowledge gained to facilitate this result.

NATURE OF COOPERATION. Alter and Hage (1993) classified JVs according to the type of cooperation that develops between partners as a result of being in similar or different industry sectors. Competitive cooperation exists between same-sector organizations, and symbiotic cooperation exists between different-sector organizations. These authors suggest that symbiotic JVs are more influenced by opportunities for mutual learning because of complementary competencies, whereas competitive JVs are more likely to be created to offset the high costs and risks of product development. It is possible that IJVs formed by parents from the same industry sector have greater opportunities for transfer of relative technologies between them, because they have a need and use for their partners' technologies and they already have a basic understanding of those technologies. However, the potential of the IJV may not be realized if proprietary knowledge that is believed to embody a competitive advantage is protected by one of the partners. It is also possible that IJVs formed by parents in related but different industry sectors have greater opportunities for transformation of technological knowledge through the integration of processes.

CULTURAL CONTEXT. Besides an understanding of the mechanisms of knowledge management, we must understand the effect of cultural differences inherent in managing in a global environment (Wright, Lane, and Beamish 1988). Alliances between parents from culturally dissimilar countries are more likely to fail than alliances between those from culturally similar countries (Li and Guisinger 1991). A Conference Board survey (1994) of more than 350 CEOs in the U.S., Canada, Mexico, and the European Union showed that CEOs in the U.S. and Mexico consider cultural differences as the leading cause of strategic alliance failure.

The organizational and national cultures of the parent companies may influence all aspects of this framework, from the initial conditions surrounding IJV formation through the knowledge management process to the outcomes. Conflict within the IJV about the definition of acceptable learning outcomes, for example, could arise because of the different mental maps and interpretive schema used by different nationalities. Organizational and national cultures also contribute to the personal values held by the people chosen by the companies to manage the IJV, determining their assumptions about what is right, wrong, appropriate and inappropriate. Their assumptions, in turn, influence how they communicate, interact, manage, interpret, report, and evaluate (Lane and DiStefano 1992). Different values increase the difficulty of assessing one another's judgments and decisions, thereby affecting the effectiveness and cohesiveness of the IJV management team (Killing 1983).

To overcome these operational difficulties, the managers assigned to the IJV must have the cultural knowledge required to be effective communicators (Lane and DiStefano 1992) and must be sensitive to the difficulties of managing cross-cultural relationships. The need for understanding the impact of cultural diversity becomes even more important when the methods by which the culturally diverse partners learn and manage their knowledge resources vary. Cultural factors have been found to exert different influences on organizational development in Western and Japanese firms (Hedlund 1994), to result in different manufacturing techniques in Mexican and Japanese firms (Lawrence and Yeh 1994), and to lead to different management styles in U.S. managers and Mexican managers (Kras 1989). Therefore, it is readily apparent that a firm must manage these differences to prevent difficulties that may impede learning and the knowledge management process. Learning how to integrate diverse organizational and national cultures in an IJV is a significant component of the ultimate success of the venture.

The Knowledge Management Process

To understand the process by which knowledge is managed, we first define our use of the word *knowledge*. As research on OL forms the theoretical underpinnings for the knowledge management process, we also provide a brief description of OL, followed by the phases of KMP.

DIMENSIONS OF KNOWLEDGE. We differentiate between two dimensions of knowledge that are important to the IJV context. The first is the application of knowledge; this includes firm-specific knowledge, market-specific knowledge (Blodgett 1991; Dunning 1988), partnering knowledge, and resource integration knowledge. The second dimension, prominence of knowledge, includes explicit (more prominent) and tacit (less prominent) knowledge (Polanyi 1958, 1966).

The first dimension comprises four categories. *Firm-specific knowledge* is knowledge accumulated about the business itself, such as the technology used, the products and operations, the services provided, the management of the employees, the history of the firm, and the systems and structures supporting the firm's internal activities. *Market-specific knowledge* is knowledge accumulated about the factors that affect the firm's activities within a particular location, such as the laws and regulations governing business activities, the customer and supplier base, the availability of raw materials, distribution channels, and political influences.

As much of the work on IJVs has cited the difficulty of managing the relationship as an important factor (Beamish 1988; Gomes-Casseres 1994; Harrigan 1985; Helleloid and Simonin 1994; Killing 1983), a third category relevant to IJVs is *partnering knowledge,* or the know-how required to work with a partner (Gulati 1995; Hagedoorn 1995; Helleloid and Simonin 1994; Lyles 1988). Kanter (1994b) discusses how learning about alliance partners and the partnering process provides partners with a significant competitive advantage. She concludes that top executives have committed too much energy to financial and control issues in the relationship and not enough to the human and relational issues. Gomes-Casseres (1994: 74), however, points out that for many firms collaborating is new territory, and that even "pioneers in the field are still learning how to initiate, build and manage networks of alliances." Another hypothesis is that collaborating might be a learned skill and that greater experience leads to higher rates of alliance success (Conference Board 1994).

There is an interesting relationship between market-specific knowledge and partnering knowledge that is being uncovered through current IJV research. Some means is needed to acquire market knowledge, either within an organizational structure such as a wholly owned subsidiary, or between organizations through collaborations (Makino and Delios 1997). If the latter is chosen, in the process of gaining the market knowledge through a local partner, partnering experience is also gained. One might assume that once market knowledge is acquired partnering is no longer necessary, and if no other benefit were gained this would probably be true. Yet, Bell, Barkema and Verbeke (1997) found that while having general international experience decreases the likelihood of choosing a JV as a mode of foreign entry, having host country experience increases the likelihood of choosing a host country JV as an entry mode. Their interpretation is that knowing something about the culture increases the comfort level of partnering with a local firm. An additional interpretation is that partnering offers more than just market-specific knowledge.

A fourth category is *resource integration knowledge,* encompassing the technical know-how required to transform the available resources so that they function in the IJV context. To their IJV, the partners contribute resources that they have developed and acquired in their individual environments. However, the IJV must then integrate these pools of resources to function cohesively and effectively in the new environment. In essence, resource integration knowledge is knowing how to combine knowledge that is both firm-specific and market-specific into a new configuration.

The second dimension, the prominence of knowledge, was first categorized by Polanyi (1958, 1966) as being explicit or tacit. *Explicit knowledge* represents facts that are codifiable in a systematic language such as words and numbers and are formally transmittable through written or electronic media. *Tacit knowledge,* in contrast, is difficult to formalize and communicate (Nonaka 1994). It is highly context-specific, anchored in personal experience, and includes underlying systems of rules and beliefs that guide actions. It is generally carried in the minds of individuals and communicated through manifest behaviors and decisions. Johanson and Vahlne (1977) called this type of knowledge "experiential" because one can learn it only through personal experience. An example of this distinction is the maintaining of safety standards in an IJV that exceed local regulations (explicit knowledge); this practice is based on the recognition that the IJV competes with local firms for skilled labor, and that provision of high safety standards attracts high-quality skilled labor (tacit knowledge).

ORGANIZATIONAL LEARNING. As suggested, the OL field provides an understanding of how developments in organizational knowledge and its application are achieved. To properly use this understanding, we should summarize some of the research on OL. There has been a dramatic increase in this field because of a number of internal and external factors driving organizations to increase their learning capabilities. The internal forces stem from the belief that OL is a means of achieving and sustaining competitive advantage. The external forces stem from the growing rate of change in political, economic, and social forces influencing the business community and creating need for faster learning, and from increasingly complex technology that creates need for knowledge-based organization forms (Schein 1993).

Many authors have summarized the OL literature (Fiol and Lyles 1985; Hawkins 1994; Huber 1991; Levitt and March 1988; Lundberg 1989; Shrivastava 1983; Ulrich, Jick, and Von Glinow 1993; Watkins and Marsick 1993). The framework shown in Figure 14.2 encompasses four microprocesses—intuiting, interpreting, integrating, and institutionalizing—that take place through intraorganizational interactions between levels of the organization—individual, group, and organization—and interorganizationally between the parent firms and the IJV. The unique aspect of these microprocesses is that they encompass both the cognitive and behavioral aspects of learning. Many OL theorists consider one or the other. For example, Nonaka and Takeuchi's model (1995) focuses on the cognitive processes of socialization, externalization, internalization, and combination by which tacit and explicit knowledge are interchanged. While they discuss behavioral activities in their descriptions of knowledge-creating situations, their model does not include these activities.

LEARNING LEVELS. Although the OL framework in Figure 14.2 encompasses four learning levels, OL researchers have not agreed on the appropriate unit(s) of analysis. A brief discussion of each of the levels conveys insight into the present state of OL research and the implicit assumptions that researchers have made about the level of learning in IJVs.

Theories of learning that take the perspective of the individual assume that learning is done only by humans and that an organization is the sum of its individual members. Therefore, when an individual acquires new knowledge or adapts an existing pool of knowledge, the organization has learned (March and Olsen 1975; Simon 1991; Simonin 1991). Research on IJVs has often implicitly assumed a model of individual learning, and concluded organizational learning as a result. However, the model of individual learning is usually a black box, with little recognition of the more subtle cognitive processes at work.

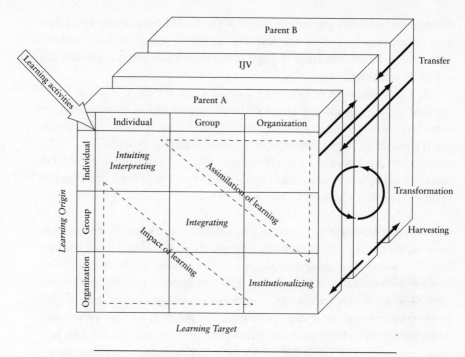

Figure 14.2. 4i³ Learning Network.

OL theories that take the group perspective assume that an organization is more than the sum of its individual members, and that some communication and integration of individual learning needs to happen for the organization to learn. These learning interactions have been described as dialogue processes (Daft and Weick 1984; Huber 1991; Isaacs 1993; Senge 1990) within communities of practice (Seely Brown and Duguid 1991) and in groups that operate in the margin between equilibrium and chaos (Stacey 1991). The ability to articulate and communicate is fundamental to developing shared group knowledge. Dialogue allows for the unfolding of meaning, which may be perceived differently by different people and which allows individuals to raise or uncover assumptions so they can learn how to think together. Understanding the elements of group learning is vital in IJVs where the partners and the JV inevitably deal with different culturally bound assumptions.

Several theorists have asserted that OL is not simply the learning arising from individuals and groups, but that there is a role for the organization as well (Argyris and Schon 1978; Hedberg 1981; Shrivastava 1983; Weick 1979), and attribute knowledge structures to organizations (Duncan and Weiss 1979; Lyles and Schwenk 1992). The distinguishing characteristic of organization-level learning is that it is embedded in systems, structures, and procedures such that the learning endures even though individuals comprising the organization change. IJV research has often neglected this aspect of learning.

The OL framework in Figure 14.2 depicts that the three levels of learning (individual, group, organization) in one organization interact with the same levels of learning in another. In the case of IJVs, a third organization, the IJV itself, engages in interorganizational learning as well. The OL literature has not considered interorganizational learning. By applying OL theory to IJVs, we not only learn about the process of knowledge management in IJVs, but also extend the reach of OL.

LEARNING PROCESSES. Central to the OL framework are the processes of learning that occur across each of the levels. At an individual level, learning activities involve intuiting and interpreting. *Intuiting* is the subconscious process of creating tacit knowledge. This can happen through pattern recognition, an expert's ability to develop solutions quickly by assimilating existing knowledge; or it can result from the creation of new knowledge, an entrepreneur's ability to develop new relationships and discern new possibilities (Cohen and Levinthal 1990). *Interpreting* is the conscious process of giving meaning to events, behavior, and data. This process of converting tacit knowledge into explicit knowledge (Nonaka 1991) is fundamental to the individual learning process (Reed and DeFillippi 1990). This interplay between tacit and explicit knowledge is the most powerful process in creating knowledge in organizations (Nonaka 1991).

At a group level, learning involves *integrating*: the process of sharing, comparing, and resolving individual views into a shared understanding. It is the process of trading and comparing information (Schrader 1991), either directly through verbal discussions and nonverbal representations or indirectly through actions. The result is the transformation of explicit knowledge into articulated knowledge through human interactions. Integration is dependent on shared information, on the existence of a shared language and belief system so that the information has common meaning, and on a continuous, direct dialogue (Isaacs 1993; Senge 1990) through which conflicts are resolved between contradictory pieces of information.

At an organizational level, learning involves *institutionalizing*: the process of incorporating new knowledge and skills into the systems, structures, and procedures of the organization. A substantial component of new knowledge can depreciate rapidly because of new information, shortness of memory, and the transience of individuals. For organizations to retain knowledge, the knowledge must become embedded in structures, systems, and procedures as part of the organization's memory (Argote, Beckman, and Epple 1990; Lewis and Seibold 1993).

A unique characteristic of the OL framework is the interaction between the levels and the processes as conveyed in the matrix structure of the framework. The matrix structure highlights, for example, the impact of organizational-level learning in the form of institutionalized systems and structures on intuiting and interpreting at the individual level (cell 3,1), and the distinction between individual intuiting and interpreting (cell 1,1) and institutionalized intuiting and interpreting (cell 1,3). The area to the right and above the diagonal represents a feed-forward loop, or the transfer of learning from individuals to the group and organization levels: the assimilation of learning within an organization. The area below and to the left of the diagonal represents a feedback loop, or the patterns, routines, and systems of past institutionalized learning that direct groups and individuals in an organization: the impact of learning. At the interorganizational level, the same processes and interactions are at work, but the process is complicated by the involvement of three or more organizations and people from different cultures.

OUTCOMES. We added outcomes to the framework to recognize that researchers and managers are clearly concerned about where knowledge management processes lead. However, there are trade-offs inherent in deciding which of the three strategic objectives suggested by Ghoshal (1987) multinationals should follow: achieving efficiency, managing risk, or learning. One must consider which objective confers the longest sustainable advantage. The decision is often presented as a dichotomous choice between doing things efficiently or doing the right things effectively. The obvious answer is an appropriate mix of both. The same paradox exists within the learning process. Continual promotion of innovation, experimentation, and reassessment can hinder the systematizing and routinizing of factors that have already been tested and justified. Yet to follow existing procedures to gain efficiencies without assessing them in the light of new knowledge or improving them by incorporating new competencies is to follow a short path to competitive disaster.

A firm has *"competitive advantage* when it is implementing a value-creating strategy not simultaneously being implemented by any current or potential competitors;" when those competitors are also "unable to duplicate the benefits of this strategy" the firm has *sustained competitive advantage* (Barney 1991: 102). Sustained competitive advantage is a function of the firm's resources, particularly its unique and imperfectly imitable characteristics. Developing knowledge resources through experience and intended effort can lead to sustained competitive advantage because those resources will be unique and difficult to acquire or copy.

Some researchers have suggested that those MNCs that are able to learn from their globally dispersed subsidiaries achieve higher performance (Kanter 1994a; Ohmae 1989; Perlmutter and Heenan 1986). Bartlett and Ghoshal (1991) argued that "the enhanced organizational learning that results from the diversity internalized by the multinational may be a key explanator of its ongoing success, while its initial stock of knowledge may well be the strength that allows it to create such organizational diversity in the first place" (quoted from Ghoshal 1987: 431). Ghoshal (1987) uses the example of Procter & Gamble's global development of Liquid Tide™ to show the strategic advantages that accrue from internalized diverse learning.

Although OL should lead to long-term performance enhancement, learning often requires taking one step backward before taking two steps forward: that is, making mistakes. Furthermore, enhanced performance may arise from factors other than learning, such as changes in exchange rates or the diminished competitiveness of an ailing rival. In addition, firms that equate learning and performance are more likely to discount learning arising from poorly performing JVs (Inkpen 1995). Focusing solely on performance as the outcome of the knowledge management process is misguided. As a result, we have distinguished between learning outcomes and performance outcomes in the knowledge management framework.

Knowledge Management Phases

The OL framework describes general learning processes. In IJVs there are three explicit knowledge management phases that need to be managed to foster learning. When firms form an IJV, they transfer or contribute resources that reflect their existing stock of competencies. Through joint activities, whether development, production, or promotion, these competencies can be transformed and enhanced to reflect the combined pool of knowledge and skills, as well as new knowledge created from the alliance. However, for firms to draw upon the new knowledge and skills in other endeavors, they must be harvested and brought back from the IJV (in other words, integrated and institutionalized). The following sections describe each of the three phases of IJV knowledge management.

TRANSFER. Most of the literature on collaborative learning has looked at the transfer of firm-specific technology (Davies 1977; Hamel 1991; Inkpen 1992; Kogut and Zander 1993; Mariti and Smiley 1983; Pucik 1991). This focus on the foreign direct investment tradition considers the actual transfer of existing know-how rather than the learning of new competencies (Simonin 1991).

Transfer is the movement of knowledge between parent firms, either directly or through the IJV, through activities such as buying technology, observing and imitating technology used by the partner, or changing existing technologies according to directions given by a partner. Transfer essentially means accepting what the partner does, integrating it into one's own systems or changing one's own resources to imitate it. The transfer phase is important in the context of an IJV because often it is the IJV channel through which transfer occurs (Benvignati 1983; Von Glinow and Teagarden 1988). Transfer is also an important determinant of IJV performance, as the IJV needs to acquire knowledge from the parent in order to carry out the activities the parent intends (Lyles and Salk 1997).

Transfer is easiest when the knowledge is easily transported, easily interpreted, and easily absorbed (Hamel, Doz, and Prahalad 1989). Badaracco (1991) termed this "migratory knowledge" because it can be clearly and fully articulated and is very mobile. The danger, however, is that the underlying tacit knowledge is not transferred or developed, in which case only imitation is achieved. When problems arise in the application of the explicit knowledge—for example, in the operation of a piece of equipment—it is difficult to know how to correct them (Killing 1983; Von Glinow and Teagarden 1988). In addition, there is the problem of integrating the transferred technological knowledge with existing systems, particularly market-specific systems based on different tacit knowledge (Tallman and Shenkar 1994). It is possible to develop an understanding of the underlying tacit knowledge by transfer and imitation, a process Nonaka calls (1994) internalization, but only if the knowledge management processes are well articulated.

TRANSFORMATION. The transformation of knowledge is the extension of existing knowledge and the creation of new knowledge, usually within the IJV. Casson (1993) notes that the successful exploitation of an advantage internationally may require adaptation of the technology, the system, or the management practices (or all of the above), to the local environment, especially given cultural differences in new markets. Often it is difficult for the management team to be good at adapting both production systems and marketing techniques. Hence, collaborating with a local partner ensures correct adaptation and also allows the management team to improve its own capabilities. As Beamish (1988) argued, the MNC takes firm-specific knowledge of production or marketing and exchanges it for market-specific knowledge of the local economy, politics, and customs through its IJVs. The transformation or creation of new knowledge resources are the products of the joint operational activities. In this process of collaboration, existing competencies may be enhanced if the new knowledge is captured by a well-articulated knowledge management system. This adaptation process creates the two kinds of new knowledge previously discussed, resource integration knowledge and partnering knowledge.

Researchers have long realized that the transfer of knowledge through collaborations is a way to extend the organization into new areas; however, they have only recently recognized the important potential for partners to learn something new through the joint activities. Hedlund (1994) incorporates the processes of transfer and transformation of knowledge into his theory of knowledge creation. He suggests that most of the literature "speaks primarily in terms of storage of information, and only secondarily about its transfer, whereas its transformation is left outside most analyses" (p. 76). The knowledge management framework positions the traditional view of knowledge creation as an organizational learning process within the context of an international alliance where both the need and opportunity for learning are magnified. The four learning processes previously identified are also the processes that should operate within an IJV to facilitate learning and the creation of new knowledge at that level.

HARVESTING. Of the three phases of the knowledge management process, harvesting is a term that has been previously implied (see Chapter Thirteen; Ghoshal 1987; Lyles 1988) but not explicitly articulated. Harvesting involves retrieving knowledge that has already been created and tested from the JV resources in which it resides, and then internalizing it into the parent firm so it can be recalled and used in other applications. Although the harvesting of knowledge sounds like a straightforward activity, it is a completely different process from those of transfer and transformation, and is neither easy nor automatic.

The theoretical framework developed by Lyles (1988) suggests that two types of learning occur through JVs: lower-level learning that incorporates what is learned into routine operating procedures and management systems, and higher-level learning that adjusts the missions, beliefs, and norms that guide the operations of the JV. Lyles found that in order for the parent firms to harvest the new knowledge created by JV activities, top management must play an active role in overseeing the JV and must communicate with the JV managers.

In a study of North American–Japanese IJVs, the IJVs did provide the opportunity for learning both within the JV and by the parent firms (Inkpen 1992). For the parents, however, learning was often a secondary motive, and learning opportunities frequently went unexploited. Interestingly, the study found that performance satisfaction determined the degree to which parents engaged in learning efforts. This observation implies that the evaluation of performance determines acquisition and harvesting efforts.

In a further study (described in Chapter Thirteen), Inkpen identified four processes critical to the incorporation of alliance knowledge into the parent company's systems and structures: technology sharing, interorganizational interaction, personnel movement, and strategic integration. The preconditions necessary for these knowledge connections to occur are intent, managerial commitment, redundancy, and trust.

Barriers to Knowledge Enhancement

Effective knowledge management can contribute to sustaining competitive advantage. However, as in other management processes, problems exist. By integrating the traditional IJV research on structure and conditions, with a process understanding of learning and knowledge management, we discover a number of barriers. For example, while partner choice determines the pool of available resources and makes clear the differences between the partners, it simply represents the potential to learn. In the first, or transfer, phase of the KMP, barriers to actual transfer of knowledge can occur at all levels of learning. The individuals assigned to the IJV by one partner may not be able to interpret the resources being transferred by the other partner. Or, given different points of view arising from different organization and country cultures, individuals may not be able to integrate their knowledge within the IJV or in their interactions with parents. In addition, the systems and structures of the parent organizations may impede the transfer of knowledge.

In the second phase of the KMP, barriers to transformation may arise because individuals lack sufficient knowledge to interpret the idiosyncrasies of a local context, or disagreements arise about the modifications because of the potentially wide diversity of interpretations. In this phase, the institutionalized learning of the parent organizations may create a great deal of inertia toward effecting changes.

In the harvesting phase, barriers arise because individuals in the parent organization have often had very little interaction with the IJV, and therefore have difficulty interpreting its highly specific and sometimes newly created assets. The problem is compounded by the fact that those individuals who act as parent-level contacts for the IJV, and who may see a benefit in adapting the parent-level operations to reflect new knowledge gained, will need support from senior management in the organization who similarly have had little interaction with the IJV. Finally, the inertia arising from the parent's institutionalized learning, which impedes transformation of knowledge in the IJV, increases as those parent-level contacts attempt to alter the systems, structures, or procedures of the parent to harvest knowledge from the IJV.

Control as a condition of IJVs can be linked directly to the institutionalized learning that affects the transfer, transformation, and harvesting of knowledge. Control is an example of learning that becomes embodied as a mechanism or artifact of the organization. Beliefs about how the IJV should be managed are captured by the control mechanism and will endure, even when the individuals who devised them leave the organization. The control mechanisms affect what gets interpreted, integrated, and subsequently institutionalized, and by whom.

Rather than being facilitators, motivation and expectations can become significant barriers to learning when they do not distinguish between learning and performance, and thus become misaligned with the knowledge management process. Without an appreciation for the KMP and the learning-performance relationship, misaligned expectations may cause premature evaluation of IJV performance. Expectations focused only on the visible achievement of productivity and financial goals may obscure the recognition of more subtle learning outcomes such as improved partnering skills or improved market-specific knowledge.

Although learning intent may be present, habitual behaviors may prevent learning from taking place. Margolis (1993) wrote about "habits of mind" and suggested that such entrenched responses ordinarily occur without any conscious attention and are difficult to change. He characterized learning as the modification of these patterned habits. Organizations work with familiar procedures and patterns that are habits of the corporate mind reinforced by structures and systems. Changing these corporate habits is a difficult task, requiring practice and repeated experience, a recognition of the need to change, a recognition of existing habits, and a conscious effort to adapt habits in order to coordinate with those of others, particularly partners with different cultural backgrounds. For these reasons, a clear understanding of how to manage the processes of learning is imperative.

Learning may not take place in MNCs for three reasons (Ghoshal 1987). First, subsidiaries may not be sufficiently sensitive, analytical, or responsive to local environments to learn from them. Second, a tight rein on decision making by the parent companies increases their chances of being insensitive to knowledge transfer opportunities by subsidiaries compared with other subsidiaries that are given more autonomy and flexibility. Third, firms may lack the ability to transfer learned competencies between units. The crux of Ghoshal's argument is that the entity in the local environment must be able to learn, the home entity must be open to learning from the local entity, and the home entity must have learning mechanisms in place.

It is important to note that the barriers to learning raised here are challenges that, if surmounted, present a tremendous opportunity to IJV parents. A fundamental building block of learning is recognizing and integrating differences: the greater the differences, the greater the challenge and the opportunity.

Conclusion

The knowledge management framework provides a comprehensive view of the knowledge management process, incorporating what we know about the structures and conditions that facilitate or inhibit learning with new developments in our understanding of the process of IJV learning and knowledge transfer, transformation, and harvesting.

Several implications for researchers arise from the framework:

1. Learning is a complex process that encounters many barriers.

2. Knowledge is not as mobile as has often been assumed.

3. Explicit assumptions about the level of learning are preferable to ambiguous ones. For example, if one or two individuals in the JV have gained knowledge, this does not mean that the organization has learned.

4. By recognizing the multiple levels of learning and the interaction among the levels, researchers have a better frame of reference to develop future research questions as well as to perceive the impact that the different levels have on learning. For example, they will be more likely to ask how the structures and systems of the organization (institutionalized learning) affect what individuals see, with whom they interact, what they do, and what they have learned (intuiting and interpreting), and whether and how this knowledge is shared (integrated) and institutionalized.

5. Researchers can begin to link structures and conditions with the process of knowledge management to develop an understanding of how elements such as partner choice, control mechanisms, motivation, expectation, and experience affect the process of knowledge management.

6. Processes of learning can be linked to specific outcomes, which should be divided into learning and performance outcomes.

7. Researchers can become more attuned to the types of knowledge to manage: in addition to firm-specific and market-specific knowledge, they need to consider resource integration and partnering knowledge.

8. Researchers can become more attuned to the phases of knowledge management: transfer, transformation, and harvesting.

For managers, one of the first steps to managing knowledge transfer, transformation, and harvesting is to recognize the challenge and complexity inherent in the process. Without being consumed by the complexity, they need to be aware that learning occurs across a variety of levels (individual, group, organization, interorganization), through a variety of processes (intuiting, interpreting, integrating, institutionalizing), and through three primary phases in the case of IJVs (transfer, transformation, harvesting). Being attuned to these aspects of knowledge management will help managers be more reflective, institutionalizing and supporting those conditions and processes that facilitate both financial performance and learning outcomes. In particular, managers must distinguish between learning and performance outcomes in their expectations of IJVs.

We are not suggesting the simplistic view that all IJVs provide learning opportunities and that all firms should take advantage of these opportunities. There may be some cases where an IJV serves a specific functional purpose that, once achieved, signals an end to the relationship. Such IJVs can be clearly specified and controlled using ownership-centered approaches (Madhok 1995). However, the ability to improve existing skills and learn new ones will be the most defensible competitive advantage a firm can hold (Hamel and Prahalad 1989). With strong support for partnering as an important factor in the global business arena (Kanter 1994a; Ohmae 1989; Perlmutter and Heenan 1986), understanding how to manage partnerships to hone learning skills, as well as to enhance and develop competencies, is in itself becoming a core competency.

BIBLIOGRAPHY

Alter, C., and J. Hage. 1993. *Organizations Working Together*. Thousand Oaks, Calif.: Sage.

Anderson, E., and H. Gatignon. 1986. Modes of foreign entry: A transaction cost analysis and propositions. *Journal of International Business Studies*, 17(3): 1–26.

Argote, L., S. Beckman, and D. Epple. 1990. The persistence and transfer of learning in industrial settings. *Management Science*, 36(2): 140–154.

Argyris, C., and D. A. Schon. 1978. What is an organization that it may learn? *Organizational Learning: A Theory of Action Perspective.* Reading, Mass.: Addison-Wesley.

Badaracco, J. L. 1991. *The Knowledge Link.* Boston: Harvard Business School Press.

Barney, J. 1991. Firm resources and sustained competitive advantage. *Journal of Management,* 17(1): 99–120.

Bartlett, C. A., and S. Ghoshal. 1991. *Managing Across Borders.* Boston: Harvard Business School Press.

Beamish, P. W. 1985. The characteristics of joint ventures in developed and developing countries. *Columbia Journal of World Business,* 20(3): 13–19.

Beamish, P. W. 1988. *Multinational Joint Ventures in Developing Countries.* London: Routledge.

Bell, J.H.J., H. G. Barkema, and A. Verbeke. 1997. An eclectic model of the choice between wholly owned subsidiaries and joint ventures as modes of foreign entry. In P. W. Beamish and J. P. Killing, editors, *Cooperative Strategies: European Perspectives.* San Francisco: New Lexington Press.

Benvignati, A. 1983. International technology transfer patterns in a traditional industry. *Journal of International Business Studies,* 14(3): 63–76.

Blodgett, L. L. 1991. Partner contribution as predictors of equity share in international joint ventures. *Journal of International Business Studies,* 22(1): 63–78.

Boisot, M. H. 1995. Is your firm a creative destroyer? Competitive learning and knowledge flows in the technological strategies of firms. *Research Policy,* 24: 489–506.

Buckley, P. J. 1991. The frontiers of international business research. *Management International Review,* 31 (Special Issue): 7–22.

Buckley, P., and M. Casson. 1988. A theory of cooperation in international business. In F. Contractor and P. Lorange, editors, *Cooperative Strategies in International Business,* 31–53. San Francisco: New Lexington Press.

Calvet, A. L. 1981. A synthesis of foreign direct investment theories and theories of the multinational firm. *Journal of International Business Studies,* Spring/Summer: 43–59.

Cangelosi, V. E., and W. R. Dill. 1965. Organizational learning: Observations toward a theory. *Administrative Science Quarterly,* 10: 175–203.

Casson, M. 1993. Contractual arrangements for technology transfer: New evidence from business history. In G. Jones, editor, *Coalitions and Collaboration in International Business,* 18–50. Hants, England: E. Elgar.

Chang, S. J. 1995. International expansion strategy of Japanese firms: Capability building through sequential entry. *Academy of Management Journal*, 38(2): 383–407.

Cohen, W., and D. Levinthal. 1990. Absorptive capacity: A new perspective on learning and innovation. *Administrative Science Quarterly*, 35: 128–152.

Conference Board, Inc. 1994. Strategic alliances survey. *James W. McKee Forum on International Management*, 11, May.

Crossan, M., H. Lane, R. E. White, and L. Djurfeldt. 1995. Organizational learning: Dimensions for a theory. *The International Journal of Organizational Analysis*, 3(4): 383–406.

Daft, R. L., and K. E. Weick. 1984. Towards a model of organizations as interpretive systems. *Academy of Management Review*, 9(2): 284–295.

Davies, H. 1977. Technology transfer through commercial transactions. *The Journal of Industrial Economics*, 26(2).

Dorroh, J. R., T. R. Gulledge, and N. K. Womer. 1994. Investment in knowledge: A generalization of learning by experience. *Management Science*, 40(8): 947–958.

Duncan, R., and A. Weiss. 1979. Organizational learning: Implications for organizational design. *Research in Organizational Behavior*, 1: 75–123.

Dunning, J. H. 1988. The eclectic paradigm of international production: A restatement and some possible extensions. *Journal of International Business Studies*, 19(1): 1–31.

Ernst and Young. 1995. Sustaining advantage: Managing knowledge in practice. *Mastering Information and Technology, Note no. 6*, February.

Fiol, C. M., and M. A. Lyles. 1985. Organizational learning. *Academy of Management Review*, 10(4): 803–813.

Geringer, M. 1988a. *Joint Venture Partner Selection*. Westport, Conn.: Greenwood Press.

Geringer, M. 1988b. Partner selection criteria for developed country joint ventures. *Business Quarterly*, Summer: 55–68.

Geringer, M. 1991. Strategic determinants of partner selection criteria in international joint ventures. *Journal of International Business Studies*, 22(1): 41–62.

Geringer, M., and L. Hébert. 1989. Control and performance in international joint ventures. *Journal of International Business Studies*, 20(2): 235–254.

Ghoshal, S. 1987. Global strategy: An organizing framework. *Strategic Management Journal*, 8: 425–440.

Gomes-Casseres, B. 1994. Group versus group: How alliance networks compete. *Harvard Business Review*, July-August: 62–74.

Gulati, R. 1995. Does familiarity breed trust? The implications of repeated ties for contractual choice in alliances. *Academy of Management Journal*, 38(1): 85–112.

Gupta, A. K., and V. Govindarajan. 1991. Knowledge flows and the structure of control within multinational corporations. *Academy of Management Review*, 16(4): 768–792.

Hagedoorn, J. 1995. Strategic technology partnering during the 1980's: Trends, networks and corporate patterns in non-core technologies. *Research Policy*, 24: 207–231.

Hamel, G. 1991. Competition for competence and inter-partner learning within international strategic alliances. *Strategic Management Journal*, 12: 83–103.

Hamel, G., Y. L. Doz, and C. K. Prahalad. 1989. Collaborate with your competitors—and win. *Harvard Business Review*, January-February: 133–139.

Hamel, G., and C. K. Prahalad. 1989. Strategic intent. *Harvard Business Review*, 67(3): 63–76.

Harbison, J. R., and P. Pekar Jr. 1993. *A Practical Guide to Alliances: Leapfrogging the Learning Curve*. Los Angeles: Booz-Allen and Hamilton.

Harrigan, K. R. 1985. *Strategies for Joint Ventures*. San Francisco: New Lexington Press.

Hawkins, P. 1994. Organizational learning: Taking stock and facing the challenge. *Management Learning*, 25(1): 71–82.

Hedberg, B. 1981. How organizations learn and unlearn. In P. C. Nystrom and W. H. Starbuck, editors, *Handbook of Organizational Design*. New York: Oxford University Press.

Hedlund, G. 1994. A model of knowledge management and the N-form corporation. *Strategic Management Journal*, 15: 73–90.

Helleloid, D., and B. L. Simonin. 1994. Collaborative know-how: The construct, measurement and theoretical links. Paper presented at the Academy of Management 1994 Annual Meeting, Dallas; Organization and Management Theory Division Program, AMA Proceedings.

Huber, G. P. 1991. Organizational learning: The contributing processes and the literatures. *Organization Science*, 2(1): 88–115.

Inkpen, A. 1992. *Learning and collaboration: An examination of North American–Japanese joint ventures*. Unpublished Ph.D. dissertation, Western Business School, University of Western Ontario.

Inkpen, A. 1995. Organizational learning and international joint ventures. *Journal of International Management*, 1: 165–198.

Isaacs, W. 1993. Taking flight: Dialogue, collective thinking, and organizational learning. *Organizational Dynamics,* 22(2): 24–39.

Johanson, J., and J.-E. Vahlne. 1977. The internationalization process of the firm: A model of knowledge development and increasing foreign market commitments. *Journal of International Business Studies,* 8(1): 23–32.

Kanter, R. M. 1994a. What "thinking globally" really means. Afterword in *Global Strategies: Insights from the World's Leading Thinkers.* Harvard Business Review Book: 227–232.

Kanter, R. M. 1994b. Collaborative advantage: The art of alliances. *Harvard Business Review,* July-August: 96–108.

Killing, J. P. 1982. How to make global joint ventures work. *Harvard Business Review,* May-June: 120–127.

Killing, J. P. 1983. *Strategies for Joint Venture Success.* New York: Praeger.

Kim, D. H. 1993. The link between individual and organizational learning. *Sloan Management Review,* Fall: 37–50.

Kim, W. C., and P. Hwang. 1992. Global strategy and multinationals entry mode choice. *Journal of International Business Studies,* 23(1): 29–54.

Kogut, B. 1989. The stability of joint ventures: Reciprocity and competitive rivalry. *Journal of Industrial Economics,* 38(2): 183–198.

Kogut, B., and U. Zander. 1993. Knowledge of the firm and the evolutionary theory of the multinational corporation. *Journal of International Business Studies,* 24(4): 625–646.

Kras, E. S. 1989. *Management in Two Cultures.* Yarmouth, Maine: Intercultural Press.

Lane, H. W., and J. J. DiStefano. 1992. *International Management Behavior.* Boston: PWS-Kent.

Lawrence, J. J., and R.-S. Yeh. 1994. The influence of Mexican culture on the use of Japanese manufacturing techniques in Mexico. *Management International Review,* 34(1): 49–66.

Levitt, B., and J. G. March. 1988. Organizational learning. *Annual Review of Sociology,* 14: 319–340.

Lewis, L., and D. Seibold. 1993. Innovation modification during intraorganizational adoption. *Academy of Management Review,* 18(2): 322–354.

Li, J., and S. Guisinger. 1991. Comparative business failures of foreign-controlled firms in the United States. *Journal of International Business Studies,* 22(2): 209–224.

Lundberg, C. 1989. On organizational learning: Implications and opportunities for expanding organizational development. *Research in Organizational Change and Development,* 3: 61–82.

Lyles, M. A. 1988. Learning among joint venture sophisticated firms. *Management International Review,* Special Issue: 85–98.

Lyles, M. A., and J. E. Salk. 1997. Knowledge acquisition from foreign parents in international joint ventures: An empirical examination in the Hungarian context. In P. W. Beamish and J. P. Killing, editors, *Cooperative Strategies: European Perspectives.* San Francisco: New Lexington Press.

Lyles, M. A., and C. R. Schwenk. 1992. Top management, strategy and organizational knowledge structures. *Journal of Management Studies,* 29(2): 155–174.

Madhok, A. 1995. Revisiting multinational firms' tolerance for joint ventures: A trust-based approach. *Journal for International Business Studies,* 26(1): 117–138.

Makino, S., and A. Delios. 1997. Local knowledge transfer and performance: Implications for alliance formation in Asia. In P. W. Beamish and J. P. Killing, editors, *Cooperative Strategies: Asian Pacific Perspectives.* San Francisco: New Lexington Press.

March, J. G., and J. P. Olsen. 1975. Organizational learning under ambiguity. *European Journal of Policy Review,* 3(2): 147–171.

Margolis, H. 1993. *Paradigms and Barriers: How Habits of Mind Govern Scientific Beliefs.* Chicago: University of Chicago Press.

Mariti, O., and R. H. Smiley. 1983. Co-operative agreements and the organization of industry. *The Journal of Industrial Economics,* 31(4), 437–451.

Nonaka, I. 1991. The knowledge-creating company. *Harvard Business Review,* November-December: 96–104.

Nonaka, I. 1994. A dynamic theory of organizational knowledge creation. *Organization Science,* 5(1): 14–37.

Nonaka, I., and H. Takeuchi. 1995. *The Knowledge-Creating Company.* New York: Oxford University Press.

Ohmae, K. 1989. The global logic of strategic alliances. Reprinted in *Global Strategies: Insights from the World's Leading Thinkers.* Harvard Business Review Book, 109–128.

Parkhe, A. 1991. Interfirm diversity, organizational learning, and longevity in global strategic alliances. *Journal of International Business Studies,* 22(4): 579–602.

Parkhe, A. 1993. "Messy" research, methodological predispositions, and theory development in international joint ventures. *Academy of Management Review,* 18(2): 227–268.

Perlmutter, H. V., and D. A. Heenan. 1986. Thinking ahead: cooperate to compete globally. *Harvard Business Review,* 64(2): 136–152.

Pfeffer, J. 1993. Barrier to the advance of organizational science: Paradigm development as a dependent variable. *Academy of Management Review,* 18(4): 599–620.

Polanyi, M. 1958. *Personal Knowledge.* Chicago: University of Chicago Press.

Polanyi, M. 1966. *The Tacit Dimension.* London: Routledge.

Powell, W. 1987. Hybrid organizational arrangements: New form or transitional development? *California Management Review,* 67–87.

Pucik, V. 1991. Technology transfer in strategic alliances: Competitive collaboration and organizational learning. In T. Agmon and M. A. Von Glinow, editors, *Technology Transfer in International Business,* 121–142. New York: Oxford University Press.

Reed, R., and R. DeFillippi. 1990. Causal ambiguity, barriers to imitation and sustainable competitive advantage. *Academy of Management Review,* 15(1): 88–102.

Root, F. 1988. Some taxonomies of international cooperative arrangements. In F. Contractor and P. Lorange, editors, *Cooperative Strategies in International Business,* 69–80. San Francisco: New Lexington Press.

Schaan, J.-L. 1983. *Parent Control and Joint Venture Success: The Case of Mexico.* Unpublished Ph.D. dissertation, Western Business School, University of Western Ontario, London.

Schein, E. H. 1993. On dialogue, culture and organizational learning. *Organizational Dynamics,* 22(2): 40–51.

Schrader, S. 1991. Informal technology transfer between firms: Cooperation through information trading. *Research Policy,* 20(2): 153–170.

Seely Brown, J., and P. Duguid. 1991. Organizational learning and communities of practice: Toward a unifying view of working, learning and innovation. *Organization Science,* 2(1): 40–56.

Senge, P. M. 1990. The leaders' new work: Building learning organizations. *Sloan Management Review,* 32(1): 7–23.

Shrivastava, P. 1983. A typology of organizational learning systems. *Journal of Management Studies,* 20(1): 7–28.

Simon, H. A. 1991. Bounded rationality and organizational learning. *Organization Science,* 2(1): 125–133.

Simonin, B. 1991. *Transfer of Knowledge in International Strategic Alliances: A Structural Approach.* Unpublished Ph.D. dissertation, University of Michigan, Ann Arbor.

Stacey, R. 1991. *The Chaos Frontier: Creative Strategic Control for Business.* London: Butterworth-Heinemann.

Tallman, S. B., and O. Shenkar. 1994. A managerial decision model of international cooperative venture formation. *Journal of International Business Studies,* 25(1): 91–113.

Toyne, B. 1989. International exchange: A foundation for theory building in international business. *Journal of International Business Studies,* 20(1): 1–17.

Ulrich, D., T. Jick, and M. A. Von Glinow. 1993. High impact learning: Building and diffusing learning capability. *Organizational Dynamics,* 22(2): 52–66.

Von Glinow, M. A., and M. Teagarden. 1988. The transfer of human resource management technology in Sino-US cooperative ventures: Problems and solutions. *Human Resource Management,* 27(2): 201–229.

Watkins, K., and V. Marsick. 1993. *Sculpting the Learning Organization: Lessons in the Art and Science of Systemic Change.* San Francisco: Jossey-Bass.

Weick, K. E. 1979. *The Social Psychology of Organizing.* Reading, Mass.: Addison-Wesley.

Wernerfelt, B. 1984. A resource-based view of the firm. *Strategic Management Journal,* 5: 171–180.

Westney, D. E. 1988. Domestic and foreign learning curves in managing international cooperative strategies. In F. Contractor and P. Lorange, editors, *Cooperative Strategies in International Business,* 339–346. San Francisco: New Lexington Press.

Wright, L., H. Lane, and P. Beamish. 1988. International management research: Lessons from the field. *International Studies of Management and Organization,* 18(3): 55–71.

PART FIVE

STRATEGY AND PERFORMANCE OF COOPERATIVE ALLIANCES

15

CHARACTERISTICS OF CANADA-BASED INTERNATIONAL JOINT VENTURES

Louis Hébert and Paul Beamish

THIS CHAPTER INVESTIGATES *foreign investment in Canada using joint ventures. Selected characteristics of these international joint ventures (IJVs) are reviewed, providing insights on the relationships linking their strategic motivations, structure, and performance. The research demonstrates that IJVs are formed to speed up market entry, that they generally involve fifty-fifty equity splits, and that they exhibit relatively high performance rates. Furthermore, several differences are observed between the IJV strategy of European firms and that of American ones.*

IN THE PAST, international joint ventures (IJVs) were most often used to exploit peripheral markets or technologies, or involved activities of marginal importance to the parent firm's competitive position. However, these shared equity and decision-making arrangements are now viewed as critical components of an organization's business unit network (Porter and Fuller 1986); JVs have become strategic weapons for competing within a firm's core markets and technologies (Harrigan 1988a). The frequency and number of JVs have also skyrocketed in recent years, a trend expected to con-

The authors would like to thank the Center for International Business Studies and the Plan for Excellence of the Richard Ivey School of Business and the Faculty Research Development Program of Concordia University for the assistance provided for this research.

tinue in the current decade (Deloitte, Haskins and Sells International 1989; Anderson 1990). In this context, the effective management of IJVs achieves considerable importance; it relies on, among other things, a thorough understanding of their dynamics as well as of their benefits and pitfalls.

This chapter investigates foreign investments in Canada that take the form of IJVs, and reviews selected characteristics of them. The objective is to provide insights on the relationships linking the strategic motivations, structure, and performance of these organizations. Prior research has studied IJVs from developed and less developed countries (Beamish 1985; 1988), and from newly industrialized countries (Lee and Beamish 1995; Erden 1997). Early research also examined some general characteristics of U.S.-based domestic and international JVs (Harrigan 1985; 1988b) as well as trends in international cooperative agreements in the 1980s (Hergert and Morris 1988) and the 1990s (Beamish and Delios 1997b). Here, we build on these earlier efforts and present new, up-to-date material on developed-country IJVs, specifically those in operation in Canada. It provides a greater emphasis on characteristics related to the management of IJVs, as has been recommended previously (for example, Beamish 1993). Our basic proposition is that parent firms pursue different IJV strategies that are associated with the firms' structures. In examining the characteristics of these IJVs, attention will also be given to ventures involving American and European parent firms. These firms represent the majority of the foreign investors in Canada who use the JV form of investment. Prior research has shown differences in the patterns of international cooperation across countries and economic blocs (Hergert and Morris 1988; Beamish and Delios 1997b); similarly, it has been suggested that the dynamics of IJVs vary with the nationality of the parent firms (Gerlach 1987; Hamel, Doz, and Prahalad 1989; Parkhe 1993; Olson and Singsuwan 1997). Therefore, this chapter also investigates whether firms with different national origins, in this case American and European, rely on distinct IJV strategies and structural arrangements.

In addition, results are reported of a 1991–1993 study on Canada-based IJVs (that is, JVs with at least one parent firm headquartered outside Canada). The study focused on two-parent manufacturing IJVs, where none of the parent firms held more than 75 percent of the equity. Qualifying ventures included those in operation in 1985 and those formed between then and 1992. These parameters resulted in a sample of terminated and surviving IJVs, and limited the bias toward surviving ventures. In the study, data were collected from parent firm managers responsible for the IJVs and general managers of the ventures. In-person interviews and a survey questionnaire were used for data collection on seventy IJVs, out of an estimated population of ninety-three. The limited purpose here did not permit extensive use of sophisticated statistical techniques, but when possible, statistical tests (mostly *t*-tests) were performed to assess the significance of the differences observed among IJVs with American and European parent firms. The steps and procedures followed for data analysis, as well as the definitions, measures, and scales used for all constructs, are included in the chapter appendix.

The chapter is divided into three sections. The first presents characteristics of Canada-based IJVs, providing information on the motives of foreign firms for establishing them in Canada. The second section looks at their structure and management. In the third section, statistics on their performance are presented.

The Strategic Dynamics of Canada-Based IJVs

Though few attempts have been made to provide a demographic and statistical image of IJVs in a single country—Canada or any other—such an image appears essential to understanding the motives and other factors underlying decisions to form them. Therefore, the profiles of Canada-based IJVs are reviewed here: the origins of their parent firms, their size, their industry, their technological advancement, their export orientation, the motives behind their formation, and their strategic relationships with their foreign parents.

Origins of Foreign Parent Firms

The nationalities of foreign parent firms involved in IJVs in Canada reflect the country's main international trade partners, as demonstrated in Figure 15.1. A majority originate in the U.S. and Europe. In the study sample of seventy IJVs, Canadian firms were associated with thirty-four American firms, thirteen European firms, four Japanese firms, and one Australian firm. There were also seven IJVs between pairs of American firms and one between two European firms. The others are American firms associated in Canada with other than Canadian partners: six European, three Japanese, and one Australian.

Size of IJVs

Canada-based IJVs were found to be of various sizes, measured in terms of sales in Canadian dollars. Most could be characterized as small or medium-sized firms (see Table 15.1). Approximately 55 percent had sales of $25 million or less; only 9 percent had sales over $100 million. IJVs involving European parent firms tended to be smaller than those with American

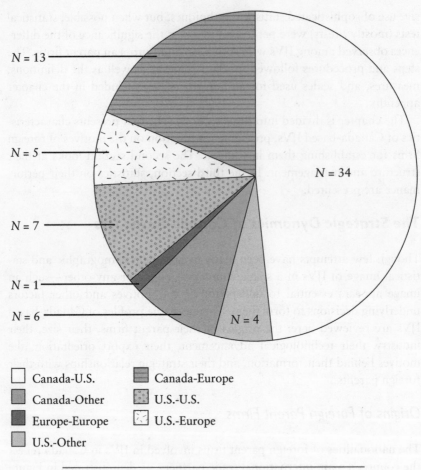

$N = 13$

$N = 5$

$N = 7$

$N = 1$

$N = 6$

$N = 34$

$N = 4$

☐ Canada-U.S.   ▨ Canada-Europe

▨ Canada-Other   ▨ U.S.-U.S.

▨ Europe-Europe   ▨ U.S.-Europe

☐ U.S.-Other

Figure 15.1. Origins of Parent Firms ($N = 70$).

parents. The relatively small average size of Canada-based IJVs mirrors the structure of Canadian industry, in which small and medium enterprises dominate.

Industry

Most Canada-based IJVs were found to be in the manufacturing industries. As is often the case with foreign investment in Canada, more than a third of these are traditional and resource-based industries such as the textile, wood, and paper product industries. A notable proportion of IJVs were also in capital-intensive industries such as fabricated metal and machinery (10 percent) and chemical products (16 percent). This may underline that reducing capital investments as well as sharing costs and risks are

	All IJVs (N = 70)	IJVs with American Parents (N = 41)	IJVs with European Parents (N = 20)
SIZE (in percent of all IJVs)			
Less than $25 million	55	52	65
$26 to $50 million	29	31	23
$51 to $100 million	6	7	6
More than $100 million	9	9	6
INDUSTRY (in percent of all IJVs)			
Food	7	9	—
Plastic products	7	7	5
Textiles and clothing	4	4	5
Wood and furniture	9	9	9
Pulp and paper	11	15	5
Printing	4	—	5
Primary metal	1	2	—
Fabricated metal	10	9	10
Transportation equipment	7	4	5
Electrical products	4	4	5
Nonmetal. mineral products	4	4	—
Chemicals	16	15	33
Other manufacturing	9	11	5
Not identified	6	7	13
TECHNOLOGICAL ADVANCEMENT[a]			
Product technology	4.1	4.0	4.7*
Process technology	4.1	4.1	4.3
LEVEL OF EXPORTS (in percent of all IJVs)			
Less than 15 percent of sales	50	60	39
16–49 percent of sales	24	28	22
50 percent of sales and more	26	12	39

Table 15.1. General Characteristics of Canada-Based IJVs.
[a]N = 55; Scale: 1 = Less advanced than competitors. 3 = Similar to competitors.
5 = More advanced than competitors.
*$p < 0.05$

objectives often associated with the formation of IJVs. IJVs with an American parent firm were typically found in the traditional, resource-based industries (43 percent), as compared to technology-intensive industries such as transportation equipment, electrical products, and chemicals (25 percent). The distribution of IJVs with European parents was almost exactly opposite: a larger proportion of ventures in technology-intensive industries (43 percent) than in traditional ones (24 percent).

Technological Advancement

Participants in the study were asked to assess the degree of advancement of their IJV's product and process technology, compared to that of their primary competitors. The objective of this was to evaluate whether IJVs provide access to technologies considered common or more advanced. On a five-point scale, IJVs were thought to involve both product (4.1) and process technology (4.1) more advanced than the competition. This characteristic was especially salient for the product technology of IJVs with European parents. These ventures' technological gap with competitors was thought to be significantly greater ($p < 0.05$) than in the case of American-parent IJVs. Such figures suggest that IJVs can represent sources of advanced technologies for Canadian firms. The formation of IJVs could even represent an approach to modernize certain sectors of Canadian industry, or at least to gain access to technological resources more advanced than usual North American standards.

Level of Exports

Examination of exports of Canada-based IJVs revealed two basic types of orientation. The first type had a Canadian market focus; representing 50 percent of all IJVs, these ventures have less than 15 percent of their sales in the form of exports (see Table 15.1). The second type, accounting for 26 percent of sample IJVs, export more than 50 percent of their sales.

A comparison of American- and European-parent IJVs revealed some notable differences. IJVs with American parents appeared to focus on the Canadian domestic market (on average, 28 percent of sales in exports), while a significant number of European-parent IJVs devoted more attention to export markets (39 percent of sales; $p < 0.10$). These differences suggest that Canada-based IJVs can serve two distinct purposes. For a majority of foreign firms, particularly American parent firms, IJVs were formed to cater primarily to the Canadian domestic market. Other foreign firms, mostly with European origins, used their Canadian jointly owned operations as a base for accessing other markets. Nonetheless, the presence of IJVs could be interpreted as a source of important export revenues for Canadian industry.

Motives of Formation

Foreign parent firms were asked to indicate the importance of various objectives in their decisions to establish jointly owned operations in Canada (see Table 15.2). Globally, they suggested that facilitating rapid market entry and exploiting the firm's technology were the most important objectives. The importance given to these may reflect the role JVs can play in firms' internationalization strategies and their attempts to exploit distinctive technologies or products in the Canadian market. This interpretation would also be consistent with the importance given to accessing already established distribution channels. In addition, compared to American firms, European firms attached greater importance to the exploitation of their technology and the development of new products, and less importance to obtaining their partner's technology and raw materials. Finally, it is interesting to note the limited importance all foreign parents attributed to accessing their partner's skills (and probably their Canadian partner's skills) in marketing and technology.

Building from the JV literature, these results stress the importance of technological and market access–related motivations in firms' decisions to participate in IJVs. Nevertheless, investigation of the partner firms' respective contributions, specifically of the Canadian and foreign firms, sheds more light on the formation dynamics of IJVs in Canada. In the formation of such IJVs, the following pattern of contributions emerges:

- Both parent firms contribute management and financial resources.
- Foreign parents assume responsibility for providing product and process technology, patents and trademarks, and R&D resources.
- Canadian firms assume responsibility for contributing marketing, distribution channels, and manufacturing facilities.

This division of contributions shows that Canada-based IJVs follow the most common formation pattern: one parent firm provides technology, and its partner contributes marketing resources. It suggests also that Canadian parent firms contribute the marketing and distribution resources, which can be more easily replaced or learned than those of the foreign partners (Blodgett 1991). From a more critical perspective, this situation could

Objectives[a]	All Foreign Parents (N = 55)	American Parents (N = 29)	European Parents (N = 12)
Spread risk by having partner	2.8	2.7	3.7
Reduce capital investment	2.5	2.3	3.3
Obtain access to marketing skills	2.2	2.3	2.0
Access distribution channels	2.9	3.0	3.1
Obtain partner's technology, patent, etc.	2.5	2.7	1.7*
Facilitate rapid market entry	4.5	4.4	4.2
Promote development of new product	2.9	2.9	3.3*
Obtain raw materials	2.9	3.0	2.0***
Exploit your firm's technology	3.9	3.8	4.3**
Reduce costs, risks of technology development	3.2	3.2	3.6

**Table 15.2. Importance of Various Objectives in Foreign Parents'
Decisions to Establish IJVs in Canada.**
[a]*1 = Not important. 3 = Moderately important. 5 = Very important.*
$*p < 0.10$ $**p < 0.05$ $***p < 0.01$

reflect that several Canadian firms have little to offer to foreign firms besides their Canadian identity and their distribution channels. They join in IJVs to facilitate access to the Canadian environment and to provide local manufacturing of products developed in another country.

Strategic Relationships with Foreign Parent Firms

Further understanding of the motives behind forming IJVs can be obtained by examining how the ventures are related to the product and market focus of foreign parent firms. IJVs were classified into different categories depending on whether they were in the same product and market segment as their foreign parent, whether they involved some form of product or geographical market diversification, or whether they represented some form of vertical integration. From Table 15.3, it is evident that the formation of Canada-based IJVs is most frequently done to achieve diversification, particularly in geographical terms. A significant portion of IJVs also involve

Strategic Relationships	All IJVs (N = 70)	IJVs with American Parents (N = 41)	IJVs with European Parents (N = 20)
Same product and market segment	10	10	10
Product diversification	23	23	24
Geographical market diversification	36	36	33
Product and market diversification	15	19	10
Upstream vertical integration	12	10	14
Downstream vertical integration	1	—	5
Not available	3	3	3

Table 15.3. Strategic Relationships of IJVs with Foreign Parent Firms.
Note: Figures are percentages of the total of IJVs.

product diversification. They are less often used for vertical integration, or in product and market segments where foreign firms are already present.

Examination of the strategic relationships confirms earlier observations on the motivations and dynamics of IJV formation in Canada. Essentially, foreign firms perceive IJVs as a means to exploit their distinctive products and technologies in a new market, the Canadian one. They use the joint form of investment primarily to speed up market entry, to gain access to existing distribution channels, and to reduce the risks and capital investment associated with the creation of local manufacturing facilities. Yet beyond these similarities, American and European parent firms appear to pursue different strategies. European firms typically invest in technology-intensive industries and introduce relatively advanced technology products. They also use their Canadian jointly owned operations as a base to access the entire North America market. In contrast, the American firms' strategies appear more conventional, focusing on industries traditionally favored by foreign investors and on serving Canadian domestic demand.

The Structure of Canada-Based IJVS

Division of Equity

In 66 percent of Canada-based IJVs, equity was found to be divided fifty-fifty between the partners (see Table 15.4). In few IJVs do the foreign partners express a preference for a minority or a majority portion of equity,

	All IJVs (N = 70)	IJVs with American Parents (N = 41)	IJVs with European Parents (N = 20)
Foreign minority ownership	10	15	5
50–50 JVs	66	67	62
Foreign majority ownership	24	16	33

Table 15.4. Division of Equity in Canada-Based IJVs.
Note: Figures are percentages of the total of IJVs.

which is believed to be consistent with the most common patterns of division of control in developed-country IJVs. No significant differences were observed between American-parent and European-parent IJVs in this regard, although European parents more often sought a majority ownership position.

Patterns of Division of Control

The division of management responsibilities, or division of control, between IJVs' parent firms has often been described as an important factor in IJV success. To examine this characteristic, this study builds on Killing (1982), who identified three distinct structures of control: dominant control structures (where only one parent firm plays a role in decision making), shared control structures (where both parents play an active role in decision making) and autonomous structures (where the JV enjoys extensive autonomy).

This classification was used in studying the division of control in Canada-based IJVs, particularly the extent to which control is shared between parent firms and the extent of autonomy enjoyed by these ventures. The extent of control sharing and JV autonomy was examined in three groups of activities: operation control, including nine decision areas of an operational nature (hiring and firing of technical, nontechnical, and management personnel; pricing; distribution; marketing; day-to-day management; cost control; and manufacturing); technological control, involving four technology-related decisions and activities (patents and trademarks, product technology, process technology, and R&D activities); and strategic control, including four strategy-related decisions (financing of the JV, nomination of the JV general manager [JVGM], location of the JV, and capital expenditure). The extent of control sharing was measured on a 3-point scale, where 1 indicates that *one parent firm controls the venture,*

2 indicates that *one parent firm exercises greater but not complete control,* and 3 indicates that *parent firms share control.*

Using these three dimensions of control, the extent of control sharing was found to vary considerably across activities of IJVs (see Table 15.5). For instance, control over strategic decisions appears to be more shared than other decisions and activities, a situation interpreted as reflecting the shared decision-making nature of IJVs. These decisions are also commonly involved in veto rights found in typical IJV agreements (Killing 1982; Schaan 1983). Dominant control appears to be more frequently exercised over technological activities. Parent firms' attempts to ensure protection of their technological assets and competencies may explain this; dominant control over technology-related decisions would be expected to reduce the risks of leakages or of undesired transfers of technology to the partner firm or even to third parties. Patterns of division of control over operational decisions and activities were more diversified. Overall, operational decisions fell between strategic and technological ones in terms of control sharing. Finally, no significant differences (at the 0.05 level) were found in the division of control between American-parent and European-parent IJVs.

In addition to the extent of control sharing found in IJVs, which parent firm exercises more or less control was also identified in order to evaluate the extent of control exercised by foreign firms compared to Canadian ones. The number of IJVs with dominant control by the foreign partner was compared to the number with shared control and Canadian or local dominant control using the three dimensions of control identified earlier.

For operational control, none of the three possibilities is dominant (see Table 15.6). Again, shared strategic control is most common, and the foreign partner most frequently (50 percent of the time) dominates technological control. Shared control and Canadian dominant control were used in only 15 percent and 35 percent of IJVs, respectively. The presence of foreign dominant control is more evident when comparing IJVs with American and European parents. European parent firms showed preferences toward the exercise of dominant control over operational activities, and especially over technological activities and decisions. In sum, not only do foreign firms form JVs to exploit their technological resources in the Canadian market, but they also tend to maintain dominant control over these resources. These results are consistent with recent studies linking parent firms' motivations and contributions with IJV control structures (Child, Yan, and Lu 1997; Lin, Yu, and Seetoo 1997). They also support the common relationship between ownership and control observed in developed-country IJVs (Killing 1982; Beamish 1985, 1993). An equal or fifty-fifty equity split was generally associated with shared control, and majority equity with dominant control.

CONTROL SHARING

	All IJVs (N = 70)	IJVs with American Parents (N = 41)	IJVs with European Parents (N = 20)
Operational control			
Hiring and firing nontechnical personnel	1.85	1.77	1.88
Hiring and firing technical personnel	1.83	1.75	1.83
Pricing	1.94	1.83	2.06
Distribution	1.81	1.65	1.98
Marketing	1.72	1.58	1.68
Day-to-day management	1.63	1.62	1.48
Hiring and firing JV senior managers	2.03	1.87	2.11
Cost control	2.07	1.95	2.23
Manufacturing	1.80	1.79	1.64
Total	1.92	1.81	1.99
Technological control			
Patents and trademarks	1.51	1.51	1.46
Technology or engineering of product	1.64	1.69	1.54
Process technology	1.76	1.77	1.83
R&D	1.76	1.77	1.59
Total	1.70	1.68	1.61
Strategic control			
Hiring and firing JV general manager	2.38	2.27	2.45
Financing of the JV	2.37	2.36	2.11*
Deciding capital expenditures	2.74	2.67	2.78
Location of the JV	2.31	2.26	2.20
Total	2.45	2.39	2.38

Table 15.5. Division of Control in Canada-Based IJVs.

*Note: Numbers represent the IJV's position on the following scale:
1 = One parent firm controls the venture. 2 = One parent firm exercises
greater but not complete control. 3 = Parent firms share control.*

*p < 0.10

	All IJVs (N = 70)	IJVs with American Parents (N = 41)	IJVs with European Parents (N = 20)
Operational control			
Foreign dominant control	32	28	50
Shared control	31	34	25
Canadian or local dominant control	37	38	25
Technological control			
Foreign dominant control	50	41	63
Shared control	15	21	13
Canadian or local dominant control	35	38	24
Strategic control			
Foreign dominant control	18	17	25
Shared control	65	62	75
Canadian or local dominant control	17	21	0

Table 15.6. Division of Control Structures in IJVs.
Note: Numbers are percentages of the total IJVs.

Patterns of Autonomy

The autonomy of Canada-based IJVs was assessed along the same dimensions as the division of control: operational, technological, and strategic. As seen in Table 15.7, IJVs generally enjoy extensive operational autonomy. Decisions over these activities appear to be made mostly by IJV managers, rather than by parent firm managers. In turn, these IJVs have considerably less technological autonomy, and especially limited strategic autonomy; strategic decision making is usually assumed by parent firm managers. This limited autonomy for technological and strategic decisions suggests that parent firms attempt to achieve significant coordination between their activities and those of their IJVs. However, IJVs with European parents exhibit less operational and technological autonomy than ventures with American parents.

An attempt was also made to identify independent IJVs—ones that are entirely autonomous. Only 10 percent of all IJVs were found to be independent for strategic decisions, in contrast to 43 percent and 81 percent

	All IJVs (N = 70)	IJVs with American Parents (N = 41)	IJVs with European Parents (N = 20)
AUTONOMY			
Operational autonomy			
Hiring and firing nontechnical personnel	1.66	1.54	1.89
Hiring and firing technical personnel	1.78	1.68	2.00
Pricing	2.42	2.41	2.61
Distribution	2.36	2.32	2.63
Marketing	2.42	2.41	2.61
Day-to-day management	1.82	1.77	2.14
Hiring and firing JV senior managers	2.78	2.66	2.83
Cost control	2.17	2.06	2.43
Manufacturing	2.11	2.09	2.29
Total	2.21	2.14	2.42
Technological autonomoy			
Patents and trademarks	3.68	3.67	3.88
Technology or engineering of product	3.19	3.17	3.23
Process technology	2.49	2.41	2.98
R&D	3.13	3.07	3.51
Total	3.10	3.12	3.40
Strategic autonomy			
Financing of the JV	3.92	3.92	3.67
Deciding capital expenditures	3.61	3.57	3.64
Location of the JV	3.69	3.52	3.91
Total	3.74	3.67	3.74

Table 15.7. Autonomy of Canada-Based IJVs.
Note: Numbers represent the IJV's position on the following scale:
1 = Decided totally by JV managers. 3 = Shared equally by JV and
parent managers. 5 = Decided totally by parent firm managers.

for technological and operational decisions, respectively. Consistent with prior research (Beamish 1993), the proportion of IJVs classified as independent overall was modest (6 percent—four IJVs). Fewer European-parent IJVs were identified as independent overall (just one, as opposed to three American-parent IJVs) or in each of the decision areas.

In sum, European and American firms appear to pursue different IJV strategies and to rely on different structures for their IJVs. The structure of IJVs with American parents reflect the conventionality of their strategies, with greater autonomy and reliance on a fifty-fifty division of equity. European parents maintain closer control over their IJVs; probably as a result of their technological emphasis, they more frequently tend to exercise dominant control and to leave less autonomy to their Canada-based IJVs compared to other foreign investors.

The Performance and Success of Canada-Based IJVs

The performance and success of Canada-based IJVs was evaluated through two perceptual measures of success: the satisfaction of the parent firms and the business performance of the IJVs. The former was selected because it is one of the most frequently used performance variables in the JV literature; it has been found to be an effective predictor of parent firms' future actions in partnerships and a necessary precursor to long-term performance (Beamish 1984; Anderson and Weitz 1989; Anderson and Narus 1990). Satisfaction of the parent firms was assessed with respect to the IJV in general, its performance, and the relationship between the parent firms. The second variable, business performance of the IJV, can be defined as the extent to which an IJV has achieved the expectations the parent firm had of it when the IJV was formed (Geringer and Hébert 1991). It was measured along ten performance dimensions, ranging from sales to product technology and overall performance.

Levels of Satisfaction and Performance

In general, Canada-based IJVs exhibit relatively high performance (see Table 15.8). For instance, based on mean scores, parent firms appear to be at least moderately satisfied with their IJVs in general, with their performance, and with the relationship with their partners. Fewer than 13 percent of IJVs had dissatisfied parent firms, and 47 percent were associated with some degree of mutual satisfaction. Foreign parent firms also expressed at least some satisfaction with their IJVs, although in a smaller and not statistically significant manner. Similarly, a majority of IJVs performed at or above parent firms' initial expectations: overall performance was judged to

	All IJVs (N = 70)	IJVs with American Parents (N = 41)	IJVs with European Parents (N = 20)
Satisfaction[a]			
JV	3.71	3.59	3.60
JV's performance	3.72	3.68	3.66
Relationship between partners	3.53	3.44	3.35
Total	3.65	3.57	3.54
Business performance[b]			
Sales	2.97	3.00	3.07
Profitability	2.92	2.88	2.96
Market share	3.14	3.18	3.09
Management of the JV	3.37	3.29	3.38
Technology or engineering of product	3.31	3.23	3.36
Process technology	3.39	3.36	3.37
Manufacturing	3.38	3.39	3.24
Marketing	3.07	3.06	3.00
Distribution	3.16	3.18	3.01
Overall performance	3.03	3.00	3.00
Total	3.18	3.16	3.15

Table 15.8. Performance of Canada-Based IJVs.

[a]*1 = Very dissatisifed. 3 = Neither dissatisfied nor satisfied. 5 = Very satisfied.*
[b]*1 = Much below initial expectations. 3 = About equal to expectations.*
5 = Much above initial expectations.

be equal to or above initial expectations for 60 percent of all IJVs. Sales and profitability performance were described as being equal to or above initial expectations for 63 percent and 64 percent percent of IJVs, respectively.

In sum, these results suggest that the performance of Canada-based IJVs is satisfactory, better than that reported in the JV literature generally (Anderson 1990; Beamish and Delios 1997a), even though the results were obtained during a period of less than ideal economic conditions. Essentially, these ventures met their parent firms' expectations.

The Control-Performance Relationship

Division of control has traditionally been perceived to be a critical determinant of the performance of IJVs. Perhaps because of this, considerable attention has been given to the relationship between the division of control and the performance of IJVs. In his pioneering research, Killing (1982) suggested that in developed-country IJVs, dominant control, rather than shared control, was associated with greater success. IJVs enjoying extensive autonomy were also found to achieve higher performance. However, not all subsequent studies support Killing's conclusion. Empirical evidence remains scant, and results are most often contradictory (see Geringer and Hébert 1989 and Hébert 1994 for reviews). Therefore, the relationship between control and performance is frequently considered inconclusive (Beamish 1993). In a recent study of developed-country IJVs, Blodgett (1992) suggested that fifty-fifty equity JVs typically exhibit higher performance, and the present study supports this: fifty-fifty IJVs exhibited significantly higher business performance ($p < 0.05$) and overall performance ($p < 0.05$) than majority or minority ventures. Similar results were obtained for IJVs with American and European parent firms.

In addition, two hypotheses related to the relationship between control sharing and autonomy structures with the performance of IJVs were investigated (see Hébert 1994 for complete results). These hypotheses proposed that both control sharing and autonomy are positively related to performance. The results show that the relationships linking the dimensions of control sharing and autonomy with performance are less direct and more complex than expected (see Table 15.9). Essentially, the sharing of operational and strategic control is positively related to the overall performance of IJVs. Strategic autonomy was also a significant factor of satisfaction and business performance, while technological autonomy was negatively related to both overall and business performance. The corresponding case of IJVs with European and American parents was not examined because of small sample size. However, analyses of these two types of IJVs together yielded similar results.

This investigation of the division of control revealed that not all dimensions of control sharing and autonomy have the same impact and importance for IJV performance. Such results may explain the limited and contradictory evidence found in previous studies. Nevertheless, overall the results suggest that IJVs with shared operational and strategic control, with extensive strategic autonomy but with limited technological autonomy, could be expected to exhibit higher performance.

Structures	All IJVs	IJVs with European and American Parents
Sharing of operational control	Overall performance (+)	Business performance (+) Overall performance (+)
Sharing of technological control	—	Satisfaction (+)
Sharing of strategic control	Satisfaction (+) Overall performance (+)	Satisfaction (+)
Operational autonomy	—	Satisfaction (+)
Technological autonomy	Overall performance (−) Business performance (−)	Satisfaction (−) Business performance (−) Overall performance (−)
Strategic autonomy	Satisfaction (+) Business performance (+)	Satisfaction (+) Business performance (+) Overall performance (+)

Table 15.9. Control Sharing and Autonomy Structures
in Canada-Based IJVs.
(+) positive relationship   (−) negative relationship

Conclusion

The study outlined in this chapter investigated foreign investment using joint ventures in Canada and reviewed different characteristics of Canada-based IJVs. It shows that foreign firms form IJVs in Canada to geographically diversify their activities and to exchange skills, rather than to meet government pressures and regulations. They choose the JV form to achieve more rapid market entry and to reduce the cost and risk associated with exploiting their firms' technology in a new market. They seek partner firms that can provide them with established distribution channels. In IJV management, foreign firms generally rely on a fifty-fifty equity split and shared strategic control, and on dominant control over technological decisions and activities. IJVs exhibit extensive operational autonomy, but relatively limited strategic autonomy. Furthermore, they display a relatively high success rate. In sum, as expected, Canada-based IJVs exhibit characteristics typical of developed-country IJVs.

The study also attempted to provide insights on the relationships linking the strategic motivations, structure, and performance of IJVs. As a result, two broad types of IJV strategy were identified that share several similarities with the two international strategies discussed by Franko (1971). The first type, frequently used by American parent firms, exhibits characteristics of a "national responsiveness" strategy whereby parent firms form IJVs in traditional and resource-based industries with the objective of catering primarily to domestic demand. Emphasizing rapid market entry and access to distribution channels and raw materials, these generally result in the creation of fifty-fifty IJVs enjoying considerable operational autonomy with shared or split control.

In the second type of strategy, IJVs are formed in more technology-intensive industries and involve the exploitation of a proprietary, and relatively more advanced, technology. These IJVs also serve as a Canadian base for gaining access to foreign markets. Parent firms rely more often on majority ownership and dominant control, as well as on limited technological autonomy that helps protect their proprietary technological assets and ensure effective coordination. This "internationally integrated" strategy is generally pursued by European parent firms.

These two strategies or strategy-structure linkages were found to be equally successful, consistent with the contingent perspective of the strategy-structure-performance paradigm. Such results and conclusions underline that subsidiaries, jointly as well as wholly owned, can assume distinct strategic roles depending on their competitive environment, their parent firms' strategy, and their competencies (Child, Yan and Lu 1997). In addition, these roles have different organizational requirements (Stopford and Wells 1972; Bartlett and Ghoshal 1986, 1989; Anand, Ainuddin, and Makino 1997). The performance of IJVs could thus be a function of the fit achieved between their strategic roles and the structure of their relationships with parent firms.

These results have implications for research and management. Specifically, they emphasize the importance of studying alliances such as IJVs within the context of the parent firms' strategies; the strategies discussed above may represent an empirically grounded base for the identification of effective strategies and structures for IJVs. The results also suggest the importance of accounting for the national origins of parent firms when studying IJVs. However, the present study focused on differences between American and European firms and did not investigate industry-related differences; building on Harrigan (1988a), one might expect that characteristics such as the volatility, capital intensity, and technological intensity of industry environments influence IJV strategies and the structures adopted by parent firms.

For firms and managers currently involved or contemplating involvement in IJVs, this study shows that an IJV can be a viable and successful form of investment compared to greenfield and entrepreneurial ventures. Indeed, despite the inherent difficulties associated with the selection of an appropriate partner firm and their joint-ownership nature, IJVs were typically found to be successful. In forming or managing these ventures, Canadian firms should take into consideration that existing or potential partner firms from different countries may have distinct strategic objectives and preferences toward IJV structures. Furthermore, as IJVs frequently involve more advanced technologies than Canadian standards, they may also offer interesting learning opportunities. Similarly, an IJV may be a suitable option for internationalizing a Canadian firm's activities and exploring exporting opportunities.

Finally, the study outlined here has implications for government policy. The formation of IJVs appears to have several benefits for the local economy. IJVs have emerged as potential sources of advanced technology for Canadian firms, thereby supporting the modernization of industry; they may also generate important export revenues when Canada-based IJVs are used to access other foreign markets. Therefore, government policy could play a role in supporting, or at least not obstructing, the formation of Canada-based IJVs. Attempts to promote investment in Canada using the JV form could emphasize positive aspects such as the availability of Canadian firms with complementary skills and resources, the possibility of using a Canada-based IJV as an export base for foreign markets (especially the American and Mexican markets), and the track record and satisfactory performance of previous and existing IJVs.

Appendix

Constructs and Measures

ORIGINS OF PARENT FIRMS. This variable was defined as the country in which a parent firm is headquartered. Six countries and regions were identified: Canada, United States, Europe, Australia, Japan, and other country.

SIZE. This variable was measured with the sales in CDN$ at the time of data collection or for the IJV's most recent year of operation.

TECHNOLOGY ADVANCEMENT. Participants were asked: "When the JV was formed, how advanced was the JV's technology compared to what was used by primary competitors?" The response scale was a Likert-type 5-point scale (-2 = much less advanced, 0 = same, $+2$ = much more advanced).

EXPORTS. Exports were defined as sales outside of Canada.

MOTIVES OF FORMATION. Participants were asked "How important were the following objectives in their decision to establish this JV?" along ten different objectives (see Table 15.2 for a complete list). The response scale was a Likert-type 5-point scale (1 = not important, 5 = very important).

STRATEGIC RELATIONSHIP WITH PARENT FIRMS. Participants were asked ("Which of the following best describes the relationship between the JV and your firm's activities?") to check one of the six following statements: "The JV is in the same product and geographic market area as my firm's existing activities"; "The JV provides product diversification for my firm's existing activities"; "The JV provides market diversification for my firm's existing activities"; "The JV provides product and market diversification for my firm's existing activities"; "The JV provides backward integration for my firm's existing activities"; "The JV provides forward integration for my firm's existing activities"; "Other (specify)."

THE DIVISION OF CONTROL, OR CONTROL SHARING. This variable was measured using a scale similar to the one used in Geringer (1986), which is an adapted version of Killing's (1982) multi-item scale. Respondents were asked "How was control over each of the following decisions allocated between your firm and your partner?" for seventeen categories of decisions and activities of the JV. The response scale was a Likert-type 5-point scale where 1 is associated with "Your firm controls," 3 with "Shared control between your firm and your partner," and 5 with "Your partner controls." JVGMs were asked whether one of the parent controls (1 or 5), or if both parents shared control (3). IJVs were classified as shared or dominant control IJVs according to the average control sharing across all activities. Using a 3-point scale (where 1 indicates that one of the parent controls and 3 that they share control), IJVs were classified as shared or dominant control if their mean was above or below 2.25, respectively.

AUTONOMY. This variable was measured with a scale similar to the division of control. Respondents were asked "How was control over each of the following decisions allocated between JV managers and the parent firms?" for the same decisions and/or activities. The response scale was a

Likert-type 5-point scale (1 = decided totally by JV managers, 3 = shared control by parent and JV managers, 5 = decided totally by parent firms). An IJV was considered independent if its average extent of autonomy for each dimension was equal to or greater than 4.

SATISFACTION. Satisfaction was measured with a three-item scale derived from Anderson and Narus (1990). Participants were asked: "How satisfied has your firm been with the following aspects of the JV?" They indicated their satisfaction (+2 = very satisfied, 0 = neither satisfied nor satisfied, −2 = very dissatisfied) along three dimensions of the JV ("the JV in general," "the JV's performance," and "the relationship between the partners").

BUSINESS PERFORMANCE. This variable was measured with a scale assessing performance versus expectations along twelve dimensions (sales, profitability, market share, costs, JV management, R&D, product and process technology, manufacturing, raw materials, marketing, distribution, and overall performance). A single-item scale for the overall performance of the JV was also used. In both cases, the response scale was a Likert-type 5-point scale (−2 = below expectations, 0 = equal to expectations, +2 = above expectations).

Data Analysis

SPSS-X was used for all analyses. The consistency and reliability of the perceptual constructs were assessed with Cronbach's alpha and exploratory principal-component factor analysis. These analyses indicated that all multi-item constructs, except control sharing and autonomy, were unidimensional and reliable (with Cronbach's alphas greater than 0.85). In turn, factor analyses identified three control factors with eigenvalues greater than one that accounted for over 75 percent of total variance and had an alpha greater than 0.75. The first factor (operational control and autonomy) involved control over nine operational decisions such as hiring and firing personnel, distribution, pricing, marketing, day-to-day management of the JV, manufacturing, and so on. The second factor (technological control and autonomy) involved control over four decisions related to technology (product and process technology, patents, and R&D). Finally, the third factor (strategic control and autonomy) was related to control over four strategic areas (financing, capital expenditures, location of the JV, and nomination of the JVGM). For testing the hypotheses regarding the relationships between control sharing and autonomy, OLS regression analysis was used. Factor scores were computed using varimax rotation when required.

BIBLIOGRAPHY

Anand, J., A. Ainuddin, and S. Makino. 1997. An empirical analysis of multi-national strategy and international joint venture characteristics in Japanese MNCs. In P. W. Beamish and J. P. Killing, editors, *Cooperative Strategies: Asian Pacific Perspectives.* San Francisco: New Lexington Press.

Anderson, E. 1990. Two firms, one frontier: On assessing joint venture perfor-mance. *Sloan Management Review,* 31(2): 19–30.

Anderson, E., and B. Weitz. 1989. Determinants of continuity in conventional industrial channel dyads. *Marketing Science,* 8(4): 310–323.

Anderson, J. C., and J. A. Narus. 1990. A model of distributor firm and manufac-turer firm working partnerships. *Journal of Marketing,* 54 (January): 42–58.

Bartlett, C. A., and S. Ghoshal. 1986. Tap your subsidiaries for global reach. *Harvard Business Review,* November-December: 87–94.

Bartlett, C. A., and S. Ghoshal. 1989. *Managing Across Borders—The Trans-national Solution.* Boston: Harvard Business School Press.

Beamish, P. W. 1984. Joint venture performance in developing countries. Unpub-lished doctoral dissertation, University of Western Ontario, London.

Beamish, P. W. 1985. The characteristics of joint ventures in developed and devel-oping countries. *Columbia Journal of World Business,* 20(3): 13–19.

Beamish, P. W. 1988. *Multinational Joint Ventures in Developing Countries.* London: Routledge.

Beamish, P. W. 1993. The characteristics of joint ventures in the People's Republic of China. *Journal of International Marketing,* 1(2): 29–49.

Beamish, P. W., and A. Delios. 1997a. Improving joint venture performance through congruent measures of success. In P. W. Beamish and J. P. Killing, editors, *Cooperative Strategies: European Perspectives.* San Francisco: New Lexington Press.

Beamish, P. W., and A. Delios. 1997b. Incidence and propensity of alliance formation by U.S., Japanese and European MNEs. In P. W. Beamish and J. P. Killing, editors, *Cooperative Strategies: Asian Pacific Perspectives.* San Francisco: New Lexington Press.

Blodgett, L. L. 1991. Partner contributions as predictors of equity share in inter-national ventures. *Journal of International Business Studies,* 22(1): 63–78.

Blodgett, L. L. 1992. Factors in the instability of international joint ventures. *Strategic Management Journal,* 13(6): 475–481.

Child, J., Y. Yan, and Y. Lu. 1997. Ownership and control in Sino-foreign joint ventures. In P. W. Beamish and J. P. Killing, editors, *Cooperative Strategies: Asian Pacific Perspectives.* San Francisco: New Lexington Press.

Deloitte, Haskins and Sells International. 1989. *Teaming up for the Nineties—Can You Survive Without a Partner?* New York: Deloitte, Haskins and Sells.

Erden, D. 1997. Cooperative FDI in NICs: Partnerships in Turkey. In P. W. Beamish and J. P. Killing, editors, *Cooperative Strategies: European Perspectives.* San Francisco: New Lexington Press.

Franko, L. G. 1971. *Joint Venture Survival in Multinational Corporations.* New York: Praeger.

Geringer, J. M. 1986. Criteria for selecting partners for joint ventures in industrialized market economies. Unpublished doctoral dissertation, University of Washington, Seattle.

Geringer, J. M., and L. Hébert. 1989. Control and performance of international joint ventures. *Journal of International Business Studies,* 20(2): 235–254.

Geringer, J. M., and L. Hébert. 1991. Measuring joint venture performance. *Journal of International Business Studies,* 22(2): 249–263.

Gerlach, M. 1987. Business alliances and the strategy of the Japanese firm. *California Management Review,* Fall: 126–142.

Hamel, G., Y. Doz, and C. K. Prahalad. 1989. Collaborate with your competitors—and win. *Harvard Business Review,* January-February: 133–139.

Harrigan, K. R. 1985. *Strategies for Joint Ventures.* San Francisco: New Lexington Press.

Harrigan, K. R. 1988a. Joint ventures and competitive strategy. *Strategic Management Journal,* 9(2): 141–158.

Harrigan, K. R. 1988b. Strategic alliances and partner asymmetries. In F. Contractor and P. Lorange, editors, *Cooperative Strategies in International Business,* 205–226. San Francisco: New Lexington Press.

Hébert, L. 1994. Division of control, relationship dynamics and joint venture performance. Unpublished doctoral dissertation, University of Western Ontario, London.

Hergert, M., and D. Morris. 1988. Trends in international collaborative agreements. In F. Contractor and P. Lorange (eds.), *Cooperative Strategies in International Business,* 99–109. San Francisco: New Lexington Press.

Killing, J. P. 1982. How to make a global joint venture work. *Harvard Business Review,* May-June: 120–127.

Lee, C., and P. W. Beamish. 1995. The characteristics and performance of Korean joint ventures in LDCs. *Journal of International Business Studies,* 26(3): 637–654.

Lin, J. L., C.-M. J. Yu, and D.-H. W. Seetoo. 1997. Motivations, partners' contributions and control of international joint ventures. In P. W. Beamish and J. P. Killing, editors, *Cooperative Strategies: Asian Pacific Perspectives.* San Francisco: New Lexington Press.

Olson, L. B., and K. Singsuwan. 1997. The effect of partnership, communication and conflict resolution behaviors on performance success of strategic alliances: American and Thai perspectives. In P. W. Beamish and J. P. Killing, editors, *Cooperative Strategies: Asian Pacific Perspectives.* San Francisco: New Lexington Press.

Parkhe, A. 1993. Strategic alliance structuring: A game theoretic and transaction cost examination of interfirm cooperation. *Academy of Management Journal,* 36(4): 794–829.

Porter, M. E., and M. B. Fuller. 1986. Coalitions and global strategy. In M. E. Porter, editor, *Competition in Global Industries,* 315–344. Boston: Harvard Business School Press.

Schaan, J.-L. 1983. Parent control and joint venture success: The case of Mexico. Ph.D. dissertation, University of Western Ontario.

Stopford, J. M., and L. T. Wells. 1972. *Managing the Multinational Enterprise.* New York: Basic Books.

16

INTERNATIONAL JOINT VENTURE PERFORMANCE OF FIRMS IN THE NONMANUFACTURING SECTOR

Hemant Merchant

EMPIRICAL STUDIES ON *the international joint venture (IJV) performance of firms in the nonmanufacturing sector are uncommon at best. The limitations of the few studies that do exist indicate a need to investigate the IJV performance of non-manufacturing firms from an alternative viewpoint—that of capital markets. Hence, this study investigates the extent to which IJVs create economic value for participating nonmanufacturing firms. The research protocol employs the event-study methodology to examine the effect of 100 IJV formation announcements on the capital market value of participating firms. Results indicate that participation in IJVs creates economic value for only about 40 percent of firms in the sample. An attempt is then made to identify conditions under which IJVs lead to value creation for the sample of firms included in this study.*

This chapter has benefited from the feedback of participants at the Global Perspectives on Cooperative Strategies: North American Perspectives Conference. In particular, I am thankful to Paul Beamish, Chris Garmston, Anju Seth, and three anonymous reviewers for their suggestions for improving this work. I am also thankful to Praveen Nayyar for his constructive comments on an earlier draft.

EMPIRICAL EVIDENCE REGARDING the economic performance of international joint ventures (IJVs) involving firms in the nonmanufacturing sector is scarce at best, despite their growing significance in foreign direct investment and world trade (Mathe and Perras 1994; World Investment Report 1993) and the recent increase in frequency of this category of IJVs (Culpan and Kostelac 1993; Ghemawat, Porter, and Rawlinson 1986; Sakullelarasmi 1991; also see Harrigan 1988; Hergert and Morris 1988). Admittedly, however, studies have begun focusing on the broadly defined performance of IJVs in the nonmanufacturing sector (for example, see Harrigan 1988; Lorange and Roos 1992 and relevant citations therein; also see Brooks, Blundel, and Bidgood 1992). Nevertheless, the limitations of these studies appear to have concealed the nature of their empirical findings.

One limitation of these studies is that their findings usually are based on managerial assessments of corporate performance, and such assessments have been found biased (Chen, Farh, and MacMillan 1993). It is possible that the IJV performance of nonmanufacturing firms is unlike that reported in earlier empirical studies. Perhaps more importantly, the case-based nature of the earlier studies limits the extent to which their conclusions about the nature of IJV performance of nonmanufacturing firms can be meaningfully generalized to a larger and more diverse set of comparable IJVs.[1] Taken together, these limitations highlight the need to investigate the IJV performance of firms in the nonmanufacturing sector from an alternative viewpoint—that of capital markets.

One key advantage of using the capital market perspective to evaluate IJV performance is that its judgments are believed (Allen 1993; Salter and Weinhold 1979) and empirically validated (Chen, Farh, and MacMillan 1993) to be least biased when compared to those of corporate managers and academics. More positively, capital market–based measures of firm performance do not suffer from the measurement problems caused by multi-industry participation (Nayyar 1992). Such measures also reflect the risk-adjusted performance of firms (Jensen 1969). In principle, moreover, a capital market perspective enables a study of all publicly traded nonmanufacturing firms participating in IJVs over a given period. Another less obvious but important advantage is that it permits a comparison of the capital market performance of nonmanufacturing firms participating in IJVs with that of their counterparts in the manufacturing sector—firms whose IJV-based capital market performance is well documented (Crutchley, Guo, and Hansen 1991; Chen, Hu, and Shieh 1991; Chung, Koford, and Lee 1993; Finnerty, Owers, and Rogers 1986).[2]

In a seminal study, Fama, Fisher, Jensen, and Roll (1969) argued that the event-study methodology can be used to assess the performance impact of announcements of corporate activity, including corporate participation in IJVs. According to financial theorists, a firm's capital market value must increase if the net discounted cash flows from corporate investment in (say) an IJV are positive, and vice versa. If capital markets are efficient, changes in a firm's market value will be incorporated very quickly in the firm's stock price, thus permitting the changes to be measured. Consequently, it would be possible to estimate the impact of proposed IJV activity on the profitability of the participating firms.

The next section of this chapter provides a theoretical explanation of why announcements of IJV formation should lead to positive changes in the capital market value of nonmanufacturing firms participating in IJVs. Following that is a description of the study's research protocol and the event-study methodology. After a presentation of empirical results, the final section discusses empirical findings, offers conclusions about the efficacy of IJVs for nonmanufacturing firms, and highlights potential areas for future research.

Value Creation in International Joint Ventures: The Case of Nonmanufacturing Sector Firms

Financial theory suggests that value creation occurs to the extent that public announcements of IJV formation contain unanticipated information about the value of IJV partners' assets in place or IJV-based earnings opportunities available to these firms (Ravichandran 1986). In the case of nonmanufacturing firms in IJVs, these explanations of value creation can be better understood in terms of two distinct but interrelated perspectives: one based on resources and the other on transaction costs.

A resource-based view of firms (for example, Penrose 1959; Wernerfelt 1984) suggests that the value of IJV partners' assets in place—the unexploited economic potential of excess productive resources held by firms participating in IJVs—fundamentally is a function of the characteristics of firm resources. Complementing this is the transaction costs view (for example, Coase 1937; Williamson 1975), which suggests that the IJV-based earnings opportunity—the potential net income that can be generated via IJVs—is a function of the extent to which firms efficiently circumvent market failures and thus overcome impediments to economic growth.

Clearly, to understand more thoroughly why economic value should be created for nonmanufacturing firms participating in IJVs, it would be useful to focus on the salient economic characteristics of nonmanufacturing firms, and to highlight the profitability implications of intangibility, inseparability,

Characteristics	Resulting Challenges	Profitability Implications
Intangibility		
Skills-based core competence	Restricts the business scope of economic activity of firms	Joint ventures in horizontal and/or related businesses facilitate opportunities for economies of scale and scope.
	Leads to nontradability of proprietary skills	Joint ventures circumvent failures in markets for proprietary skills.
Inseparability		
Jointness of production and consumption	Creates the need for high level of interaction	Joint ventures allow the use of impermanent and perishable firm resources.
	Leads to wastage of (unstorable) service capacity	IJVs offer potential location-specific advantages.
Heterogeneity		
Uncontrollable variance in production, quality, and level of service	Increases risk of operating in unpredictable industries characterized by variance of consumer preferences and creative talent	Joint ventures allow firms to diversify the risks of operating under uncertain conditions, and to gain economies of scope.
Variability		
Asymmetries in demand for and supply of service offerings	Leads to underutilization of corporate resources when supply exceeds demand	Joint ventures increase resource utilization by permitting manipulation of demand.
	Limits earnings opportunity when demand exceeds supply	Joint ventures enable pooling of resources to fulfill unmet demand.
Regulation		
Government-induced market impediments	Obstructs cross-border provision of services and slows international services growth	IJVs circumvent artificial entry barriers and may create first-mover advantages for partners.

Table 16.1. Characteristics of Services and Their Profitability Implications for Joint Venture Partners.

heterogeneity, variability, and regulation (Dunning 1989; Enderwick 1989a, 1989b; Nusbaumer 1987). Table 16.1 summarizes the linkage between these characteristics and the profitability implications of each for joint venture partners.

Intangibility

Intangibility refers to the concept that the core competence of nonmanufacturing firms is largely based on skills, not assets. As skills are usually tacit and often uncodifiable (for example, Polanyi 1962), the IJV participation of nonmanufacturing firms will usually be confined to horizontal or related businesses (Enderwick 1992). Tacitness enhances the value of participating nonmanufacturing firms' assets in place in at least two ways. First, the deployment of excess productive resources to horizontal or related businesses essentially increases their utilization rate, thereby generating economies of scale for IJV partners. Likewise, relatedness facilitates the transfer of skills and resources across different value chains (Porter 1987), thereby generating economies of scope for the involved firms—assuming other conditions regarding the creation of these economies are fulfilled (Teece 1980). Second, the value of participating firms' assets-in-place increases to the extent that joint ventures provide them with opportunities to develop learning routines that better exploit the efficiency of available corporate resources (Badaracco 1991).

The intangibility-induced pursuit of horizontal or related business activity by nonmanufacturing firms participating in IJVs has other implications for firm profitability. Above all, these types of undertakings hint at reduction in the marginal costs of resource utilization (Chatterjee 1990). Intangibility, moreover, confers a sustainable competitive advantage upon joint venture partners to the extent that certain types of skills are difficult to imitate (Dierickx and Cool 1989; Rumelt 1987; Winter 1987) and, hence, less prone to competitive appropriation. Implicitly, joint ventures (including those involving nonmanufacturing firms) circumvent failures in markets for hard-to-imitate skills (for example, reliability of service delivery), as such attributes cannot be traded in open markets (Arrow 1962; Williamson 1975). Alternatively, market failures indicate a breakdown in the market for the output of services and therefore eliminate earnings opportunities that otherwise would accrue to joint venture partners. By announcing their participation in joint ventures, firms can better signal the removal of market infirmities and, as a result, credibly communicate their access to the earnings stream of unserved markets.

Inseparability

Inseparability refers to the joint production and consumption of services brought about by the impermanent and perishable nature of many non-manufacturing firms' resources (Enderwick 1992). The need for a high level of interaction between nonmanufacturing firms and their customers implies that inseparability can result in market failures on supply as well as demand sides. Arguably, the participation of nonmanufacturing firms in joint ventures circumvents both types of market failures, thus creating economic value for them.

On the supply side, participation in joint ventures increases the usage of nonmanufacturing firms' resources, many of which are not only impermanent and perishable in nature but also subject to a high rate of obsolescence. Indeed, a "great deal of available service capacity often is wasted because it is perishable and must be held in reserve for just those moments when customers need it" (Heskett, Sasser, and Hart 1990: 9). In other words, the value of nonmanufacturing firms' assets in place increases to the extent joint ventures efficiently exploit the unused productivity of excess corporate resources by creating time and place utilities for consumers.

The availability of resources does not, however, mean a demand market for nonmanufacturing firms. Inseparability creates the dual challenges of gaining access to potential markets and assuring the quality of intangible service offerings to them (Enderwick 1989b). In other words, inseparability can result in impediments that limit the participating firms' earnings in potential markets. Fortunately, corporate participation in joint ventures can alleviate these challenges; joint ventures are a mechanism to combine and therefore capitalize on stand-alone firms' complementary resources, such as service technology and service delivery systems.

On the demand side, announcements of IJV formation hint at location-specific advantages such as market access and access to relatively inexpensive factors of production. These advantages can generate additional earnings for joint venture partners (Enderwick 1989a). To illustrate, firms can generate sales by serving previously untapped markets that may have resulted at least partly from inseparability-induced market failures. Moreover, the pooling of complementary assets can reduce entry costs while increasing the speed of market entry. In some cases, firms can increase their earnings by gaining access to relatively inexpensive factors of production, particularly when these factors are cospecialized (for example, scientists, their scientific community, and research labs) such that they are subject to a significant loss of value when removed from the context from which they obtain.

Heterogeneity

Heterogeneity is the uncontrollable variance in production and quality of service offerings and in differences in the level service performance. It arises primarily because of the human element embedded in most services (Campbell and Verbeke 1994). One implication of such variance is that nonmanufacturing firms can diversify the risks associated with heterogeneity by participating in joint ventures. Joint ventures can, for example, permit firms to reduce the costs of operating in unpredictable industries characterized by variability of consumer preferences and creative talent, as in the entertainment industry and biotechnology research industry, while enabling firms to quickly exploit opportunities when they arise.

As a corollary, firms can optimize the value of their assets-in-place by deploying older service technologies—either alone or in combination with other technologies (Garud and Nayyar 1994)—to relatively less-developed consumer markets. Joint ventures thus allow firms to continue to exploit the productivity of otherwise dormant resources. Such exploitation is particularly viable in nonmanufacturing industries characterized by high fixed costs, a majority of which may already have been written off. The redeployment of older technologies to less-developed markets may even permit nonmanufacturing firms to obtain, relatively inexpensively, first-mover advantages and perhaps a dominant competitive position.

In principle, heterogeneity facilitates a broader range of offerings to the extent it is possible to combine different levels of services within a joint venture. All else being equal, nonmanufacturing firms participating in IJVs therefore can position themselves differently across markets to take advantage of opportunities to increase earnings. Arguably, earnings can be optimized if the performance differentials that exist between service providers can be matched to the services demanded across different markets, or to distinct segments within a given market. Nonmanufacturing firms participating in IJVs thus can increase the input efficiency of resources and, in doing so, economize on the real costs of service offerings. That is, nonmanufacturing firms can increase the IJV-based earnings accruable to them.

Variability

Variability refers to asymmetries in the demand and supply of services, rather than in service quality (Enderwick 1992). In that sense, variability implies market failures that result in underutilized resources when the supply of services exceeds demand, and limited earnings opportunities when the demand for services exceeds supply. Nonmanufacturing firms that participate in joint ventures can address both types of challenge, thus creating economic value.

In the first case, corporate participation in joint ventures allows firms to engage unused capacity to serve markets where there is unfulfilled demand or where the demand is insufficient to justify market entry by stand-alone firms. They can better manipulate the demand for services by entering into joint ventures with others possessing complementary resources or offering complementary services. For example, a ski resort may enter into a venture with an outdoor exploration company to increase utilization of the firm's hotel service during summer months. Clearly, joint ventures would be a mechanism to increase the value of nonmanufacturing firms' assets-in-place in such cases.

Likewise, joint ventures provide a growth mechanism to improve the earnings of participating nonmanufacturing firms when the demand for these firms' services exceeds their supply. In this case, the creation of a joint venture facilitates economic growth by enabling them to pool their competencies, thus increasing the supply of resources while lowering the risks associated with unfulfilled demand, and potentially increasing their earnings.

Regulation

In general, service industries are subject to very high levels of government intervention and regulation (Enderwick 1989c). This may limit the growth and earnings of nonmanufacturing firms; as Trondsen and Edfelt (1987) note, "from a regulatory perspective, services have historically been an overprotected and overcontrolled sector of economic activity. Government monopolies have supplied a number of major services . . . and there have been restrictions on foreign investment in some subsectors. . . . These factors have tended to *obstruct* the crossborder provision of services and slow international services growth in many countries and regions" (Trondsen and Edfelt 1987: 55–56; emphasis added). Admittedly, however, recent years have witnessed a deregulation of services (Enderwick 1992) in many countries.

One implication of this trend is that corporate participation in IJVs permits firms to circumvent government-induced market imperfections. In principle, firms can enter previously closed markets and create economic value in terms of both the value of assets-in-place and IJV-based earnings. To illustrate, servicing new markets often requires increased utilization of existing corporate resources; this generates economies of scale and improves the output efficiency of available resources, leading to an increase in the value of firms' in-place assets. Likewise, corporate participation in IJVs improves the earnings potential of firms servicing markets opened by deregulation or differential regulation. They can then reach previously inaccessible customers, possibly with a broader range of and more sophisticated offerings than what the customers were used to before. This could result in first-mover advantages. Moreover, firms can reduce the risks and costs of entering such markets if they enter into a joint venture with local firms who bring local market expertise. Joint ventures with local firms can also legitimize a nondomestic firm's involvement in recently deregulated or nationalistic markets.

In summary, nonmanufacturing firms' participation in IJVs confers upon them both asset-based and location-based advantages (Dunning 1989; Enderwick 1989b). Joint ventures provide a mechanism to increase the efficiency of corporate resources and give access to unfulfilled market potential. Together, these mechanisms hint at a low-risk and high-payoff duality that may create value for nonmanufacturing firms participating in IJVs. Unfortunately, empirical work that might prove it is limited at best. It would be useful therefore to conduct an empirical analysis of the economic performance of IJVs involving nonmanufacturing firms. This is done next.

Methodology

This study includes announcements of IJVs involving U.S. nonmanufacturing firms and non-U.S. partners from January 1986 through December 1990 obtained from the Dow Jones News Retrieval Service.

The Sample

The search produced an initial sample of approximately 250 headlines referring to various possible corporate investments in IJVs. Consistent with its objective, the search retained only those reports that likely contained news about IJV formations involving nonmanufacturing firms. The full texts of the screened reports were then obtained and examined to verify whether they exclusively contained IJV formation news, so as to ensure that changes in market value announced in them pertained only to new IJV activity. All announcements about other types of corporate activity were eliminated. When two news reports referred to the same IJV, which was very infrequent, only the earlier news item was retained. A final requirement was that firms be publicly traded either on the New York, American, or NASDAQ stock exchanges. The result was a sample of 100 IJV formation announcements. Table 16.2 presents the distribution of these an-

					SECTOR[a]				
Year	Exchange[b]	1	2	3	4	5	6	7	Total
1986	NYAM	2	1	4	3	0	1	2	13
	NSDQ	0	0	0	0	0	0	0	0
1987	NYAM	0	1	2	0	0	2	2	7
	NSDQ	2	0	2	1	0	2	2	7
1988	NYAM	1	2	4	1	0	1	2	11
	NSDQ	0	0	1	0	1	0	2	4
1989	NYAM	2	3	1	0	1	3	3	13
	NSDQ	1	0	1	1	0	0	2	5
1990	NYAM	2	1	7	2	1	6	3	22
	NSDQ	0	0	5	1	0	3	9	18
	Total	**10**	**8**	**27**	**9**	**3**	**16**	**27**	**100**

Table 16.2. Distribution of IJV Formation Announcements.
Note: N = 100.
[a] 1 = mining; 2 = construction; 3 = transportation; 4 = wholesale trade;
5 = retail trade; 6 = finance, insurance, and real estate; 7 = other services.
[b] NYAM = New York or American stock exchange;
NSDQ = NASDAQ stock exchange.

nouncements across time, industry sectors, and stock exchanges. The predominantly uniform distribution of IJV formation announcements suggests that the IJV-based capital market performance of firms in the sample will not be overly influenced by characteristics of the data set (Brown and Warner 1985). This conjecture was confirmed during data analysis.

Event-Study Methodology

The impact of IJV formation announcements on the participating firms' stock price was assessed using the event-study methodology commonly employed in the empirical literature of finance and accounting. As mentioned earlier, the event of interest was the announcement of IJV formation between a U.S. nonmanufacturing firm and a non-U.S. partner. The day on which the announcement was first reported by Dow Jones News Retrieval Service was labeled event day $t = -1$.[3] Trading days prior to that day were numbered $t = -2$, $t = -3$, and so on; subsequent trading days were numbered $t = 0$, $t = +1$, and so on.

It was expected that IJV formation announcements would lead capital markets to revalue the earnings streams of involved firms, if the announcements contained unanticipated news about the economic prospects attending IJV activity. To determine how much these announcements affected a firm's stock price, it was necessary to first estimate the firm's stock price in absence of such announcements. It was assumed that the daily stock returns were described by the Capital Asset Pricing Model (CAPM) relation:

$$R_{it} = A_i + B_i{}^*R_{mt} + E_i \qquad (1)$$

where

R_{it} = rate of return for firm i on day t

R_{mt} = rate of return on the value-weighted market portfolio on day t

A_i, B_i = intercept and slope parameters (respectively) for firm i

E_i = firm-specific disturbance term

The above CAPM relation was estimated for each firm in the sample for a 200-day estimation period beginning fifty-one days before the announcement day. It was expected that the returns-generating process defined above was unbiased in that it estimated normal returns (as if the firm's IJV had not been announced or not been entered into) approximately ten trading weeks (two and a half trading months) before the particular announcement. The estimated parameters, a_i and b_i, and the firm's actual returns were then used to predict normal returns for the two-day announcement period, defined as $t = -1$ and $t = 0$. The resulting prediction errors, the difference between actual and normal returns, are unbiased estimates of abnormal returns, that is, changes in the stock price of firms whose participation in IJVs was publicly announced. These changes signify capital markets' expectations regarding the performance of IJVs.[4] The abnormal return on day t for each firm i was computed as

$$AR_{it} = R_{it} - (a_i + b_i{}^*R_{mt}) \qquad (2)$$

Next, abnormal returns (obtained via equation 2) were standardized to facilitate tests of statistical significance (Mikkelson and Partch 1986). Such standardization was necessary to account for firm-specific influences on economic performance (Lubatkin and Shrieves 1986; Seth 1990).[5] The standardized abnormal return for firm i on day t was defined as

$$SAR_{it} = AR_{it}/\text{s.e.}(AR_{it}) \qquad (3)$$

where

SAR_{it} = standardized abnormal return to firm i on day t

s.e.(AR_{it}) = standard error of AR_{it}

Following convention, standardized abnormal returns were accumulated over the announcement period for each firm in the sample. This aggregation formed the basic statistic for evaluating the performance of IJVs.

Tests of Statistical Significance

Over the event period defined by (t_1, t_2), where $t_1 < t_2$, which may differ among firms, the mean interval abnormal return for a sample of N firms was computed as

$$CASAR(t_1, t_2) = \frac{1}{\sqrt{t_2 - t_1 + 1}} \times \sum_{t=t_1}^{t_2} ASAR_t \qquad (4)$$

where

$$ASAR_t = \frac{1}{N} \times \sum_{i=1}^{N} SAR_{it}$$

A special case—one of particular interest to this study—of equation 4 pertained to firm i's abnormal returns cumulated over the interval $t = -1$ and $t = 0$, the announcement period. This was necessary to test whether the mean abnormal return for the sample of N firms was statistically significant over the announcement period.

PARAMETRIC TEST. Some empirical studies in the finance literature, for example Mikkelson and Partch (1986), determine that the test statistic for assessing the statistical significance of the mean abnormal return for a sample of N firms over the interval (t_1, t_2) is given by

$$Z_I = \sqrt{N} \times CASAR_{(t_1, t_2)} \qquad (5)$$

where Z_I follows the unit normal distribution, under the null hypothesis that the mean abnormal return for N firms over the interval (t_1, t_2) is zero. That is, on average, IJVs do not create economic value over the interval (t_1, t_2).

NONPARAMETRIC TEST. The statistical significance of the above mean return assumes, however, that the average return over the announcement period is not influenced by outlier values. The assumption necessitates the use of the Wilcoxon test to circumvent potential distortions introduced by any outlier values. The Wilcoxon test is given by the statistic (Siegel 1956: 79):

$$W = \frac{T - \dfrac{N(N + 1)}{4}}{\sqrt{\dfrac{N(N + 1)(2N + 1)}{24}}} \qquad (6)$$

where T is the smaller of the like-signed ranks. The W follows the unit normal distribution under the null hypothesis that the sum(s) of positive and negative ranks are equal to each other (that is, IJVs create as much positive as negative value for the participating firms).

Empirical Results

Table 16.3 summarizes empirical findings pertaining to announcements of IJV formation involving nonmanufacturing firms. Above all, the results indicate that firms in the sample obtained average standardized abnormal returns of 5.44 percent (n.s.) over the announcement period; these translate into an average standardized increase of approximately $5.7 million in the firms' capital market value.[6] (For comparison, unstandardized abnormal returns are also reported.) The results also indicate that less than half of firms in the sample (43 percent) obtained positive returns, albeit this proportion is not statistically significant at the 10 percent level. Given the lack of statistical significance of these returns, it was necessary to verify that capital markets had not already anticipated the IJV formation announcements included in this study and, by extension, adjusted the studied firms' capital market performance. Further data analysis (not reported) indicated, however, that the mean abnormal return to firms in the sample was not significant at the 10 percent level for three other conventionally defined event windows preceding the announcement period. Thus, "information leakage" about the sample of IJV formation announcements can be ruled out as an explanation for the modest empirical results reported above.

Likewise, it was necessary to ascertain whether the modest returns merely were an artifact of the magnitude of financial investment in IJVs. To the extent there is some relationship between a project's size (initial total capital investment) and cash flows (McConnell and Nantell 1985), it is possible that the reported lack of significance is due to usually smaller investments in joint ventures as opposed to large investments made through vehicles such as mergers and acquisitions. Additional data analysis (not reported), however, indicated little support for the above-mentioned conjecture. For the subsample of seventeen firms for which data on initial total capital outlays was available, the average investment in IJVs was nearly 150 percent of their capital market value. Nonetheless, it is useful to note that the initial total capital outlay variable had a large variance.

At a finer level, the results show that mean standardized abnormal returns are positive for firms in several industries: construction; transportation and public utilities; finance, insurance, and real estate; and service sectors designated as "other." In contrast, these returns are negative for firms in mining, wholesale trade, and retail trade sectors. Note, however, that all of these sector-specific returns lack statistical significance at the 10 percent level. It is useful to note that the apparent discrepancy between the sign of standardized and unstandardized mean abnormal returns merely is an artifact of construction (refer to Note 6). The relatively large mean values for wholesale trade, retail trade, and finance, insurance, and real estate sectors suggest that at least some firms in these sectors may represent outlier cases. The proportion of firms with positive returns varies between 30 and 63 percent, with a modal value of about 33 percent. The lack of significance for the Wilcoxon test suggests that the proportion of nonmanufacturing firms with positive returns is statistically equal to that of nonmanufacturing firms with negative returns.

To ascertain the possible impact of outlier cases, the results in Table 16.4 are based on a reduced sample ($N^* = 90$) that deletes five observations each from subsamples of firms with positive and negative returns. The deleted observations were identified based on a univariate analysis of data (available upon request). An analysis of the cluster plot clearly identified that each of these sets of extreme values comprised observations that were noticeably distant from the cluster of remaining observations.

Above all, the results in Table 16.4 indicate the general robustness of results presented Table 16.3. The results in Table 16.4 show that after deleting outliers, remaining firms in the sample obtain average standardized returns of nearly −5.75 percent (n.s.); the average standardized capital market value of these firms decreases by approximately $44 million, on average. Nearly 42 percent of these firms obtain positive returns, but this figure is not significant at the 10 percent level. The mean standardized abnormal returns remain positive for firms in the construction, finance, insurance and real estate, and other services sectors. In contrast, the returns are negative for firms in mining, transportation and public utilities, wholesale trade, and retail trade sectors. Note that all sector-specific returns lack statistical significance at the 10 percent level except the wholesale trade sector. The mean return for the latter sector is statistically significant at the 5 percent level. Relatedly, results of the Wilcoxon test suggest that the proportion of nonmanufacturing firms obtaining positive returns is significantly

	Abnormal Returns	Z Test	$ Value of Gains	Firms with Positive Returns	W'cox Test
All sectors					
Standardized	5.44%	n.s.	$5.71 mil.	43.0%	n.s.
Unstandardized	0.16%		0.09 mil.		
Specific sector					
Mining (n = 10)					
Standardized	−15.66%	n.s.	−81.1 mil.	30.0%	n.s.
Unstandardized	−0.64		−4.0 mil.		
Construction (n = 8)					
Standardized	10.27%	n.s.	100.1 mil.	62.5%	n.s.
Unstandardized	0.40%		3.3 mil.		
Transportation and public utilities (n = 27)					
Standardized	0.55%	n.s.	48.9 mil.	33.3%	n.s.
Unstandardized	−0.29%		−0.2 mil.		
Wholesale trade (n = 9)					
Standardized	−13.40%	n.s.	−366.5 mil.	33.3%	n.s.
Unstandardized	0.90%		−2.7 mil.		
Retail trade (n = 3)					
Standardized	−12.78%	n.s.	−1241.8 mil.	33.3%	n.s.
Unstandardized	−1.53%		−17.9 mil.		
Finance, insurance, and real estate (n = 16)					
Standardized	37.41%	n.s.	226.1 mil.	56.3%	n.s.
Unstandardized	0.85%		4.6 mil.		
Other services (n = 27)					
Standardized	18.84%	n.s.	98.7 mil.	48.1%	n.s.
Unstandardized	0.37%		1.1 mil.		

Table 16.3. Announcement Period Mean Abnormal Returns.
Note: N = 100

	Abnormal Returns	Z Test	$ Value of Gains	Firms with Positive Returns	W'cox Test
All sectors					
Standardized	−5.75%	n.s.	−43.48 mil.	42.2%	n.s.
Unstandardized	−0.09%		−0.86 mil.		
Specific sector					
Mining (n = 10)					
Standardized	−15.66%	n.s.	−81.1 mil.	30.0%	n.s.
Unstandardized	−0.64%		−4.0 mil.		
Construction (n = 8)					
Standardized	10.27%	n.s.	100.1 mil.	62.5%	n.s.
Unstandardized	0.40%		3.3 mil.		
Transportation and public utilities (n = 23)					
Standardized	−22.87%	n.s.	−111.0 mil.	30.4%	n.s.
Unstandardized	−0.74%		−3.1 mil.		
Wholesale trade (n = 8)					
Standardized	−76.67%	$p < 0.05$	−548.2 mil.	25.0%	$p < 0.08$
Unstandardized	−0.91%		−7.3 mil.		
Retail trade (n = 2)					
Standardized	−17.69%	n.s.	−434.7 mil.	50.0%	n.s.
Unstandardized	0.30%		−5.5 mil.		
Finance, insurance, and real estate (n = 16)					
Standardized	37.41%	n.s.	226.1 mil.	56.3%	n.s.
Unstandardized	0.85%		4.6 mil.		
Other services (n = 23)					
Standardized	5.80%	n.s.	12.5 mil.	47.8%	n.s.
Unstandardized	0.23%		0.2 mil.		

Table 16.4. Announcement Period Mean Abnormal Returns (Outlier Observations Deleted).

Note: N* = 90

lower than that of nonmanufacturing firms obtaining negative returns ($p <$ 0.08) in the wholesale trade sector. In general, the proportion of firms with positive, as opposed to negative, returns varies between 25 percent and 63 percent with a modal value of about 30 percent.

Clearly, the modest results presented above call for further analysis to generate a better understanding of the unexpected findings. To that end, this study first reports the pattern of empirical results across different sectors within the nonmanufacturing economy. It then explores possible differences between subgroups of firms with positive and negative returns with respect to certain salient firm- and venture-specific variables.

The results in Table 16.5 present the distribution of nonmanufacturing firms in the above-mentioned subgroups across industry sectors. Above all, the findings indicate that the number of nonmanufacturing firms with negative returns usually is twice the number of firms with positive returns. This pattern occurs in five out of seven sectors within the nonmanufacturing economy, with the construction and the finance, insurance, and real estate sectors being the exceptions. The above-mentioned pattern is nearly identical when outliers are excluded from the sample (results not shown). Interestingly, however, the results in Table 16.6 indicate that firm- and venture-specific contrasts between the subgroups of firms generally are less noticeable. Among variables for which additional data were readily available, only political risk variables were statistically significant at the 3 percent level: nonmanufacturing firms with negative returns apparently ventured into politically riskier countries than did nonmanufacturing firms with positive returns. Relatedly, it is useful to note that relatively more firms entered into IJVs for offensive reasons (for example, to capitalize on their core skills) than for defensive reasons (for example, competitive pressures) (for example, Porter 1990). Interestingly, nonetheless a majority of firms in the former category (approximately 58 percent, or twenty-three of forty firms) obtained negative returns.

The results in Table 16.7 indicate that the distribution of foreign partner countries appears to be uniform across the two subgroups, except for those of European origin. Firms with negative returns seem to have a relatively greater affinity for entering into joint ventures with European partners than do firms with positive returns. Similarly, Table 16.8 shows that the distribution of joint venture host countries appears to be uniform across the two subgroups except with respect to North American countries. Firms with negative returns seem to have relatively greater affinity for locating their joint ventures within North America than do firms with positive returns. The results in Table 16.9 indicate that, in general, nonmanufacturing firms

Sector	n	Firms with Negative Returns	Firms with Positive Returns
Mining	10	7	3
Construction	8	3	5
Transporation and public utilities	27	18	9
Wholesale trade	9	6	3
Retail trade	3	2	1
Finance, insurance, and real estate	16	7	9
Other services	27	14	13
Total	**100**	**57**	**43**

Table 16.5. Distribution of Returns Across the
Nonmanufacturing Economy.
Note: N = 100

with negative returns simultaneously undertake more types of IJV activities than do nonmanufacturing firms with positive returns.

Conclusion

Above all, the findings of this study indicate that U.S. capital markets' assessment of nonmanufacturing firms participating in IJVs is modest. It seems they do not believe participation in IJVs will yield positive net benefits to firms in the sample. In other words, it is possible that the costs of servicing international markets via IJVs are expected to equal the benefits of doing so for firms included in this study—assuming that an IJV was the most appropriate mechanism for economic value creation for these firms.[7] Carman and Langeard (1980) cautioned service firms about the challenges of international market expansion, noting that the costs, real or otherwise, associated with such growth are considerably higher for service as opposed to manufacturing firms. These authors argued that differences in costs arise to the extent that certain mechanisms (for example, exporting) may be inefficient for service firms who, therefore, must—at the onset—undertake direct investment in international markets to serve customers face-to-face. The hinted lack of experience that could be generated via a less resource-intensive entry mode suggests that nonmanufacturing firms will

Variables	FIRMS WITH NEGATIVE RETURNS (n = 57 Firms)		FIRMS WITH POSITIVE RETURNS (n = 43 Firms)		t-Test (p-Value)
	n	Mean	n	Mean	
IJVs with SOEs	4 firms		4 firms		
IJVs with private firms	53 firms		39 firms		
IJV size: Capital outlay (in million $)	8	70.98	9	73.51	n.s.
Political risk: Resource transfer	56	2.96	43	2.14	$p < 0.03$
Political risk: Exports	56	3.95	43	3.09	$p < 0.02$
U.S. partners: Equity held (%)	33	46.09	21	45.71	n.s.
U.S. partners: Sales ($ bil.)	48	4.74	35	7.83	n.s.
U.S. partners: Assets ($ bil.)	48	12.43	30	15.16	n.s.
U.S. partners: Employees (000s)	48	34.89	34	34.48	n.s.
Non-U.S. partners: Employees (000s)	31	74.89	19	56.94	n.s.
U.S. partners: Strategic motivation for IJV formation					
Offensive	23 firms		17 firms		n.m.
Defensive	7 firms		4 firms		n.m.
Unclear	27 firms		22 firms		n.m.

Table 16.6. Selected Mean Comparisons.

Note: N = 100

Country Groupings	Firms with Negative Returns	Firms with Positive Returns
Americas		
North America	5	3
South America	4	0
Europe		
Eastern Europe	2	4
Western Europe	29	20
Asia		
Southeast Asia	2	0
Rest of Asia/Pacific	12	13
Rest of world	3	3
Total	**57**	**43**

Table 16.7. Distribution of Returns Across Partner Countries.
Note: N = 100

Country Groupings	Firms with Negative Returns	Firms with Positive Returns
Americas		
North America	26	13
South America	3	0
Europe		
Eastern Europe	2	4
Western Europe	15	16
Asia		
Southeast Asia	4	1
Rest of Asia/Pacific	5	7
Rest of world	2	2
Total	**57**	**43**

Table 16.8. Distribution of Returns Across Joint
Venture Host Countries.
Note: N = 100

TYPE OF VALUE-CHAIN ACTIVITY			Firms with Negative Returns	Firms with Positive Returns
Upstream	Midstream	Downstream		
Unclear classification			3	0
No	No	Yes	18	21
No	Yes	No	19	14
No	Yes	Yes	8	3
Yes	No	No	4	3
Yes	No	Yes	2	0
Yes	Yes	No	2	1
Yes	Yes	Yes	1	1
		Total	57	43
Summary[a]				
All three value-chain activities			1	1
Any two value-chain activities			12	4
Any one value-chain activity			41	38

Table 16.9. Distribution of Returns Across Value-Chain Activities.
Note: N = 100
[a]Numbers do not add up to 100 because of multiple responses.

have to incur higher servicing costs relative to those incurred by manufacturing firms. For example, they may have to expend more resources on acquiring knowledge of local markets or credibly communicating the value of certain types of services offered. Providing some empirical support for this, Channon (1978) reported a decline in return on capital with increasing levels of international activity for a sample of British service firms.

The modest capital market performance of firms in the sample may also be explained by further examining the principal characteristics of services. Capital markets may be conservative in their performance evaluation of nonmanufacturing firms participating in IJVs to the extent that the intangible nature of services obscures a better understanding of incremental advantages of an IJV's offerings in relation to services offered by existing firms (Campbell and Verbeke 1994). Indeed, as one study argued, it is conceivable that incumbents possess sustainable advantages that render absolute benefits of new service offerings less attractive—albeit only in a relative sense: "Contrary to the widely held view that geographical dispersion, small firm size and market fragmentation apparent within many domestic services prevent the erection of significant barriers to entry, the international case [of firm-specific advantages possessed by service firms] appears untypical. Here the returns to quality maintenance and branding as well as the benefits of incumbency suggest that *established firms may enjoy significant advantages over newcomers*" (Enderwick 1989b: 22; emphasis added). There is some empirical support for the above-mentioned view in that many successful U.S. service firms have been unable to replicate their success abroad. For example, a *Wall Street Journal* article reported that Federal Express sustained a nine-month loss of $200 million from its non-U.S. operations and that United Parcel Service has also experienced losses from its overseas operations (Pearl 1991).

The challenge of isolating incremental benefits offered by IJVs will be intensified due to the heterogeneous nature of services. To the extent that the efficacy of some types of services is "hard to assess even after services are performed" (Heskett, Sasser, and Hart 1990: 5), it must be even harder to assess *before* the services are rendered (as when IJVs are first publicly announced). The modest performance of firms in the sample thus hints that U.S. capital markets may not be convinced whether these firms can ultimately realize the potential benefits of their IJV activity. Perhaps heterogeneity creates hesitancy about the competent delivery of service offerings (Campbell and Verbeke 1994; Heskett, Sasser, and Hart 1990). In that vein, Nayyar (1992) found a negative empirical relationship between corporate economic performance and U.S. service firms' focus on their internal capabilities. Nayyar concluded that "firms that have attempted to benefit from economies of scope [by leveraging their internal capabilities] have been unable to capture those benefits. . . . Although a focus on distinctive internal capabilities might be attractive because it appears to apply existing resources across multiple services, implementing this strategy seems to be difficult" (Nayyar 1992: 1000–1001).

Notwithstanding capital markets' moderate assessment of the IJV performance of nonmanufacturing firms, it is useful to note that performance expectations can be quite skewed. At best, capital markets expect IJVs to increase the cash flows for about half the sample of firms included in this study (the average return to firms in this subgroup is highly significant: $p < 0.0001$). This figure varies across specific sectors within the nonmanufacturing economy, suggesting that capital markets perceive IJVs to be potentially more remunerative not only for firms in certain nonmanufacturing sectors, but also for some types of firms within each sector. Apparently, in the estimation of capital markets the potential net benefits attending IJV activity are greater for some firms than they are for others. Although data limitations constrain sector-specific analysis, it is possible to draw a few preliminary inferences about firm- and venture-specific characteristics that seem to be associated with value creation for the nonmanufacturing firms included in this study. Clearly, however, it is imperative that future studies more systematically identify conditions under which nonmanufacturing firms' IJVs are deemed profitable.

The results of this study suggest that value creation for firms in the sample is associated with the level of joint venture host-country political risk. Economic value is created when joint ventures are located in less politically risky countries, and vice versa (Keller 1992). This is consistent with observations that government regulations increase the real costs of servicing markets (Heskett 1986; Trondsen and Edfelt 1987). For example, government regulations can impose a ceiling on the equity held by foreign firms, thus diluting the firms' hold over the transfer of specialized corporate resources. Likewise, government regulations increase entry costs for nonmanufacturing firms by creating nontariff barriers that impede efficient transfer of resources needed to serve local markets (Pearl 1991). The nontariff-barriers argument perhaps explains the lack of value creation for some nonmanufacturing firms that enter into joint ventures with European partners (Rapoport 1992). Admittedly, however, the level of host country political risk is not the only reason why some nonmanufacturing firms in the sample lose economic value. It is conceivable that geographical distance between firms in the sample, their non-U.S. partners, and their respective IJVs increases the challenge of coordinating resources (Keller 1992). Indeed, as one study observed, "not all companies are convinced that global service providers can meet their needs, especially when the support arena extends beyond [certain geographic territory]" (DeVoe 1995: 44). Clearly, however, more analysis is needed before definitive inferences can be drawn about the impact of geographic location of joint ventures involving nonmanufacturing firms and these firms' ability to be locally responsive. Likewise, it would be useful to investigate the association between strategic motivation and the performance of IJV partners.

The results pertaining to the distribution of returns over joint venture functional roles suggest that value creation is also associated with the number of value-chain activities to be concurrently performed within IJVs. Firms with positive returns seem able to *a priori* reduce the complexity attending simultaneous pursuit of distinct types of value-chain activities (Killing 1988; Campbell and Verbeke 1994; Koh and Venkatraman 1991), thus hinting at the increased efficacy of joint ventures in which they participate. Nevertheless, more research is needed before definitive conclusions can be drawn. Indeed, it may be useful to further investigate whether, as it appears, value creation is a joint function of political risk levels and the number of value-chain activities concurrently pursued within a joint venture.

In conclusion, future studies need to continue the identification of conditions under which IJVs involving nonmanufacturing firms are deemed more profitable by capital markets. Of course, it is just as important to identify factors associated with other dimensions of firm profitability. Only by undertaking such research will it be possible to strengthen the knowledge base created by previous IJV performance studies and identify profitable IJV conditions for practicing corporate managers.

NOTES

1. It is useful to note just how much the markets for IJVs have changed in recent years. Specifically, IJVs are increasing both in terms of frequency (Culpan and Kostelac 1993) and dollar value (*Wall Street Journal* 1991). Likewise, IJVs involving relatively small firms (Badaracco 1988) as well as firms in the service sector (Culpan and Kostelac 1993) are becoming less uncommon. Moreover, the geographical scope of IJVs seems to be widening both in terms of partners' nationalities as well as the ventures' locations. Most important, recent IJVs seem to be motivated by strategic, as opposed to tactical, reasons (Porter and Fuller 1986).

2. A comparison between the capital market performance of nonmanufacturing and manufacturing firms is not presented due to space constraints. In general, however, U.S. manufacturing firms participating in IJVs obtain (unstandardized) returns of less than 1 percent. Approximately 45 to 50 percent of these firms obtain positive returns; the remainder obtain negative returns.

3. Labeling the announcement day as $t = -1$, instead of $t = 0$, departs from convention but does not alter either the substance or interpretation of empirical results. The break from tradition is required to avoid possible confusion effected by this study's use of an online data source to generate its sample.

4. Financial theory holds that abnormal returns attending a particular event, here announcement of corporate participation in IJVs, indicate changes in firms' cash flows associated with that event. Presumably, these cash flows highlight the profitability of that event for a given firm (Sakullelarasmi 1991) and thus the firm's long-term performance in the presence of that event. Interpreted from the perspective of this study, positive abnormal returns suggest that capital markets expect firm i's participation in an IJV to be profitable (successful) in the long term whereas negative values suggest the opposite.

5. Standardizing the abnormal returns essentially sharpens the contrast between firms' historical performance. As constructed, standardization inflates the value of abnormal return to a firm whose historical performance exhibits a smaller variance, and vice versa. Thus, standardization implies that a return of (say) 15 percent to consistent performers will be valued more than a 15 percent return to firms whose performance exhibits less consistency.

6. The dollar equivalent of abnormal returns was first introduced by Singh and Montgomery (1987) to present abnormal returns in a more understandable manner. In the present study, the dollar equivalent is defined as the product of firm i's announcement period standardized abnormal return and market capitalization during that period.

7. Some empirical studies point to the differential impact of various resource-linkage mechanisms, such as joint ventures and mergers and acquisitions, on the capital market performance of firms (Woolridge and Snow 1990; Woodcock, Beamish, and Makino 1994). Thus, it is useful to note that the differential impact of various types of resource-linkage mechanisms on the capital market performance of firms is partly due to the magnitude of the investment undertaken by firms. For example, it is widely held that corporate investment (capital outlay) in joint ventures is usually smaller than it is in mergers and acquisitions. More fundamentally, however, these performance differentials are argued to arise from the feasibility of engaging a particular type of resource-linkage mechanism, given the characteristics of firm resources (Gupta and Singh 1991).

BIBLIOGRAPHY

Allen, F. 1993. Strategic management and financial markets. *Strategic Management Journal,* 14 (Special Issue): 11–22.

Arrow, K. J. 1962. Economic welfare and the allocation of resources of invention. In National Bureau of Economic Research, editor, *The Rate and Direction of Inventive Activity: Economic and Social Factors.* Princeton, N.J.: Princeton University Press.

Badaracco, J. L. 1988. Changing forms of the corporation. In J. R. Meyer and J. M. Gustafson, editors, *The U.S. Business Corporation: An Institution in Transition.* New York: Ballinger.

Badaracco, J. L. 1991. *The Knowledge Link: How Firms Compete Through Strategic Alliances.* Boston: Harvard University Press.

Brooks, M. R., R. G. Blundel, and C. I. Bidgood. 1992. Strategic alliances in the global container industry. In R. Culpan, editor, *Multinational Strategic Alliances.* New York: International Business Press.

Brown, S. J., and J. B. Warner. 1985. Using daily stock returns: The case of event studies. *Journal of Financial Economics*, 14: 3–31.

Campbell, A. J., and A. Verbeke. 1994. The globalization of service multinationals. *Long Range Planning*, 27(2): 95–102.

Carman, J., and E. Langeard. 1980. Growth strategies for service firms. *Strategic Management Journal*, 1(1): 7–22.

Channon, D. 1978. *The Service Industries: Strategy, Structure, and Financial Performance*. Old Tappan, N.J.: Macmillan.

Chatterjee, S. 1990. Excess resources, utilization costs, and mode of entry. *Academy of Management Journal*, 33(4): 780–800.

Chen, H., M. Y. Hu, and J. C. Shieh. 1991. The wealth effect of international joint ventures: The case of U.S. investment in China. *Financial Management*, Winter: 31–41.

Chen, M.-J., J.-L. Farh, and I. C. MacMillan. 1993. An exploration of the expertness of outside informants. *Academy of Management Review*, 36(6): 1614–1632.

Chung, I. Y., K. J. Koford, and I. Lee. 1993. Stock market views of corporate multinationalism: Some evidence from announcements of international joint ventures. *Quarterly Review of Economics and Finance*, 33(3): 275–293.

Coase, R. H. 1937. The nature of the firm. *Economica*, 386–405.

Crutchley, C., E. Guo, and R. S. Hansen. 1991. Stockholder benefits from Japanese-U.S. joint ventures. *Financial Management*, Winter: 22–30.

Culpan, R., and E. A. Kostelac. 1993. Cross-national corporate partnerships: Trends in alliance formation. In R. Culpan, editor, *Multinational Strategic Alliances*. New York: International Business Press.

DeVoe, D. 1995. Support organizations link up to provide global service. *InfoWorld*, May 8: 44.

Dierickx, I., and K. Cool. 1989. Asset stock accumulation and the sustainability of competitive advantage. *Management Science*, 1504–1511.

Dunning, J. H. 1989. *Transnational Corporations and the Growth of Services: Some Conceptual and Theoretical Issues*. UNCTC Current Series, New York: United Nations.

Enderwick, P. 1989a. *Multinational Service Firms*. London: Routledge.

Enderwick, P. 1989b. Some economics of service-sector multinational enterprises. In Peter Enderwick, editor, *Multinational Service Firms*. London: Routledge.

Enderwick, P. 1989c. Policy issues in international trade and investment in services. In P. Enderwick, editor, *Multinational Service Firms*. London: Routledge.

Enderwick, P. 1992. The scale and scope of service sector multinationals. In P. Buckley and M. Casson, editors, *Multinational Enterprises in the World Economy: Essays in the Honor of John Dunning*. Brookfield, Vt.: Edward Elgar.

Fama, E. F., L. Fisher, M. C. Jensen, and R. Roll. 1969. The adjustment of stock prices to new information. *International Economic Review,* 10: 1–21.

Finnerty, J. E., J. E. Owers, and R. C. Rogers. 1986. The valuation impact of joint ventures. *Management International Review,* 26(2): 14–26.

Garud, R., and P. R. Nayyar. 1994. Transformative capacity: Continual structuring by intertemporal technology transfers. *Strategic Management Journal,* 15(5): 365–385.

Ghemawat, P., M. E. Porter, and R. A. Rawlinson. 1986. Patterns of international coalition activity. In M. E. Porter, editor, *Competition in Global Industries*. Boston: Harvard Business School Press.

Gupta, A., and H. Singh. 1991. Exploiting synergies: External alliances versus inter-SBU coordination. Paper presented at the annual Academy of Management Meeting, Miami Beach, Florida.

Harrigan, K. R. 1988. Strategic alliances and partner asymmetries. In F. Contractor and P. Lorange, editors, *Cooperative Strategies in International Business*. San Francisco: New Lexington Press.

Hergert, M., and D. Morris. 1988. Trends in international collaboration agreements. In F. Contractor and P. Lorange, editors, *Cooperative Strategies in International Business*. San Francisco: New Lexington Press.

Heskett, J. L. 1986. *Managing in the Service Economy*. Boston: Harvard Business School Press.

Heskett, J. L., E. Sasser, and C.W.L. Hart. 1990. *Service Breakthroughs*. New York: Free Press.

Jensen, M. C. 1969. Risk, the pricing of capital assets, and the evaluation of investment portfolios. *Journal of Business,* 29: 167–247.

Keller, J. J. 1992. AT&T, Cable and Wireless suspend talks on global telecommunications alliance. *Wall Street Journal,* January 23.

Killing, J. P. 1988. Understanding alliances: The role of organizational complexity. In F. J. Contractor and P. Lorange, editors, *Cooperative Strategies in International Business,* 55–67. San Francisco: New Lexington Press.

Koh, J., and N. Venkatraman. 1991. Joint venture formations and stock market reactions: An assessment in the information technology sector. *Academy of Management Journal,* 34: 869–892.

Lorange, P., and J. Roos. 1992. *Strategic Alliances: Formation, Implementation, and Evolution*. Cambridge, Mass.: Blackwell.

Lubatkin, M. H., and R. Shrieves. 1986. Towards reconciliation of market measures to strategic management research. *Academy of Management Review,* 11(3): 497–512.

Mathe, H., and C. Perras. 1994. Successful global strategies for multinational companies. *Long Range Planning,* 27(1): 36–49.

McConnell, J. J., and T. J. Nantell. 1985. Corporate combinations and common stock returns: The case of joint ventures. *Journal of Finance,* 49(2): 519–536.

Mikkelson, W. H., and M. M. Partch. 1986. Valuation effects of security offerings and the issuance process. *Journal of Financial Economics,* 15: 31–60.

Nayyar, P. R. 1992. Performance effects of three foci in service firms. *Academy of Management Journal,* 35(5): 985–1009.

Nusbaumer, J. 1987. *Services in the Global Market.* Norwell, Mass.: Kluwer.

Pearl, D. 1991. Innocents abroad: Federal Express finds its pioneering formula falls flat overseas. *Wall Street Journal,* April 15: A1.

Penrose, E. T. 1959. *The Theory of the Growth of the Firm.* Oxford: Blackwell.

Polanyi, M. 1962. *Personal Knowledge: Towards a Post-Critical Philosophy.* New York: HarperCollins.

Porter, M. E. 1987. From competitive advantage to corporate strategy. *Harvard Business Review,* May-June: 43–59.

Porter, M. E. 1990. *Competitive Advantage of Nations.* New York: Free Press.

Porter, M. E., and M. Fuller. 1986. Coalitions and global strategy. In M. E. Porter, editor, *Competition in Global Industries,* 315–344. Boston, Mass.: Harvard Business School Press.

Rapoport, C. 1992. Europe looks ahead to hard choices. *Fortune.* December 14: 144–146, 148–149.

Ravichandran, R. 1986. An investigation of domestic joint ventures. Unpublished doctoral dissertation, University of Iowa.

Rumelt, R. P. 1987. Theory, strategy, and entrepreneurship. In D. Teece, editor, *The Competitive Challenge: Strategies for Industrial Innovation and Renewal.* New York: Ballinger.

Sakullelarasmi, P. 1991. International joint ventures: An analysis of the effects of joint venture formation on shareholder wealth. Unpublished doctoral dissertation, University of North Texas.

Salter, M. S., and W. A. Weinhold. 1979. *Diversification Through Acquisition: Strategies for Creating Economic Value.* New York: Free Press.

Seth, A. 1990. Sources of value creation in acquisitions: An empirical investigation. *Strategic Management Journal,* 11: 431–446.

Siegel, S. 1956. *Nonparametric Statistics for the Behavioral Sciences.* New York: McGraw-Hill.

Singh, H., and C. Montgomery. 1987. Corporate acquisition strategies and economic performance. *Strategic Management Journal,* 8: 377–386.

Teece, D. 1980. Economies of scope and scope of the enterprise. *Journal of Economic Behavior and Organization,* 1: 223–247.

Trondsen, E., and R. Edfelt. 1987. New opportunities in global services. *Long Range Planning,* 20(5): 53–61.

Wall Street Journal. 1991. Cross-border deals decline, July 1.

Wernerfelt, B. 1984. A resource-based view of the firm. *Strategic Management Journal,* 5: 171–180.

Williamson, O. E. 1975. *Markets and Hierarchies: Analysis and Antitrust Implications.* New York: Free Press.

Winter, S. 1987. Knowledge and competence as strategic assets. In D. Teece, editor, *The Competitive Challenge: Strategies for Industrial Innovation and Renewal.* New York: Ballinger.

Woodcock, P. C., P. W. Beamish, and S. Makino. 1994. Ownership-based entry mode strategies and international performance. *Journal of International Business Studies,* 25(2): 253–273.

Woolridge, R. J., and C. C. Snow. 1990. Stock market reactions to strategic investment decisions. *Strategic Management Journal,* 11: 353–363.

World Investment Report. 1993. *Transnational corporations and integrated international production.* New York: United Nations.

NAME INDEX

A

Abegglen, J. C., 360, 365
Abernathy, W. J., 92, 102, 107
Abrahamson, E., 4, 20
Achrol, R., 258, 260, 261, 262, 279, 280, 282
Adams, J. S., 198, 221, 311, 329
Adobor, H., 111*n*
Aguilar, F. J., 342, 365
Ainuddin, A., 421, 425
Ajzen, I., 317, 320, 330
Alchian, A. A., 6, 22, 60, 68, 69, 82
Alderson, W., 257, 260, 280
Alexander, S., 222
Allen, F., 429, 452
Allen, N. J., 199, 222, 225
Alpert, F., 237, 251
Alter, C., 309, 330, 378, 392
Anand, J., 421, 425
Anderson, E., 26, 29, 36, 39, 44, 45, 46, 57, 83, 136, 147, 156, 169, 170, 171, 172, 193, 262, 280, 371, 376, 392, 404, 417, 418, 425
Anderson, J. C., 155, 158, 166, 170, 192, 193, 258, 264, 280, 311, 312, 318, 326, 330, 332, 417, 423, 425
Argote, L., 385, 392
Argyris, C., 295, 303, 383, 393
Armstrong, J. S., 142, 156, 174, 193
Arrow, K. J., 310, 330, 432, 452
Ashby, G., 312, 332
Ashforth, B. E., 172, 193
Aulakh, P. S., 163, 170, 191, 194

Auster, E. R., 9, 20, 257, 280
Axelrod, R., 7–8, 20, 167, 193, 245, 251
Axelsson, B., 303

B

Bacharach, S. B., 12, 20, 315, 330, 355, 365
Badaracco, J. L., Jr., 93, 102, 107, 261, 263, 264, 280, 371, 377, 387, 393, 432, 451, 452
Baird, I., 134, 156
Bamford, J., 19, 20
Banks, J. C., 9, 14, 21, 52, 82, 93, 94, 107, 165, 167, 193, 257, 263, 266, 280, 309, 330
Barber, B., 310, 330
Barclay, D. W., 261, 264, 284
Barkema, H. G., 116, 129, 381, 393
Barley, S. R., 303, 304
Barney, J. B., 8, 12, 13, 14, 20, 32, 49, 114, 115, 129, 302, 304, 385, 393
Baron, R. M., 18, 20
Bartlett, C. A., 118, 130, 386, 393, 421, 425
Baughn, C. C., 26, 31, 33, 35, 36, 37, 48, 92, 93, 96, 109, 134, 159, 305–306
Beamish, P. W., 9, 11, 14, 21, 51*n*, 52, 82, 89*n*, 90, 93, 94, 107, 111*n*, 118, 131, 134, 137, 138, 140, 156–157, 158, 159, 164, 165, 167, 193, 198, 206, 222, 224, 228, 245, 251, 257, 263, 266, 280, 304, 309,

SUBJECT INDEX

A

Academy of Management, 308n, 337n

Agency theory: assumptions of, 60; and joint ventures, 63, 70–74, 79–80; propositions on, 70–74; and residual claims and risk, 68–70

Alliances: culture for, 94–96; formation of cooperative, 87–159; for technology, 89–110; Types I and II of, 134, 376. *See also* Collaborations; International cooperative alliances; International joint ventures; Joint ventures; Partnerships

Alpha JV, and knowledge creation, 346, 349–350, 352, 355–358, 360, 362–363

Alpha Mines, and process patterns, 289, 290–291, 294, 297, 298

American Graduate School of International Management Research, 337n

Argentina: partnerships in, 176

Armani, and industry dynamics, 122

Asea Brown Boveri, and industry dynamics, 120

Asia: industry dynamics in, 122, 123, 128; nonmanufacturing sector in, 447; process patterns in, 290; trust in partnerships in, 175, 176, 180, 186, 276

Asset specificity: and environmental dynamism, 39–40; kinds of, 82; and specialization, 20; and transaction costs, 6–7; and trust in partnerships, 177, 181, 184, 185, 190–191, 192

Assets: as bundles of rights, 59; non-separability of, 65–66; optimal usage of, 61, 64, 66–67

Atkinson, Guy F., in collaboration, 280

Australia: collaborations in, 270, 405; process patterns in, 290, 299–300

Austrian school of economics, 81, 114

Automotive industry: knowledge creation in, 344–364; trust in, 316–326

Autonomy, in international joint ventures, 413, 415–417, 423

B

Bahrain, collaborations in, 270

Baird Textile, and industry dynamics, 124

Bechtel, and industry dynamics, 121, 127

Belgium, collaborations in, 270

Benevolence, and trust in alliances, 229, 237, 246, 249

Beta JV, and knowledge creation, 346, 349, 351, 353, 358

Beta Trading Co., and process patterns, 290–291, 297–301

Boundary choices, and entry mode, 30

Boundary role persons (BRPs), and trust, 311–312, 317–318, 326

Bouygues, and industry dynamics, 127

Brazil: collaborations in, 270; partnerships in, 176

Brown and Root, in collaboration, 280

International Office Contact Information

Canada
Prentice Hall Canada
1870 Birchmount Road
Scarborough, Ontario M1P 2J7
tel: 800 567 3800
fax: 800 263 7733
Canadian booksellers order through:
Distican Inc.
35 Fulton Way
Richmond Hill, Ontario L4B 2N4
tel: 905 764 0073
fax: 905 764 0086
1 800 Numbers:
Ontario 800 387 0446
Canada w800 268 3216

United Kingdom/Europe/
Middle East/Africa
Simon and Schuster International
Campus 400
Marylands Avenue
Hemel Hempstead
Herts HP2 7EZ
England
tel: 44 442 881900
fax: 44 442 882277

Northern Europe
Paramount Publishing Nederland B.V.
Postbus 9255
1006 AG Amsterdam
The Netherlands
tel: 31 20 669 4419
fax: 31 20 615 3043

Japan
Prentice Hall Regents
Nishi Shinjuku KF Building, 602
8-14-24, Nishi Shinjuku
Shinjuku-ku Tokyo 160
Japan
tel: 81 3 3365 9004
fax: 81 3 3365 9009

Australia/New Zealand
Prentice Hall Australia Pty Ltd.
P.O. Box 151
7 Grosvenor Place
Brookvale, New South Wales 2100
Australia
tel: 61 2 9939 1333
fax: 61 2 9938 6826

South East Asia
Simon and Schuster Asia
Pte. Ltd.
317 Alexandra Road
#04-01 Ikea Building
Singapore 159965
tel: 65 476 4788
fax: 65 378 0373